The Rise
of English
Nationalism

1. 1756. "Degenerate Britons," aided by upper-class folly, effeminacy, bribery, and favoritism, are about to bury Britannia below. On the frieze of the collapsing state: "Noble Trophies of old English Vallour but much Defaced and allmost forgot." At the left, fickle patriots resign themselves to the general ruin; "manufacturers" languish below. Britannia prophetically exclaims, "Oh thoughtless Sons know you not in destroying me you destroy your selves."

The Rise
of English
Nationalism

A CULTURAL HISTORY
1740–1830

Gerald Newman

But in spite of all temptations
To belong to other nations
He remains an Englishman!
—W. S. GILBERT, *H.M.S. Pinafore* (1878)

St. Martin's Press · New York

First published in the United States of America in 1987

Printed in the U.S.A.

ISBN 0-312-68247-6

Library of Congress Cataloging in Publication Data

Newman, Gerald.
    The rise of English nationalism.

    Includes index.
    1. National characteristics, English.
2. Nationalism—England—History.   3. England—
Civilization.   4. Great Britain—History—
1714-1837.   I. Title.
DA118.N48   1987   941.07   86-17676
ISBN 0-312-68247-6

To Peter and Livia

CONTENTS

LIST OF ILLUSTRATIONS

Illustrations 1–10 are reproduced by courtesy of the Print Collection, Lewis Walpole Library, Yale University; illustration no. 11 is reproduced by courtesy of John R. Freeman & Co., Ltd., London.

ACKNOWLEDGMENTS

I HAVE RUN UP many debts in the course of writing this book, and would like to take this opportunity to thank many people who encouraged and helped me during this pleasant but arduous journey. Special appreciation is due to those who read portions of the draft in one form or another. I am deeply indebted to my mentors John Clive and H. J. Hanham for their criticisms and encouragement, and for the inspiration of their own writings. W. H. G. Armytage very kindly took time to read and criticize the first part of the draft, and the result owes much to his patience and cheery lucidity. Frank O'Gorman gave me the benefit of his written criticisms on the whole pattern of ideas I have developed here, and I also owe much to conversations with him. My thanks go also to R. K. Webb, who supplied many very helpful criticisms and suggestions. In addition, I wish to thank Martha Vicinus, J. J. Hecht, Harold T. Parker, Boyd Shafer, and William H. McNeill for criticisms and encouragement given me along the way. Walter Arnstein's suggestions on an early version of Chapter Eight were of great value. I have benefited greatly from conversations with many talented colleagues, including Jack Breihan, Earl Reitan, Linda Colley, and Mike McCahill. Christine Worobec helped me acquire several of the book's illustrations, and I am very grateful also to Joan Sussler of the Lewis Walpole Library for her advice and help with many others. Thanks also go to Kermit Hummel, Director of the Scholarly and Reference Books Division of St. Martin's Press, for his friendly support and excellent editorial advice. Finally, I wish to acknowledge with much affection the help and encouragement of Ruth Warner, Giovanni and Amne Costigan, Barbara Clements, Lynn and Tom Benediktsson, and my parents, Leonard and Loree Newman. The manuscript has benefited from the intelligence and generosity of all these people; I hope they will take pleasure in the result and see their beneficial influences in it.

A NOTE ON FOOTNOTES
AND PUNCTUATION

I HAVE ATTEMPTED to keep the potentially over-large number of foot-notes in bounds by following the practice of consolidating multiple references within a single note wherever possible. In punctuation I have employed a small device that might be thought quirky unless explained. Where I quote a given author for the first time, I use the standard double quotation marks of American usage: "thus." But if I should use the same author's phrase later, 'thus,' or any other specialized term or phrase of the sort which we ordinarily surround with quotations marks, such as, for example, 'Victorianism,' I have borrowed for that purpose the English single quotation marks, with the purpose of showing more clearly on the page the difference between material directly quoted there and that which is not.

PREFACE

I T IS STRANGE to think how greatly English nationalism has eluded our scholarly attention. Its nature has not been debated, and its power, though often sensed, has escaped analysis. Its historic creators have not been enumerated or considered as a group, its workings in English literature have received little attention, its connections with English industrialization and modernization have gone unnoticed. Nor, it would seem, has anyone attempted to piece together a theory that might shed light on the many symptomatic struggles in modern England to banish 'National Apostasies' from the land and to create in their place what might well be called, with equally large application of phrase, 'National Conventions.' When we consider the professional study of the eighteenth and nineteenth centuries, we may come to feel that scholarship has been too unattuned to the possibility that the moral, social, and intellectual discipline that we loosely call 'Victorianism' might be well understood rather in the same way that we understand German culture in the later nineteenth century, as the expression and fulfillment of a powerful nationalist movement that began some decades before the French Revolution.

The academic specialists on nationalism, the historians and political scientists who concern themselves with its global expanse, general features, and comparative differences, might have been expected to voice suspicions over this apparent failure, but few have done so. Undoubtedly there are good reasons for this; for example, most of these specialists are today interested primarily in the Third World. But characteristic of this failure is the comment of Professor K. R. Minogue, in his excellent little handbook on nationalism, that England is a nation that apparently has had "relatively little nationalist experience." A. D. Smith, another of our foremost authorities on nationalism, writes that "England presents a difficulty. It can be argued that . . . England has experienced no fully developed nationalist movement." In another book the same author lists every 'Developed Nationalist Movement' known to scholarship and comes up with one hundred ten of them: French, German, Russian, Indian, Japanese, American, Brazilian, and more than eight dozen others, including "Slovenian," "Trinidadian," and "Mongol." Neither "English" nor "British" appears on this gigantic list. In truth it is no oddity but rather commonplace to find general accounts of nationalism like the recent one by Professor Isaiah Berlin in which "the first true nationalists—the Germans" dominate the entire discussion, without there being even a curious glance at the way the English experience might fit the categories of analysis.[1] The occasional reference to Shakespeare as a focus of German cultural awakening is made as though in unawareness of the English Shakespeare revival that made the German one possible, while the occasional mention of Edmund Burke as a philosopher of nationalistic ideas is thrown in without an English context and as though Burke, a sort of honorary German in such discussions, had written with the aim of elucidating Fichte, Arndt, and Jahn.

The same unawareness is revealed in scholarly periodical literature. Just a few years ago I ran a computerized search through *Historical Abstracts* of more than eighty thousand articles published worldwide since 1972 on all aspects of history and literature. The search was designed to catch every article dealing directly with English or British patriotism or nationalism. It produced but two essays in rather obscure journals (one concerned itself with recent Welsh nationalism, the other with nationalistic sentiment in late-Victorian chambers of commerce), whereas identical searches keyed to German and Irish nationalism produced more than seventy references. There is in fact only one document in the entire bibliography of nationalism which focuses squarely on the general problem of an English variety, a short article by Hans Kohn, nearly half a century old, published during the Battle of Britain and written more in the spirit of passionate encouragement than calm analysis, which anachronistically pinpoints the English manifestation, contrary to the whole canon of theory on nationalist development, in the seventeenth century—an age still dominated by religious, rather than secular, perspectives. Beyond this, proclaiming their obsolescence in their very titles, there are only the still older and even more romantic treatments of English 'patriotism' that date from the first decade or so of the present century.[2]

Of course it is only fair to point out that Kohn, Minogue, Smith, and the other analysts of nationalism as a global phenomenon have been obliged to work with what England's own historians and critics have given them. Their fogginess on England only reflects the state of specialized thinking about English history and literature. The truth is that one of the most interesting and central problems of English culture has somehow gotten largely overlooked by people working close to it. I have in my possession a letter of 1981, written to me by an American friend, a co-author of a well-known textbook on modern English history. Its wording is interesting because it reveals the degree to which the Anglo-American historiographical consciousness has been trained in the absence of any technically meaningful idea of English nationalism. "Nationalism," my friend observes, "is not a word often used in connection with the English. Patriotism, Anglo-Saxon racialism, imperialism are the substitutes." The same outlook may be seen in what is perhaps the finest published study of English attitudes in the nineteenth century, Walter Houghton's *The Victorian Frame of Mind, 1830–1870*. Professor Houghton does not entirely ignore nationalism—would it be possible to do so in a book covering the whole period of Podsnap and Palmerston and Pax Britannica?—but in a work of more than four hundred pages he gives it less than two pages of sustained discussion, treating it as a tiny subheading under "Hero Worship."[3] He is far from presenting it as a mighty, historic force helping to produce or hold together the thirteen major 'Attitudes' he so impressively catalogs and describes—Optimism, The Will to Believe, The Commercial Spirit, The Worship of Force, Earnestness, Enthusiasm, etc.

Sooner or later one might begin to wonder whether there is not something wrong here. And there would seem to be only two alternative explanations of the puzzle. Either England was so unlike all the rest of the nations that she declined to participate in something that, without exception, engulfed all of them; or else England's past cultural interpreters, many of them, were so influenced by national myths that we ourselves, inheriting their concepts, have not quite yet gotten so far above these myths as to be able to understand their multifarious workings—to see, for example, how they still affect our own vision, and to see also how, as all-embracing historic ideological phenomena, they underlay and secretly imparted hidden directionality to the particular events and movements we ordinarily study and write about.

Perhaps it might be suggested that what we have here is a manifestation in the academic world of the fond old idea that God is an Englishman. Other peoples—the French, the Germans, the Mexicans and Irish—have their nationalisms, their amusing beliefs, and silly prejudices about themselves. The English and their many benevolent foreign commentators have—what? A curious little book of 1840, *Heads of the People: Or, Portraits of the English,* begins with a wry preface on John Bull: "He, and he alone, knows and does that which is 'wisest, discreetest, virtuousest, best;' that he has no prejudices—none; or, if indeed he have any, that they exist and have been nurtured so very near his virtues, that if he cannot detect the slightest difference between them, it is not likely that any vagabond foreigner can make so tremendous a discovery."[4]

The whimsical A. A. Milne might have suggested that what we have found is a Thing Without a Name. Professor J. G. A. Pocock, in an important article written "In Search of the Unknown Subject," believes that the thing that we do not understand, whatever it is, is of much importance. What is the British Nation? "The English ruling structure," he writes, "may have organized a geographically defined culture into a nation and in some sort a state; the history of how it has done so is not free from blind spots but constitutes one of the great historiographical enterprises of the world." Yet not even he, though writing very much in the vicinity of the thing Unknown, speaks its seemingly unpronounceable name. The same element of perplexity, the vague sense that something important has been too widely overlooked, is conveyed by Professor Ian Christie as he introduces his excellent new account of the reign of George III. Contemplating Britain's successful emergence "from the great power-struggle against France . . . unshattered from the age of revolutions," he confesses that "it has been borne in upon the author during the preparation of this book, that there is much about this process of survival that as yet remains unexplained. Historians have hardly begun to ask the right questions, which will lead to the proper elucidation of it." C. P. Wormald, discussing an earlier period, rightly complains of the common historical notion that "the making of England was somehow inevitable."[5]

And so we come to the interesting question: How would it affect our understanding if modern English history were to be reconsidered from this novel point of view, keeping most prominently before us those facts and circumstances that apparently were most critically connected with the launching and later success of English nationalism? To answer this question, or to take a first step toward answering it, is the aim of this book.

Such an investigation must, of course, run occasionally against the grain of current understanding. Nationalism bears a certain relatedness to nearly every aspect of national culture, and hence to look at any historic society for the first time by this light is, necessarily, to discover new items of interest, and for the same reason to acquire suspicions about some of the truths by which existing knowledge is organized. Indeed we have the basis here for quite a new historical perspective. Owing to the novel angle of approach and to a rather embracing viewpoint upon the material, imposed by the multifaceted nature of nationalism itself, this book attempts to outline an improved general picture of modern English culture and to offer a body of connected ideas by which many pieces of the familiar old puzzle might possibly be fitted together a little more satisfactorily. The aim is to do so, however, not quite so much by dropping a newfangled bomb, 'Nationalism,' into existing knowledge (though, of course, there is some of that), as by adjusting innumerable emphases that can be shown to be mistaken, and mistaken in consequence of original causes that can now be more satisfactorily explained. For in setting out with this new compass to assess the process of English nation-building in the eighteenth and nineteenth centuries, one is led also, by just the same avenue, to the mythic process by which many important facts of this development became disguised and thus eluded subsequent notice.

This will not, I hope, be taken as an arrogant suggestion that earlier writers who concerned themselves only indirectly with what we are going to concentrate on here, the circumstances and manifestations of English nationalist development, have gotten everything wrong. Asking other questions, they naturally came up with other answers. My own aim has been to synthesize many of their findings where these touch upon our own problem, and the reader will see how much I owe even to those earlier authors whose conclusions I feel it necessary to criticize. Unfortunately it is nearly impossible in these well-worked fields to say anything new without contradicting something old, so I have indeed paused occasionally to take issue with concepts which I consider mistaken. But the reader will understand, I hope, that if I have sometimes become warm in criticism of existing assumptions, it is only through vexation over injuries wrought by them upon men and women in the past. Voltaire once said that history is a pack of cards with which we play tricks on the dead. I believe that quite a few have been played on men and women of the age of George III, and that it is possible to regard them and their literature in a rather different way.

And so I have attempted to review and reconsider the main characteristics of England's participation in the cosmopolitan European civilization of the eighteenth century, and then to project an outline of the formation of English nationalism in that same century and of its chief effects in the nineteenth. At the same time I have attempted to suggest some of the effects which scholarly acceptance of a sophisticated description of English nationalism—a description more refined than the inevitably preliminary one offered here—might have upon our understanding of English literature and society. Of course I have been unable to address myself to every aspect of this question. Indeed I have not addressed myself in great detail to any of them, for this would have meant subordinating the breadth of the discussion to interminable refinements of argument. The main effort has been on synthetic interpretative adjustments, the reordering of many emphases. I am quite aware that some of my own emphases might be wrong; one reader, for example, might complain that I do not begin at a period earlier than the eighteenth century, another that I ignore the Empire. And though I could argue in justification of such omissions, I hope I may find some absolution on the simple plea that it is never easy to account fully for movements essentially spiritual, and on the ground, too, that with a problem of such complexity I could easily have spent the rest of my life on this book before feeling that I had done justice to its subject.

So I do not delude myself that I have discussed everything of importance; and the opposite complaint will probably be true too, that I have attempted to explain too much. But a fuller and rounder general understanding may nonetheless emerge, for there can be little question that the serious study of English nationalism which this book is intended to promote will help to unlock some of the still elusive secrets of English literary, social, economic, and political evolution of the reign of George III, a period still regarded by many people as the most interesting, if also the most tangled and confusing, in the whole development of English civilization. Such study may also help to clarify our understanding of what has been called the 'Code' of the Victorian society that followed, and hence may prove enlightening to students of still more recent British history. Beyond that, such study, by exploring some of the achievements of the mythmakers of the eighteenth and nineteenth centuries, may assist us all to a fresher appreciation of the literary and historical remains of that long period, as well as to a clearer understanding of the origins and unconscious organization of our own scholarly understanding, which was in many cases formally launched by those very mythmakers.

Moreover, the same study may help to answer a modern need by investigating the process by which England's legendary 'uniqueness,' her 'differentness' from Continental society, arose from her very commonness with it. The study of English nationalism may help to satisfy the desire,

increasingly expressed in recent years, to renovate English historical understanding in such a way that the English experience may be seen more
satisfactorily not only within the larger British context but within the
whole context of European history as well. In today's post-imperial times,
times of a diminished British role in the world and of renewed ties with
other European nations, the English national mind and with it the national historiographical precepts have begun to change. Pocock, whose
richly imaginative work has always tended to cast doubt on the uniqueness
of the English experience, recently mounted one of the most skeptical
attacks to date on that immense body of historiographical opinion which
"presupposes the uniqueness and [independent] intelligibility of England."
There is perhaps, as he suggests, a new willingness to accept the notion that
British history "is and always has been part of 'European history.'" It is
interesting to see that Roy Porter, an excellent writer of the younger generation, has recently applied the same controlling idea to the supposed differences between English and European thought during the Enlightenment, vigorously attacking both the notion of the separateness of the
English Enlightenment and the existing scholarship in which this idea is
embedded. "Modern scholarship," he complains, "reads like a paternity-
denying alibi, proving that England's kinship with the family of *philosophes*
was no closer than a maiden aunt." Still more recently Theodore Zeldin,
the eminent historian of France, commented even more scathingly on what
he treated as the near bankruptcy of the English historiographical tradition, expressing his own view "that a national perspective cannot be sustained in historical study much longer and that such a perspective survives
only because of inertia and the difficulty of developing a satisfactory alternative."[6]

There is too much truth in this criticism, and this book may be looked
upon as an attempt to break that inertia and initiate that 'satisfactory alternative' on solid ground, namely on the supposition of deep similarities,
during both the age of cosmopolitanism and the age of nationalism that
followed, between England's experience and the experience of many
other nations. England is indeed unique, quite as unique in the technical
sense as any other modern nation with a long and complex past, but it
was not this but rather her pioneering passage, her flagship voyage
through an experience now common to all of today's peoples, which made
her truly great and powerful and distinguished among nations. The more
extreme Anglophiles would do well, I think, to relinquish a bit of England's supposed uniqueness in return for a clearer comparative understanding. I have at least attempted here to visualize the feelings and
thoughts and achievements of Englishmen within a much larger multina-
tional setting. One may hope that the exercise may have permanent value
even if it only proves again what ought not to be done, and confirms
again by a novel test the ineffable Englishness of the English. Little, at
least, can be lost through the exercise, for as regards nationalism, England, according to the present state of thinking, has nothing to lose.

There is, finally, an important corollary to all this. Some readers will be aware that our understanding of many other cross-cultural phenomena, international phenomena rooted in the eighteenth and nineteenth centuries, is at present organized in patterns that more or less complacently admit the separateness of the English experience. English history is a little like the house guest who, whether from pride or some other reason, refuses to attend the party and thereby withholds through his absence some of the importance and much of the general significance of whatever occurs there. It is high time for us to consider the hidden effects upon other bodies of theory of what might simply be the delusion of England's separateness, her non-participation in movements common to other nations. The English historian Alan Macfarlane only exaggerates a common view when he states that England historically was "a society in which almost every aspect of the culture was diametrically opposed to that of the surrounding nations." The American professor of English Literature Donald Greene only reaffirms a deeply rooted conviction of English-speaking scholarship in his assertion that "it is dangerous at any time for the student to lump together English literary and intellectual phenomena such as 'the Enlightenment' or 'Romanticism' without making due allowance for the stubborn idiosyncrasy of the English."[7]

But what if this is just stuff and nonsense? What if it is just the reflection of a myth—one of the central myths, perhaps, of English nationalism? What if the real obstacle to understanding is simply the stubborn immobility of certain academic prejudices? It would not be the first time that intelligent men and women, looking at their cultural motherland, had begun with pleasant illusions and then woven from these a mythology that passed for common sense and obvious fact. Surely it might be argued, contrary to the faith expressed by these authors, that abandonment of the idea of England's 'stubborn idiosyncrasy' might prove less dangerous than beneficial by permitting us, indeed encouraging us, to find ways to unify many bodies of theory which can never become truly *international* and *global* so long as England stands silently in the background as a supposed non-participant, hence a missing link, in what might otherwise instantly be seen as common patterns of historical experience. There are reasons to suspect, for example, that the supposed uniqueness of England has acted as a hidden brake on our grasp of such things as 'modernization,' class consciousness, and European 'romantic' literature in the nineteenth century, and even, to take a later example from still another field, the mythology and psychodynamics of fascism in the twentieth. This last may seem farfetched, but at any rate it will be conceded by many thoughtful people that there is one body of theory today, an exceedingly important one for the understanding and even perhaps—is it too farfetched to say so?—the salvation of the modern world, which must be very much enriched by the recognition and study of English nationalism, and that is the body of understanding on the nature of nationalism itself.

The Rise
of English
Nationalism

2. *1778, Bunbury. A rather oafish young English gentleman, bearing a cane in one hand and a volume of Chesterfield's 'Letters' in the other, approaches a smiling French hotel-keeper holding a bill of fare. An English man-servant hauls thick books from the young traveler's chaise while his tutor prompts him to converse in French. A postillion looks on; cooks prepare a meal.*

CHAPTER ONE

Fine Fellow Traveling in the Age of Cosmopolitanism

The knowledge of the world is only to be acquired in the world, not in a closet.

—CHESTERFIELD

T O UNDERSTAND the genesis of nationalism in England, or for that matter in any European country, it is first necessary to understand the foundations of eighteenth-century cosmopolitanism. This is a complicated and amorphous subject, but our task requires a review of it. It is possible to conduct one from an angle particularly revealing of English civilization by keeping in view the career, the ideas, and the English contacts of Voltaire, whom many people in the eighteenth century, Englishmen included, admired as the very personification of the cosmopolitan spirit.

Cosmopolitanism, as an ideal handed down through many centuries of western culture, has never attained such wide influence and respect as it did during Voltaire's lifetime (1694–1778). Its essential ideas, rooted in the concept of the underlying unity of mankind, had originated in pagan antiquity, but then been only partially absorbed into the Christian proclamation of salvation for the entire human race. After centuries of relative dormancy it gradually revived as a secular ideal in Renaissance humanism, the renewed study of Stoic doctrines, the spread of global exploration, and the tendency to man-in-general theorizing that was greatly strengthened by the Scientific Revolution of the seventeenth century. Such were some of the chief sources of what has been styled "the neo-Stoic cosmopolitanism of the seventeenth and eighteenth centuries." Cosmopolitanism was "a sentiment uniting cultured minds" down through the ages,[1] one which in various ways touched thinkers as diverse as Zeno and Cicero and Marcus Aurelius, St. Augustine and Erasmus, Bacon and Montaigne, Voltaire and Alexander Pope. The cosmopolitan ideal, like others deeply rooted in constant human aspirations, thus possessed a sort of historical life and momentum of its own, an internal power capable of carrying it without external help into the mental life of the eighteenth century.

1. ANGLO-FRENCH INTERCHANGE

But behind the enthusiastic acceptance and considerable influence of cosmopolitanism during the age of Enlightenment was a remarkable combination of contemporary circumstances as well. Of great importance

among these was the quickened tempo of intellectual and social interchange between the two Great Powers of the day, France and Britain.
Voltaire, commenting admiringly on Pope's writings in a late edition of
his *Lettres philosophiques,* characteristically observed that "when a
Frenchman and an Englishman think the same, they must certainly be
right." The remark captured both the dissimilarity of the two national
patterns of thought, and the conviction that truth was a province specially
shared between them. This belief was widespread during the eighteenth
century, and there is something to recommend it still. Modern writers
have aptly pictured France and Britain as "unruly twins," sibling carriers
of European culture, over the centuries constantly exchanging "ideas,
customs, blows, compliments or complaints," with Britain sometimes
striving for ascendancy (as during the Elizabethan Age), or France (as in
the Age of Louis XIV), but together weaving through their strife, agreement, and mutual influence a wider pattern whose original threads cannot be easily traced to the one or the other. One historian (Jarrett)
persuasively argues that neither society, in the later eighteenth century at
least, can be understood without studying the other. Another historian
takes this so far as to maintain that "as the influence of France and England has radiated throughout the world and often given a lead to universal life, there are few general questions that can be solved without active
investigations conducted jointly by the historians of both countries." This
is excessive, but it was nonetheless shrewd of Kipling to observe (in his
poem "France 1913") that within this tangled Anglo-French relationship it
was the fate of each nation "to mould the other's fate as he wrought his
own," and this no less in the realm of thought than on the fields of war
and empire: "We have learned by keenest use to know each other's
mind." Nor has war always obstructed positive interchange. The intensity
of mutual attraction and influence, the cordial "minuet" of ideas and
customs (as the literary historian F. C. Green happily puts it), has never
been greater than it was at the mid-eighteenth century, when, despite
dissonant clashes of war in the background, cultivated Englishmen and
Frenchmen disparaged local attachments, openly expressed their Francophilism and Anglomania, and moved easily from these affinities to intellectual ideals which embraced the whole of Europe, indeed the whole
of mankind.[2]

The chief mediator of this Anglo-French accord, as of the philosophic
cosmopolitanism connected with it, was Voltaire. To France and the rest
of Europe he was by the 1750s the foremost exponent and interpreter of
English ideas and taste. To the British, on the other hand, he was far the
most conspicuous and eminent representative of French culture. An astonishing number of Englishmen and Scotsmen knew him personally.
This fertile association had begun in 1726 when Voltaire, aged thirty-two,
carrying letters of introduction from the British ambassador and other
Englishmen in Paris, crossed to London and began a stay that was to last
more than two years. When he arrived he was greeted warmly not only as
a favored Parisian wit but as the rising poet of France, thanks to the suc-

cess of his first tragedy, *Oedipe* (1718), and to the promise of his epic poem *La Henriade,* a glorification of the popular French monarch Henri IV and of the spirit of toleration. In London, he was received and given handsome gifts by King George I and by his successor, George II, and was introduced to many of the greatest figures of the contemporary political and intellectual world—Walpole, Newcastle, Pulteney, Dodington, Chesterfield, Hervey, Richmond, Peterborough, Argyll, Lyttelton, Pope, Swift, Gay, Cibber, Young, Thomson, Clarke, Woolston, and Morgan, among others.[3] It was through their goodwill and patronage that he was enabled to publish in London a lavish edition of his *Henriade* (1728). The work's subscription list, comprising nearly 350 names, reads like a contemporary *Who's Who.* Sir Robert Walpole himself collected subscriptions from his cabinet colleagues. The first lord of the treasury, unlike most upper-class Englishmen, knew little French; but he knew how to please the queen, who, with the king and their entourage, spoke little else. Voltaire dedicated the work to Queen Caroline, one of his ardent patrons and well-wishers.

Thus began a remarkable network of acquaintance and mutual attraction between Britain's chief opinion-makers and the man who was destined by the 1750s to be hailed universally as the leader of the European Enlightenment. Voltaire never visited Britain again, but during his residence in France in the 1730s and 1740s, and in Prussia during the 1750s, he maintained a correspondence with his old British friends; and after establishing himself at Ferney on the French-Swiss border in 1758 he enlarged and strengthened this personal connection still more by receiving in his home some 150 or more British visitors before he died in 1778, at the advanced age of eighty-three. His relations with these visitors, most of them members of the aristocracy and wealthy gentleman-officials, have been studied in detail, and they present a picture of Voltaire's influence widening and at the same time extending down through two and even three generations of notable British families. Lord Chesterfield, for instance, Voltaire's contemporary (both were born in 1694), not only visited him on the Continent and kept up an exchange of notes and letters with him, but assured with letters of recommendation that parties of younger men, such as Francis Hastings (tenth earl of Huntingdon) and young Stanhope (Chesterfield's cousin and godson, successor to his earldom), would receive a cordial welcome at Ferney. Other old acquaintances did the same: Dodington, Stair (ambassador to France, commander-in-chief of British forces in the 1740s), Fawkener (ambassador to Constantinople, postmaster-general), Beckford (mayor of London), and Fox (leader of the House of Commons, paymaster of the forces). The touring sons, nephews and younger friends of these older men were themselves often destined to achieve eminence, and many of the tutors, guides, and traveling companions who accompanied them to Ferney would do so as well. Politicians, diplomats, artists and writers as diverse and well-known as Charles James Fox, George Macartney, John Wilkes, Edward Gibbon, Horace Walpole, James Boswell, Oliver Goldsmith, Allan Ramsay, George Keate, John

Moore, and Adam Ferguson all made the philosopher's acquaintance, and some visited him on many occasions—Gibbon, for instance, and Adam Smith, who later fondly recalled that he had seen Voltaire five or six times in the course of his travels.[4]

Ferney to these 'second-generation' pilgrims was more than a fixed attraction of the Grand Tour, a place not to be missed; often it figured in their minds as the shrine of a living deity whose fame was already, even before his death, passing into the sphere of heroic legend. In their letters we may sense the awe that they felt on first being admitted to the great man's presence. Take Charles Burney's account of his visit in 1770. There was Voltaire's house. The English musicologist approached it "with reverence, and a curiosity of the most most minute kind." The philosopher was just quitting his garden. On two legs, he was actually walking across the courtyard. "My heart leaped at the sight of so extraordinary a man. . . . He approached the place where I stood, motionless . . . I found myself drawn by some irresistible power towards him; and, without knowing what I did, I insensibly met him halfway." No sooner had they met than Burney began to think of taking his leave, "for fear of breaking in upon his time, being unwilling to rob the public of things so precious as the few remaining moments of this great and universal genius." Voltaire, however, who had charmed the greatest monarchs in Europe, knew how to make his British visitors welcome. He exchanged flattery and gossip with them, made them laugh, entertained them in his private theater, showed them his deist church with its prominent motto DEO EREXIT VOLTAIRE (Voltaire has built this for God), and when they left, often charged them with diplomatic and literary errands. He showered upon them his wit and learning, and sometimes drolly undertook their spiritual guidance as well. A member of Charles Fox's traveling party reported that toward the end of a lively visit in 1768 Voltaire "gave us a list of some of his works, adding, *'Ce sont des livres de quoi il faut se munir,'* they were such as would fortify our young minds against religious prejudices." The philosopher never tired of declaring his Anglomania, and many a visitor proudly recorded it—often in the profane idiom of the 1720s, when Voltaire had learned his English: "By G——I do love de Ingles G——d dammee, if I don't love them bettre dan de French by G——." Yet his visitors admired in him a spirit which transcended the great nations of Europe. Typical were the praises of Harry Temple, Second Viscount Palmerston (father of the Victorian prime minister), in a letter back to England (1763):

> You have no notion how amiable the old man is in private, and [even if] he was not one of the greatest geniuses he would be one of the best creatures in the world. I have seen him receive English, French, Italian and German travellers who all find him equally well acquainted with their country and its literature. His genius is too great to be contained within the limits of his own nation, it belongs to the whole earth. I believe he received from heaven the gift of languages and the knowledge of folio vols, for it is impossible to conceive when he could find time to learn the first, or read the last. . . .[5]

2. Unifying Intellectual Trends

Of course it would be a mistake to think that the cosmopolitanism of the age had no deeper roots than Anglo-French friendship, or more fruitful manifestations than Voltaire-worship among the young and fashionable. One need not deny contemporary reports, for example that Voltaire in 1759 was "as much in fashion among the English as Chinese furniture," or that still ten years later in Scotland "it was in the middle of the age of Voltaire, and his doctrines and his wit had been adopted by all the soi-disant Scotch wits," or that still fifteen years after that, in 1785, this "universal genius" remained, in the view of sophisticated Englishmen, "the most celebrated writer in all of Europe."[6] But widespread attraction to Voltaire was the result of something much deeper, a widespread acceptance of the body of cosmopolitan ideas which, in so many of his writings and activities, he seemed to symbolize.

The European Enlightenment has been pictured in many ways, as a spreading campaign for liberty and humanity, a spreading contagion against authority, a drive for practical reforms, a throwback to medieval ideals. There is no firm agreement on whether it began in the eighteenth century, the seventeenth, or even the sixteenth. Yet from the standpoint of world history, one of the most striking things about it is that it marked a long era of general intellectual unity between the crazy-quilt age of the Reformation, torn by religious divisions, and the age which we ourselves inhabit, fragmented by secular ideologies as well. One may say that this unity was based on two things, a widespread faith in the power of human reason to penetrate nature, and a complementary conception of nature as a machinelike structure governed everywhere by fundamental laws, whether in celestial mechanics or terrestrial physics, anatomy or psychology, politics or international relations or history. The result was a generalizing, indeed a universalizing system of thought which emphasized the rationality of God, the regularity of natural processes, the oneness of humanity, the value of life and of intellectual freedom; and which implicitly opposed revealed religions, arbitrary governments, national enthusiasms and war as artificial and costly barriers to human understanding and brotherhood.

At bottom, this faith in intellect and natural law was itself the product of tradition; or rather of the convergence in the early eighteenth century, most notably and productively in the mind and writings of Voltaire himself, of three powerful secular traditions of thought: French rationalism, British mechanico-empiricism, and the classical moral philosophy common to all European nations. Its patron saints, apart from Grotius and the ancients, were mostly French and English—Descartes and Bacon, Boileau and Bayle, Locke and Newton. Its chief synthesizers and popularizers were Pope, an Englishman thoroughly impregnated with French ideas—he was, by the way, the first English intellectual to take notice of Voltaire (in a letter to Bolingbroke, 1724)—and Voltaire, one of the first Frenchmen of note even to learn the English language, much less apply himself, as he did from the later 1720s on, to the translation and propagation of Lockeian and Newtonian ideas on the Continent. Far more attractive than the writings of Newton and Locke themselves, his popularizations in such works as the *Lettres philosophiques* (1734) and the *Éléments de la philosophie de Newton* (1738) even helped to spread English philosophical ideas in Britain; a fact generously acknowledged by the Royal Societies of London and Edinburgh when they elected him to their memberships in 1743 and 1745. But by this period he was emerging as something more than merely the best-known propagandist of enlightened ideas. Thanks to his unusual longevity, to the primacy in that day of French as the language of international communication, and above all to Voltaire's incredible productivity in nearly all fields of literature, he was coming to be looked upon as the guiding spirit, the high priest of the movement as well.

3. CLASSICAL EDUCATION

The 'mature' Enlightenment was thus primarily an Anglo-French intellectual product, the result of what the great Victorian writer W. E. H. Lecky called a "remarkable junction of the French and English intellect"—so much so indeed that a congress of modern scholars meeting in Warsaw deemed it sufficient to investigate the movement of eighteenth-century thought under the simple heading of 'Franco-British Influence on the Continent.' But, as was suggested earlier, one should not underestimate the extent to which this influence was supported by older assumptions derived from the heritage of classical philosophy and literature, a pagan heritage rediscovered by Renaissance humanists and then synthesized and disseminated by the great French authors of the seventeenth century. When Pope declared, in his *Essay on Criticism* (1711), that "Those Rules of old discovered, not devised,/ Are Nature still, but Nature methodized," he spoke with the authority not only of Locke's psychology and Newton's physics, but of aesthetic and moral philosophy gleaned from Aristotle and Horace, and formulated in Boileau's *L'Art poétique*. Bolingbroke, Voltaire's first British patron, wrote under similar influences when he observed (in his 'Reflections on Exile,' 1716) that "a wise man looks on himself as a citizen of the world: and, when you ask him where his country lies, points, like ANAXAGORAS, with his finger to the heavens." In short, the generalizing character of enlightened opinion was indeed powerfully shaped by the leveling and rationalizing epistemologies and cosmologies of the Scientific Revolution, but it was laid in soil prepared by much earlier 'citizens of the world' who also had contemplated nature, religion, art and manners as 'things in general,' *sub specie aeternitatis*. Education in the classics helped to promote the cosmopolitan cast of mind. McKillop makes the point succinctly in an essay on eighteenth-century cosmopolitanism: "The more direct the influence from classical moral philosophy, the more reluctance there was to grant validity to inexplicable special attachments."[7]

4. ENLIGHTENED TOLERATION AND ANTI-PATRIOTISM

There were, as is well known, two characteristic targets of this potent mistrust of 'special attachments.' National sentiment was one, and the famous anti-patriotic expressions of writers so diverse as Voltaire, Johnson, and Goethe arose from this frame of mind. It was only in such a context that Voltaire, despising patriotic enthusiasms, could have embarked hopefully in 1761 on his second great literary subscription project, a campaign to underwrite his own monumental edition of the *Théâtre de Pierre Corneille,* the collected works of the great seventeenth-century dramatist—a project which envious or unenlightened foreigners might easily have condemned as an indirect glorification of French national literature and of the neoclassical literary and dramatic rules that were linked to it with such special intimacy. Yet no such condemnation was voiced, and more than a hundred well-to-do Britons even joined the international subscription list.[8] The campaign's success is the more significant when one recalls that France and England and the other major European powers were then locked in bitter warfare.

The other 'special attachment' that suffered from the expanding influence of enlightened thought was, of course, Christianity. It is true that certain social and political forces were working in the same direction. Religious enthusiasm of any sort was an object of suspicion among peoples and governments still struggling to emerge from nearly two centuries of religious warfare. But it is no secret that the premises of enlightened thought were often at odds with the traditions and authority of Christian belief, and that no matter how ingeniously Christian apologists tried to reconcile the two, it was religious enthusiasm that suffered. The result, as Tocqueville later remarked in a famous chapter on 'anti-religious feeling' under the ancien régime, was that Christianity lost much of its hold on men's minds throughout Europe. Deism and other forms of natural religion, championed not only by Voltaire but certainly very effectively by him, became prevalent among the upper classes. It became fashionable to doubt whether any of the world's revealed religions had a monopoly on truth; and then, by the third quarter of the century, whether they possessed even a little of it. Christianity as an intellectual system survived chiefly because it was watered down and made 'reasonable.' The ideal of religious toleration, forming since the later sixteenth century, emerged as a powerful force. And it became increasingly sharp and influential not only because it seemed the correct attitude but also because, in the minds of those who mattered—the wealthy and educated—the older, essentially political and social fear of 'fanaticism' was now sometimes mixed with a new intellectual contempt and moral indignation at the sight of persecution.

5. PERSONAL INFLUENCE OF VOLTAIRE

Here too, in the central attack on 'superstition' and the crusade for general toleration, Voltaire served as Europe's schoolmaster. John Wilkes was but one among thousands who believed that this "universal genius, the most amiable, as well as the wittiest of our species," born "for the advancement of true philosophy and the polite arts, and to free mankind from the gloomy terrors of superstition," had "done more to persuade the practice of a general toleration, of humanity and benevolence, than [even] the greatest philosophers of antiquity." Horace Walpole phrased the general applause more elegantly when he lauded Voltaire as not only the greatest literary stylist but the most powerful moralist in Europe, the "countryman *du coté du coeur*" of all men. More tangible tributes were proffered in the impressive European response to still another great Voltairean subscription campaign which began in 1762. This grew out of the notorious Calas affair, aptly dubbed by Brailsford "the Dreyfus case of the eighteenth century." France, though not unaffected by the spirit of toleration, remained a Catholic nation, with pockets of extreme anti-Protestant fanaticism still existing in provincial centers such as Toulouse. Protestants labored under heavy disabilities, and the preaching of Protestantism was a capital crime; the pastor Rochette was executed for it in Toulouse in early 1762. Later that year in the same city another Protestant, the draper Jean Calas, was barbarously tortured and finally killed by the local authorities on the charge, never substantiated even under torture, that he had murdered his own son; who, the authorities alleged, had been contemplating conversion to the Catholic faith. In fact the son had simply committed suicide. Voltaire, on learning all this, became so enraged that he put aside everything else in an effort to vindicate Calas and exonerate and indemnify his widow and two younger sons who remained under suspicion. With the Corneille subscription he had taught all Europe a lesson in contempt for the patriotic prejudices which were apt to divide peoples; similarly, in the Calas case he labored to bring together all friends of toleration in a single great cause. While helping to engage and write memoranda for lawyers (who ultimately fought the case up to the King's Court of Appeal, where in 1765 the dead man was finally acquitted and his judicial murderers humiliated), Voltaire simultaneously enlisted the salons, the presses, the leading figures and opinion-makers of every nation in a subscription to defray legal costs and support Calas's widow. The campaign was a huge success. In Britain alone 137 wealthy subscribers came forth in a group headed by the king's prime minister (the earl of Bute), the Archbishop of Canterbury, ten bishops, twelve dukes, and a cloud of lesser noblemen and gentlemen. Voltaire was particularly gratified to see that among all Europeans it was the English and French who outdid each other in generosity, "*à qui secourerait le mieux la vertu si cruellement opprimée.*"[9]

Writing on this affair, the late Theodore Besterman remarked that "by his activity in the Calas case Voltaire created public opinion as a new and increasingly weighty factor in the life of a civilised community." Perhaps we should take this statement in the same liberal spirit with which we understand, for example, Benjamin Franklin's comment in his autobiography that "Voltaire's *Treatise on Toleration* has had so sudden and so great an Effect on the Bigotry of Europe, as almost entirely to disarm it." It is convenient to explain trends in opinion by reference to a single event such as the Calas affair, or a single powerful book such as the treatise that Voltaire published in the midst of it (1764). But the response to his subscription campaign and his treatise, like the responses to the contemporaneous expulsion and papal dissolution of the Society of Jesus, were more in the nature of spectacular results of the drift of contemporary opinion than causes of it. Voltaire himself, not to mention other writers, had labored to spread the gospel of toleration for many decades. His first great literary production, *Oedipe,* contained lines which, as Lecky observed, clearly foreshadowed the mission of his life—*"Nos prêtres ne son pas ce qu'un vain peuple pense,/ Notre crédulité fait toute leur science."* The *Henriade* was an untiring celebration of the royal author of the Edict of Nantes. The *Lettres philosophiques,* in which Voltaire contrasted French conditions unfavorably with English ones, was a witty and incisive exposition of the good effects of toleration and intellectual freedom; and though the work was promptly condemned (1734) by the French censors as subversive of order and religion, it nevertheless constituted a landmark in the history of European opinion and so figured, in the famous words of the critic Gustave Lanson, as "the first bomb thrown at the *ancien régime.*"[10] The same philosophical message, emphasizing the positive relationship between toleration, free thought, and social progress, reappears in many of Voltaire's later works—histories such as *Le Siècle de Louis XIV* (1751) and the much-admired *Essai sur les moeurs* (1756), fiction such as *Zadig* (1747) and *Candide* (1759), miscellaneous works of all sorts such as the *Dictionnaire philosophique* (1764) and *Questions sur l'Encyclopédie* (1770). The same was true of many of his twenty-odd plays; *Zaire* (1732), for example, teaches humanity through a sentimental confrontation between Muslim and Christian, *Alzire* (1736) through portrayal of the brutal conquest of Peruvian natives by Spaniards, *Mahomet* (1742) through a more comprehensive attack on fanaticism and revealed religion of every kind, not excluding Christianity—and the play's dedication to the pope deceived no one except perhaps the pope himself, who responded with a complimentary letter.

Nor can it be doubted that these works were influential, far more so than those of any other eighteenth-century writer. Dr. John Moore—traveler and man of letters, surgeon, father of Sir John Moore and Admiral Sir Graham Moore—looked back from the 1790s and, with reference to European opinion during the preceding half century, commented that "the writings of Voltaire, distinguished for wit, and a happiness of expression which baffles imitation, contributed more than all the rest to form the taste and bias the opinions of the age. They were more universally read than the works of any other author." And there is much other evidence to the same effect. The historian Preserved Smith discovered that in Europe at large Voltaire's collected works (entirely apart from the publication and reprinting of individual works) went through nineteen editions between 1740 and 1778. A bibliographer (Evans) found that

Voltaire's writings were so much in demand in England that the first translated edition of his collected works (in thirty-six volumes, published in 1761–65) went through three printings by 1770 and led to still another complete edition in 1779–81. R. S. Crane, the noted literary scholar, found in a painstaking study of the reception of Voltaire's works in England that these were so "extraordinarily" popular as to have overshadowed not only the works of all other foreign writers but those of all contemporary British authors as well. In an examination of the contents of more than two hundred private libraries owned by a wide variety of officials, clergymen, professionals, and assorted men of leisure he arrived at the "remarkable fact" that Voltaire's writings, whether in French or in English translation or in combinations of the two, were represented in nearly 80 percent, eight out of ten, of these holdings; the next most popular writers were Pope (represented in just over 50 percent of the libraries), Young (28 percent), Thomson (nearly 24 percent), and Rousseau (23 percent). Of course it is more difficult to establish how seriously these books were read. One cannot often find such direct testimony as that of Chesterfield, for instance, in which, writing to his son, he noted that he had read all of Voltaire's works more than once, and one of them, the *Siècle de Louis XIV*, four times. But Crane's statistics are very significant. So too are other measurements, such as that afforded by examination of Voltaire's place in the pages of contemporary British periodicals. So frequently did his letters and miscellaneous pieces appear there that when he died in 1778, the periodicals broke out in italicized lamentations: *"We have lost an excellent contributor to our journal, at least in the article of entertainment!—What shall we do for another Voltaire?"*[11]

6. INSTITUTIONAL UNIFORMITIES

And thus when the British and other Europeans responded generously to the Calas campaign, they did so because public opinion had already been conditioned by Voltaire and by the intellectual influences of the Enlightenment. But the international confluences and solidarities of opinion that existed in that age, the 'European consciousness' that was so widely remarked upon at the time, was the result also of a level of understanding between men and nations which had little to do with the climate of contemporary ideas, favorable though this was. The cosmopolitan spirit derived from deeper structural influences as well. It originated, as Edmund Burke observed—and his view simply echoed a widely held opinion—in a great range of institutional resemblances between the European states, provided by history and made known through travel and "habitual intercourse," which, to continue in his words, tended to "approximate men to men without their knowledge, and sometimes against their intentions," so that when a man traveled "from his own country, he never felt himself quite abroad." At bottom, Burke continued, the religion, laws, manners, classes, orders and systems of Europe, and "the whole form and fashion of life" were "all the same." Europe was not so much an aggregate of nations as a single commonwealth, "virtually one great state, having the same basis of general law, with some diversity of provincial customs and local establishments."[12] Europeans were tied to one another by great institutional uniformities, and by instinctive understandings and sympathies resulting from them.

Burke wrote these lines with reference to all Europe, but thoughts of France and his own country were uppermost in his mind. Resemblances between the two nations were all too evident to his experienced eye. Of course there were obvious differences between them, often to France's advantage. France, geographically the largest nation in Europe outside Russia, with a population at mid-century of more than twenty million, was three times as populous as England, and this power was backed by impressive economic resources, superior political and diplomatic weight, and an army capable not only of defeating any other army in Europe but of successfully resisting any combination of powers opposed to it. So widespread was French cultural influence and so effective was France's long-standing policy of foreign subsidies and bribes that it is indeed "not surprising," as a noted diplomatic historian has written, that English statesmen "were often despondent about their chances of competing successfully with France in foreign courts."[13] But Britain's power and influence had risen greatly since the Revolution of 1688, thanks both to the intellectual discoveries, constitutional freedoms and financial arrangements hailed by Voltaire in his *Lettres philosophiques,* and to her success since the days of the French-sponsored Stuarts and Jacobites in winning independent Great Power status, free from French political interference. These two states were, by the middle of the eighteenth century, the only two Great Powers in Europe, in the sense of having the capacity to wage war without dependence on other powers. Both were great maritime and colonial states, and both had seen during the first half of the century an impressive rise of commercial activity and wealth. They were the two richest and most advanced nations in the world. In the application of new techniques to industrial processes they were, as late as 1789, about equal, though France was still probably ahead of Britain in total industrial as well as agricultural production. On the other hand, the pace of technological change was faster in Britain—an important point upon which we may be able to cast some light later. And both countries were just beginning to experience some of the social stress and political ferment of societies approaching the era of industrialization.

7. ARISTOCRATIC CULTURE

Yet as Burke emphasized, it was primarily the feudal and agricultural past, rather than new developments leading to the future, which provided the great underlying uniformities and psychological affinities of European society. Britain and France, like most other European nations in the eighteenth century, were monarchies of the ancien régime, dominated in church and state by hereditary or quasi-hereditary oligarchies as yet scarcely challenged by the forces of competitive and individualistic modern society. The progressive middle classes of both countries, tiny by today's standards, without organization and still trained in deferential attitudes toward the nobility, had little political influence before the French Revolution, and indeed the Revolution itself was at the outset instigated and led by noblemen. Eighteenth-century European culture was an aristocratic culture, the product of centuries of aristocratic leadership and domination, and it was among the courts and wealthy nobilities of Europe that the instinctive moral and social internationalism to which Burke referred was most pronounced.

J.-P. Labatut, the French historian, has attempted in his recent study of the European nobilities to disentangle and define the many causes of this internationalist sentiment.[14] The oldest of these lay in the common values and traditions engendered among all noble families by their superior wealth and position. In common they were the possessors of inherited landed wealth, family estates, titles and armorial bearings, privileges in government and at the bar of justice. They shared privileges of dress, special hunting rights, and common expectations of high occupational preferment in civil governments, religious establishments, the armed forces, and the diplomatic services. They enjoyed a sense of superiority which traditionally had been cultivated in religious precepts, enshrined in the doctrine of nobility of blood, recognized in law by institutions such as primogeniture and entail, sanctioned by their leadership functions and by the ancient tradition of noblesse oblige, and accepted by their inferiors and by society at large. Their wealth, opportunities, and status led them through similar educational institutions and encouraged in them similar pursuits of honors and distinctions, similar patterns of deportment before equals and inferiors, similar reliances on favor and loyal service as roads to fortune and advancement. Their venerable place in military affairs furnished common standards of honor and a sense of aristocratic brotherhood which often overrode whatever kinship they felt with their lesser-born countrymen. There is hidden social significance in stories such as that of the Battle of Fontenoy, at which the gallant French officers politely invited the gallant English officers to shoot first: *"Messieurs les Anglais, tirez les premiers!"*

In the eighteenth century these unifying tendencies among Europe's upper classes were strengthened into important forces by a marked expansion of international communication and travel, by general acceptance of common standards of genteel speech and manners, and by still other aspects of the aristocratic resurgence which in most countries accompanied these developments. The Grand Tour, an established feature of English aristocratic education by mid-century, was mirrored in the *'voyage de gentilhomme'* pursued by well-born French, German, Italian, Russian, Spanish, and Polish youths as they crisscrossed Europe, often for periods lasting more than three years, spending princely sums, visiting foreign courts, cities, family homes, and salons. The announced purpose of the tour, apart from its myriad pleasures, was to give a man 'parts'; to polish his conversation and manners, deepen his experience of the world, sharpen his judgment of art, habits and character, and, not least, provide him an easy fluency in foreign languages, especially French, which, like French manners, was accepted as the common vehicle of this intercourse, and which was in addition an essential prerequisite for careers in diplomacy. France, "an irresistible magnet to young English gentlemen," as Mingay observes, was the centerpiece of the tour, after which the young nobleman made his way to Italy (usually via Geneva and Ferney) and then to other countries, chiefly Germany and Holland, for shorter visits. Since the tour was expensive, "a couple of years in France" was deemed sufficient for younger sons. So great was the dependence of certain Parisian hotelkeepers on young English gentlemen that some of them blamed their bankruptcies on a recession of English clientele during a phase of Anglo-French warfare. But then, as Gay says of Voltaire, "where he was, there was Paris," and the most popular salon in Europe was open to young milords with the right credentials at any time, during peace or war.[15] Voltaire aptly styled himself "the innkeeper of Europe," and it would be hard to find any historical scene which better captures the attunement of intellectual ideals to social realities, of philosophical cosmopolitanism to social internationalism, than that portrayed in the letter by young Palmerston quoted earlier, in which young bluebloods from all countries, pursuing their amiable wanderings, joined at Ferney to share the hospitality of the intellectual wonder and genius of all nations, of 'the whole earth.'

David Hume, watching all this, shrewdly observed that "where any set of men, scatter'd over distant nations, have a close society or communication together, they acquire a similitude of manners, and have but little in common with the nations amongst whom they live." The institutionalization of foreign travel, the development of international friendships and marriages, the acceptance of French as the language of international communication, the propagation through the great courts and through dozens of published manuals of a single system of deportment, the tendency to extend formal recognition to foreign noblemen (the houses of La Force and Mazarin, for example, were recognized in the English peerage, while those of Portsmouth and Richmond achieved recognition in France)—all of these tendencies, together with the traditional affinities mentioned earlier, were, in the opinion of many historians who have looked closely at the matter, working together to promote, just as Burke suggested, a single aristocratic civilization throughout Europe. This is the central thesis of Labatut's book, that the early modern era saw a "progressive unity of the nobilities," intensifying in the eighteenth century to produce a single aristocratic personality type and style of life. Hampson in his penetrating study of the Enlightenment maintains a similar thesis in his commentary on how "the gentlemen of Europe formed more of a social club in the eighteenth century than at any time before or since." The same basic idea is instrumental in Palmer's important study of this era, in which intensifying aristocratic consciousness and social exclusiveness are seen as mainsprings of general revolutionary change.[16]

8. LA BELLE FRANCE

Of course it would be very wrong to infer from all this that regional and national differences did not exist. A British statute was not a Russian *ukaz,* a soufflé was not a potato, the barefoot nobles of Poland were not the Pelhams of Sussex, bagpipes were not the fashion in Naples or Vienna. The point is not that life was everywhere the same or that national institutions were interchangeably similar, but that common structural features of social organization were working together with an increasing circulation of people and the elaboration of a unifying pattern of secular ideas to produce a common consciousness at the upper levels of European society, distinctively marked by cosmopolitan ideals and by related inhibitions against the assertion of provincial attachments.

Indeed the very differences that existed between societies were made the subject of selective importation by these same sophisticated circles, with the effect that the 'great' and 'fashionable' world became more homogeneous still. A growing awareness among educated Frenchmen of England's superior religious and intellectual freedom encouraged the spread of related ideals in France, and perception of the political power directly enjoyed by the English landed classes encouraged French desires for, and increasing emphasis on, whiggish constitutional forms. Intensifying interest in English life led to such an unprecedented influx of distinguished French visitors during the first decades of George III's reign that English observers began to notice that there was "a considerable tendency to approximation between the two nations." Lecky's phrase is reminiscent of Arthur Young's comment, on visiting the homes of French noblemen in the later 1780s, that "there is a great approximation in the modes of living at present in the different countries of Europe."[17]

In the same way, English importations of French culture reveal the selective influence of the cosmopolitan upper classes. Of course there was nothing new in this, since so many features of upper-class English culture had been French to begin with. As Fisher writes, "the Norman Conquest had made of England a province of French civilization. The language of the aristocracy, of the government, of the law courts, was French. It was from the île de France that England derived its Gothic architecture. . . . Feudalism, chivalry, the Crusades, were French. The university movement, so far as England was concerned, originated in Paris." And so on, with many other reminders of how "intermingled were the two countries," how "indistinct were the spiritual frontiers," especially between upper classes, during the centuries of Norman and Angevin rule.[18]

And these were only the beginnings of Norman and French influences. Anglo-French was the natural speech of the English upper classes into the fourteenth century, and in various forms, as in law and in the writing of law reports, it survived to the eighteenth. The royal motto and the formal royal assent and dissent on parliamentary bills came from the French. All English noble titles, even the word *peerage* itself, were taken from the French. A number of aristocratic houses, aided by resourceful heralds, traced their descent from the Normans—the Percies of Northumberland, the Greys of Howick, the Lowthers, Montagus, Grosvenors, Stanleys. English terms surrounding the 'noble' arts of war, hunting, hawking, heraldry, and cookery were French, as were those pertaining to luxurious pastimes such as cards, dancing, and dice. And then in addition to these many influences from the past there were very heavy influences later, as during the Restoration, which of course coincided with the beginning of the great age of Louis XIV in France, so widely imitated throughout Europe. This era of the later Stuarts, themselves partly of French blood, nourished in French culture, and sustained by French bribes as well, saw a regenerated Francophilism which deeply affected all aspects of English taste and manners until late in the eighteenth century, indeed later. 'Jack would be a gentleman—if he could speak French' was still a proverb in the nineteenth century. Even in the twentieth century one may easily find traces of the mental associations left by these ancient historic connections between class, breeding, and French influence. A novelist such as Michael Innes (J. I. M. Stewart) will introduce one of his English bluebloods as "the product of centuries of breeding. His appearance was as thoroughly Anglo-Norman as was that of his castle." Nancy Mitford introduces two of her characters as members of a large group of upper-class Francophiles: "They both belonged to the category of English person, not rare among the cultivated classes, and not the least respectable of their race, who can find almost literally nothing to criticize where the French are concerned."[19]

Though there were, then, many strands of Anglo-French 'intermingling,' the age of Louis XIV was particularly important in strengthening the Francophilism of the English upper classes. Later generations, considering such influences disreputable, have minimized and even denied them, but so great in fact was the international splendor of the court of Versailles, so well rooted became the acceptance of French superiority in fashions, manners, and taste that a 'Gallic stamp' was imposed on these things in England as well as elsewhere. Jarrett rightly remarks that "early eighteenth-century England was unsure of itself in many ways, acutely conscious of the long shadow of France and French culture," and there are signs that London was in some respects as much a cultural colony of Paris as Rome, Madrid, or St. Petersburg. The supremacy of French fashions in dress was so well established by the age of Queen Anne that Richard Steele could write humorously of a friend at the club, "the gallant Will Honeycomb," who "knows the history of every mode, and can inform you from which of the French king's wenches our wives and daughters had this manner of curling their hair, that way of placing their hoods; and whose vanity to show her foot made that part of the dress so short in such a year." A similar pattern held sway in many other domains where fashion reigned. There was a great thirst for French cosmetics, jewelry, plate, and tapestries. English cooking was held to be as inferior to French as French religious toleration was to English—indeed Voltaire's quip that England had a hundred religions and only one sauce, that France had just the reverse, captures some of the facts of contemporary cultural interchange. French cooks were so sought-after in England that, as Mingay writes, they "ranked among the proudest possessions of wealthy aristocrats."[20] Much the same was long true of fashions in furniture, interior decoration and gardening; landscape gardens such as those at Oakley Park and Riskins, so admired by Pope, were modeled on those at Versailles and Fontainebleu.

As to standards of literature, the international supremacy of the French language—and, behind it, the century-old authority of the Académie Française, an official literary institution with no counterpart in England—ensured the overwhelming dominance of French models. In English literature the whole era from Dryden to Johnson was, as Clark has demonstrated, powerfully influenced by the authority of French critics, authors and playwrights; it was "a time when every one was aping French fashions." One understands what Victorian critics, Leslie Stephen for example, meant when writing of "the Gallicised neatness of Addison and Pope." Moreover in the English theater, as Pope graciously acknowledged in his 'Imitations of Horace,' "Exact Racine and Corneille's noble fire/ Show'd us that France had something to admire"—a sentiment which, as we noted previously, still lived in the early 1760s when Voltaire launched his Corneille subscription. In the twentieth century it requires some effort of the imagination to grasp that as late as 1759, prior to the English Shakespeare revival, it was not Shakespeare but the 'Gallicised' Pope whom Englishmen unhesitatingly thought of as "our favorite British bard." Arthur Young was still marveling in the late 1780s at the superiority of the French theater "to all I have ever seen," and in view of this it cannot be thought too surprising that Voltaire, France's greatest contemporary playwright, Corneille's successor, should have enjoyed such tremendous popularity on the English stage. Sixteen or more of his plays were adapted for the London stage. "There was no living dramatist in England to challenge comparison with Voltaire," writes Bruce.[21]

In the realm of poetry, distinguished English judges were not unwilling to acknowledge French excellence. "Voltaire's *Henriad* may be placed at the head of the modern epic," wrote Thomas Warton, and he, like many others, hailed the greatness of Voltaire's achievements in the writing of history. The Frenchman was "the first who has displayed the literature and customs of the dark ages with any degree of penetration and comprehension." In fact in virtually all departments of literature, wrote Sir William Jones, Voltaire "excels all writers of his age and country in the elegance of his style, and the wonderful variety of his talents."[22] Yet Voltaire, the most respected cosmopolitan writer of the age, was but the most dazzling light in the firmament of encyclopedists, essayists, historians, poets, mathematicians, scientists, musicians, and artists who shone forth from the Académie Française and the salons of Paris—themselves much admired and imitated by the fashionable hostesses, the 'bas blue,' of London.

Finally, as to importations of social manners, there was a persistent effort in eighteenth-century England to spread what many fastidious observers regarded as France's much superior standards of courtesy, address, deportment, table manners, and habits of personal cleanliness. The English dancing-master, often an elegant Frenchman himself, and a specialist in manners as well as dancing and physical deportment, was a characteristic sign of this effort. Most Englishmen, says Jarrett, "felt a little awkward and self-conscious in the presence of the polished suavity of the French." By the 1780s, however, French visitors such as the Duc de la Rochefoucauld were apt to find themselves very much at home with the manners of their English hosts; though even under the roof of the Duke of Grafton there survived unpleasant traces of former local deficiencies— excessive spitting, we are told, together with drunkenness, indecency of conversation, the rinsing of the mouth at table, indifference to table linen, the free resort to chamber pots in the dining room after the retirement of ladies and servants, and much scratching. Edmund Burke summed things up when he asked, looking back over the centuries, whether England had learned manners from France or vice versa, then handed the palm to France: "You seem to me to be—*gentis incunabula nostrae*. France has always more or less influenced manners in England; and when your fountain is choked up and polluted, the stream will not run long, or run clear, with us, or perhaps any nation."[23] In these phrases he again voiced his conviction that Europe was a morally, intellectually and institutionally unified civilization, and added the notion, a mere truism among European historians today, that the pervasive influence of French tastes and cultural models was still another binding element in this 'one great state, having the same basis of general law, with some diversity of provincial customs and local establishments.' To the English as well as to all the other peoples surrounding France, the cosmopolitan spirit was bolstered by a diffused spirit of Francophilism as well, and not infrequently confused with it.

The 'European consciousness' of the eighteenth century was thus the product of many influences, so many indeed that in this brief survey there is little room for details of the cosmopolitan intellectual movement itself (though this has been well handled already by Gay, Schlereth, and others), for discussion of the lines of international communication among bankers, traders, booksellers, etc., or for consideration of lesser influences such as the interesting role played by colonies of resident aliens—there were, for example, populous colonies of Englishmen in most of the larger cities of France, Switzerland, and Italy. But without taking the matter further one may say in summary that European society was in a general way unified by similar institutions and modes of social organization, that it was still more unified at the top by personal contacts, nomadic families, an international social network, cross-cultural borrowings, French fashions and manners, and the similarity of life at the great courts; and, further, that the capstone of all this was a system of cosmopolitan ideals which seemed authenticated in the advanced ideas of the day, which received the blessing of the prestigious philosophical movement, and which promoted the international interests and pleasures of Europe's upper classes.

3. 1735, Hogarth, "A Rake's Progress." *The man of fashion, wearing slippers and nightcap, holds his morning levee. Suggestive of his expensive foreign tastes are the French fencing master, the dancing master, the paintings behind, the new clothes brought by attendants at the left, and the whole display in the left foreground. From the back of the harpsichordist's chair there hangs a long scroll which begins: "A list of the rich Presents Signor Farinelli the Italian Singer Condescended to Accept of ye English Nobility & Gentry for one Nights Performance in the Opera Artaxerses." The scroll ends on the floor near an engraving of the same singer on a pedestal, to whom a throng of infatuated English ladies sacrifice their hearts.*

CHAPTER TWO

Cosmopolitanism and Aristocratic Supremacy

*Philosophy had no apostles more well disposed than the grand seigneurs,
. . . even more than men of letters.*

—VICOMTESSE DE NOAILLES

The ideas of the ruling class are, in every age, the ruling ideas.

—MARX

MODERN THOUGHT has been conditioned by Marx and his followers
to look suspiciously at every ideological system as in part a conceal-
ment, in part a rationalization, of underlying arrangements of power.
Was this true of eighteenth-century cosmopolitanism? Did cosmopolitanism underwrite aristocratic society? Oddly enough, the question
has received little attention. We cannot ignore it here, for cosmopolitan
culture was the soil from which European nationalism burst forth.

1. SINEWS OF ARISTOCRATIC POWER

Obviously the answer depends on the true nature of aristocratic power in
that age. Certain aspects of this have been extensively studied and are well
understood. The most visible side of aristocratic power was economic.
The great landlords' ownership of immense agricultural estates conferred
upon them innumerable powers which deeply affected the livelihood,
even the survival, of their countrymen. And this power of superior wealth
was on the upswing throughout the century. The reigns of the first two
Hanoverian kings saw a steady enlargement of aristocratic estates. The
great magnates "owned a much larger, and the lesser rustic squires a
much smaller acreage of England in 1760 than in 1660." Further, by 1760
these long-term tendencies began to receive powerful new stimuli from an
unexpected acceleration of population growth that resulted in a phenomenal rise of agricultural profits—profits which rose by forty or fifty percent between 1760 and 1790, and as Mingay adds, "even more where
much land was enclosed."[1]

These attractive profits had the effect of hastening the enlargement of
landed estates and their concentration in fewer hands through the passing of parliamentary enclosure acts. Soon the great landlords possessed
not only commons and wastes that formerly had not belonged to them,
but also many properties which smaller farmers, victims of this process,
could no longer farm competitively. The enclosure acts, "hurried through
every Parliament of George III," constituted a "radicalism of the rich." It
was not chiefly the traders from the towns who took over these properties,
"it was the men who already owned land that were buying more land."[2]
The landed rich became still richer, but as they did so they passed many
costs on to their tenants, relieving themselves of inherited paternalistic

responsibilities and giving still larger rein to their increasingly insatiable passions for home-building, landscape gardening, gambling, and other conspicuous consumption.

A second important source of the landlords' power lay in their control of political activity. Not since the Middle Ages had they exercised such complete political dominance as that which they began to enjoy under the Hanoverian kings. Here also the pattern during much of the century was one of continuing concentration at the uppermost reaches of landed society. Even in the counties, traditionally the preserve of the gentry, justices of the peace were increasingly appointed on the recommendation of the Lords Lieutenant, great noblemen sitting in the central government who now began to take over much of the patronage in the localities as well. There was a gradual monopolization of power. From a high level of popular involvement and party strife throughout the nation's constituencies in the age of Queen Anne, there emerged a tendency to concentrate power in the hands of a select oligarchy by narrowing the electoral franchise, lengthening the period between elections, reducing party strife and the number of electoral contests, eliminating unwanted voters, and managing and disciplining those who remained. By mid-century "the individual who possessed a political franchise very rarely had the opportunity to exercise it." Political power at both the national and local levels had been absorbed by aristocratic political managers whose actions were only too often dictated by considerations of self-interest. "What was increasingly obvious to the world at large was the development of a self-gratifying oligarchy that held power for its own profit."[3]

Manifestations of this enhanced power could be seen in new game laws, criminal laws and turnpike acts, all establishing new conveniences and privileges for the elite, matched by new hardships and more severe penalties for the many. Special hunting rights allowed gentlemen to ride roughshod over their tenants' land while prohibiting the latter from hunting. Exemptions from turnpike tolls for gentlemen's carriages were laid down even while penalties for toll-gate offenses were raised from whipping and imprisonment to transportation and death.[4] Other such phenomena, expressive of growing political concentration and social stratification, could be listed. The effect would only be to dispel still further the old rosy generalizations on eighteenth-century England and erase other sentimental distinctions between English life and the harsh existence elsewhere.

A third aspect of aristocratic power, the vertical structure of rewards and services, has also been studied in detail. So pervasive indeed was the practice of 'patronage and clientage' that historians have taken this as their prototypical organizing concept in thinking about the entire eighteenth-century social structure. The power of the landed classes is visualized in terms of a reciprocal flow of favors and services from the top of society to the bottom, from elite families through a pyramidal structure ultimately touching everyone. Such are the terms in which Perkin, for example, in his now classic survey, pictures the English ancien régime.

And this notion of an ubiquitous godfatherism does seem to capture the inner facts of contemporary political organization. Nothing is more famil iar in our history books than the vision of great magnates—Pelhams, Grenvilles, Bedfords, etc.—gathering around themselves by nepotism and the distribution of favors larger followings of loyal dependants, them-selves commanding trains of electors and other people no less influenced by considerations of private advantage. "The great Chain of political Self-Interest," cried its nearly impotent critics, extended "from the *lowest Cobler* in a *Borough,* to the *King's first Minister.*" Elevated notions of principle and the public good were inevitably at low ebb, and the tale of eighteenth-century politics is largely an unedifying one of shifting coalitions of pow-erful landholders maneuvering and grappling for plunder, all the while talking solemnly of Whig principles and luring into their camps younger men to talk the same stuff even better. Flattery and insincere declamation were the meat and potatoes of politics, and it is no wonder that modern political biographers, momentarily overcome by exasperation, will some-times remark of their subjects that they were "as promiscuous in . . . pol-itics" as their mothers were "in . . . love affairs."[5]

Yet these were the same ineffably charming people whom Cecil, in a marvelous little essay, saluted as "the most agreeable society England has ever known." There is truth to this, but also to the charge that they ex-ploited every advantage to keep things agreeable for themselves and their kin. Patronage began at home. Virtually everything belonging to the gov-ernment had prior claims on it by the barnacle sons of the elite. In the House of Commons in 1761 there were five Townshends, five Mannerses, four Cavendishes, four Yorkes, three Walpoles, three Cornwallises—as Namier coyly writes, "the 'predestination' of Parliament extended even to younger sons." Mingay says it was "not very extraordinary" for a member of parliament to have fifty relatives in the House of Commons, and it is a fact that more than half the men who sat there during the entire century before 1832 were sons, nephews or grandsons of earlier members. The sides and bottom of the iceberg were equally encrusted. Nepotism and favoritism prevailed throughout the civil services and the fighting ser-vices—where, of course, the purchase of army commissions provided still another special advantage to the sons of the great. Yet there were never enough jobs to go around, "the lucrative *Employs* of our *Country* not being near so numerous as the Claimants are," as the critics impotently thun-dered; and while the number of bureaucratic posts remained small throughout the century, the number of needy applicants rose continually. Early in the century there were some 20,000 younger males of the upper class "who having but a small estate get preferments one way or other"; there were probably at least twice or three times that number by the six-ties and seventies. By that period, says Baugh, the pressure to place aristo-cratic nominees was becoming intense. Botsford finds that in colonial administration, "government positions in the West Indies alone" were taken by "thousands of younger sons." There was a belief in the seventies that the rupture with America had been precipitated in part by aristo-

cratic pressure to find places in the colonies for "their wretched dependants," "the same train of vermin to which this country has been so long a
prey."[6]

Of course the Church furnished other picking-grounds closer to home.
It too, like colonial administration, was in one respect nothing more than
a branch of political society, exhibiting the same vertical linkages and
exuding the same noxious vapors over matters of principle and the public
good. The Church perpetuated the comfortable ideas of Society. Its only
indispensable qualification for high office was political reliability—that
and a good pedigree, for it is conceded even by Sykes, its ablest defender,
that the episcopate was regarded as "the providentially appointed portion
of younger sons of the temporal nobility." The rise of the 'squarson' sig-
naled a parallel at the level of the parish clergy. "Throughout the Eighteenth Century, country gentlemen came more and more to regard
livings in their gift as worth the acceptance of their younger sons."[7]

In view of all this it should come as no shock that Voltaire's writings
were, as Professor Crane observed, 'remarkably' well represented in these
clergymen's private libraries. Like the rest of society, they admired his
histories, laughed at his stories, respected his literary criticism, and had a
very high tolerance for his skepticism. He was a Whig like them, wary of
kings, loving liberty, despising the mob. They loved and hated many of
the things that he loved and hated, and condemned religious enthusiasm
no less than he; for it was intellectually insupportable, it tended towards
cruelty, it threatened society, and, not least, no hope for advancement lay
in it. 'Enthusiasm' in the parlance of the day meant "ill-regulated or mis-
directed religious emotion, extravagance of religious speculation." Deism
"had shaken Christianity badly," says Stromberg; it had given a worldly
twist to the latitudinarian theology of the day, and done nothing to discourage the worldly concerns of the clergy. Voltaire in his *Lettres philosophiques* waggishly remarked that though there were many faiths in
England, Anglicanism was "their genuine Religion, the one in which people make their fortune." The higher clergy, appointees of the crown,
comfortably remunerated for service in the House of Lords as well as for
ecclesiastical duties, lived luxuriously, so often occupying themselves
rather with mundane than pastoral concerns that it was said of some that
they never entered their churches till the day of their funeral. William
Cowper published many complaints in his 'Tirocinium' (1784): "Behold
your bishop! well he plays his part, / Christian in name, and infidel in
heart, / Ghostly in office, earthly in his plan, / A slave at court, elsewhere
a lady's man." The clergy's corruption was most evident at the heart of
fashionable society in London. C. P. Moritz, a German visitor, commented
in 1782 that "the English clergy, especially in London, are notorious for
their free and easy way of life," and went on to tell the amusing story of
one young cleric who, having recently killed his opponent at a duel in
Hyde Park, was sentenced to be branded on the hand—"with a *cold* iron,"
he remarked, "this being a privilege the nobility and clergy enjoy over
other murderers."[8]

Of course it would be a gross distortion to suggest that the Anglican clergy was nothing but a pack of time-serving infidel playboys and mouldering overstuffed pensionaries. It is no less true, however, that parasitism, servility, and worldliness were encouraged in a system standing so much upon nepotism and patronage. But it may be observed that the Anglican church, though in all these respects it resembled the established church in France, did possess one great comparative advantage, its weakness. England, unlike France, had passed through two religious revolutions, and freedom of opinion, anchored in the Toleration Act of 1689, posed no serious threat to a church which had learned to live with it. True, dissenters continued to suffer from discrimination, and efforts to relieve Catholics from disabilities provoked riots. But the position of religious minorities was far less precarious than in France, where their marriages, property, and even lives were insecure. Ecclesiastical selfishness and worldliness might give rise to anticlerical irritation, even contempt, but not to the increasingly furious hatred that the French Church began to experience by the 1750s—partly, it is true, due to its arrogant attacks on the *parlements,* but more largely as a result of its overlordship, backed by censors and hangmen, of French intellectual and spiritual life; and this in an increasingly skeptical age. In France a battle-to-the-death against the Church began to take shape; in England, churchmen continued their pleasant exercises in 'practical divinity,' ignoring signs of discontent and rumbling warnings that (as Adam Smith put it in 1776) in their excessive attentions "to the higher ranks of life" they were "very apt to neglect altogether the means of maintaining their influence and authority with the lower."[9]

2. GHOSTLY AUTHORITY

Smith's phrases recall us to our starting point, the problem of aristocratic power in general. We have surveyed the economic and political expressions of this power, and found these on the rise: there was, unquestionably, an aristocratic resurgence in England like the better-known one in France. The same resurgence was reflected in the third great dimension of aristocratic power, the social. It was the sinuous social authority of the elite which provided the context and enveloping psychological conditions in which the more direct and naked economic and political acts of power occurred, and for this reason this nebulous source of power was ultimately more important than they; for it conferred *legitimacy* on raw economic and political power.

This nebulous and ghostly power has long been acknowledged by English poets and fiction writers. George Meredith caught it perfectly when he wrote that the claims of the governing class were "built on birth, acres, tailoring, style, and an air." Few historians have troubled much to analyze this power, perhaps deeming it obvious and self-evident. Thus Townsend, writing on the "almost irresistible" power of England's "great governing families," simply traced this to "their influence, partly direct and used through their property, partly and chiefly indirect and exerted through social position." Brooke, whose pages are often sprinkled with wise observations on behavior and on human nature in politics, remarks that "social qualities count for as much as political ideas" in the management of men, but cautions that such qualities "are almost impossible to transmit to posterity by the printed word and in consequence are apt to be undervalued by historians." Laslett also points to the empirical difficulty of determining "how the *élite*, the ruling segment, was related to the rest" of society, and dwells especially upon the importance of understanding "their symbols of status." Mingay similarly writes that "to a crucial extent the social supremacy of the landlords rested on their superior education and culture." Thompson takes all this further, imaginatively arguing that "ruling-class control in the eighteenth century was located primarily in a cultural hegemony, and only secondarily in an expression of economic or physical (military) power." Observing that established power only rarely asserts itself in the form of the policeman, the prison or the gibbet, he says that England's elite maintained its dominance chiefly through a calculated array of everyday appearances, "gestures and postures," a "theatre of greatness," manifest in innumerable small tokens and signs of prestige—the wig, the cane, the ornamental clothing, the hunt, the segregated pew, "the rehearsed patrician gestures and the hauteur of bearing and expression," etc. In short, he distinguishes "a studied and elaborate hegemonic style, a theatrical role in which the great were schooled in infancy and which they maintained till death." He also vaguely suggests that the patterns of deference sustained by this 'theater of greatness' were in some way reaching a period of prolonged crisis from about the 1750s or 1760s. Unfortunately he then passes too quickly from this vision of how the ruling class "imposed their presence" to a parallel discussion of the counterculture and "countertheater" of "the plebs," omitting analysis of the attitudes of the middling orders, and explanation of how this aristocratic "presence" actually bore down upon society.[10]

What he leaves out, of course, is the phenomenon of emulation, of social imitation. The 'theater of greatness' was not just 'imposed' on the body of the people but also actively supported by them. It was theater-in-the-round, and mass participation was what gave it such a long run. Contemporaries understood its workings. Chesterfield, one of the coolest and shrewdest social observers of that age (indeed of any age), wrote that it was "the fine lady and the fine gentleman" who "absolutely give the law of wit, language, fashion, and taste, to the rest of . . . society." And he fully appreciated that this dictatorial power rested on the snobbish ambitions of inferiors: "Manner is all, in everything; it is by manner only that you can please, and consequently rise." As Forster, a contemporary, remarked, it was "a perpetual restless ambition in each of the inferior ranks to raise themselves to the level of those immediately above them" which gave rise to "a strong emulation in all the several stations." He concluded that "in such a state as this fashion must have an uncontrolled sway."[11]

These phenomena of emulation and fashion, vitally important to a full understanding of aristocratic power, have received growing attention in recent decades. Perkin, arguing that pre-industrial England was not yet a horizontally stratified "class society" but instead a vertically organized "classless hierarchy," is typical in calling attention to the way in which society was finely graduated from top to bottom "through layer after contiguous layer of status," with all men and women not only acutely conscious of their status but proclaiming it "by every outward sign: manner, speech, deportment, dress, liveried equipage, size of house and household, the kind and quantity of the food they ate." Indeed this idea of social imitation has gained such currency that there is perhaps some danger of its becoming a hobbyhorse. Perkin elsewhere suggests that it might have been the single most important cause of the English industrial revolution! But so many authors, studying unrelated bodies of evidence, have called attention to it that we cannot doubt its importance. Hecht, in his excellent book on servants, presents a lucid discussion of it. Hart also remarks upon the strong patterns of imitative behavior exhibited by social inferiors. Mingay comments frequently on "the downward percolation of fashions set by the aristocracy," and the same is true of Porter, whose very entertainingly written survey provides much suggestive information on the subject. Marshall, another insightful social historian, makes two particularly valuable contributions. Portraying the familiar structure of manners and fashions dispensed from London's high society, she detects in this a clear evolutionary trend—by mid-century, the growth for the first time of "a definite code of social politeness," animated by "an appreciation of the graces of social refinement, which is so clearly mirrored in Lord Chesterfield's letters," but which by the seventies and eighties was, among some at least, becoming extreme, "affected," even "ridiculous." She also emphasizes how closely related were aristocratic political power and social authority, the junction between these being the patronage system, and hence behind that the personal relationships established in social encounters. "Before the day of the great competitive examination the great man's levée was the door to a successful career." Humphreys neatly underlines this in his comment that "the twentieth century controls party loyalties by party discipline, the eighteenth century by *douceurs*."[12]

We thus have here many interesting points, in fact a collection of mini-theories, on the nature of aristocratic social authority—on the mysterious power of the fancy stuffed shirt. Though vague and immaterial, this power was tremendously potent; its essence was cultural and it was wielded theatrically, through gestures and the brandishing of status symbols; these, imitated by the rest of society, won a blanket assent to many of the less pleasant doings of the upper crust; a sort of codification of these gestures was occurring around the middle of the eighteenth century, precipitating a crisis not yet over by the 1780s.

Now let us consider these points from a still more general plane. Are these not simply the normal evolutionary characteristics of oligarchy, of oligarchies in general? Ever since Weber it has been perceived that maturing oligarchies produce 'status' (not modern 'class') societies of the sort pictured by Perkin and these other English historians. The driving force is the elite's desire to *restrict access* to valued resources (such as land, power, knowledge, and other 'rewards and opportunities') to itself and its nearest relations—to what the sociologists call 'a limited circle of eligibles.' Of course the impulse is perfectly natural, a universal one. "Men and women occupying positions of high status generally endeavor to preserve their privileges for their kin and heirs," note the sociologists. "A 'good' father is one who tries to pass the status he enjoys on to his children, and . . . to near and distant relatives as well. Hence . . . there is . . . a straining towards aristocracy and a limitation of mobility."[13]

A limitation of mobility! Could this explain why this model, a model of ever-intensifying oligarchy, has not been applied to England? Has the fond legend of English social mobility simply ruled it out of consciousness? The accepted view, rarely questioned, and perennially endorsed even by our most keen-eyed guides to the age, is that "Britain on the eve of the Industrial Revolution may be called an open aristocracy," that the picture is one of "an open aristocracy in which every member of society trod closely on the heels of the next above."[14]

But let us put this aside and attempt to look at things afresh. Now what, in general, were the secrets of aristocratic power in pre-modern societies? The sociologists tell us that social organization in such societies was at bottom dualistic, reflecting a fundamental distinction between those who were qualified to lead and those who were not. Fundamentally the picture (as Talcott Parsons writes) is that of "a two-class society," divided between aristocratic elite and people. Of course this does not mean that there were *only* two social groups (something which the mere thought of historic India should illustrate), simply that the single most important division within these societies was that between the 'superior men' who ran things and everyone else, the dividing line being one of culture. And that is the key point. The innermost secret of aristocratic power—it was like that of the later British Raj in India—was that of the elite's believed *personification* or *embodiment* of cultural excellence: "The culturally qualified group took over control of society . . . by virtue of its embodiment of the ideal cultural patterns [and] a fundamental line was drawn between them and the 'common people' [although] it was quite possible for individual sublineages to cross the line through upward (or downward) mobility." Note that this last also has suggestive implications for a better understanding of eighteenth-century England. Oligarchies are not necessarily *totally* inimical to upward and downward social movement; indeed such movement may help to keep them in business. Social risings and fallings, when confined to a few select areas, may bolster rather than weaken oligarchical control by nurturing illusions of social mobility. In China, for instance, the "universalistic emphasis" in bureaucratic recruiting provided "a 'differential joint,' the flexibility of which made possible the maintenance of . . . the social structure."[15] 'Tokenism,' in other words, works; it can fool people. But later observers, unless unconsciously perpetuating socially useful ideas, are not often fooled to the same degree.

Cultural differentiation is thus a central and indispensable feature of aristocratic society. And this helps to explain why the *displaying of cultural excellence* at the top of society, the perpetual flashing and checking of credentials of 'eligibility' (cultural superiority), becomes the prototype of social activity at lower levels. The sociologists explain how the elite's desire to monopolize 'rewards and opportunities' helps give rise to the pyramid of social differentiation and vertically graduated statuses. The key mechanism is 'social closure,' which, a little like the closing of a door, has two aspects. The first is the elite's self-enclosure or self-definition, its elaboration of 'a definite style of living' (a 'theater of greatness,' replete with costumes, symbols and gestures) not easily attainable by the mass of society. The 'limited circle of eligibles' thus defines itself through a pattern of special cultural characteristics. As an inevitable byproduct of this it is also historically the first 'class' to acquire 'self-consciousness.' The elaboration of a definite style of living with distinctive characteristics of dress, speech, etiquette, taste, intellectual tone, and so on, helps to solidify internal self-esteem within the elite group. At the same time this activity has the effect of shutting others out, of creating beneath the elite a mesh of 'exclusionary mechanisms' (cultural ones, in addition to marital, residential, and professional barriers, legislated privileges, and so on) which obstruct the rise of parvenus to 'eligibility.' The group of 'eligibles,' in other words, both defines itself and simultaneously creates "another group or stratum of ineligibles beneath it." This in turn tries to close off and monopolize "remaining rewards and opportunities" against newcomers from below while imitating the life-style of those above, and in this way the sub-strata continue to replicate themselves all the way down to the bottom of the social structure.[16]

Will these concepts help us to picture the drift of English social life in the later eighteenth century? One might certainly think so, especially when we recall the rising tide of 'ineligibles.' For it is well known that by the sixties the aristocracy, despite its rising profits, its monopolization of government, and its many successes in restricting 'opportunities and rewards' to its own nominees, was beginning to experience a challenge to its economic predominance by financiers, traders, and other 'new' men. It was not only the great magnates who were getting richer as the century passed; the great bankers and traders were, too. "Men are every day starting up from obscurity to wealth," declared Samuel Johnson. Something very similar was happening in France at the same time, and Palmer had both countries in mind when he underlined a tendency during the quarter-century before the French Revolution "for society to become, so to speak, both more aristocratic and more bourgeois at the same time, or for both aristocracy and bourgeoisie to make increasing claims to recognition, with resulting conflict."[17] In fact the aristocratic response in both countries was very similar: to set up, or, where these were already in existence, to tighten up, a wide variety of 'exclusionary mechanisms,' political, social, occupational, marital, and physical.

French historians have been meticulous in cataloging these, for together they constituted the so-called feudal or aristocratic reaction, directed against both bourgeoisie and a reforming monarchy, which precipitated the revolution of 1789. In fact a similar development was taking place in England, even though English historians have had much less incentive to study it. As Goodwin remarked some years ago (his point is still fairly true today), "English historians find it difficult to [detect] even a quasi-revolutionary pattern" during this period. There is an astigmatism here which must be addressed later (in Chapter Seven). At any rate, the signs of growing aristocratic exclusiveness in France are well known. New members of the *parlements* and the officer corps became required to prove four generations of noble descent, there was a revival of feudal rights and dues on landed estates, there was growing emphasis on the badges of landowning and on points of manners and precedence, there were efforts by the older nobles to show that they were racially different from the rest of society, there was an increasing tendency among courtiers and young heirs to flaunt their leisured status, their wealth and their superiority to bourgeois virtues by extravagant gambling, libertinism, and free thought.[18]

But were there not many parallels to this in England? Palmer, with England in mind, vaguely states that it is "by no means certain" that "the class problem" was "most acute in France." Some English historians so far agree with this as to discard temporarily the old clichés of eighteenth-century social 'mobility' and 'harmony' and to comment on the apparent growth of "social competitiveness" during this period. Jarrett believes that the aristocracy "had more success in keeping out intruders during the eighteenth century than at any other time in modern history." Mingay, writing on the sixties and seventies, declares that the English landlords felt "a mounting dislike, not to say a contemptuous hostility, towards the men of business." Marshall sees a deepening "social and even emotional gulf" separating the Quality from the sober and prosperous citizens whom they regarded as "inferior beings," even "animals." Porter comments that "in some ways social fluidity was silting up." Baugh flatly declares that while "it is hard to see a situation of 'closed ranks' before 1750," afterwards "the lines appear to harden"; and he goes on to quote Stone's even bolder suggestion that "the reputation enjoyed by pre-industrial England as an unusually mobile society is largely an illusion based on false assumptions and a dearth of statistical evidence." Lecky, in the nineteenth century, agreed with much of this. Comparing the seventies and eighties with the earlier part of the century, he wrote: "The connection between the English nobility and the trading or commercial classes, which I have already had occasion more than once to notice, seemed to have disappeared." The earlier harmony had become a clash; and he added insightfully that "an attentive reader of the light literature of the time will, I think, be struck with the degree in which the distinction between peer and commoner is accentuated." Adam Smith, a shrewd contemporary observer, seems to confirm much of this in his observations of the seventies on the disproportionate respect then accorded to "ancient greatness" over "upstart greatness," and on the "indignation" aroused by the thought of "upstarts" assuming authority. In the eighties, the travel writer John Andrews observed that foreigners found Englishmen extremely haughty and ceremonious towards their social inferiors. The relationship to domestic servants was symptomatic. "The English," he wrote, believed that foreigners were "too easy and condescending" towards their servants: "They highly censure that reciprocally unceremonious behaviour which . . . they think totally inconsistent and incompatible between a gentleman and his domestic."[19]

These are ugly offerings to set before the old household deity of English Social Mobility. But worse than that, Peter Burke, comparatively examining all the European national cultures of the ancien régime, suggests that *in both France and England* the gulf was actually *widening* between elite and popular cultures. This certainly is just the light in which we should visualize English social life as it passed into the second half of the century. There are in fact many signs of growing social exclusiveness, increasing markedly from the 1750s, and tending to underline every differential aspect of 'eligibility.' Have we not encountered many already, signs of 'predestination' and 'providential appointment' to an entire gamut of offices and emoluments, as we surveyed the solidification of aristocratic power in parliamentary government, the services, and the Church? Many other signs, turned up by a great variety of historians plowing unrelated fields, could be laid out and studied in the same harsh light: the huge 'aristocratic dole' from the secret service funds, by which financially embarrassed noblemen, regardless of their politics, were kept afloat at state expense (Namier); the decline of "new men" permitted to buy land "in the second half of the century" (Habakkuk); the increasingly intense "social exclusiveness among the justices [of the peace] which led them to object to anyone engaged in trade or manufacture" (Holdsworth); the notable decline as the century passed in the number of landed men who went into trade, so that "by 1760 the stratification . . . roughly blocked out the division of functions between different groups of the community" (G. N. Clark); the fact that marriages between aristocrats and bourgeois heiresses were quite uncommon—there was perhaps more "proof of their rarity . . . than of their frequency" (Habakkuk); the shrinkage of the baronetage and knightage during much of the century, and, when a few merchants did gain baronetcies, the growing stress on antiquity of distinctions (Baugh); the static size of the peerage throughout the century till the 1780s—and even then the new creations of 1784 basically reflected political adjustments within the landed class rather than the admission of 'new men.'[20]

Yet even today it would sound very strange to hear it declared flatly that English society was not mobile and harmonious. A characteristic formulation (from one of the best and most up-to-date textbooks in print) is: "Britain was more 'open' to both wealth and talent than any European society, but *fine gradations* of hierarchy and status survived."[21] The fault, being deeply engrained in historiography, may never be fully corrected.

Sir Lewis Namier himself, the dean of eighteenth-century studies, repeatedly stressed the importance of studying realities, of ignoring historiographical precepts, but despite the wealth of his own evidence supporting the raw fact of intensifying aristocratic solidarity, he too seems to have been unwilling to acknowledge it. When he came, for example, to the fact that merchant M.P.s could expect nothing more than baronetcies (or, later, Irish peerages), and that it was only "with much repugnance" that George III created his first merchant peer, it was evidently his own historiographical preconceptions which led him to suggest that this snobbery belonged to the king alone: "Although George III gloried 'in the name of Britain', he still clung to certain German court prejudices."[22] In fact the German-descended king was less opposed to 'upstarts' than the great English aristocrats he detested.

Even those writers who do acknowledge social frictions like to repeat the fond dogma that England was 'nevertheless not a caste society'—as if any other western European country were. This distinction, for all its pleasant sound and seeming usefulness, has no real meaning. Caste, after all, implies the most rigid stress on kinship ties, endogamy, inheritance of occupations, and physical exclusion. None of these existed in a pure form anywhere in western Europe, but castlelike tendencies were appearing in England just as in France and elsewhere. For example, with regard to residential segregation, M. D. George points to the growing social "stigma of living among 'cits,'" i.e., among the businessmen and traders of the City of London: "The cleavage between the City and St. James's—'the polite end of town'—was profound, fostered by social, political, and commercial jealousies." No such 'profound' cleavage existed before the 1740s. To take another example, Rudé, generalizing upon a variety of studies of London building patterns, property values, water supplies and the like, asserts that from the fifties on "a growing gulf was drawn between the eastern and western districts of London," between "the industrious and poor" and "the fashionable and rich." Henry Fielding in 1752 puckishly described the internal migration already underway as a mad pursuit of "People of Fashion" by an enemy or foe which was continually "breaking in" and forcing "the circle of the people of Fascination" westward from one great district to another. Margetson and other social historians have turned up other parallels, such as the decay in social egalitarianism represented by the declining popularity of coffeehouses amongst the Quality, and their replacement in the sixties and seventies by the palatial new clubs of St. James's Street.[23]

3. SHARPENING CULTURAL DIFFERENTIATION

All these facts may be read in the light of a growing and many-sided attempt to 'exclude ineligibles,' an effort paralleling the concentration of power in the economic and political areas. But what of the other aspect of social closure, the attempt to elaborate and sharpen a 'definite style of living,' not easily attainable by inferiors, by which the 'eligibles' might recognize themselves and be recognized by everyone else? Was there not a pattern of sharpening cultural differentiation during this period, expressing itself through significant alterations in dress, speech, etiquette, taste, intellectual tone, manners, and morality?

There certainly was. In fact one might even speculate that the English elite's power rested more heavily than did that of others on the outward impressiveness of its cultural style, thanks to a greater freedom of criticism in England and to fewer *legal* barriers to upward mobility. At any rate, though Englishmen have always loved jolly good shows and excel at putting them on, there really was something absolutely manic in the showmanship of this era. McKendrick, pioneering a fascinating new history of consumerism, shrewdly remarks that "the extreme fashions" of this era were "symptomatic of the lengths to which the rich were prepared to go to proclaim their wealth, their rank, their 'insignia of leisure.'"[24]

It was the younger members of the elite, the young 'eligibles,' who were most concerned to parade these marks of superiority. Earlier we touched upon various aspects of their effort to sharpen their 'distinctive style of living.' Marshall found one in her discussion of the growth by mid-century of a 'definite code of politeness' which by the 1780s was being carried to a point of extreme affectation and 'ridiculous excess'—ridiculous perhaps, but not without social significance. To this elaborate attention to manners (related undoubtedly to the increasingly intense competition for places) was joined a growing spirit of irresponsibility and an increasingly ostentatious contempt for thrift and other bourgeois virtues—a side of the picture noticed by Habakkuk in discussing the phenomenal rise of landed wealth during the same period: "In the 60s and 70s the temptation to 'show the spirit of an heir' seems to have grown stronger," he writes, adding that simultaneously "there is a perceptible change in the social climate, of which the most obvious mark is the increase in speculation and gambling."[25]

Gambling is, of course, in one respect an affirmation of superior social status, a statement of disregard for money, especially if the sums are very large; and the colossal sums lost and won by the 'bucks,' 'bloods,' and 'macaronis' of the St. James clubs were not only the talk of the town but, inevitably in view of the gamblers' social position, furnished the basis of general imitation. Familiar are Horace Walpole's strictures, dating from the 1770s, on "the outrageous spirit of gaming [which has] spread from the fashionable young men of quality to the ladies and to the lowest rank of the people." A decade later he wrote that "even the loss of £100,000 is not rare enough to be surprising." Unfortunately such activity, irrational on the face of it and peripheral anyway to the main (political) concerns of most historians, has often been treated only anecdotally as a mere amusing oddity of eighteenth-century life. We forget that to the cultural anthropologist such activity is not only intelligible but expressive of important undercurrents and often of tremendous efforts to assert or maintain social status. In the notorious gambling of this period there was a level of 'deep play' or competitive social exhibitionism comparable to that so brilliantly described by Geertz in his classic essay on the Balinese Cockfight.[26]

The Quality displayed their distinctive style of life and set themselves off from 'cits' and lesser folk in countless other ways. Even the bizarre hours they kept represented a social statement. By the later seventies the West End had gone onto Moonlight Saving Time. The day did not begin there till late in the morning; a Man of Quality would stroll about openly in the streets till two in the afternoon in "a sort of negligée or morning dress"; dinner was no longer eaten (as it had been during the first half of the century) at the same hour with "that part of the population which was engaged in business," but instead in fashionable circles "the tendency was for the hour of dinner to become later and later"; the same was true of supper. David Garrick in 1771 ridiculed the habits of the "superior beings" of the West End: "Til noon they sleep, from noon till night they dress, / From night till morn they game it more or less." Walpole's letters again yield much of sociological interest. In 1777 he wrote:

> Silly dissipation rather increases and without an object. The present folly is late hours. Everybody tries to be particular by being too late; and, as everybody tries it, nobody is so. It is the fashion now to go to Ranelagh two hours after it is over. You may not believe this, but it is literal. The music ends at ten; the [fashionable] company go at twelve. Lord Derby's cook lately gave him warning. The man owned he liked his place, but said he should be killed by dressing suppers at three in the morning.[27]

This was extreme cultural differentiation, even more effective in underscoring social boundaries than physical flight westward. The morning hours belonged to men of industry and sobriety, those of the night to men of leisure and pleasure. And of course the latter's colorful and expensive dress, no less than their fancy manners, costly pastimes, and impossible hours, set them off spectacularly from 'the industrious part of the population.' Costume, we know, always furnishes the first emblems of social status. Cunnington writes that "snobbery was in full blossom. The prosperous merchant and the nabob . . . were equally intent on pushing into the world of fashion, and round the outskirts of it were grades of would-be gentry, the Spruce Fellow, the Smart, the Flap, the Dapper, the Spark, the Blood, each distinguishable by contemporaries through subtle difference of costume. To escape from these vulgar imitators the Quality must needs devise modes more exclusive."[28]

Here again it was the 'eligibles,' the smart young men-about-town, who set the style: "The 'macaronis,' led by [Charles] Fox, were imitated at more or less distance by all who affected the 'ton.'" In their clothes, their manners, and the often fantastic hairstyles of their ladies, there was something distinctly foreign, something too that smacked of the will to *épater le bourgeois*. The fashionable young buck displayed himself in clothes bought in Paris—a coat trimmed with silver and gold, a hat laced with gold *point d'Espagne*, silver-buckled slippers or red-heeled boots, a gold-headed cane. At Vauxhall and Ranelagh, the Cockpit and the theaters, the young nobleman wore his star, the gentleman his order of knighthood. Often he flaunted his rakish immorality and enlightened irreligion, for it was accepted "that infidelity, like hair-powder, could only be worn by the aristocracy" (Trevelyan). Aristocrats' sexual habits had never been too austere; indeed the genealogist might grow "quite giddy as he tries to disentangle the complications of heredity consequent on [their] free and easy habits," chuckles the aristocratic Cecil. But even here, where there was so little opportunity for excess, there was an increasing social differentiation producing what Stone calls "bizarre upper-class manifestations." In 1780 the Earl of Pembroke suggested that the ladies of his acquaintance were promiscuous as sheep: *"Nos dames, douces commes des agneaux, se laissent monter par tout le monde."*[29]

The smart young gentleman cared as little for the prejudices of 'cits' as for those of the bumpkin gentry, and laughed up his sleeve at both. He complained that "the commercial interest" had "almost levelled every distinction but that of money among us," and blamed the men of business "for bringing on wars which had to be fought at the cost of landowners." The threat to his pleasant mode of living came not from abroad, not from France, but from below. Indeed if (as Martelli writes) "patriotism was not at all fashionable," then it became a still greater object of suspicion in the seventies: "After Wilkes, the word 'patriot' become synonymous with what today would be called 'bolshy'—while France, the perpetual enemy, was much more admired and imitated as the centre of fashion than hated or feared as a rival power." So deep and antagonistic became the patterns of cultural differentiation between the two ends of London that foreign visitors were moved to comment upon it: "This difference which holds even in the hours of eating and drinking, in the kind of amusements, the dress and manner of speaking etc. has given rise to a degree of mutual contempt by the inhabitants of each of these quarters for the other," wrote Archenholz. The people of the West End "never mention an inhabitant of the city but as an animal gross and barbarous, whose only merit is his strong box"; while "those of the city reproach them of the other end for their idleness, manner of living, and desire to imitate everything that is French."[30]

4. COSMOPOLITAN TASTES AND MANNERS

And so we come back again to the important question raised at the start of this chapter. To what extent was the Francophiliac cosmopolitanism of the age essentially a mere pose, helping somehow to justify and uphold aristocratic power? Trevelyan, who knew the eighteenth century well, registered his astonishment at the "singular fact" that at a time "when the common people despised and hated everything French with a fierce ignorance and prejudice," English taste "was to an unusual degree subjected to French and Italian ideas."[31] Was this some mechanism by which the Quality proclaimed their own superiority, and simultaneously the inferiority of their countrymen?

The problem, though it defies exact analysis, must be faced. On the one side, there is no denying the genuineness of the attraction to things French and foreign. We saw earlier that the English elite had many traditions and tastes from across the Channel, and it would be absurd to suggest that these were merely devices for keeping the hoi polloi in awe. Connoisseurship ignores frontiers. The surroundings of the Quality, their food, dress, and entertainments, all testify to attractions which set them apart from their beef-eating countrymen. They were more aware of English provinciality than lesser folk, and better able to escape it. 'Lord Ogleby,' a character in a London play of 1766, was not accused of affectation though he sprinkled his conversation with French bons mots, employed a continental man of fashion as his companion, surrounded himself with foreign luxury goods, and unostentatiously discriminated against domestic products: "My lord's chocolate is remarkably good, he won't touch a drop but what comes from Italy." Real-life parallels existed in innumerable Chesterfields, Richmonds, Walpoles, Herveys, Selwyns, Palmerstons. The young second Duke of Kingston loved France so much that he considered abandoning life in England altogether; Charles Fox, at fourteen a self-styled *"petit maître de Paris,"* so delighted in the French capital that he swore off a planned Christmas trip there for fear that he could not afterwards bring himself to return to Eton; Richard Bingham, later second Earl of Lucan, spent much of his adolescence in France before returning to nest in Parliament. The playwright Samuel Foote's theatrical portrayals of 'The Englishman Returned from Paris' caricatured young men like these: fashionable young men who came home from the gaiety, warmth and sunny skies of Paris proclaiming "that the French are the first people of the universe," that "in the arts of living, they do or ought to give laws to the whole world," that the *véritables Anglois* were "rustic rude ruffians," that there was nothing so unrefined as the "blood and blank verse" of Shakespeare, or "so soft, so musical, and so natural" as "the rich rhimes of the *theatre François,*" the inimitable beauties of "Mr. Voltaire"; and who, though sprinkling their speech with French phrases at every turn, nonetheless lamented that from "the barbarity of [their] education" they could never escape being taken for Englishmen.[32]

It was not a far cry from this to the contempt felt by a real-life Walpole or Chesterfield toward "our Bumpkin Countrymen," those "mountains of roast beef," or to the attitudes memorably captured in Gibbon's comment that a fortnight in Paris yielded "more conversation worth remembering" than "two or three winters in London." Contemporary moralists chronically complained of "how enamoured of France" their highborn countrymen were, how given to lauding that nation "even in those things wherein its inferiority is apparent." The same was true of Society's women. Typical was Elizabeth Montagu, 'Queen' of the London salon: "She loved Paris," comments West. Even Mrs. Carter, bluenose of the Bluestockings, was transformed into a *gaie parisienne* the moment she left her native shores; her friend Mrs. Montagu laughingly described the event, with their jolly pilgrimage from Calais to the Tuileries, as "the met-amorphosis of Mrs. Carter." Comparable attitudes existed in the English hinterland, where, according to French travelers, country gentlemen ex-hibited a courteous appreciation of their country "and would take all pos-sible trouble to give us pleasure," trying sometimes "to mix a French word or two with their English." Even in Dorset, far away from London's direct influence, the French traveler Macky recalled how he was "unmercifully caressed and entertained by the gentlemen."[33]

It would be absurd to dismiss the genuineness of the foreign appeal. But that was not the whole story, either. Let us recall the contrary tradition of xenophobic and anti-French feeling, particularly strong at the bottom of society. The insular and anti-French sentiments of the eighteenth-century 'mob' are legendary. Macky, just before his reception by the gentlemen of Dorset, was jeered at in the street as "Frenchie." Voltaire had been harassed by unwashed Londoners. Similar animosities, though diluted, were present among more respectable groups. The city trader, despite his 'fashionable' aspirations, had not shed his fears of France, nor was the gentry, despite decades of growing 'culture' and 'polish,' entirely free of the Gallophobia of a Sir Roger de Coverley. The completely uncritical Francophile, the aggressive cosmopolitan, was only to be found among the fashionable young men and women at the top of society. But it was these who set the tone for everyone else.

A comment in the *Gentleman's Magazine* (1766) indicates the contempo-rary organization of taste: "Those who have conversed with persons of different ranks, that have been in France, will find the account favoura-ble, in proportion as their rank is high. The man of fashion is always captivated with his journey to France; the man who moves in a lower sphere always disgusted."[34] Here, in the first sentence, we have con-firmation that favorable attitudes toward France corresponded closely to social position. But also, in the second, we find an indication that within this scale of attitudes there was a particularly clear line at which 'the man of fashion' distinguished himself from everybody else.

Thus it might seem fair to say that the fashionable man's enthusiasm for France and Europe, like his manners, choice of dress, pastimes, hours, and place of residence, was one of those things which peculiarly distin-guished his style of life, set him off as one of 'the people of Fascination,' subtly excluded outsiders with less wealth, leisure and sophistication than he, constituted an inner cultural bond between himself and his fellows, and helped to establish his 'eligibility' at the door of contemporary suc-cess, 'the great man's levée.' Yet this still fails to bring out the very special importance of this extra-national identification. It will not suffice to re-gard the taste for foreign things as just another cultural trump to play in the social game, like a proper bow, compliment, wig, or waistcoat. Rather, as we saw in Chapter One, the prestige of foreign things was much more like the very suit of trumps itself, invisible as a thing apart but conferring value on many of these same individual tokens of worth. Very often the proper coat, wig, compliment or bow *was* French or foreign, and much the same was true also of the finest painting, musical composition, work of poetry or history, even the perfect cup of chocolate.

The reader, to grasp the full significance of this, may need to exercise his imagination a bit. To a degree not easily appreciated by natives of England or the United States, the entire structure of contemporary taste was dominated by the supposed excellence of foreign standards; rather as, to take perhaps a more pleasing example from our own times, taste in many formerly colonial countries is today dominated by standards which are at once cosmopolitan and identifiably English (or Anglo-American). Who can explain the respect still accorded today in Nairobi and Singapore to everything English? For that matter, who can explain why in the United States itself, after two hundred years of political independence and at least half a century of untutored cultural achievement, the 'English accent' still carries a remarkable cachet? Who can say what this suggests to Americans in the way of quality? Why do American business firms, hawking their wares, so often employ TV and radio announcers with such an accent? Cultural signs such as this, though not easily studied, are often more important than scholarship has allowed; Brooke is right to warn that they are too often missed. We sometimes forget that 'culture'—often indefinable apart from elusive essences and fleeting signs—is an historical force quite as potent as anything found in politics or economics. But we have, sad to say, no way of measuring cultural facts with precision, and for verification we must often resort to analogy and intuition.

Fortunately our problem does not resolve itself into a need to define the indefinable quality of style, of culture, as it presented itself to the eyes and ears of eighteenth-century Englishmen, so much as it is simply to appreciate that this quality, whatever it was as an impalpable essence, and however it was distinguished, was very closely identified in their minds with the sense that true value, true superiority, came from abroad. One might say that it was felt to *descend* into England from an aesthetic and intellectual imperium which was both cosmopolitan and vaguely French, a realm transcending local and national values. It is helpful to keep in mind the colonial analogy just mentioned. "Few nations in Europe," wrote an Englishman in 1781, "have retained their original characters. They have almost all adopted the French fashions and customs; it is a uniform that they all wear . . . in the large cities everything is *à la Française.*" As we saw earlier, London, like every great city outside France, was to some extent a cultural colony of Paris, a province schooled for generations in the idea that what was truly excellent was very probably foreign. English taste in the middle of the century, as portrayed by London playwrights, was so thoroughly imbued with notions of the superiority of imported goods that English paintings, porcelains, carpets, linens and hardware had to be "smuggled thro' the street," to be offered for purchase only after fitting them out with bogus foreign labels: "Should it be known that *English* are employ'd,/Our Manufacture is at once destroy'd." As to the connoisseur, the judge of true quality, "This Gentleman has Taste; he is a Foreigner";

"The Fellow should know something of something too, for he speaks broken English"; "You have no Conception how the dear Foreign Accent is to your true Virtuoso; it announces Taste, Knowledge, Veracity, and in short, every Thing." These were satirical gibes, but struck off a flinty reality. The sense of national cultural inferiority was very much greater than the more extreme Anglophile scholarship has allowed. Cunnington states that "the constant lament that 'we take our fashions from the land we hate,' and scorn for 'admirers of foreign gewgaws,' had little effect." Poets in the sixties acknowledged the truth even while trying to laugh it off: "French follies, universally embrac'd,/At once provoke our mirth, and form our taste."[35]

Socially, the scale of contemporary taste was Francophile and international at the top, local at the bottom. But as we recall, this problem of cultural definition, whose solution we have sought in the preponderating influence of international standards, overlaps what is essentially a problem of power, of authority within the nation-state. How then did the two relate to each other? One might say, as a rough approximation, that cosmopolitan taste was to aristocratic power what invisible guy wires are to a trapeze act. The ultimate source of the elite's authority, protecting its property and privileges, was something immaterial, its 'cultural hegemony'—its *style*. Domestic ascendancy depended on cultural superiority, while this was woven from participation in a cosmopolitan and recognizably Gallic international culture which transcended the nation-state and which was, by its very nature, inaccessible to the mass of Englishmen. If the 'Foreign Accent' announced 'Taste, Knowledge, Veracity, and in short, every Thing,' then to display one's foreign accents was to prove personal cultural sophistication, advertise one's 'eligibility' for favors and opportunities, identify oneself with the elite as a group, and perpetuate the oligarchical 'classless hierarchy' by upholding that one system of support which could never be touched even by armies of anti-aristocratic critics *so long as they accepted the value of that which lay beyond their ken.*

And thus the cosmopolitan cultural style was something more even than guy wires. To change the metaphor, it was nothing less than the Grand World Opera House within which the 'theater of greatness' was enacted, furnishing its backdrop, wardrobe, props, many gestures, and some of the script. The players were, to be sure, people of substance in their own right, but much of their dazzle, their magic, came from over the waves. Pocock, writing on the Whig Supremacy of mid-century, comments: "Given the vehement disrespect in which England's newly consolidated masters were held, their legitimation and acceptance remains astonishing."[36] Perhaps not, when we recall how much power depends on art.

5. TOURS OF FORCE

But there is more to learn here; the point repays further consideration. First, observe the many names applied to the elite and its satellites. Professor Hecht writes that this group was "variously styled the Ton, the Great, the Polite, the Beau Monde, the World of Fashion, and, simply, the World." These antiquated terms preserve the truisms of that age, and some of its hidden social machinery. In particular, many of them register in their very ambiguity the pattern described above, the juncture of international cultural standards with things domestically held in great esteem, of these in turn with a perceptibly international social class, and of this with habitual cultural influence and social precedence. The word 'Quality,' for example, which was used not only as a synonym for value but as another name for elite society, reveals the extremely close identification between aesthetic worth and social ascendancy, and in its specific contexts often refers also to the system of emulation operating below—"Nobody knows the qualaty better than I do"; "She is so stark quality-mad." 'World,' also used to denote high society (and seemingly acknowledging its international character), embraces in its ambiguity the close relationship between cosmopolitan cultural ideals (ideals observed the world around), personal sophistication (worldliness, man of the world), and social rank (to rise in the world, to fall in the world, to be born to move in the sphere of the world). In a play of 1752 the wife of a London Alderman inquires: "I should be glad you would inform me if there are any Lots of very fine old China. I find the Quality are grown infinitely fond of it; and I am willing to show the World, that we in the City have Taste." The poet Burns played on these associations when he wrote of the aspiration "To mak a tour, an' tak a whirl,/To learn *bon ton* an' see the worl'." The word 'Fashion' in its various usages also reveals the connections between international culture, rank, and domestic power. It was a settled axiom that "to be out of the Fashion" was to be "out of the World." Reference to "Fashion's boundless sway" was a fixture of contemporary writing, the whole expression suggesting both universalities of taste and universal blindness of imitative behavior: "The Town, as usual, knew no reason why./But fashion so directs, and Moderns raise/On Fashion's mould'ring base their transient praise."[37]

Fashion's boundless sway was indeed heavy—we shall have to ponder this more later—but it is worth pausing to note that this very overbearingness greatly enhances its entertainment value in retrospect. Few historical (or is it anthropological?) subjects are at once so intriguing and amusing as Fashion. For example, is it not hard to keep a straight face at the thought of the figure cut by the well-turned-out London man of 1785, wearing his sword in the usual way (with the handle jutting forward and the tip pointing out behind), at the same time clad from neck to calf in the baggy flannel gown, the 'banyan,' that was obligatory that year? One tortured soul, complaining that "banyans are worn in every part of town from Wapping to Westminster," wailed that the sword "sticks out of the middle behind. This however is the fashion, the ton, and what can a man do? He *must* wear a banyan."[38] The mind boggles at the thought of coffeehouses full of Englishmen milling about in banyan and sword, the crockery flying. Was this what saved England from the French Revolution?

Now this term 'ton,' noted by Professor Hecht and also, as we see, used above, is especially interesting. Like 'Great' and 'World' it denoted 'fashionable society' (the word 'tonnish' was also taken into English as a synonym for everything stylish and fine) and seized in one grasp both the cultural dimension and the social, showing the junction of international (French) standards with the domestic elite, and, further, disclosing this group's privileged place in dictating to inferiors what was acceptable and what was not. "The present fashionable *Ton* (a word used at present [1769] to express every thing that's fashionable) is a set of French puppets"; "Don't we all know that you lead the *ton* in the *beau monde?*" In considering the full import of this term it is instructive to refer to the colonial analogy suggested earlier. Today the old elites of the non-Western world, fully realizing, according to Emerson, that "the prestige of the West" is "an essential ingredient in the advancement of their children," labor to give these children "a Western style of schooling and perhaps to send them overseas to make the grand tour and finish off their higher education." In consequence, members of many African and Middle Eastern elites are today distinguishable to their countrymen by their manners, dress, accents and attitudes, all of which subtly proclaim the fact that they have received parts of their higher education abroad (often in Britain or the United States). In Nigeria and other parts of Africa such persons have in fact occasionally been referred to by their countrymen, with some mixture of respect and mockery, as 'Been-tos,' a term which cleverly summarizes all these differential cultural indicators under the key organizing fact that the ruling class have 'been to' Britain or America, and there received much of the culture which in Africa underpins their power.[39] Now is there not a resemblance between this and the eighteenth-century 'Ton'? In both cases a species of folk sociology has imprinted itself into the language, not only acknowledging but highlighting the relationship between foreign enculturation and domestic authority. We see also that in both cases the defining term is itself an importation into the native tongue, showing unmistakably the foreign port of origin.

Again it may be necessary to tread delicately here, as we are in the vicinity of another applecart held sacred in certain groves. The reader can picture the screams of frugivorous outrage, the potential damage to life and limb, were it to be stated flatly that English boys came home from France just as frenchified as those pathetic German and Russian and Polish boys we have always read about. Was not this the 'Age of Johnson'? Did not the prestige of English culture keep these youths' eyes glued to the mystic signs and figures of English 'native character'? Later we shall examine how faint these really were. Perhaps it will suffice here simply to point out that the whole system by which these boys were educated was in fact increasingly foreign as the eighteenth century passed, due to the notorious inadequacy of the English universities and the growth of wealth.

By the 1750s the continental Tour, itself an indirect confession of English cultural inferiority, was something much more than a mere pleasant jaunt for the gentleman. It was the one indispensable element of his education.

We glanced at the Grand Tour earlier, noting the crisscrossing of many paths at Ferney. No sociological analysis of the touring phenomenon exists, but it is quite obvious that the so-called 'vogue of touring' was in fact a central event in the contemporary struggle for eligibility and status, a struggle being fought with increasing desperation on many fronts from the 1750s by Englishmen as well as Frenchmen. McKendrick, examining English business activity in this period, distinguishes, as we saw earlier, an absolutely manic "fashion frenzy early in the reign of George III" which "had never happened before" and which he believes is attributable to "new levels of spending" by both ordinary people and by "those in the higher ranks who felt for the first time threatened by the loss of their distinctive badge of identity." This is just the right formula, and it applies with special force to the phenomenon of the Tour. What made the Tour so important socially was the fact that here there were few obstacles, many fewer than in ordinary town or country life, to prevent a man of lower status from simply slapping down the money and carrying off with him the choicest counterfeit credentials of a gentleman and 'man of the world.' Mead, the great historian of the Tour, vaguely observes that while it was the English upper crust alone which toured during the first half of the century, afterwards there was "a large increase in the number of young tourists, with a very short pedigree but a very long purse, who wished to gain whatever social distinction travel might confer."[40] The truth is that while landed estates, coronets, aristocratic marriages and knightly ribbons were increasingly difficult to obtain, a young man could nevertheless cross the Channel, see the sights, change his clothes and manners, hobnob with and imitate the poses of his betters, come home with them in the character of a frenchified young lord, and with them lay claim to an educational and social superiority quite inaccessible by any other route.

The purpose of the Tour had been educational ever since its inception around the 1670s. Mead sums up its objectives: "The studious and open-minded tourist enlarged his view of mankind, learned tolerance, discovered what was worthy of imitation, grew more polished in manners, and became a citizen of the world." The Tour was thus the equivalent of a good liberal arts education today, a typical Oxbridge or Ivy League education. But, similarly, its completion brought certificates of social acceptability and tickets to worldly advantages. No man who had not seen Paris, no man who had not treasured up a fund of anecdotes on Europe's principal sights or acquired "that knowledge of the world which marked the cosmopolitan," could hope to make a mark in fashionable society. "Something provincial, some lack of *savoir-faire*, would inevitably betray him."[41]

Thus a line separating the traveler from the stay-at-home lay across the structure of higher education, and, as on the other meters of eligibility which we considered earlier, encouraged a consciousness of superiority above it, feelings of inferiority below it, and hence a thirst for imitation as well. Samuel Johnson confessed that a man who had not traveled was "always conscious of an inferiority, from his not having seen what it is expected a man should see"; nor was it always easy to shake these feelings even after crossing the Channel, if his own behavior is any indication. Arriving in Paris in 1775, he felt so insecure despite his fancy new Parisian clothes and wig that he declined to converse in anything but Latin, justifying this on the ground that "a man should not let himself down by speaking a language which he speaks imperfectly."[42] This was a sad parry in social one-upmanship, the embarrassed Englishman discarding the rules of social play and substituting others more to his advantage. It is not clear what the Parisians made of it.

Johnson was hardly the only Briton out to ogle them that year. Many historians have noted with Lecky that "in the latter half of the century the movement towards the Continent was much more general, and foreign travel became the predominating passion of a large portion of the English people." When Edward Gibbon reached Boulogne in 1763 with three English lords, "they found the Paris road so jammed with British travellers that there were not enough post-horses to go around." Walpole complained in 1765 of the swarms of Englishmen in Paris; "it certainly was not my countrymen that I came to live with," he sniffed. Perhaps as many as 12,000 Englishmen a year were now visiting the Continent.[43] And the pace was accelerating. In 1772 another observer wrote that "where one Englishman travelled in the reigns of the first two Georges, ten now go on a grand tour . . . there is scarce a citizen of large fortune but takes a flying view of France, Italy, and Germany in a summer's excursion." Adam Smith declared in 1776 that it was "every day more and more the custom to send young people to travel in foreign countries"—and he did not mean the Hessians then traveling to America. There were, according to French customs officials, more than 40,000 Englishmen, masters and servants, upon the Continent in 1785. Some of this may have been due to conditions at home (it being the year of the banyan plague) but the tally is amazing nonetheless. The tally would seem to suggest that perhaps one out of every twenty inhabitants of Great Britain might have seen the European continent during the early decades of George III—a virtual epidemic of traveling. This makes it all the more important to reflect carefully upon Mead's conclusion that the touring experience, coming for so many at the most impressionable period of life, "shaped the ideals and character of a multitude of the most influential citizens of England."[44]

But of course the Tour's educational value fell as its social value was strip-mined. The aristocratic young tourist of the earlier part of the century, his sketchpads and language dictionaries in hand, sheltered and instructed by his 'bear-leader,' was increasingly an anachronism as hordes of English travelers began to pour onto the Continent; and as a great volume of contemporary discussion shows, many of these newcomers were nearly indifferent to the intellectual and cultural merits of the trip. Letters, commentaries, and travel books of the period 1750–90 increasingly focus on the growing rudeness, drunkenness, and lust for gambling of young English travelers; on their strange conception of "their whole business abroad" as being "to buy new cloathes, in which they shine in some obscure coffee-house, where they are sure of meeting only one another"; on their growing tendency to band together into traveling colonies, "*fighting* their way through Europe," speaking nothing but English, observing "routes rather than the country," ignoring the architectural wonders around them, coming away from Rome "without knowing where the Coliseum is," offending the sensibilities of cultivated Europeans yet "striving by their insolent ostentation of riches to pass for gentlemen to the manner born." Cowper, writing on the tourist's return to London, caricatured its intended social effect: "Returning he proclaims by many a grace,/By shrugs and strange contortions of his face,/How much a dunce, that has been sent to roam,/Excels a dunce, that has been kept at home."[45]

Of course the real Been-tos fought back. The aristocrat defended his superiority by ridiculing the upstart and by exaggerating the purity of his own cosmopolitan tastes. In travel as in dress he was driven to 'devise modes more exclusive.' The unmistakable sign of this was the founding in the late sixties of the Macaroni Club, whose members distinguished themselves by gulping pasta from their butter plates. While thousands were now rattling across the Channel "for a brief round of travel, with no intention of making the elaborate grand tour," the Beau Monde, brandishing spaghetti, showed that they had gone all the way to Italy, the farthest point in the tour—visited by "scarcely one Englishman in ten thousand," according to Mead.[46] In fact the tonnish struggle against the 'animal' bourgeois pretender is discernible from the fifties. Symptomatic was Chesterfield's contribution to *The World* (1753), savagely lampooning the throngs who "now, in a manner, overrun France, a second incursion of the Goths and Vandals," their purpose being to "expose themselves there as English, and here, after their return, as French," henceforth displaying in their own land "their affected broken English, and mangled French," and ceaselessly speaking "of nothing but *le bon ton.*" Another 'eligible' satirically lamented that touring was becoming so common that no one gathered round when he began unfolding his anecdotes gathered through "four years of expense, danger, and fatigue": if one wanted attentive auditors "he must have recourse to his tenants in the country, or seek them about four o'clock on a bench in St. James's park." Another grumbled that "all men are not born for all things," that the tour was educationally valuable only to those young minds "to which Nature has been originally kind, and which culture has duly prepared." Another complained that touring did not suit men of the lower ranks because it might give one "a relish for foreign manners, and a taste for the society of a set of men, with whom neither his station nor his fortune entitle him to associate in the after-part of his life."[47] Again, as though fleetingly through a corner of the curtain, we glimpse the spidery network of international values upholding the stagecraft of local power.

6. SOCIAL STATUS, EUROPEAN CONSCIOUSNESS, NATIONAL IDENTITY

All this international intercourse, while in many respects helping to 'polish' the Englishman and make of him a 'citizen of the world,' was also in some obscure way denaturing him. There was an ironic parallel to this in the mid-nineteenth century, when the Germans, having at last (like the English earlier) shaken the 'yoke' of French culture, began to ape the Victorians: "Germans," wrote Alexander Herzen around 1860, "do not really become Englishmen, but affect to be English, and partly cease to be Germans." A century earlier, around 1760, young Englishmen were affecting to be French, and partly ceasing to be English. What was happening was that many English travelers, though increasingly inclined while traveling to depreciate lands which they neither really saw nor understood, dropped these critical attitudes on returning to England and there metamorphosed themselves into Frenchmen. The literature of the period often dwelt upon this apparent paradox. Foote makes one of his Englishmen in Paris observe that "Fashion has ordained, that as you employ none but foreigners at home, you must take up with your own countrymen here [i.e., in Paris]"; to which another responds that "it is not in this instance alone we are particular, Mr. Subtle; I have observ'd many of our pretty gentlemen, who condescend to use entirely their native language here, sputter nothing but bad French in the side-boxes at home." Dr. John Moore, one of the most experienced travelers of the age, captured the same seemingly paradoxical phenomenon when he spoke of "Englishmen, who, while on their travels, shock foreigners by an ostentatious preference of England to all the rest of the world, and ridicule the manners, customs, and opinions of every nation; yet on their return to their own country, immediately assume foreign manners, and continue during the remainder of their lives to express the highest contempt for everything that is English."[48]

To Mead these polar variations in individual attitude seemed "strangely contradictory,"[49] but of course they were not, when seen from the standpoint outlined in this chapter. Interpretatively it is indeed hard to say whether the frantic social imitativeness of this period signified a welcoming consciousness of the opportunities of the new age or instead a neurotic pressure building against the heavily guarded gates of the age that was passing: vanity and conformity would seem to be signs of insecurity, not of opportunity, and perhaps there were simply too many hopeful and increasingly well-off people chasing too few opportunities. But however that question may be decided, there is no paradox in the two-faced behavior of the traveler. What explains it is the struggle for status and everything that that implied. On tour, an Englishman might display his personal superiority before both Continentals and other Englishmen by despising the best and costliest that Europe could produce; at home, nothing English could compare with what he had seen abroad. A parallel might be sought in the African wearing a dashiki in New York and a leisure suit in Timbuktu.

The whole phenomenon of foreign travel, like so many other patterns of the period, lends itself to Palmer's contention that the three or four decades before the French Revolution exhibited a tendency 'for society to become, so to speak, both more aristocratic and more bourgeois at the same time, or for both aristocracy and bourgeoisie to make increasing claims to recognition, with resulting conflict.' What is ironical is the fact that these conflicting claims were in many ways operating together to raise English culture from its age-old provinciality and draw it further and further towards standards, endorsed by The World, which were both cosmopolitan and French. Jarrett rightly suggests that the English "world of fashionable pleasure" was becoming "more and more French" as time passed.[50] By virtue of both genuine attractions and the snob appeal connected with superior taste and education, the culture of the English bourgeoisie, that of the great unthinking mass of it, was becoming as cosmopolitanized and frenchified as that of the aristocracy. Increasingly excluded from the land and from other stations of power by the 'self-gratifying oligarchy that held power for its own profit,' yet increasingly wealthy and obliged to jostle within itself for 'remaining rewards and opportunities,' the bourgeoisie sought cultural distinction and social credit by aping the distinctive cultural style of The World, and thus entered by one port or another into that 'gentlemanly international social club,' European in consciousness and French in manners, which has so often been remarked upon as the key feature of European social life in the later eighteenth century.

At the same time, naturally, the English sense of national identity drifted entirely out of shape; and the same was happening in other countries outside France. In fact there are signs that a version of the same thing was beginning to occur in France itself, where the elite and then their many imitators began to underline their threatened superiority by aping foreigners, especially *the English*. "We are all metamorphosed into English," wrote the comte de Lauraguais in 1769. Everywhere, Europeans by taste were pursued by Europeans by imitation. The wise French author Marivaux caught the inner meaning of it when he wrote:

> Think highly of anything made in our own country! Why, whatever should we come to if we had to praise our fellow-countrymen? They would get too conceited, and we should be too much humiliated. No, no! It will never do to give such an advantage to men we spend all our lives with, and may meet wherever we go. Let us praise foreigners, by all means. . . . When he ranks foreigners above his own country . . . *Monsieur* is no longer a native of it, he is the man of every nation.[51]

Thus it should be clear, with reference to the important question posed at the beginning of this chapter, that cosmopolitanism did play a valuable role in rationalizing, maintaining and even extending the scope of aristocratic power in the eighteenth century. The 'great governing families' of

Europe were like sunlit clouds, basking and floating together in a supporting cultural medium as real yet nearly as invisible as air, and it was very much by virtue of this aerial position that they cast their shadows over the several national landscapes below. Beneath them in each country the vertical linkages of fashion and favor, of imitation and patronage, facilitated the diffusion of sophisticated ideals and international culture. *But, by the same token, these linkages impeded the growth of national consciousness, and blocked the formation of class consciousness at levels below the great landed elites.*

To anyone pondering the matter from this angle it would seem fairly obvious that in the era to come, the era emerging in the later eighteenth century, the self-promotion of new elites would therefore wait upon the repudiation of 'Fashion,' the destruction of cosmopolitanism, and the elaboration of nationalist ideology. Unfortunately this line of reasoning has not received much attention from English historians. In fact, to tell the truth, it has not received much attention from anyone at all. Recently the French historian Suratteau, expressing his surprise at an apparent gap in our understanding of that age, confirmed that the implications of eighteenth-century cosmopolitanism and of its reverse ethic, national patriotism, remain something of a mystery to international scholarship even today. It seems clear, he observed, that cosmopolitanism belonged primarily to "the elites" and developed "at the expense of the notion of the native land," but still less is understood about the social dimensions of patriotism during the ancien régime. In particular, "it is surprising to learn that most of those who have studied these two 'themes' of the Enlightenment, whether in analyzing them separately or in comparing them," have "barely paid attention to and in any case have hardly exploited" the "simple idea" that toward the end of the ancien régime, "patriotism, or what existed of it, was anchored in the popular classes, the 'people', the 'populace'."[52]

This emerging dualism does deserve much more study. For there are many signs that, in England at least, the domestic social cleavage of the later eighteenth century was translating itself into a general and intensifying clash between two patterns of belief and culture, cosmopolitan on one side, aggressively local on the other. We must turn now to investigate the latter, and the great historic *Kulturkampf* built up from it.

4. 1756. *The Duke of Newcastle (with magnifying glass) and Henry Fox. Note the fleurs-de-lis on their clothing, the Gallic cock crowing on the overturned ship, and the punning association between Gaul and the gallows, all insinuating subservience to France.*

5. 1762. *This is one of the earliest known caricatures of John Bull. Blind, with cuckold's horns, and burdened by ugly Scotland, he is led to disaster by Fox and Newcastle (here a goose). Sinister Francophile influences are suggested in the simian figure (holding an olive branch and French gold) secretly consorting with Scotland.*

CHAPTER THREE

What is Nationalism?

In history, as in traveling, men usually see only what they already had in their own minds; and few learn much from history, who do not bring much with them to its study.

—MILL

IN 1898 the French historian Joseph Texte wrote a contented little essay on France's eighteenth-century literary and intellectual hegemony. He began by quoting Schiller's advice to his fellow Germans: "Do not seek to form a nation, content yourselves with being men." This, Texte proudly wrote, was an echo of French thought: "It is we who taught the nations of Europe to detach themselves from a narrowly national ideal and to march resolutely towards a human ideal. These are our philosophers who have appealed to the fraternity of the peoples, and who, disregarding frontiers in the order of thought, prepared the unification of the world in the order of the heart." France had not imposed these divine universal values on others; she had simply been chosen as their special earthly vessel and mediary:

> Certainly it was not we who imposed our art and our thought on Europe, but rather it was Europe which, freely and joyfully, came to us, lured by the unusual prestige of our doctrines and by the communicative warmth of our language, by the entirely novel generosity of our ideal and by the inexpressible charm of that nation truly representing humanity, a nation which others might hate, but which could never hate others.[1]

In the 1890s these pleasant but rather pseudohistorical reflections had their humane uses. In that age of imperialism, war clouds, and racism, the historian wanted to remind France, and, if he could get its ear, the whole world, of the spirit of international brotherhood. But would it be too unkind to point out that he got to have things both ways? The French patriot was able to laud France with every word devoted to the spirit of internationalism. To a sophisticated observer it might seem surprising that Academe still today accepts this tradition very uncritically. We find gowns for our ideas no less than for our bodies, and the 'universal' character of French thought and of the French Revolution is one of our most sacred banyans. Each generation of teacher-scholars hands it down to the next, and each brings it out for reasons similar to Texte's in that year of Fashoda and Dreyfus and the cry: "Remember the Maine!"

1. THE MINGLED NOTES OF THE 1780s

This is certainly not to suggest that the brotherhood of man is a bad thing, or that Texte was wrong in crediting Voltaire and French philosophy with helping to spread it. Prior to the French Revolution, the culture of Europe's upper classes was indeed marked by a cosmopolitan sentiment, a spirit of worldly sophistication and tolerance, a genuine attachment to international ideals of reason, progress and civilized behavior, and all this for reasons intellectual as well as social. There was, as Texte implied, a gravitational drift in the direction of 'humanity,' and a filtering down through the social ranks of the sense of being Europeans, citizens of an expanding and improving world. But at the same time, and to some degree as a direct result of this broader international contact, these pre-revolutionary decades also witnessed an awakening of national pride, a proliferation of national cultural institutions, an attempt to elaborate specifically national intellectual and moral styles, and myriad attempts to excavate the foundations and define the type of the national self.

There were many contemporaries who seemingly experienced no sharp contradiction between this international culture and these nationalistic impulses. By 1789 there were in England many humane and civilized men and women who, like Franklin and Jefferson in America, Lafayette and Brissot in France, Herder and Lessing in Germany, seem to have held the one in balance with the other, and to have visualized the civilized world as a great international community, a garden as Herder pictured it, to which all the varying national flowers, the English rose and German Kaiserblume as well as the French fleur-de-lis, contributed in some measure. Such a one was Josiah Wedgwood, a friend to humanitarian causes, a generous internationalist, yet also a dedicated improver of life in his own nation, and—in this he was quite typical also—the inventor of a specifically English style of earthenware. His universally admired medallion of a kneeling slave in chains, pathetically inquiring whether he too was not 'a man and a brother,' a medallion wrought in the clays of Devon but expressing an universal ideal of liberty, may be regarded as a symbol of this admirably balanced frame of mind. As Kohn has written with general reference to European society in that era, "Cosmopolitanism or internationalism and patriotism or awakening nationalism intermingled in that age of promise and hope under the aegis of liberty and peace."[2]

Yet the relationship between this cosmopolitan internationalism and this 'awakening' patriotism or nationalism was far more complex, more contradictory yet more progenitive, than Kohn suggests. With reference to England at least, it would be truer to say that beneath the spirit, undoubtedly genuine, of international awareness and benevolence, and of commitment to the best cosmopolitan and classical values, the first phase of a massive nationalist revolution had begun, pricked into being by a general sense, cultural and aesthetic as well as political, social, economic and religious, that all was not well; a sense that the dominant culture of the nation was far too much under the spell of France, and, simultaneously, too much the bastion of an overbearing and selfish oligarchy, a Fashionable World excessively contaminated by corrupting spiritual influences originating (so it was increasingly suggested) in France.

2. COMPONENTS OF NATIONALISM

To trace this revolution we will need to keep the basic concepts of nationalism in hand as a compass. And since these are not widely studied even in the universities, it will be necessary to provide a brief and (with apologies to the specialists) simple primer here. Is it not amazing how little attention nationalism receives in the schools? If a poll were to be taken among educated people as to which of history's great ideologies is now most powerful and widely influential, the winning entry would surely not be communism, socialism, Christianity, or Islam, but nationalism. Is it not strange then that so few scholars have devoted themselves to exploration of this great phenomenon?

Perhaps this rather dangerous neglect might be remedied if we addressed its causes. One cause might be that while most history-writing is done by nationals, by citizens of the country written about, the study of nationalism requires a degree of detachment from the whole system of national values which few active citizens can, or perhaps should, strive to attain. More history-writing tends to the perpetuation of national beliefs than to their dissection, and scholarship in some countries, not to mention officialdom looking over its shoulder, might surely discourage the analysis and perhaps deflation of those very myths which hold nations together. And of course the same would hold true for empires and other sorts of polyethnic states. It is hard to imagine English historians, before Indian independence at least, exposing the historical roots and analyzing the rise of England's feelings of international superiority. And then too there is also a tendency in the more advanced countries to look upon nationalism as a sort of disease that peculiarly affects 'underdeveloped' foreigners. In addition, it is probable that the inattention to English nationalism has helped to foster a similar negligence in other English-speaking countries. Further, there is also the possibility that mental associations with fascism and Hitler have served to obscure nationalism's universality and its special connection with the whole process of nation-building in every country. "Nationalism," says Berlin, "—an ideology to which German and Italian thinkers seemed particularly prone." Chadwick must have had much the same assumption in mind when in 1945 he wrote of nationalism's nonexistence in his own country. It is perplexing to read his comments on what he calls "the non-existence of any feeling for English nationality" and his perfectly sober suggestion that this in turn may explain why "English people frequently find it difficult to understand the feeling for nationality shown by other peoples."[3]

But the chief stumbling block may simply be the difficulty of analyzing this complex phenomenon, of attempting to understand and describe anything so seemingly nebulous in its essence yet vast in its effects. The investigator of nationalism must be prepared to try on many scholarly roles in the course of his study. He must attempt to approach social development as a sociologist, literature as a critic, myth as a cultural anthropologist, biography as a psychologist, politics as a political historian, and so on. Yet very few scholars, the present one included, can pretend to expertise in more than one or two areas, and the professionalization of university disciplines and the ethic of 'publish or perish' discourage the intellectual bush pilot. Perhaps the real wonder then is that anyone has had the face to write upon nationalism at all. The thing is certainly not perfectly understood even by the few experts who bother with it. Even German nationalism, about which so much has been written, still remains obscure in fundamental ways, as is evidenced by the continuing debate over its social orientations.

i. nationalism not 'mere patriotism'

To begin then with this simple primer, let us start with the difference between patriotism and nationalism. It is important to understand that historians, when they speak of nationalism, have in mind (or ought to) something much larger and more complicated than mere chauvinistic flag-waving. Journalists and others, careless of the difference, often use the terms 'patriotism' and 'nationalism' interchangeably, but to anyone acquainted with the subject this is a little like confusing alchemy with polymer science. It is true that both terms do refer to very strong emotional identifications between individual and group, and this is why they are often confused. Doob, who has devoted a book to this particular problem, distinguishes between patriotism as a group-oriented feeling or psychological predisposition which exists *universally,* wherever human beings are joined in societies, and nationalism as a much more complex, programmatic and historically conditioned elaboration of this simple feeling into *patterns of demands and actions* deeply affecting group policy; a distinction which necessarily rests therefore on the historic growth of a sense of active participation or citizenship in the individual as he relates himself to his group. Many other writers agree with this elementary distinction. Gellner, for instance, writes in his excellent new survey that "nationalism is a very distinctive species of patriotism, and one which becomes pervasive and dominant only under certain social conditions, which in fact prevail in the modern world, and nowhere else." Similarly, Kedourie maintains that patriotism "is a sentiment known among all kinds of men," whereas nationalism, though it may "annex" this sentiment, is a product of modern thought, *"a comprehensive doctrine"* particularly distinguished by its "anthropological and metaphysical ideas" and by its "distinctive style of politics."[4]

Patriotism is a mere primitive feeling of loyalty. Of course even this presupposes at least a rudimentary consciousness of the historic land, people and culture of the nation. But, as is suggested in the fact that most of today's 'patriotic societies' are in some way connected with military matters, the patriotic sentiment should be regarded as primarily an attachment to the country's prestige in a context of foreign relations; to its arms, flags, and power in the international sphere. In early times this sentiment usually focused upon the king as the nation's chief in battle and the personification of political unity against the foreigner, and also upon the native land, the realm, which he guarded—hence, for example, Shakespeare's identification of king with nation (Fortinbras is the nephew of 'Norway') and his famous patriotic evocation in *Richard II* of England as a 'royal throne of kings,' a 'sceptred isle,' a fortress and realm inhabited by a 'happy breed of men.'

One may see characteristic adjustments of this patriotic sentiment in the age of aristocracy, the eighteenth century. Kiernan, referring to the eighteenth-century landowning classes, observes that "when such men 'loved their country,' they were thinking of it as a glorified private estate owned by themselves and their friends. About most of its inhabitants, and their wants, they preferred not to think: instead they idealised the 'sacred soil', the territory inalienable as an entailed patrimony." Such nationalism as did exist was looked upon as something marked by "intensely vulgar sentiments" and as "an invasion of the sphere of public life by plebians."[5]

Such was the mere patriotism of early modern Europe. Minogue goes so far as to say that "nationalism, far from being similar to patriotism, often comes close to being its opposite." Certainly such patriotism was very different from the all-consuming, civic, and egalitarian sentiment of the Victorian era—that is, the nationalistic spirit of the nineteenth century. Consider George Eliot's description of this in 1879:

> Not only the nobleness of a nation depends upon the presence of this national consciousness, but also the nobleness of each individual citizen. Our dignity and rectitude are proportioned to our sense of relationship with something great, admirable, pregnant with high possibilities, worthy of sacrifice, a continual inspiration to self-repression and discipline by the presentation of aims larger and more attractive to our generous part than the securing of personal ease or prosperity.[6]

Nineteenth-century nationalism meant much more than support of national military power and of freedom from foreign domination. The idea of national freedom now also carried with it a complex idea of *national solidarity* in peace as well as war, and, necessarily, of opposition to internal obstacles to this solidarity. Koht, the Norwegian historian, attempting to capture the essential transition from primitive patriotism to modern nationalism, wrote that "the idea of national solidarity replaced boastful pride." An example exists in the Victorian intellectual J. A. Froude, whose conception of English greatness and freedom combined an admiration of military power with a passion for internal solidarity. Froude enthusiastically wrote in 1870, after the parliamentary reform act of 1867, that "the people have at last political power. All interests are now represented in Parliament. All are sure of consideration. Class government is at an

end. Aristocracies, landowners, established churches, can abuse their privileges no longer. The age of monopolies is gone. England belongs to herself. We are at last free."[7]

ii. eighteenth-century roots and relation to modernization

Patriotism, we see, is an old and familiar phenomenon, while nationalism, as Minogue also explains, is something much more complex
and much more attached to ideals of internal solidarity under an
egalitarian moral discipline. Patriotism focuses outward, while nationalism
takes *all the nation's affairs,* internal as well as external, into its compass.
Nationalism is thus considered a *modern* phenomenon, something of recent historical growth. "Writers about nationalism mostly agree that there
was little or none of it in the world until the end of the eighteenth century," writes Plamenatz. Snyder, typifying the views of many authors, defines nationalism as "a powerful emotion that has dominated the political
thought and actions of most peoples since the time of the French Revolution. It is not a natural, but an historic phenomenon, that has emerged as
a response to *specific political, economic, and social conditions.*" So much does
this appear to have been the case that many analysts, Gellner most recently, have portrayed it in its broadest dimensions as the inseparable
ideological counterpart of modernization, of the transition from agricultural to
industrial society, in every country of the world. In 1939 E. H. Carr and a
distinguished panel of scholars wrote that "nationalism cannot be properly appreciated if it is treated as an isolated political or psychological
phenomenon. It must be regarded as a special case of the more general
and permanent problem of group integration. Far-reaching questions of
sociology and group psychology are involved, questions which admit of
wide differences of opinion and to which scientific methods of study cannot be easily applied."[8]

Since the Second World War the specialists, seeing the proliferation of
many anti-colonial nationalist movements, have begun to understand even
more clearly the way in which such ideology provides an *integrative* structure both assisting and easing the shocks of modernization in all its facets—the breaking down of tribal, social and intellectual barriers, the
reorientation of politics, the spread of education and literacy, the expansion of equal opportunity, the introduction of agricultural and industrial
techniques and disciplines aimed at general national betterment. Minogue
asks whether it is possible to "find a general condition of things from
which nationalism seems primordially to spring," and suggests a general
answer: "Our clue may be that nationalism in both France and Germany
became the spearhead of an attack on feudalism."[9]

iii. aspects of the ideological transformation

In its broadest dimensions, then, nationalism is viewed as a manifold
force assisting the attack upon traditional society through a leveling and

simultaneously reintegrative *transformation of the emotional and intellectual bonds of group identification.* Although it is therefore a very complex phenomenon with important social, economic, and political aspects, it is above all—one should rather say beneath all—an *ideological* fact, an ideological development which passes through definable historic stages in its movement towards fulfillment and realization. Nationalism is an ideology; its primary facts are facts of human consciousness; and its movement is towards an ideal if unattainable goal of uniform collective consciousness, and hence concerted discipline and action for the good of the whole. The passage from George Eliot, quoted earlier, includes a fine exposition of this relationship between 'national consciousness' and individual 'self-repression and discipline,' and it would be hard to find in the modern scholarly literature on nationalism a more acute description of its psychological significance and shaping power.

Kohn emphasizes a second point helpful in understanding nationalist psychology, the indispensable importance of an out-group (or groups) in the formation of in-group consciousness and discipline. The reader may note that Kohn, the only specialist to address English nationalism—four years before writing this passage he had attempted to trace its flowering in the seventeenth century—seems here to have forgotten or changed his mind about England as he joins other scholars in tracing the general movement from 1789:

> Nationalism is first and foremost a state of mind, an act of consciousness, which since the French Revolution has become more and more common to mankind. The mental life of man is as much dominated by an ego-consciousness as it is by a group-consciousness. Both are complex states of mind at which we arrive through experiences of differentiation and opposition, of the ego and the surrounding world, of the we-group and those outside the group. The collective or group consciousness . . . will strive towards creating homogeneity within the group, a conformity and like-mindedness which will lead to and facilitate concerted common action.[10]

For our lengthening list of concepts the significant new point here is the importance of *aliens and outsiders* to the formation of group consciousness. This consciousness does not simply form itself, as an ineluctable fact of the natural world. Doob explains that the group's members' "*anxiety* must first be aroused before they will acknowledge the threat [of an apparently hostile out-group or enemy] and hence be stirred to nationalistic activity." This activity, the theorists say, is *initially a cultural activity,* though it may later take on political and other manifestations also. The activity is cultural at the outset, its causation is originally defensive and reactive, and its purpose is to create or revive, by conscious self-comparisons with the alien culture, a more distinct sense of we-group identity. Many theorists maintain also that such activity could not really have taken place before the Age of Reason; that it could not have arisen except in *an intellectual milieu prepared by secular ideas* and especially by the rise of a secular ideal of progress. Plamenatz summarizes these very noteworthy points in an excellent essay:

> Nationalism, as I shall speak of it, is the desire to preserve or enhance a people's national or cultural identity when that identity is threatened, or the desire to transform or even create it where it is felt to be inadequate or lacking. I say *national* or *cultural,* for what distinguishes a people from other peoples in their own eyes consists of ways of thinking, feeling and behaving which are, or which they believe to be, peculiar to them. Thus nationalism is primarily a cultural phenomenon, though it can, and often does, take a political form. . . . Nationalism, as distinct from mere national consciousness, arises when peoples are aware, not only of cultural diversity, but of cultural change and share some idea of progress which moves them to compare their own achievements and capacities with those of others. . . . Thus nationalism is a reaction of peoples who feel culturally at a disadvantage. Not any reaction that comes of a sense of weakness or insecurity but a reaction when certain conditions hold.[11]

iv. central role of the artist-intellectual

Other analysts, accepting this picture, explain more fully the central role played in it by *the artist-intellectual.* It is he who first senses these differences, makes these comparisons, and mounts these reactions. It is he who creates and organizes nationalist ideology, the machinery at the heart of the nationalist movement. In an especially intense way he is the first to feel the illness of his nation's culture and to sense himself a lonely exile from its true sources. "One is, indeed, tempted to generalise the idea of exile," writes Minogue, and regard nationalism "as a recourse of those who feel spiritually exiled . . . the alienated, the excluded." Berlin explains that nationalism emerges from a sleeping state of "mere national consciousness" (patriotic consciousness) in response to perceived *slights against the value and dignity of the national inheritance,* slights which, he suggests, are felt most keenly by "socially conscious" members of the bourgeois intelligentsia. He outlines the stages of their response, the evolution of what he regards as the typical nationalist intellectual movement:

> It may be true that nationalism, as distinct from mere national consciousness—the sense of belonging to a nation—is in the first place a response to a patronising or disparaging attitude towards the traditional values of a society, the result of wounded pride and a sense of humiliation in its most socially conscious members, which in due course produce anger and self-assertion. This appears to be supported by the career of the paradigm of modern nationalism in the German reaction—from the conscious defence of German culture in the relatively mild literary patriotism of Thomasius and Lessing and their seventeenth-century forerunners, to Herder's assertion of cultural autonomy, until it leads to an outburst of aggressive chauvinism in Arndt, Jahn, Korner, Goerres, during and after the Napoleonic invasion.[12]

v. provocations, war, institutional disintegration, a sense of crisis

Thus the nationalist movement, according to the specialists, is initially roused into action by cultural provocations and social humiliations experienced by writers and intellectuals—by an articulate minority. Obviously the source of these provocations and humiliations cannot be entirely foreign and external to the nation, or otherwise there could not arise the sense of a substantial threat to native culture and identity. In most cases the critical stimulus to nationalist 'anger and self-assertion' is the patronizing and culturally disparaging—the anti-national—attitudes of *the domestic elite, perceived as cooperating too freely with a foreign power.* As Chadwick observes, the rise of nationalist sentiment "would seem to need the stimulus of a powerful antagonistic force, either within the same country or beyond, but not too far beyond, its borders." In such circumstances the enemy of the despised and oppressed nation is seen confusedly as a combination of foreign and domestic conspirers and oppressors—of real and 'surrogate' aliens, "honorary foreigners," as Minogue denominates them. Alexander Herzen noted that Russian nationalism originated as antagonism to "an exclusively foreign influence" yet also as a confused "domestic struggle" against an alien elite: "We have had to set up our nationalism against the Germanised government and our own renegades." Much the same has traditionally been true of Latin American nationalism, directed against native elites as well as their backers and cultural exemplars in Europe and the United States.[13]

This helps to explain why *war with the external enemy* has often helped, as it did, for example, in the Spanish reaction to Napoleonic France, to kindle nationalism into frenzied activity. Handman suggests the way in which external threats and provocations can affect the individual's more or less organized idea of the group, and hence his behavior:

Under proper conditions, this system [of ideas and traditional doctrines concerning the group] . . . may show itself in behavior as *an agitated and agitating concern with the life and honor of the group.* When this agitation is more or less *chronic* it becomes the sentiment of nationalism. This chronic agitation assumes a correspondingly chronic provocation and the workings of the sentiment of nationalism cannot be understood except in the light of this provocation. What makes this provocation sure of a response is not only the provocation itself, but the whole attitude of animosity toward another group, historically developed and maintained by a process of education. . . . Every group has experienced series of events which have led it to regard some other group as competitor, aggressor, oppressor, plunderer, defiler, enslaver and destroyer.[14]

Foreign and domestic provocations, a chronic state of agitation over the life and honor of the group, and an historically conditioned awareness and suspicion of a particular foreign rival, are thus regarded as fundamental also to the formation of nationalist movements. From the standpoint of the would-be nationalist there is special piquancy in the old maxim, reaffirmed in modern psychoanalytic theory, that one's worst enemy may turn out to be one's best friend.

But this brings us back from the 'agitated and agitating' sentiment of nationalism to the half-conscious creators of nationalist ideology and their backers and receptive supporters. Berlin emphasizes that provocations such as those discussed above, provocations from both internal and external sources, provide a necessary condition for the birth of nationalism, but not a sufficient one. The provocations must fall on peculiarly receptive terrain, properly conditioned by emerging historical forces, consequently marked by *internal political, cultural and social alienation, and fertile with momentous change.* What he says in effect is that society must be ripening, and must be *sensed* to be ripening, towards fundamental institutional disintegration and breakdown—a 'Machiavellian Moment,' as it were, of the sort which has in fact been ascribed by Pocock to English civilization on the eve of the American Revolution. Berlin writes:

> The society must, at least potentially, contain within itself a group or class of persons who are in search of a focus for loyalty or self-identification, or perhaps a base for power, no longer supplied by earlier forces for cohesion—tribal, or religious, or feudal, or dynastic, or military. . . . In some cases, these conditions are created by the emergence of new social classes seeking control of a society against older rulers, secular or clerical. If to this is added the wound of conquest, or even cultural disparagement from without, of a society which has at any rate the beginnings of a national culture, the soil for the rise of nationalism may be prepared.[15]

3. AN ENGLISH PATTERN?

Let us now take inventory and attempt to match some of these concepts to the general facts of English history in the eighteenth century. We have at this point a number of theoretical elements which are all considered necessary in some degree to the development of the typical nationalist movement: a pre-existent consciousness of land, culture and people, an instinct to defend these, an historic external enemy; war with this historic enemy; cultural provocations, social humiliations, and other grievances often experienced as impositions by aliens; the sense of a betrayed past, the search for loyalty and self-identification in a present which is experienced as incohesive, fractured, yet restrictive; an intellectual thrust, initially defensive and intensely cultural in character, shaped by restive and socially sensitive bourgeois intellectuals and supported by a wider class seeking liberation, resulting gradually in the establishment of a comprehensive doctrine ultimately tending towards profound and general social, political, religious and cultural reorientation; a disintegrative and revolutionary ideological thrust, therefore, which nevertheless has as its objective the reintegration of the entire national group through the expansion of a uniform national consciousness and discipline based on the ideals of complete national unity, freedom and power. Then add to all this the fact that in Europe the typical nationalist movement is agreed to have begun and been timed with the economic, social and political dynamics of the later eighteenth century, together with the broad concurrent acceptance of secular ideals of progress, and it becomes clear that we have already the elements of a general theory that might shed much light on the nature of England's transformation during that decisive period.

The presence in England of many of these preconditions seems only too obvious, and in a sense the only task remaining before us in this book is to trace out their workings in some detail and show their meaning for a clearer understanding of what was going on from roughly 1740 to 1830 or a little later. Of course this inevitably means bumping into more scholarly applecarts already set up on the scene, questioning the value of some, and trying to move others around so that they all, on questions related to the making of the nation, point in roughly the same direction. Consider, to take a characteristic example, the question of the extent to which Englishmen in general experienced social and political discontentment during the period from roughly 1750 to 1789. Professor Caroline Robbins, in her fine history of liberal thought during this period, has suggested that "whatever discontent there may have been in any class" during this era (and she does not think there was much), "it found expression chiefly in the works of Real Whigs or Commonwealthmen. These were articulate and generally from the middle classes of society." But this, if we accept it without qualifications, would seem to tie our own problem too closely to the political attitudes and activities of a very small group of chiefly dissenting intellectuals and businessmen, too small indeed, as Professor Robbins herself suggests, to have carried much weight with their countrymen even if the members of this group had been the foremost pioneers of English nationalism (which they were not). One certainly should not underestimate the efforts of these 'Commonwealthmen' in stirring up grievances and raising the general consciousness of 'provocations' and 'humiliations,' of 'agitating concerns for the life and honor of the group.' But they constituted only one small and in some ways very irregular woodwind section of a big brass band, a broad and ever-growing spectrum of national dissatisfaction, largely middle-class it is true, but one which enjoyed the occasional support of sensitive observers, no matter where they were located in the social structure. It was, after all, Horace Walpole who in 1773 asked himself "What is England now?" and bitterly answered: "A sink of Indian wealth, filled by nabobs and emptied by Maccaronies! A senate sold and despised! . . . A gaming, robbing, wrangling, railing nation, without principles, genius, character, or allies; the overgrown shadow of what it was!" [16]

No one had a monopoly on such complaints, or on the jeremiads by which, during the third quarter of the eighteenth century, they were strung together into a virtual philosophy, indeed a cosmology, attacking national corruption and decay. Luxury, conspicuous consumption, political dishonesty and venality, moral dissolution, the abandonment of national character, collective decline and the imminence of ruin: these were the major themes not only of the 'Real' Whigs of the so-called Commonwealth tradition but of a broad and expanding generational cohort of sensitive and 'socially conscious' intellectuals dating from the 1740s. In the paintings and prints of Hogarth, the dramatic productions of Foote and Garrick, the moralizing essays of the Rev. John Brown, the prose and poetry of writers as diverse as Thomson, Shenstone, Johnson, Goldsmith, Smollett, Day, Burgh, Price, Cartwright, Mary Wollstonecraft, and even Fanny Burney, we find an intensifying, in some cases a nearly obsessive—an 'agitated and agitating'—concern with national decline and with the need for thorough moral regeneration. Nor can this really be thought surprising, in view of the general patterns of development which we have already surveyed in connection with the contemporaneous growth of wealth, the concentration of power, the intensification of social exclusion and social conflict, the mad pursuit of Fashion and of the external markings of Quality. These clergymen, artists, intellectuals, educators, and political theorists were sensitive monitors of these changes, often themselves painfully experiencing their effects in the form of humiliations, frustrations, and affronts to personal dignity and achievement. It was, as we shall see, in the intimate life experiences as well as the general social and political attitudes of these men and women, and of many more like them, that the low flame of eighteenth-century English patriotism, of irrational 'local attachments,' was fanned into the consuming fire of nationalist 'demands and actions,' 'anger and self-assertion.'

W. Hogarth inv.t et del.

C. Grignion sculp.

EXOTICKS

OBIT 15..

Publish'd according to Act of Parliament May 7, 1761.

6. 1761, after Hogarth. The sly connoisseur, an ape in French clothes, wig, and solitaire necktie, nurtures lifeless antiques and aesthetic imports while pretending to find in them hidden beauties invisible to ordinary taste.

CHAPTER FOUR

The Anatomy of Cultural Protest in the Age of George II

The connoisseurs and I are at war.

—HOGARTH

OUR THEORY IS that England, like several other European countries in the eighteenth century, witnessed the birth of modern nationalism, the transformation of an older 'patriotic consciousness' into something of tremendous new force and lasting importance. The movement began as a protest against excessive foreign cultural influence in the fatherland, and at length produced its own secular ideology.

Earlier we saw that the English spirit in the age of George II lay under the shadow of French and other foreign models. The Queen, patroness of the arts, spoke nothing but French, and young Voltaire was treated almost like a visiting potentate. In such realms as painting and music the native genius suffocated under the influence of foreign-born artists like Kneller and Handel. Commentators today harbor no doubts about the great extent to which English patrons and connoisseurs lavished their attentions upon foreigners at the expense of English creativity.[1] The upshot was a sense of both personal and national 'grievances and humiliations' which naturally was felt most keenly by native artists, still crucially dependent upon aristocratic tastes and encouragement. Together these conditions produced cries of simultaneously anti-foreign and anti-aristocratic cultural protest which by the 1750s were becoming a full-blooded chorus of lament and execration.

1. THEMES OF ARISTOCRATIC CULTURAL TREASON AND MORAL POLLUTION

The dynamics of this early movement sprang from the interaction of history and psychology, not the guiding influence of any particular individual. Yet if any patron saint of the movement were to be singled out, the obvious candidate for the honor would be William Hogarth (1697–1764), the first great English-born master of pictorial art. He was one of the earliest figures to express the artist's angry response to what presented itself as a rising tide of foreign cultural influence. From his extremely vulnerable point of view the yoke of foreign taste was already unendurable in the 1720s when he produced his print *Masquerades and Operas* (1724), a ferocious attack on foreign arts and their domestic aristocratic admirers, coupled with bitter commentary on the neglect of native genius (the print shows the works of Shakespeare and other English authors being hauled away to be pulped). Gaunt rightly observes that the print attacks "the patron . . . favouring the foreigner to the detriment of home-grown art." Moore comments that it may be said to furnish "the keynote of nearly all Hogarth's future works." Pinto maintains that Hogarth's entire subsequent career should be read as a sustained protest against alien cultural invasion and the "culture-snobbery" which so powerfully abetted it.[2]

Certainly Hogarth's pictorial essays and scattered writings do convey a sense of both personal outrage and projected national shame over what he repeatedly treated as a sort of cultural treason by the Great and their artistic suppliers. His ire was directed not so much at the foreign artist as at the domestic "connoisseurs," the cosmopolitan aesthetic establishment and its supporters, who, he wrote in 1737, "depreciate every English work . . . and fix on us poor Englishmen the character of *universal dupes.*" "The connoisseurs and I are at war," he declared; "and because I hate *them,* they think I hate *Titian*—and let them!"[3] Here is the paradigmatic 'reaction' of those 'who feel culturally at a disadvantage.'

In his 'war' on the connoisseurs Hogarth employed and gradually gave wider currency to what was to become a standard strategy of the mature nationalist movement, the subtle portrayal of the Ton as the enemy of domestic virtue as well as of domestic culture. Portraying it thus, as an alien race polluting the tastes and morality of the people, he embraced and refashioned for his own purposes an older strain of anti-aristocratic feeling. The strategy may be discerned in many of his productions. It appears in his most famous set of works, *Marriage à la Mode* (1743), the portrayal of a marriage of convenience between the foppish young Earl of Squanderfield and the daughter of a wealthy tradesman—a marriage which ends in adultery, murder and suicide. The fourth picture in the series, 'The Countess's Morning Levée,' furnishes a particularly good example. In considering it one should keep in mind what Gaunt, following Charles Lamb, has called "'the dumb rhetoric of the scenery', the way in which inanimate objects in lieu of the minor players of the stage became living things in their silent comment on the action going forward."[4] That is, Hogarth's details carry the brunt of his philosophical and moral comment, and do so the more powerfully because the message is conveyed by suggestion rather than explicit statement. In this representation of the young countess's levee in her boudoir the three figures of the lady, her husband and the lawyer Silvertongue convey the central action. The count, foppishly dressed, his hair in curlers, sits bemusedly sipping coffee while his wife and the lawyer seem to moon over each other as they admire a 'black master,' a murky old painting near the lawyer's couch—just the sort of foreign work of art that Hogarth deplored. The ideas of moral betrayal and cultural treason are thus suggested in the central action. But it is the background details and minor characters which enforce these 'pictur'd Morals' (a phrase coined by Garrick in his 'Epitaph on Hogarth'). The worship of un-English arts and fashions is condemned not only through the artificiality of the action but by the skillful placement around the room of several ridiculous foreign musicians, a French hairdresser (his face plastered with makeup), a French novel, a voluptuous Correggio on the wall; while the theme of carnality and moral betrayal is reinforced through lustful activities portrayed in the decorative paintings in the background and the gesture of the black page-boy in the foreground, who grinningly addresses the viewer while pointing significantly to the large horns of a semi-human statuette which he holds—horns which laughably resemble the glassy-eyed count's curlers.

The 'World' repaid Hogarth's shafts with ridicule and neglect, but his campaign in favor of domestic art and virtue gained a sympathetic audience among many younger artists and intellectuals. His great influence on literature, particularly on the rising art of the novel—a propaganda force of ever-growing importance in the eighteenth century—is held to have been equal to his influence on the graphic arts. There can be little doubt of his tremendous influence on Henry Fielding, who in 1740 praised "the ingenious Mr Hogarth" as one of the most "useful *Satyrists* that any Age hath produced."[5] It is difficult to say whether Fielding consciously set out in *Joseph Andrews* (1742), his first novel, to embody in literature any of Hogarth's ideas (though he again praised Hogarth in the preface of it), but the point is unimportant. What concerns us is the theme of cultural protest itself and its expression in literary as well as graphic channels of communication. And indeed the key pattern, an allegorical extension of the patriotic, moralizing and anti-aristocratic protest voiced by Hogarth, does appear in *Joseph Andrews* and may be regarded as the pattern for much subsequent propaganda on the same theme.

In this novel Fielding expresses an awakening cultural nationalism in many ways, but the subject may be handled most conveniently by examining the short tale or 'history' of Leonora told by one of Parson Adams's acquaintances.[6] Every detail lends weight to its 'pictur'd Moral.' Young Leonora and her suitor, Horatio, live in a northern English town. She is beautiful and much admired, too vain and "an extreme lover of gaiety," but not without modesty, conscience and self-respect. The lovers pledge themselves to each other, but shortly before their marriage Horatio must make a brief trip away from the town. No sooner has he gone than Leonora spies through her window a coach and six passing by, "which she declared to be the completest, genteelest, prettiest equipage she ever saw, adding these remarkable words, 'Oh, I am in love with that equipage!'" At the assembly that night she is dazzled by its owner, Bellarmine, a young, handsome and splendidly dressed English aristocrat "just arrived from Paris." Ignoring her pledge to Horatio, she dances the night away with Bellarmine. The latter's principal attractions, apart from his equipage, flattering attentions, and lovely French-sounding name (which like Hogarth's 'à la mode' subtly tags the surrounding action as un-English), are his speech—a mixture, particularly in his letters to Leonora, of English constructions interlarded with French phrases—and his fine gold-embroidered clothes: "'All French,' says he, 'I assure you, except the great-coats; I never trust anything more than a great-coat to an Englishman. . . . I would see the dirty island at the bottom of the sea rather than wear a single rag of English work about me, and I am sure, after you have made one tour to Paris, you will be of the same opinion with regard to your own clothes.'"

Leonora yields to these hybrid charms and gives Bellarmine leave to consult her father about marriage. "Thus, what Horatio had by sighs and tears, love and tenderness, been so long in obtaining, the French-English Bellarmine with gaiety and gallantry possessed himself of in an instant." But Leonora's conscience troubles her, and she continues to wrestle privately with her decision. "Is not Horatio my lover—almost my husband? . . . Aye, but Bellarmine is the genteeler and the finer man." At this point Leonora's aunt casts a decisive weight into the balance, the weight of 'the World.' Leonora ponders her engagements to Horatio: "'Engagements to a fig,' cried the aunt . . . 'Bellarmine drives six, and Horatio not even a pair.' 'Yes, but madam, what will the world say?' answered Leonora; 'will they not condemn me?' 'The world is always on the side of prudence,' cries the aunt, 'and would surely condemn you if you sacrificed your interest to any motive whatever. . . . Besides, if we examine the two men, can you prefer a sneaking fellow, who hath been bred at the university, to a fine gentleman just come from his travels?'"

Thus shabbily convinced, her conscience appeased, Leonora goes on with Bellarmine to plan their marriage. But then returns the "grave and plain" Horatio. Unaware of all that has happened, he interrupts one of their trysts. His puzzlement turns to indignation and then violence against the 'French-English' seducer, whom he wounds with his sword. With Bellarmine's recovery uncertain, Leonora's worldly aunt—her other seducer (for in the nationlist logic the French and the World are always paired)— advises her to think of regaining the affections of Horatio. "No," cries Leonora, "I have lost him as well as the other, and it was your wicked advice which was the occasion of all; you seduced me, contrary to my inclinations, to abandon poor Horatio." But Bellarmine recovers, and with Leonora's renewed consent applies to her father; who, a miser, refuses to provide a sufficient dowry. The tale thus ends with the collapse of the proposed marriage, Leonora and Horatio fated to live out the rest of their lives in unhappy solitude while Bellarmine returns to his amphibious life of pleasure. After the interview with her father, Bellarmine "took his leave, but not in order to return to Leonora; he proceeded directly to his own seat, whence, after a few days' stay, he returned to Paris, to the great delight of the French and the honour of the English nation."

2. THE DREAM LOGIC OF BELIEF

Fielding's little fable thus concludes with generalized hints on French versus English morality and a pleasant symbolic excommunication of the English lord. But in truth no high-flown literary analysis is needed to bring out the few basic ideas and symbolic associations developed in this story. At bottom they are nearly identical to those of 'the Countess's

Morning Levée,' though Fielding's medium permitted him to elaborate them more fully. Later authors were able to build up much of the entire nationalist philosophy from this simple theoretical base, using it as a sort of expanding file for the storage and projection of their accumulating grievances.

What we have here is a sort of symbolic logic, a chain of cultural-social-moral reasoning or rather association, which begins in the international sphere, ends in the national, and works through a vague notion of creeping contamination. At the heart of the nationalist protest may be discerned four interconnected ideas which together constituted its inner logic, a sort of dream logic, which was to serve it for many decades. To put these as plainly as possible: (1) the World are pervaded, even neutered or hermaphroditized, by foreign cultural influence; (2) this foreign cultural influence translates itself into ruinous moral influence; (3) it is a fact that ordinary, innocent Englishmen unthinkingly admire and follow the World's lead—they are seduced by the Quality; (4) hence alien cultural influence brings collective domestic moral ruin.

This inner logic was inherently anti-cosmopolitan, anti-aristocratic, and nativist. It exploited the energies attached to crude anti-French myth and joined these to ancient notions of aristocratic moral degeneracy. Although in fact it was not so much a logic as an illogical tribalistic jumble of beliefs and perceptions combining rude notions of national character, cultural invasion, moral pollution, social transmission, and collective spiritual disintegration, it nevertheless was the plastic material from which a great variety of protests were to be raised. Indeed it was more than that, for as time passed and circumstances invited, it was capable of being amalgamated with, and hence of lending a semblance of philosophical unity to, so many allied dissatisfactions that in the end it constituted no longer a protest but the base and vehicle of an entire countercultural program of action.

This philosophical transformation took place essentially between the mid-1740s and the mid-1780s; these were the critical years in the launching of English nationalism. Many contributory factors were at work here: the rise of the novel, of graphic satire and of other forms of mass communication, the expansion of the reading public and the declining importance of aristocratic artistic patronage, the intensified sense of togetherness and collective destiny brought on by the Seven Years' War and the War of American Independence, the 'chronic' sense of military, economic and diplomatic competition with France during this entire period, the rising political activity of the middle and lower classes which also took place during the early decades of George III, the sharpening consciousness of aristocratic exclusiveness and political irresponsibility (as well as of cultural and moral betrayal). But it was apparently the well-justified sense of alien cultural invasion, linked in nationalist perceptions with the idea of aristocratic cultural and moral betrayal, which furnished the root theory of the movement.

3. THE FIFTIES: SHARPER TONES, DEEPER ELABORATIONS, AN EMERGING MOVEMENT

There are many signs that by the 1750s the theme of cultural protest was becoming more generalized, frantically hypochondriac, and strident. Take, for example, Tobias Smollett's *Ferdinand Count Fathom* (1753), which in one respect is little more than a sustained attack upon what Smollett sarcastically calls "that class, who, in the sapience of taste, are disgusted with those very flavours, in the productions of their own country, which have yielded infinite delectation to their faculties, when imported from another clime." In plot structure, characterization, symbolism, and explicit commentary as well as suggestion, the novelist knits together the ideas, apparently fused in his own mind, of alien cultural penetration and aristocratic moral pollution, again joining them dramatically through themes of seduction. Of course the native purity has its sturdy though ineffectual defenders. In certain scenes set in Paris one gets the sense of Smollett himself materializing in the "flannel waistcoat, buff breeches, hunting-boots and whip" of the redoubtable Sir Stentor Stile, the one English original in the city, a man who refuses to alter his dress, manners, speech or diet in deference either to the French, who consider him "some savage monster or maniac," or to the visiting English, who "were overwhelmed with shame and confusion, and kept a most wary silence, for fear of being recognized by their countryman." It is Smollett who vainly stalks Paris in search of "solid belly timber," a "nice buttock of beef"—a calculated reminder perhaps of Fielding's song 'The Roast Beef of Old England' and Hogarth's popular *The Gate of Calais, O the Roast Beef of Old England* (1749), which had featured deprived Frenchmen slavering over an enormous, a mystically huge joint of English beef; a symbol from his friend the 'inimitable Hogarth' which Smollett was often to exploit in the future, as in his comedy *The Reprisal* (produced by Garrick in 1757). It is Smollett in cut bob and leathern cap who cries that "a true-born Englishman needs not be afeard to shew his face, nor his backside neither, with the best Frenchman, that ever trod the ground"; who reproaches "we English, no offence Sir Giles, that seem to be ashamed of their own nation"; and who slyly associates a half-frenchified English baronet with ideas of fundamental moral betrayal: "Mercy upon thee, knight, thou art so transmogrified and bedaubed, and bedizened, that thou mought rob thy own mother without fear of information."[7]

These touches anticipate Smollett's own journies in France, memorably captured in his anti-Gallic *Travels Through France and Italy* (1766). But more significant here is the novelist's portrayal of the cultural landscape of London itself in 1753, a scene not simply of foreign intrigues but of full-scale invasions waved on by the Beau Monde. When Fathom, a smooth, swindling, half-British nobleman first comes to England, a fellow adventurer explains to him some of the established methods of infiltration—a sign here of Smollett's great anxiety on this subject. "There is a variety of shapes, in which we knights of the industry, make our appearance in London. One glides into a nobleman's house in the capacity of a valet de chambre," or else "professes the composition of musick," or else assumes the character of "dancers, fencing-masters, and French ushers," or else "breaks forth at once in all the splendor of a gay equipage, under the title and denomination of a foreign count." Any method is likely to succeed, the Ton being stupid, vain, and immoral—the English "people of fashion being, for the most part, more ignorant, indolent, vain and capricious than their inferiors, and of consequence more easily deceived; besides their morals fit generally so loose about them, that when a gentleman of our fraternity is discovered in the exercise of his profession, their contempt of his skill is the only disgrace he incurs."[8]

Fathom proceeds then to set himself up as a connoisseur of art, and, having "captivated the favour and affection of the English nobility" by means of his surface glitter, proceeds to take the whole fashionable world under his aesthetic dictation, a cover for his fraudulent dealings in old masters, antiquities, foreign musical instruments, and the like. "He himself was astonished at the infatuation he had produced. Nothing was so wretched among the productions of art, that he could not impose upon the world as a capital performance, and so fascinated were the eyes of his admirers, he could easily have persuaded them that a barber's bason was an Etrurian Patera."[9]

All this is familiar stuff to the student of nationalism. What we have here are the typical manifestations of nationalist cultural paranoia. Literary students will recognize here many familiar themes of contemporary fiction and poetry; the larger job is to see what they mean in relation to each other, to see them as parts of an expanding philosophy. One such theme is the idea of the native *Volk* being gulled by smooth operators swarming in from abroad. Samuel Johnson, trying out his poetic wings (he started his literary career in the 1730s as a translator of French), complained that "Their Air, their Dress, their Politicks import . . . on *Britain's* fond credulity they play." The poet Edward Young was so obsessed with this French influence that he experienced it as "a Satanic force"[10] —another reminder of our contemporary world, where Middle Eastern nationalists and others see the United States as a 'Great Satan' bent on gobbling their cultural hearts. A second aspect is the broadening critique of not only Paris as the principal source of foreign pollution but London itself, the domestic capital, as the beachhead and entrepôt of alien cultural influence and the associated moral disease. A third is the suggestion that this influence is part of a deeper and more sinister foreign plot against native liberty and national identity. A fourth, linked to this last, is the increasingly stylized treatment of the London Quality as a hybrid 'class' or 'race,' and the sharpening criticism of not only its aesthetic and moral values but its intellectual values as well. A fifth is the emerging tendency to generalize these cultural and ethnic concerns into a pessimistic philosophy of historic decline, a philosophy emphasizing the abandonment of national character through the abuse of wealth and the neglect and mongrelization of national culture. Connected with this, however, and equally symptomatic of the formative stages of nationalist ideology, is a sixth characteristic, an increasingly energetic call for aesthetic and moral revival, harking back to an idealized age of national greatness.

i. an intellectual awakening

But before considering these points more fully it will be useful to step back a moment and ponder the artist-intellectuals as a group. Watt has shown how the novel rose from the early 1740s to become a major channel of social criticism, one which he closely associates with the rise of distinctively bourgeois concerns and sensibilities. The novelists, he says, may be considered in the light of "a literary movement whose members had a good deal in common," both "in narrative method and in social background." Other commentators have pursued the same idea. Baker suggests that it was in the early fifties that the English novel's mood began to alter from one of lighthearted mockery to a more caustic one of "stern invective" and "downright plain speaking" against "the contemporary world, frivolous, immoral, godless." Why was this? Sometimes we forget how mistreated many of these artists were by their countrymen. Fielding, crowned with laurels in our memory, was despised by many high-born contemporaries. His greatness "remained without recognition by anyone of eminence in the world of letters," while reviewers for such magazines as the *Gentleman's* "sought to crush him with contempt or innuendo." These forgotten facts supply a clue to Fielding's social attitudes. It was in 1752, in the *Covent Garden Journal,* that he published his "Modern Glossary" which caustically defined "no body" as "all the people in Great Britain, except about 1200," a definition underlining the arrogance of the country's opinion-makers. According to the same glossary, "great" when applied to a man was to be understood as meaning "littleness, or meanness"; "fine" when applied to taste, clothes and people was just another way of saying "useless"; "gallantry" meant "fornication and adultery."[11]

If, as Baker believes, Fielding's increasingly critical social attitudes reflected those of English novelists in general, then perhaps it would not be generalizing too much to urge that the novelists themselves were part of a still broader movement which included the intelligentsia in the larger sense—graphic artists, playwrights, poets, critics, moralists, and so on, who shared essentially the same social background, professional concerns, and artistic conventions as the novelists. Certainly many contemporary playwrights and actors shared Fielding's perspectives. Garrick's early views on the neglect of English art are well known: "Virtu to such a height is grown,/All Artists are encourag'd—but our own." Such was the lament recited over and over at Drury Lane in 1752 by this rising actor, this defender of native cultural genius; the lines were written by him too.[12] Such anguished sentiments may seem natural in one whose very name was to become synonymous with the tremendous Shakespeare revival that began in the sixties, but they were shared by many of his friends in the theatrical world.

ii. a growing concern over alien manners and morals

Take Sam Foote, 'the English Aristophanes,' the comic actor and dramatist. Let us consider the nationalist fears, emotions and beliefs, the embryonic nationalist philosophy, so insistently expressed in such productions as *The Englishman in Paris* (1753) and its sequel, *The Englishman Returned from Paris* (1756). The plot in these two self-continuing works, much like that in Arthur Murphy's *The Spouter* (1756), is but a variation on the fundamental theme examined already in Hogarth, Fielding, and Smollett. The characters, action, and 'pictur'd Moral' are all built up from the same materials as well. Young John Buck is sent to Paris to polish his manners and refine his low tastes. Soon he becomes outrageously frenchified, a caricature of French values. When his father dies, he returns, accompanied by a retinue of alien cronies and hangers-on, to his now detested homeland to claim his inheritance. But his father's will requires him to deal with his earlier betrothal to the orphaned Lucinda, who figures as the elaborate personification of English purity and integrity. Opposed on principle now to marriage, he tries to seduce her. She indignantly rejects him and turns the tables on him, for good measure tricking him into destroying all his beloved French clothing and cosmetics, and sending his friends and servants back to France; the story ends with Buck repudiated and Lucinda free to accept a truly English marriage.[13]

The plot itself is thus an articulation of the basic ideas already outlined, the lateral movement from Paris to London of cultural influence, with 'the World' its carrier, betrayal and immorality its effect, English innocence its potential victim through actions of fashionable influence or outright seduction. But this last, this stress on morality, points to another distinction which should be made about the general character of the protest movement as it passed into the last years of George II's reign. In the works we examined earlier, the artist's concern fastened as much upon the preference for foreign arts and luxury goods as upon the supposedly foreign morals and manners which allegedly constituted the other major element of this international traffic. But the fifties saw a considerable enlargement of this moral complaint, and even—this is an important point—a confused tendency to look upon the whole system of 'modern' manners and morals as traceable to foreign (French) influence. The *modern* disease was the *French* disease. "So, Youngster!" exclaims one of Buck's English antagonists, "I suppose you are already practising one of your *foreign* lessons. Perverting the affections of a friend's mistress, or debauching his wife, are mere peccadilloes, in *modern* morality." Garrick conveyed the same idea in his one-act farce *Lilliput* a year later (1757): "Time was when we had as little vice here in [England] as any where; but since we imported politeness from [France], we have thought of nothing but being fine gentleman [which means] impertinence and affectation, without any one virtue."[14]

Undoubtedly the expansion of foreign travel in the fifties gave a push to this confused idea; surely another important cause was the consolidation by mid-century of the Chesterfieldian 'code of politeness,' a consolidation which evidently gave a unified and alien quality to the manners of the supremely eligible (and of course, in lesser degree, to the manners of all who imitated them). The increasingly shrill rejection of alien manners and morality constituted an important step in the enlargement of the whole anti-foreign and anti-aristocratic protest.

iii. concepts of contamination, disintegration, and decline

A few other points may be illustrated from Foote's plays before we leave them. While their plot-line registers the basic theme harped upon by so many artists of this period, Foote's characters' speeches reveal its subterranean connections with more remote questions of ethnic identification, social criticism, and historical theory. In fact what these speeches seem to reveal is the solidification by the fifties of an ideology protesting numerous grievances and holding up only one solution, moral regeneration through national rebirth. A few quotations will illustrate the growing many-sidedness of the theme: (1) Vice is virtue in France: "The customs of this gay country give sanction, and stamp merit upon vice; and vanity will here proclaim what modesty would elsewhere blush to whisper." (2) Emulation of French culture produces immorality, artificiality, snobbery and social pretension: "To *parler François,*—fib, flatter, and dance,/Which is very near all that they teach ye in France. . . . The merest John Trot in a week you shall zee/*Bien poli, bien frizé, tout à fait un Marquis.*" (3) The French cultural conquest of England is part of a larger and more sinister scheme to paralyze native resistance and virtue: "The importation of these puppies [French valets, servants, etc.] makes a part of the politics of your old friends, the French; unable to resist you, whilst you retain your ancient roughness, they have recourse to these minions, who would first, by unmanly means, sap and soften all your native spirit, and then deliver you an easy prey to their employers." (4) The international cultural treason is progressing all the time: "The French are the first people in the universe . . . This is my creed . . . and with the aid of these brother missionaries, I have no doubt of making a great many proselytes." (5) This treason must be exposed and punished: "For the wretch who is weak and wicked enough to despise his country, sins against the most laudable laws of nature; he is a traitor to the community, where Providence has placed him; and should be denied those social benefits he has rendered himself unworthy to partake." (6) Foreign influence feeds on native wealth and social affectation: "Your tawdry trappings, your foreign foppery, your washes, paints, pomades, must blaze before your door. . . . And, lastly, I'll have these exotic attendants, these instruments of your luxury, these panders to your pride, pack'd in the first cart, and sent post to the place from whence they came [Paris]." (7) Wholesale cultural disintegration is the result of all this: An appalling *loss of national character* has resulted from the "importation of every foreign folly: and thus the plain persons and principles of old England, are so confounded and jumbled with the excrementitious growth of every climate, that we have lost all our ancient characteristic, and are become a bundle of contradictions; a piece of patch-work; a mere harlequin's coat." (8) History and the memory of ancient forefathers underscore the dreadful decline of national identity and patriotic spirit, yet they also point the way to national regeneration if only the nation will awaken from its hybrid effeminacy and cultural amnesia:

> They [our prudent forefathers] scorn'd to truck, for base, unmanly arts,
> Their native plainness, and their honest hearts;
> Whene'er they deigned to visit haughty France,
> 'Twas arm'd with bearded dart, and pointed lance.
> No pompous pageants lur'd their curious eye,
> No charms for them had fops or flattery. . . .
> Far other views attract our modern race,
> Trulls, toupees, trinkets, bags, brocades, and lace;
> A flaunting form, and a fictitious face.
> Rouse! re-assume! refuse a Gallic reign,
> Nor let their arts win that their arms could never gain.[15]

iv. elements of caution, confusion, and ambivalence

Thus we have here by the mid-1750s something more than a cultural protest. What we have is an emergent nationalist philosophy, anti-French and anti-aristocratic, linked to sharpening moral, social and historical concerns as well as aesthetic and commercial ones; the beginnings of a *Kulturkampf,* a campaign over morality and taste, which, it was now dimly realized, would require the projection of an entire series of challenges to values upheld by 'the World.'

Now it is quite true, as was suggested earlier, that much of the felt oppressiveness of English social life was due in fact to an emerging domestic socioeconomic conflict and had really nothing to do with foreign influences. But such a distinction is not easily made by troubled and confused men, artists and intellectuals believing themselves borne down beneath a spreading cultural collapse. And indeed many facts of everyday experience seemed to authenticate the 'Gallic' portrayal; Foote's audience understood his terms of reference, with their suggestion of a creeping imposition of French values. And then there was, to be sure, the strategic consideration as well: the nationalist writer was moved by genuine fears and convictions—we shall explore his psychology later—but he had his eye on polemical strategy also when he presented what he disliked as vaguely French, and what he yearned for as vaguely English; when he personified his grievances in Bellarmines and Bucks, his dreams in Horatios and Lucindas, compressing the cultural, moral and social tendencies which he only half understood into opposed patterns of behavior, dressed in national uniforms. It would be a mistake to think the propagandist did not know how to manage what one was to call "the language of allusion" when attacking the powerful: "He who attacks [existing institutions], sanctified by time and custom, and interwoven with the *selfish interests* of the most powerful men in the community; had need, even in the most enlightened and liberal age, to move with circumspection; and to omit nothing . . . in making his approaches."[16]

There was an element of class warfare here in the fifties, a battle mounted by the London man of letters against the London man of fashion, and fought with the artist's weapon, the pen. But we must keep things in proportion: the world of art was a mere Punch-and-Judy show on the corner of the great stage of daily existence and historical reality, and there are other reasons why the idea of class warfare should not be exaggerated. The artist's target was not yet the aristocracy itself as a group or institution but rather aristocracry as a corrupted and corrupting moral system—personified, it is true, in the unpatriotic, arrogant, exclusive and in so many other ways insufferable young men who every day were gliding into their 'predestinated' offices and privileges. But the movement's political elaboration did not come till later. In the fifties it was still essentially a campaign for greater influence over English culture and morality by a small but irritated and growing number of anti-Gallic cultural patriots like Hogarth and Fielding, Smollett and Foote, a battle by a sensitive minority of artist-intellectuals against 'the World' and all who unthinkingly supported it, including other bourgeois artists and intellectuals. It was a campaign within the ranks of educated Britons by a discontented minority whose sleeping partner was the insular prejudice of the unwashed and only half literate multitudes, the *Volk*—not yet a very respectable ally nor a very useful one either, one to be kept at arm's length until tidied up and romanticized. We must never forget that the would-be nationalist lived as yet in an age of flourishing philosophy and cosmopolitanism, an age too when 'the great man's levée' was still the portal to success in the arts. To play the cultural bigot was to put on the fool's cap and pronounce oneself 'ineligible,' unworthy of the notice of cultivated men. This goes far to explain the fact that even on the stage and in graphic satire, the most plebeian forms of artistic expression, the campaign was fought as much through symbols, hints, 'the dumb rhetoric of the scenery,' as through explicit statement; and of course it is true also that art by its very nature works emblematically, achieving effectiveness by requiring the spectator to do some of the work. Foote breaks off his own most explicit attack on aristocratic cultural treason with a caution against "sententious lectures."[17] There are many signs that the *Kulturkampf* was fought out within the mind, sensibilities and ambitions of the literati itself as history and circumstance slowly increased the stakes, enlarged the crowd, and sharpened the enemy's profile.

4. FOLKISH GALLOPHOBIA

And though the matter seems too obvious to require detailed discussion at this point, it will do no harm to keep in mind the increasing force, increasingly important, of English popular opposition to France after the beginning of the Seven Years' War; the growing opposition, primarily mil-

itary and economic but running beyond that, to France as historic enemy—as 'competitor, aggressor, oppressor, plunderer, defiler, enslaver
and destroyer' (Handman). Clearly a very long tradition of 'animosity,
historically developed and maintained by a process of education,' stood
behind this opposition: so long indeed that it would perhaps be no exaggeration to say that a consciousness of France as England's military, commercial and diplomatic enemy was one of the foundation stones of the
national mind, perhaps in those days even more basic than the sense of
common territory and language, and one of the very few articles of belief
that in some way or another was capable of influencing all Britons beneath otherwise immense diversitites of wealth, locality, dialect, occupation, religion, and political faith.

True, this opposition has been much exaggerated by a legend-ridden
and chronologically undiscriminating historiography. In the eighteenth
century, a fixed opposition to all things French was a cretinous prejudice
of the rabble—the *canaille,* as they were called in London as well as
Paris—and an embarrassment to educated and 'polished' men. It should
be kept in mind also that the wars of the eighteenth century, during
which such popular sentiments were most likely to receive expression, had
about them a nakedly commercial character which helped to insulate sensible people against the tendency, so enlarged in our own era of mass
politics, to hate the enemy as an undifferentiated menace to existence
itself. Yet even the most devoted cosmopolite knew (just as the Francophiliac Frederick the Great, for example, knew in Germany) that the
basic commercial and territorial interests of his own country lay in opposition to those of France. In 1757, after the invasion scare of the previous
year and the appalling British disasters at Fort Duquesne, Minorca and
Calcutta, it was Chesterfield himself who lamented the extent to which
"we are undone. . . .The French are masters to do what they
please. . . .We are no longer a nation."[18] If these were his fears, then
what were those of ill-educated men during the three decades to follow, a
period of more or less perpetual excitement over the nefarious and at
last, so it was to seem by 1783, humiliatingly successful designs of England's powerful neighbor?

It is clear, on a long view of things, that the very concepts of British
strength and territorial integrity were shaped in the ancient flow of Anglo-French rivalry, or, as the British saw it, in the ongoing experience of
French 'threats and provocations.' Each major step in the consolidation of
English rule in the British Isles—1689, 1707, 1745, 1801—was taken in
the context of Anglo-French warfare, and so for that matter was each
assertion of British power in the great world beyond. The field of anti-
French conflict was the mirror of British independence and might. But to
see this is to see that military conflict with France also overlapped and
gave a specious reality to certain internal constitutional ideas, thanks to an
easy confusion in the popular mind between national self-determination
and popular liberty. In one facile sense an Englishman was a free man, a
'free-born Englishman,' simply by virtue of the fact that he was not a

Frenchman, nor born in a country that accepted French political dictation. He might be penniless, he might be politically impotent, he might
for all that be marching to die on the gallows for some trivial offense
against property, but nevertheless he was by this delusive standard a free
man in a free country; and there are grounds for suspecting that in actu-
ality the mob's sense of English liberty by the 1750s was based on about
three parts of Gallophobia to one of constitutional guarantees and the
assumed right to riot. The myth or at best the half-truth of popular liberty was sustained—some cynics might say that in many countries it still is
today—by consciousness of national rivalry with the foreign foe bent
upon 'enslavement.' And it is certain that the nationalist publicists were
never so eloquent about the splendors of the English constitution as when
defending it against the designs of France—"this ambitious, perfidious,
restless, bigoted, persecuting, plundering Power," as one pamphleteer
wrote in 1756, "which has long been the common Disturber of the western World, and as long struggled for Universal Monarchy"; this "irreconcilable and enterprizing enemy," as Arthur Young described France in his
first published work (1758).[19]

Later we will examine the nationalists' political ideas in detail. But it
should be noted here that their constitutional ideas were not nearly so
simple, so lyrically supportive of 'the matchless constitution,' as one might
carelessly think. Towards the constitution, as towards many other things,
they took two radically opposed views, depending on whether they were
thinking of it in its ideal form, its supposedly pristine original state, or its
contemporary form, which they regarded as almost hopelessly corrupted
by the combined machinations of the Ton abroad and the Ton at home,
the devils in France and those in the West End. This means, among other
things, that eighteenth-century 'tributes to English freedom' should not
be regarded as proofs of 'stability' and 'contentment' without careful scrutiny of their contexts, tone, and hidden purposes. The correct approach is
taken by Gazley in his perceptive study of Arthur Young's copious writings, a study which passes beyond Young's stock phrases on "the
GLORIOUS CONSTITUTION of this kingdom" to present materials in
which Young in fact violently attacks "the English constitution" as more
than "deficient," as "worthless; . . . so that if the nation do not make some
change in its constitution, it is much to be dreaded that the constitution
will ruin the nation." The result is that Gazley correctly (though still too
cautiously) interprets Young's patriotic ideology as "hardly that of a stand-
pat conservative": Young was instead imbued with "an extreme form of
nationalism" and "a very radical position" in domestic politics which manifested itself in an insistence that "it is not the opinion of THE PEOPLE
that has authority in this kingdom."[20] This, as shall be shown more fully
later, is the correct perspective onto what has been rather badly misunderstood as the 'conservatism' of Young and of others who thought as he
did.

But in the 1750s the political aspect of the nationalist movement still
belonged to the future. To return then to the point under discussion,

popular anti-French feeling was, to the propagandist, potentially a source of tremendous power, connected as it was with ancient ideas and feelings—myths of liberty, enslavement, oppression, and even racial defilement. The English had lived under various dynasties, constitutional forms, and religions, but they had had only one permanent enemy, the one that had conquered their island in 1066. Indeed if Christopher Hill is correct—we must return later to his brilliant essay on the 'Norman Yoke'—this anti-French sentiment was connected with the most ancient pattern of secular mythology in English history. For all these reasons it was doubly useful then in the new age of war with France, an age too in which England's rulers were themselves perceived as admirers of French ways and minions of French influence, for propagandists to reach down to these stores of popular sentiment and, increasingly, exploit them, just as Hogarth in his rage at aristocratic connoisseurship had urged the mass of struggling younger artists to reach down with him to the sentiments of the people, finding salvation and livelihood "not above, but below."[21]

5. Sleeping Beauty

And it is in fact among the prints and drawings of Hogarth's artistic disciples that the "basic preconceptions," the "semi-coherent beliefs" of contemporary popular culture, are best revealed. Such is the view set forth by Atherton in his rich and learned study of the graphic prints of this era—a veritable mine of materials awaiting the student of English nationalism. Atherton himself harbors no doubts on the existence of this nationalism: "One of the most striking developments in the mood and thought of the Georgian era is the exuberant nationalism which appears in the middle decades of the eighteenth century. . . . nationalist fervour was evidencing itself in the nation at large, in a way never seen before. Its manifestations appear everywhere."[22] Though in fact he means little more by this than that patriotism was rising, Atherton does insightfully point to the importance of contemporary fear and hatred of France. His discussions probe the manner in which stereotyped images of the French helped to shape and unify the English popular consciousness, and they also suggest the paranoid intensity of some of these anti-French feelings. But what is still more interesting is the manner in which these anti-French feelings were deliberately trained against the native oligarchy—a sign of that growing internal alienation along social and cultural lines which, in the view of authorities like Chadwick and Berlin, is so essential to the conversion of 'mere national consciousness' into full-fledged nationalist 'demands and actions' taking the nation itself as their object.

Consider the treatment of 'Britannia'—a figure which Berlin and the others, were they to look up from their meditations on Germany, would probably interpret as a mythic projection of loyal sentiments which in contemporary reality could find no authentic 'focus for loyalty or self-identification.' As Atherton explains, the patriotic anthem 'Rule, Britannia!' made its appearance in 1745 (as also did 'God Save the King!') and led to the full iconographic establishment by the 1750s of this famous female personification of both the nation and, continues Atherton, of "Virtue, especially those virtues relevant to national and public life: love of country, dedication, honesty, selflessness, discipline, simplicity." But "the decline and impending fall of Britannia is a common lament." Britannia, this representation of "virtuous innocence" and of "the nation" ("whether that nation is England or Great Britain varies with the subjects and intent of the prints"), is shown over and over as "distraught, weakened, or defeated." She is shown repeatedly as weeping, abused, insulted, cozened, persecuted, martyred, and in every way defiled—even though, writes Atherton, one sometimes finds in the midst of this "the idea of 'Britannia *redux*', that she will return. . . . 'She is not dead but sleepeth.'"[23]

These are, generically considered, common nationalist images, with obvious symbolic implications of ideal national unity and purity, present disintegration and degradation, future resurrection. Minogue begins his book on nationalism with an illuminating discussion of Germany's 'Sleeping Beauty,' put to sleep "by wicked kings and self-seeking aristocrats." And who are Britannia's persecutors and defilers? There are of course the French in France: in one print, for example, "Britannia appears tied down, half-naked, on a beach, and dismembered by invading Frenchmen." But far more frequently she is the weakened and ravished victim of the French in England: she is the victim of the aristocracy, especially of ministers of state. Atherton has no explanation of this very important point, these "vapid insinuations" as he calls them, beyond his idea that "a common assumption, perhaps inspired by memories of the intrigues of the Restoration, maintained that English ministers were in the pay of France, or at the very least, the dupes of French policy."[24]

But of course we see the answer more clearly: the identification of domestic rulers with the foreign enemy is a characteristic of nationalism, one of the key characteristics in fact which help to distinguish it from mere patriotism. And this explains why, in innumerable prints, we discover absolutely laden with symbols of Frenchness the Quality and nearly all politicians with the exception of Pitt—Walpole, the Pelhams, Bedford, Bute, Sandwich, Mansfield, the Foxes. Fleurs-de-lis peep from their hats and lapels, portraits of coiled serpents with fleurs-de-lis in their mouths adorn their walls, Gallic cocks surround them, they smilingly present their children to French tutors and dancing masters for proper education, their quarters are piled high with French luxury goods, French menus and cuisine stand on their tables (the Duke of Newcastle feasts on 'Soup À la Reigne' with 'Woodcocks Brains' and 'Popes Eyes'), French bribes pass plentifully between them, Frenchmen perched in the tree of temptation help them distribute "golden pippins," they stand in dancing poses with cloven feet beside devils and Frenchmen, tonnish French apes in French bag-wigs and solitaires hover near them. (The apes date probably from Arbuthnot's tracts of 1712 contrasting 'John Bull' with 'Lewis Baboon'; and apes, notes Atherton, also doubled as symbols for the devil). And all of this while, often in scenes truly nightmarish to behold, they dismember and disembowel the fair Britannia, administer emetics to her and force her to vomit English possessions into basins held by apish Frenchmen, garb her in French finery decorated with fleurs-de-lis, sit with their feet resting on the head of a defunct British lion, auction off English territories in Paris, defecate on a map of England, stand on the shield of the City of London and the Cap of Liberty, and trample on Justice, Honesty, Liberty, Honour, Property, Trade, and Love.[25]

This is strong evidence, evidence of a very primal sort. It is evidence from what old-fashioned German historians were wont to call the 'folk mind,' a primitive half-conscious world of tribal dreams and fantasies, of ancient forbidden fruits, of folkish memories of seduction, force, and desecration. These materials suggest how very deep, elemental, carnal, even in some way manic, was the folkish attitude toward France; and thus how electrically charged was the semi-conscious network of belief upon which the frustrated artist-intellectuals, with their Punch-and-Judy shows at the edge of daily reality, were able to play, setting up their Squanderfields, Lovelaces, Bellarmines and Bucks. It was this same underworld of irrational feelings, of fear yet fascination with the powerful alien culture, which a French visitor tried to address in more rational terms when in 1747 he sought words to express a prevailing English attitude toward France: "By their continual uneasiness, they seem to believe that we are in regard to them what the Persians were to the Athenians. . . . They fear and yet despise us: we are the nation that they pay the greatest civilities to, and yet love the least: they condemn, and yet imitate us: they adopt our manners by taste, and blame them through policy."[26] France was the 'Great Satan' of the eighteenth century, supposedly too much admired, imitated, and secretly aided by domestic leaders everywhere. Inevitably she became the scapegoat of every nationalist movement nearby.

If, as Atherton believes, the satiric prints of the mid-eighteenth century should be looked upon as "documents of cultural and intellectual history," expressing "basic assumptions and beliefs, so fundamental that they are rarely talked about or explained,"[27] then it becomes increasingly clear that the nationalist philosophy which we have attempted to trace, with its roots in the idea of pro-French aristocratic treason, was by this period approaching the status of something more than a protest, more even than a philosophy. Was it not an ideology? What, after all, is an ideology but a large and interconnected body of doctrines and myths, partly inhabiting the underworld of emotions and pre-conscious suppositions, operating intellectually more as a set of enthymemes than as explicit propositions in argument, broadly uniting some class or group (often against another), and giving direction to collective action? By the later fifties, a decade which saw the establishment of Britannia as a folkish symbol representing the oppressed and virtuous nation, one must judge that the intellectual materials of the nationalist movement were achieving the sort of fluid interconnectedness implied in the idea of ideology, while its broad social orientation, morally attacking the vicious, defiling and exploitative Man of

Quality in the name of the entire Third Estate symbolically represented, seems obvious enough by any fair measurement.

6. JOHN BROWN, SCOURGE OF NATIONAL DEGENERACY

This helps to explain why the protest was also beginning to achieve extended formal expression in works of moral and social philosophy—a fourth source of nationalist propaganda, along with prints, novels, and plays (we will consider others later). The ideology was raising up true ideologues. The great early philosophical manifesto of the movement was John Brown's *Estimate of the Manners and Principles of the Times* (1757–58), written during the early years of the Seven Years' War. This work was bolder in statement than, say, Foote's plays, which preceded it by a year or two, and it traveled much more explicitly into realms of political criticism and historical philosophy, drawing out more clearly the implications there of the central argument. Yet on the whole it was really little more than an elaborate systematization of the ideas we have already studied. The central argument, identical to that discussed earlier, was that England, thanks to its unprincipled and morally polluted ruling class, lived under a multifarious Gallic reign, and was surely destined to perish unless by some extraordinary miracle there arose a great national and moral revival, a recovery of true English identity and assertion of true English principles.

i. national strength a reflection of rulers

Rather like Smollett's 'Stentor Stile' in Paris, Brown stalks about, vainly searching for beef. It is amusing to watch him loading his flintlock at the beginning. He presents his treatise as an inquiry into the question, "How far the present ruling Manners and Principles of this Nation may tend to its Continuance or Destruction." For this reason he deliberately limits himself, he says, to an investigation of the manners and principles of "the higher Ranks in Life"; for the strength of a nation is determined by "the Manners and Principles of those who *lead,* not of those who *are led;* of those who *govern,* not of those who *are governed.*"[28]

The fact that Brown unhesitatingly identifies the strength of the nation with the qualities of the ruling class is a noteworthy reminder of how rapidly attitudes were to evolve during the '60s, the decade following. He thinks this relationship so obvious that he sets up his three basic categories of analysis on it, maintaining that national strength depends on "the *Capacity, Valour,* and *Union,* of those who *lead* the *People.* The first may be called, '*the national Capacity;* the second *the national Spirit of Defence;* the third *the national Spirit of Union.*'" With this essentially traditional and, as it were, pre-nationalist conceptual apparatus in place, and with himself (one must smile at this) pretending to assume the role of impartial inquirer into the strength and destiny of his country, Brown proceeds to "rise, or rather *descend,* to an impartial View of those who are called the *better Sort*": he proceeds, that is, to build up an absolutely withering attack upon the manners, education, habits, tastes, ideas, practices, and influence of England's ruling class, demonstrating thereby, through what he condemns as its incompetence, cowardice, and avaricious lack of principle, the nearly complete wreck of the National Capacity, Valour, and Union. "BLUSH, *if ye can,* my degenerate Contemporaries!"[29]

ii. moral disease and cultural disintegration

Brown's book is a sweeping review of the nation's institutions and of the whole trend of contemporary history, written in a style which somehow combines the apocalyptic talents of a Jeremiah with the caustic reflectiveness of a Tacitus surveying the disintegration of Rome. The work moves easily towards its conclusion, this being hidden in its premises. The argument from beginning to end, as Brown complacently acknowledges, rests on "the ruling principle of *Effeminacy,* which runs through this work," a principle which—he returns to it over and over—he takes to be realized and objectified in all he critically surveys. The grand root of the nation's ills is "the luxurious and effeminate Manners in the higher Ranks, together with a general Defect of *Principle.*" "How far this dastard Spirit of Effeminacy hath crept upon us" is something he thinks self-evident in the mini-analyses that roll from his pen, analyses of Dress ("the first and capital Article of Town-Effeminacy"), Travel (no Circumstance in Education can more surely tend to strengthen Effeminacy"), Entertainments ("modern Entertainments generally consist of such *exotic Articles,* as no *Englishman* of *middle* Rank ever heard of"), Taste (which "hath now generally supplanted *religious Principle*"—the Man of Fashion "derides and affronts" the Sabbath "as a vulgar and obsolete Institution"), Gaming, the Dissipation of Modern Assemblies, Midnight Riots, Sleep, Ignorance, Irreligion, Avarice, Rapacity, Borough-jobbing, Party Pamphlets, Fear, Cowardice, and Several Thousand Other Menaces and Bugbears, by no means excluding the great Threat from Abroad, for England's weakness has "fitted us for a Prey to the Insults and Invasions of our most powerful Enemy."[30]

The same creeping system of moral rot, "the present prevailing System of Town-Effeminacy," stands at the heart of Brown's analysis of contemporary social change (deterioration). This was to become one of the favorite hobbyhorses of social analysis for the next generation: Fashionable Dissipation is seen as the cause of increasingly prolonged residence in London, the purchase of town houses, the draining of rural wealth and labor into the city, the transmogrification of honest plowboys and milkmaids into dandified servants, the deterioration of ancient hospitality, the exploitation of the rural poor, the desertion of the village, abandonment of rustic virtues, and so on. And it is interesting to note that Brown, as though anticipating the increasingly primitivist writings of the sixties and seventies, has already begun to invert the measures of value in his comments on the rural as opposed to the sophisticated life: "It was a shrewd Observation of a good old Writer, 'How can he get Wisdom,

whose Talk is of Bullocks?' But *Rusticity* is not more an Enemy of Knowledge, than Effeminacy: With the same Propriety therefore it may now be
asked, 'How can he get Wisdom, whose Talk is of *Dress* and *Wagers, Cards*
and *Borough-jobbing, Horses, Women,* and *Dice?*'"[31]

Over and over Brown asserts that Effeminacy is the "ruling Character"
of the Great, and traces out its deplorable effects. Sooner or later, he
warns, "the Influence of the *leading People*" will form the "*leading Character*" of the nation at large. This effeminacy, he concedes, was not entirely
the result of French influence. It was, in part, an historical result of economic progress in its "third or highest period," following naturally upon
the growth of trade and wealth, and the consequent pursuit of pleasure.
It manifested itself in excessive attention to dress and the like, and of
course was brought wholesale into the country through the pleasure-seek-
ing travels of "our rising Youth," "our young *Men of Quality.*" Brown is
rigidly opposed to early foreign education and travel, going so far as to
insist, in classic nationalist fashion, that "there is not, perhaps, a more
important political principle than this, That the ruling Habits of young
Men" should be "severely and unalterably formed" to the Laws, Customs,
"the *Genius,* of their own *Country*"; and adding somewhat contradictorily
(for he often comes close to denying that England has any special character or genius left) that "the Genius of *our* Country, above all others, is
particularly distinguished from that of its Neighbour Nations" (meaning
France), he lays it down that Parliament should stop the practice of early
traveling. This would greatly help, he says, in "restoring Manners and
Principles."[32] (Note that he sees improvement as a *restoration.*) Like his
evangelical successors some forty years later, Brown would thus have re-
joiced at the nearly complete quarantine of French influence that was to
run from about 1790 to 1850.

iii. the French poison

We come then to the *fons et origo* of the modern Effeminacy. This
effeminacy, according to Brown, was part of a gigantic French plot, consciously or unconsciously abetted by England's ruling class. His belief in
this apparent conspiracy, like so much else in his *Estimate*, is symptomatic
of the 'agitated and agitating' nationalist mentality. He elaborates his view
most fully in the course of a comparative analysis of French and English
national strength—another identifying characteristic, as we have seen, of
early nationalist thought in general, and in the English case nothing short
of an obsession which was to permeate the philosophical and historical
literature, the 'Estimates,' 'Hints,' 'Thoughts,' and 'Comparative Views' of
the entire reign of George III, indeed the entire period down to Bulwer-
Lytton's *England and the English* (1833). Brown's ostensible purpose is to
answer what he anticipates to be the chief objection to his entire exposition, namely that if effeminate manners have ruined England, then have
they not ruined England's rival as well? Far from it, he replies. Applying
his analytic concepts to France, he contends that even though French

manners are "as *vain* and *effeminate* as our own, and the very Archetype from which ours are drawn," France herself has not suffered any of the dreadful consequences of this. Unlike England she is protected, he says, by the existence of *"Principle"* in both her upper and lower classes. France has escaped the debilitation of her Capacity by virtue of her excellent schools, which unlike the English schools truly instill *"Knowledge and Ability"*; of her Defence by the superior strength in the French "national Character" of "the Principle of military *Honour"*; of her Union by the superior *"Power of their Monarch,"* which gives *"Unity* and *Steddiness"* to French policy. England is weak in her effeminacy, France is strong despite hers. There is something superhuman about the French national character: "They have found, or rather invented, the Art of uniting all Extremes . . . seemingly incompatible. They are effeminate, yet brave: insincere, yet honourable: hospitable, not benevolent: vain, yet subtile . . . mercantile, yet not mean: In Trifles serious, gay in Enterprize: Women at the Toilet, Heroes in the Field: profligate in Heart; in Conduct, decent . . . *Contemptible* in *private* Life; in *public, Formidable."*[33]

From all this Brown proceeds to summon up what one might call (were there not the inevitable grain of truth in it) a totally nightmarish vision of France as a cultural and political monster, a 'Great Satan,' a steadily growing colossus employing her insidious cultural influence to numb and neutralize her rivals, herself possessing the antidote to the fatal moral poison she cunningly injects into England and her other neighbors. Brown writes that the French have now nearly completed

> their vast Plan of Power (formed by the great *Colbert* almost a Century ago) carried on . . . thro' a Variety of Reigns, Wars and Administrations. . . . Thus, in Contradiction to all known Example, *France* hath become powerful, while she seemed to lead the way in Effeminacy: and while she hath allured her neighbour Nations, by her own Example, to drink largely of her *circaean* and *poisoned Cup* of Manners, hath secured her own *Health* by the *secret Antidote* of *Principle."*[34]

It thus becomes fully apparent at last that effeminacy and dissipation are no weaknesses at all for the French, but rather magical potions of global influence and power. With this revelation Brown puts the garnish to his own mystical broth. As if the domestic effects of Effeminacy, this French-inspired *"national Debility,"* were not catastrophic enough, he reminds his readers of the even greater danger to be apprehended from France as the *"outward Enemy":*

> The French, in Land Armies, are far our Superiors: They are making large and dreadful Strides towards us, in *naval Power.* They have more *than disputed* with us the Empire of the Mediterranean. They are driving us from our Forts and Colonies in *America.* . . . Thus by a gradual and unperceived Decline, we seem gliding down to Ruin. We laugh, we sing, we feast, we play: We *adopt* every *Vanity,* and catch at every *Lure,* thrown out to us by the *Nation* that is planning our *Destruction* . . . in our *Fondness* for *French* Manners, [we] resemble the *Lamb* described by the *Poet* [which] *licks* the *Hand* that's *raised* to *shed his Blood.*[35]

iv. moral revolution for a despairing nation

Was there any remedy for this dreadful condition of weakness and disintegration? Things looked very black. Palliatives might be sought in some sort of moral coercion (an anticipation here of the vice societies established under George III). But Brown despaired because the offending class was the very class that held power: "The ruling Mischief desolates the Great. . . . A coercive Power is wanting: They who should cure the Evil are the very Delinquents: And moral or political Physic is what no distempered Mind will ever administer to itself."[36]

The only other remedy, "radical, general, and lasting," would be a comprehensive reformation, a complete and drastic "Change of Manners and Principles." But in the 1750s little hope lay in that direction either: "This may justly be regarded as an impossible Event, during the present Age; and rather to be wished than hoped for, in the next." Only *"Necessity"* in the form of some unparalleled national disaster, perhaps also of unexampled public tumult and outrage—or perhaps a combination of the two—could bring about such a monumental departure, such a tremendous reformation. "Our Deliverance," the salvation of this "despairing Nation," had to wait upon events; for as Brown darkly prophesied, "the Idea of a Public has no Place" in the minds of the Great, "nor can such Minds be ever awakened from their fatal Dream, till either the Voice of an abused People rouse them into Fear; or the State itself totter, thro' the general Incapacity, Cowardice, and Disunion of those who should support it." Then perhaps—a rather forlorn hope—"SOME GREAT MINISTER" might arise to help put all things right.[37]

THE YOUNG POLITICIAN

7. *1771. Charles Fox, made to personify young men of pleasure with political ambitions, admires himself in a glass held by his valet, at the same time tearing up Magna Carta for curl-papers for his French hairdressers.*

8. *1762. "The Hungry Mob of Scriblers and Etchers." A noble patron (Bute) tosses coins towards a crowd of ragged writers and artists. These have been identified as, from right, Johnson (clutching his £300 pension), Smollett, Churchill (in clerical habit), the printmaker Darly, and Hogarth (with the large engraving tool).*

The Literary Revolution, 1740–89

You poets, I suppose, have an exclusive right to explain one another.
—HURD

Nothing is little to him that feels it with great sensibility.
—JOHNSON

NATIONALISM IS, at the outset, a creation of writers. Thus the study of it in England must look to the practitioners of English literary history and criticism, experts in the great tradition of 'Eng. Lit.,' for help in understanding the true relationships between authors, texts, audiences, and national opinion. It is not enough merely to integrate such work with the efforts of the historians. In fact such work should guide the historians, for nationalism, as we have seen, is first and foremost an *ideology*.

Unfortunately, however, Eng. Lit. in its present state is not ready to assume this leading role. We must first formulate a wider view of the literature of the eighteenth century, one that is more plausible historically. The literary commentators themselves recognize this. In the literary groves of Academe as in the historiographical there have always been plenty of sacred applecarts, but the literary analysts—as a group more frolicsome than others—have always had a high tolerance for kicking them over. Much useful work, nearly all destructive, has already been done.

1. POTS OF MEANING

The literary history of England from roughly 1740 to 1789 has always posed great problems of structural definition. This has never been considered a period of exceptional achievement. Though the novel began its rise to prominence during this period, the non-fictional literature has often been seen as pedestrian, while poetry, still at that time the *genius loci* of literary creation, was too often merely imitative of Pope, Spenser, and Milton. The whole literary period has thus often been neglected as a sort of transitional lotus-land of strange impulses and weird experimentations between the sharply defined intellectual culture of the first third of the century, the so-called Augustan or Neoclassical Age, and the remarkable outpourings of so-called Romantic literature with which the century ended in the 1790s. This neglect was also furthered by the general absence in mid-century of any 'great events' by which the characteristics of literature might be indexed and explained; and so while the ordered forms of Augustan literature were often traced to the quest for stability after the tumults of 1685–1715, and the iconoclastic and visionary forms of Romantic literature to the impact of the French Revolution on the English mind, the literature stretching between these two turbulent periods has typically been seen as lacking connectedness with the facts of the real world.

Perhaps it was inevitable then that an excessively metaphysical web of interpretation would settle on this supposedly dull literature, with the sources of intellectual change being sought almost exclusively within the domain of artistic thought, 'aesthetic sensibility,' itself. The tendency was to view the literary age as one of dying Neoclassicism or 'Augustanism,' considered as a decaying system of aesthetic rules, and of sprouting Romanticism, considered as the birth of a very different system of aesthetics, with a dream of Creative Imagination postulated as the motive force bringing about the emergence of the one from the other. Under these formulae the literature of mid-century was thus interpreted by reference to two aesthetic-philosophic complexes which lay chronologically outside it; or, allied to this, as an evolving 'pre-romanticism' whose unconscious destiny was to produce the glories of Wordsworth and Coleridge, Blake and Burns; or, finally, in more sophisticated versions of these same very mechanical formulations, as what was vaguely called the 'Spread of Sensibility,' the 'Growth of Feeling,' the 'Rise of Primitivism,' and so on, as traced through methodologies which focused upon what one earlier author unabashedly called "the life-history of an idea as it passes through a succession of human minds."[1]

At last, inevitably, came the attack. The opening shot of interpretative revisionism was an essay by Frye (1956) in which he rejected the standard 'transitional' interpretations which treated this as "a period of reaction against Pope and anticipation of Wordsworth," and denounced as still more unacceptable the 'pre-romantic' conception for "committing us to anachronism before we start, and imposing a false teleology on everything we study." Here was good sense. Frye's revisionist message began to circulate freely, and a line began to form in the appleyard. There was a delicious thrill as everyone took a kick at the old classic-to-romantic formulation. Greene, in his influential handbook, attacked it as "childish" and "preposterous," at the same time warning that "its essential elements still hold a powerful sway." By the 1980s this same line of denunciation had become almost a purgative ritual introducing any new attempt to analyze the literature of that period. Hence Cohen began a stimulating survey of that literature by charging literary scholarship with mistaking its own concepts for historic literary reality, and then went on—quite agreeably to the theory pursued here—to assert that there occurred some sort of pervasive "intellectual reorientation at mid-century" which involved "a complex network of related assumptions rather than a set of stable [aesthetic] assertions." Gelley launched similar accusations and proceeded to argue that eighteenth-century fictional characters should be interpreted not only as artifacts of literary consciousness but in relation to the historically conditioned consciousness of the readers of those novels. Siskin sang the same refrain, attacking what he called the still prevailing tendency to resolve literary history into "a history of ideas isolated from socioeconomic and political contexts," and going on to declare that because all literature figures in one way or another as social commentary, the postulation of some central "connection between literary change and social change" is of vital importance to any further understanding of the literary products of this period. The same attitude is characteristic of such recent studies as Barrell's excellent investigation of the way in which 'correct' English usage upheld elite authority, and Kenny's exposition of the political and social symbolism of 'country-house' literature. Rogers's voluminous writings delve even more deeply into the relations between high literature and everyday life.[2]

To the historian, this all seems like a very good idea. Readers interested in 'intellectual history' will see that the practitioners of Eng. Lit. have undergone during the past thirty years a conceptual revolution resembling that which has taken place rather more fully in several continental European countries, particularly France.[3] In essence what has happened is that the rise since the 1950s of cultural history—of social history, the histories of popular culture, myth, *mentalités*, and so on—has resulted in an almost total reformulation of the history of ideas. Discredited are the classic methodologies so dear to earlier literary historians, which traced through a few 'great' texts the histories of single ideas (and systems of ideas) as seen in detachment ('disincarnation') from the objective social, psychological, economic and political conditions which surrounded them and conditioned their acceptance. Ideas are no longer seen as the products of a few savants, handed down through processes of 'influence' and 'borrowing,' or maturing through metaphysical dynamics suspended over the plane of history. Instead they are regarded from many different angles as instruments of society—as reflections of general consciousness, 'unthought' as well as articulated commentaries upon reality, linkages between groups, and, in the hands of groups of intellectuals, as themselves motors of social reality, transformers of the social order through the images and classifications which they impose upon it, these images working by popular circulation to alter the collective consciousness, modify individual demands and self-definitions, shift the frontiers between groups, and even give birth to new classes. This new and much more sophisticated emphasis on the *relationship* between literature and society has thus in a sense even turned the old intellectual history upside down by focusing attention not upon the products of individual genius but rather upon the unconscious collective assumptions which regulated these and prescribed the boundaries of the thinkable—that is, the subterranean categories of assumption, the shared 'mental tools' and 'ways of thinking and feeling' that are common to a given people in a given historical milieu, conditioned by a given cultural heritage and by specific socioeconomic and political realities.

Yet it is just here, with today's new literary investigators bursting the bonds of the old critical tradition and groping their way into social history, that we reach a serious difficulty. It is just at this point that the historians let their literary colleagues down by carrying on too casually with one of their own tribal exercises, the incessant polishing of that almost totally imaginary surface of English 'Placidity' and 'Moderation' upon which these others are trying to find a handhold. If the reader thinks this unfair, then let him open any historical survey of this period, old or new, and scrutinize the mere words and twaddle which in even our best histories may be found padding and subtly protecting the dollhouse of Stability, Mobility, and English Differentness which, it is imagined, must have been responsible for that supposedly 'conservative' English response to the French Revolution—an archetype of thought which unconsciously guides historical interpretation as surely as the teleologic 'Romanticism' used to guide literary.

What the literary investigators really need is a coherent, detailed, and drastically revisionist account of English social history in the eighteenth century, an account giving full emphasis to the social conflict that increasingly divided the country. But here is an irony. For the social historian attempting to write such a history will receive very little deliberate help from existing histories of literature. The historians have let down the critics, but the critics pay them back in full. The literary analysts must turn to the historians' concepts when working out their literary subjects, but historical researchers depend on the analysts to give them much of the biographical, intellectual, and social flavor of the times. And what do they find in these accounts? Not always, but rather too often, they find the same blends of informative factual presentation, intelligent local analysis, hair-splitting thesis-making, and numbingly conformist general interpretation which too often mark their own works. The historians seldom examine their own precepts, but Eng. Lit. is terrified of contradicting them. And that is just the trouble: Literature is afraid to lead History anywhere. Take that social resentment that we noticed among the writers of this period. How have the literary historians dealt with it? We find them encountering it, even pointing it out, then sensing themselves trespassing into the historians' sacred cow pasture of Placidity and Mobility, and at last before our very eyes denying the plain meaning of the texts they have just quoted! Thus one of the analysts mentioned earlier, in a handbook which has done much to shape the views of today's English teachers and students, may be glimpsed performing surprising feats of intellectual acrobatics as he passes from the anti-aristocratic texts of his writers to the hoary Placidity of his society, a society he has been led to believe was nearly as "homogenous," "mobile," and free of "class snobbery" as the United States in the twentieth century![4]

But the real villain of the piece is neither literary analysis nor social history but the failure of critical discourse between them. It is a failure of nerve, not intellect. The dreadful old metaphysicization of literary studies has scared fact-loving historians away from literature—a circumstance reflected in the deplorable tendency to relegate all ideas but political ones to some subchapter toward the end of a history book—while, on the other hand, the wizards of Lit.-Crit., afraid of getting supposedly obvious things wrong, are wary of trespassing into history. And meanwhile our knowledge of the eighteenth century grows more manifold than ever before, with new monographs on it appearing every day. Our knowledge is like a burgeoning house plant, fertilized and watered from every direction. Today many would agree, historians and critics alike, that it is time we searched together for a bigger and more mutually suitable pot.

2. THE WRITER AND HIS AUDIENCE

So how should we, from the present angle, regard the literature of the period 1740–89? The answer is that much of it should be regarded as the material outpouring of the nationalist movement itself. It should be regarded not only as a manifold instrument of protest but as an evolving body of texts, 'a literature' in the sense of a progression of coded and internally related messages, a new hieratic tradition indeed, which was vitally important in breaking down old resistances, implanting subversive suggestions, arousing new sensitivities, creating new dissatisfactions where before there were none, stimulating revolutionary new notions of the national heritage and hence of shared individual rights, and, in sum, outlining a radical new philosophy and exciting people to embrace it.

Let us begin by considering the personal discontentedness and alienation of the bourgeois artist-intellectual, the primary agent of the nationalist movement. The analysts of nationalism lay much stress on his inner sensibilities, his subordinate place in the social structure, and beyond that the social and psychological discontents of his audience, considered as a wider class seeking liberation. Shafer is typical in writing that "indignation at social injustice, and resentment arising from a feeling of personal inferiority," often play "a vital role" in the psychic genesis of nationalistic feelings. Now as to the general malaise of England's intellectuals in the middle and later years of the eighteenth century, there can be no doubting it. Though never explained satisfactorily, the 'ambivalence' and 'anxiety' of the poets of this period is notorious. Frye notes that "the list of poets over whom the shadows of mental breakdown fall is far too long to be coincidence." Sitter defines this as a period of "literary loneliness." There are indeed many signs of unhappiness and inner turmoil. Poor John Brown entertained no hope whatsoever of living to see the moral and national revival of which he dreamed; he committed suicide in 1766. This was just two years after Hogarth, his spiritual ally, also died in depression and Weltschmerz. The painter prophetically left behind as his last work a representation of 'The World's End' with Time itself dying and civilization falling to pieces all around (*Finis, or The Bathos*, 1764). For these and other artist-intellectuals the period was one of deepening frustration and despair, a 'Machiavellian moment,' as Pocock defines it, "a crisis in the relations between personality and society, virtue and corruption," in which all the finer old traditions and values of English society seemed even more pervasively menaced than before by the spread of 'the modern morality,' a systemic and supposedly terminal disease.[5]

Cultural despair was certainly instrumental here. In the fifties, as we saw, there was a fear of cultural disintegration, a tendency to look upon the country as already so far subject to a 'Gallic reign' that its culture resembled 'a bundle of contradictions, a piece of patch-work, a mere harlequin's coat.' In the sixties, despite the brief exultation that marked the victories of the Seven Years' War, the fear of French influence continued to grow. Atherton diagnoses the presence of "a paranoid fascination with the secretive powers of French influence." Yet was there anything in English social life to relieve this paranoia? Certainly not in the behavior of high society, in which, for example, all the evils of the age seemed personified in the character and teachings of a Lord Chesterfield, "arbiter of taste," notes his biographer, "notoriously identified with the French spirit in thought and behavior," whose posthumously published *Letters to His Son* (1774) provoked such a tempestuous but ambivalent response, with one portion of the public snapping up five editions within the year, and another, a smaller one composed largely of writers like Johnson and Cowper, unloosing blasts of indignation against these (French) "morals of a whore and manners of a dancing master," taught by this (frenchified) "polish'd and high-finish'd foe to truth,/Greybeard corrupter of our listening youth." The same paranoia was scarcely eased by the rise of the Macaronis—a race of a "neuter gender" in the eyes of their journalistic critics, portrayed amid monkeys by graphic satirists—who in the seventies seemed to personify all the worst, the most un-English aspects of Chesterfield's influence. The same cultural frustrations were fed by the spectacle of all those scores of rich young 'bucks' and 'bloods' effortlessly gliding to their 'predestinated' places in government, the services, the colonies, and the Church; and, as it must have seemed to outsiders, contemptuously mincing their way through Grosvenor Square at half-past two in the afternoon in their dressing gowns and slippers. Such men seemed only too well typified in the figure of Charles James Fox, a man of unusual polish, wit, and bilingual eloquence, the model of fashion in his Gallic clothes and feathered hat, the famous darling of the *Ton* throughout his lifetime: this notoriously frenchified young rake, the epitome of dissipated aristocratic youth, son of one of the most infamously venal men of the age, foe of 'Wilkes and Liberty,' champion of the ministerial slave Luttrell, and, not least, like his cousins of the Richmond and Grafton tribes a blooded descendant of the Stuarts (not for nothing was he Charles James) and of the Bourbon dynasty of France.[6]

Thus cultural anxiety shaded easily into social resentment as the artist-intellectual contemplated the lawgivers of London society. Can it be thought surprising that while "Francophil Englishmen . . . were perhaps more numerous in the 'eighties than in previous decades," there was also a "howl of execration" over "the mere mention of France" which "became stronger as the century advanced"?[7] The country, increasingly sensitized by its intellectuals to cultural contrasts between rulers and ruled, was undergoing an identity crisis—a prelude to basic change.

But the writers had other discontents besides cultural and social ones. They had more intimately personal grievances which also served to drive their pens in much the same anti-aristocratic line. Consider how they made their livings. Voltaire in the 1730s remarked that "men's thoughts have become an important article of commerce. The Dutch publishers make a million a year, because Frenchmen have brains." The balances of literary commerce were shifting in England too. Literary historians, tracing the growth of the reading public by means of many measuring devices, agree that at some point between the 1740s and 1780s the economic balance of literary production shifted, with booksellers and a much-enlarged reading public gradually taking up the responsibility of literary patronage which formerly had belonged to noble patrons either singly or through subscriptions.[8] The leveling effects of this change upon standards of taste have often been discussed. But what is equally clear is the psychological fact that until this larger transition was complete, the position of the artist vis-à-vis the aristocratic patron was ambiguous and unenviable, more indefinite than it had ever been before and hence more anxiety-producing—a source of great frustration and often of ill-concealed animosity.

To an intellectual priding himself particularly on independence of thought, the servility in this relationship was apt to be galling. Psychologically the choice was to humble oneself, adopt the position of an inferior, and, with it, receive the favor of the patron, or else despise this and attempt to survive in independence. The tremendous resentment born of this awkward relationship can be seen in the famous case of Johnson's rejection of Chesterfield's too lukewarm favor in the production of his English dictionary—an act of *"defensive* pride," as he characterized this to a friend;[9] that is, of *wounded* pride, as Shafer and the other experts on nationalism might see it. No longer, said Johnson in the famous letter to Chesterfield (1755), would he aspire to boast himself—he put it in language intended to impress—*"le vainqueur du vainqueur de la terre";* he would be independent. But the difficulty of surviving independently can be seen too in Johnson's subsequent acceptance of a royal pension. Hypocrisy caught up with him after all.

The same resentment, stemming from similar causes, ate away at the dignity and inner happiness of Fielding, Smollett, Foote, and Goldsmith. And just as Johnson turned his experience with Chesterfield into sundry condemnations of the obsequiousness expected by patrons, they too transformed their personal experiences, their 'provocations and social humiliations' at the hands of the Great, into subtle literary propaganda. Foote's early prefaces bristle with animosity towards patrons; one of his more biting plays, *The Patron* (1764), actually originated as a piece of revenge on Bubb Dodington, Lord Melcombe, who had humiliated him several years before. Yet aristocratic influence was difficult to resist, and in 1766 Foote's leg had to be amputated because of a nasty joke played upon him one day by the Duke of York and other men of fashion who had baited him to match their horsemanship. (No one could resist punning on the unhappy depeditated writer: "A Foot too little now you are;/Before a Foote too much.") Or again in *The Vicar of Wakefield*, in George Primrose's account of his brief and humiliating experience with his London patron as "half friend, half underling," Goldsmith's page fairly crackles with disgust at the necessity of an author's learning the arts of "pimping and pedigree." The whole novel is written in a spirit condemning "tip-top quality breeding" and the dependence of virtuous and simple people upon the corrupting influence of the great. Yet this was still a common experience for men of Goldsmith's profession, and a doubly provoking one inasmuch as it meant that personal success often depended not only on adoption of false feelings and the self-interested cultivation of the fashionable, but on the neglect of merit as a value in its own right. "In state of letters, Merit should be heard," wrote Churchill; "Let Favour speak for others, Worth for me."[10]

Here, it is important to note, was a fundamental bond, a strong point of psychic and social unity, between the writer and his ever-expanding popular audience. Early spokesmen of the nationalist movement, Hogarth for example, may in some ways be looked upon as lonely voices in the wilderness, often not terribly clear about their goals, and not always enjoying solid popular following. As time passed, however, and as the program of national renewal acquired larger scope and definition, these spokesmen came to voice ever more broadly the frustrations of the middle classes. This is nowhere more evident than in their dissatisfaction with patronage, a key issue of the later eighteenth century. The issue of artistic patronage involved and was really nothing but a special instance of the much larger and historically more significant issue of 'merit' versus inherited 'privilege'—or, as contemporaries sometimes put it, 'Fashion,' by which in this context they meant advantageous social connections. These associations in thought can be traced in many works—in successive statements, for instance, in Smollett's *Fathom*. In this work, Smollett, whose own professional fortunes were embittered by many difficulties with patrons, first angrily attacks those "consummate connoisseurs" (aesthetic cosmopolites) who, "when a British satirist, of this generation, has courage enough to call in question the talents of a Pseudo-patron, in power, accuse him of insolence, rancour and scurrility"; he then abruptly turns to general thoughts, sarcastically phrased, on "a land of freedom like this, where individuals are every day ennobled in consequence of their qualifications, without the least retrospective regard to the rank or merit of their ancestors." The discontented artist, his own abilities in question, turns to gaze contemptuously on the claims of his high-born judges. And in the process he teaches a lesson in antithetically opposed values to his readers, linking together on his own side the values of courage, truth, merit, and that which is British, presenting these as besieged by inherited privilege and power, aesthetic and other incompetence, internationalism in taste, and vaguely anti-British actions. Fielding, snubbed by the Ton, in *Amelia* dealt with the same problem in similar terms: "Are we resolved never to encourage merit; but to throw away all our preferments on those who do not deserve them? What a set of contemptible wretches do we see strutting about the town in scarlet!"[11] The associations subtly affirmed here between privilege, incompetence, arrogance, and un-English taste, and the opposition between these and merit, are plain enough. To contemporary readers they came as little whisperings in a rising wind of subversive education.

3. JOINED IN NOBLE RAGE

The writers were shaping a generic sort of resentment, felt well beyond Grub Street and Fleet Street. Middle-class businessmen, clergymen, educators, professionals, soldiers, all felt it rising in their daily lives. The troubled dependence of writers on patrons with fickle loyalties and excessive demands was but a microcosm of the dependent relations in general between middle-class producers and the Quality whose favor and 'custom' they were still obliged to seek in this era preceding the opening-up of internal transport and the organization of nationwide domestic markets. Josiah Wedgwood, who at just about this time was attempting to rescue English pottery-making from the flood of French and Belgian imports, was obliged to waste many precious hours "looking over the English Peerage to find out *lines, channels and connections*," for there were very few persons, he complained, who would dare purchase his goods without higher recommendation; few who would "dare venture at anything out of the common stile till authoris'd by their betters—by the ladies of superior spirit who set the tone." That Wedgwood, the very pattern of the new self-made industrialist, not only appreciated the difference between 'fashion' and 'merit' but detested the dominion of the former is apparent in his correspondence with his business associate, Bentley. Philosophizing ironically on the art of salesmanship, he wrote: "Fashion is infinitely superior to merit in many respects; and it is plain from a 1,000 instances that if you have a favourite child you wish the public to fondle and take notice of, you have only to make choice of proper sponsors. If you are lucky in them no matter what the brat is, black, brown or fair, its fortune is made!" Similar sentiments were shared by Wedgwood's friend and protégé Joseph Priestley, and by another friend, James Watt, the pioneer of English engineering. Throughout his life the latter was afflicted with "sensitiveness on questions of class-feeling and priority"; and, symptomatically also, he was very suspicious of the too friendly relations between the native aristocracy and his French competitors. Writing to a friend about these suspicions, he sternly commented: "Rich men may do mean actions. May you and I always persevere in our integrity, and despise such doings."[12]

All of this helps to explain why the fashion madness so enraged the intellectuals. "Rarely, if ever," says McKendrick, had social imitation "been so frequently mocked." In fact the double-edged meaning of the word 'Fashion' reveals the tension gradually developing in the age of George III. To the rich and the thoughtless many it was a justification, but to the sensitive few it was becoming an oath. "Fashion," spat Churchill, "—a word which knaves and fools may use/Their knavery and folly to excuse." And of course if Fashion so often overrode Merit in art and business, then it was still more notorious that it controlled the whole domain of political and administrative appointments as well, where (as Churchill wrote) "Those, who would gain the votes of British tribes,/Must add to force of Merit, force of Bribes"; where "those of Quality and Fortune," as Brown complained, were able to exploit their influence "as a kind of *Family-Fund,* for the provision of the younger Branches. . . . Thus in a Time when Science, Capacity, Honour, Religion, Public Spirit, are rare; the remaining *Few* who possess these Virtues, will often be shut out from these Stations which they would fill with Honour; while every public and important Employ will abound with Men, whose *Manners* and *Principles* are of the *newest Fashion.*" Fashion, a cloak for favoritism, sustained the supremacy of the rich in an age when Merit crowded up from below. Beneath the whole issue was the contrast (in the words of John Cartwright) between "merit" and all "*artificial* . . . distinctions amongst men." The issue was becoming a very sore one in political feeling, both with would-be independent politicians like the elder Pitt—"I sought for merit wherever it was to be found"—and with others equally talented but without Pitt's family advantages, such as Edmund Burke.[13]

Burke's case is symptomatic. Here again, as with Fielding, it is well to keep in mind that posterity's darling was in fact a rather small fish to many of his contemporaries. And this helps to explain why Burke was capable of extremely contradictory attitudes towards the Great. Standing in the House of Commons in 1769, he unashamedly trumpeted his adulation of his aristocratic patrons:

> I am connected; I glory in such connection. I ever shall do so. . . .When I find good men, I will cling to them, adhere to them, follow them in and out, wash the very feet they stand on. I will wash their feet and be subservient, not from interest, but from principle; it shall be my glory.[14]

This was the attitude he exhibited much of his life in service to the Whig grandees, and it is small wonder that Jeremy Bentham despised him as "reduced to that species and degree of servitude, with which sincerity is incompatible." But Burke had another side which he kept discreetly hidden until, like acid, it poured out through the walls of inhibition and self-interest:

> But as to public service, why truly it would not be more ridiculous for me to compare myself in rank, in fortune, in splendid descent, in youth, strength, or figure, with the Duke of Bedford, than to make a parallel between his services, and my attempts to be useful to my country. It would not be gross adulation, but uncivil irony, to say that he has any public merit of his own to keep alive the idea of the services by which his vast landed pensions were obtained. My merits, whatever they are, are original and personal; his are derivative. It is his ancestor, the original pensioner, that has laid up this inexhaustible fund of merit, which makes his grace so very delicate and exceptious about the merit of all other grantees of the crown. . . . Why will his Grace . . . force me reluctantly to compare my little merit with that which obtained from the Crown those prodigies of profuse donation by which he tramples on the mediocrity of humble and laborious individuals?[15]

Burke thus provides a striking example of the mentality encouraged by the tensions we have examined. The point is neatly summed up in the title of Kramnick's thoughtful study of *The Rage of Edmund Burke*. Kramnick shows that Burke's inner life was a volatile mixture blended from pride over his own ascent from insignificance, and rage against the obsequious servility imposed upon him by dependence upon the great. The historian so far peels away the cherished 'conservative' legends attached to Burke as to present him as "the prototypical rebellious son for his age. . . . His ambivalence, his hatred and love for the aristocracy, was the ambivalence of the revolutionary bourgeoisie." Tracing this neurotic ambivalence to "the profound tension between a sense of self ascribed by birth, tradition, and custom and [an opposing] sense of self as achieved by work and talent," Kramnick takes the issue into the large realm of historical generalization where it certainly belongs. Burke's neurotic ambivalence, he writes, "persisted throughout his life . . . and matched most perfectly the historical identity crisis then being experienced by the advanced societies of England and France."[16]

It would be very foolish to dismiss this as wild generalization. Consider Pitt the Elder as another example. Historians, often uncomfortable with psychological explanation, have never known what to make of him. Brooke refers to his alternating imperiousness and servility, calling him "complex, violent, and repressed," but concludes that his character remains enigmatic.[17] There was, however, a striking psychological resemblance between Pitt and Burke (and others who could be mentioned, Rousseau for example), and its occurrence was no accident; instead it was a condition imposed on many sensitive people by the circumstances of the historical transition then going on in England as well as France. This was an unique moment in history. People were simultaneously torn by two contradictory patterns of value, one old and the other new, one oriented, just as Kramnick explains, towards traditional social valuations, and the other towards new and more functional standards of worth, which history was forcing upon their attention. We must examine this historic conflict in its true historical details in the next chapter. It may suffice here to suggest a simple analogy: the case, let us say, of a cannibal society evolving dimly towards some non-cannibalistic plan of diet. Inevitably the history of that society will reveal, to persons looking at it in retrospect, a generation or two in which the strains of evolution were particularly severe, with old values and the institutions built upon them still demanding conformity, but individual black sheep internally pricked by the new values, admiring them but afraid to act them out fully, and enraged at their own hypocrisy in playing a two-faced game: a group of men who, the documents might show, in public smilingly ate people, and toasted the eating of people, but who also, so it would appear from fragmentary psychological evidence, only the more furiously gnawed on themselves in private.

We shall continue with this problem later, for it has many aspects. The point here, an aspect of the unequal contest between Fashion and Merit, is that ambitious people outside the 'circle of the People of Fascination' were particularly subject to intense mental distress, the artist-intellectual more so than anyone else. Is there not a paradigm in the well-documented case of Mary Wollstonecraft? Consider the ailments which in the later 1770s began to afflict this impoverished, obscure, and painfully sensitive young woman as she began her work as a lady's companion in Bath. Her biographer believes them to have been largely social in origin. The young woman's first responses to fashionable society were ambivalent, a mixture of delight and apprehension, but then her hopelessly inferior position began to work upon her and to produce "lassitude, depression, acute headaches, and digestive difficulties" which Flexner, working in the tradition of modern psychiatry, diagnoses as "symptoms of deeply repressed anger." "Her position grated on her temperament," writes the biographer: "An independent turn of mind, an assertive character which was to become increasingly obvious, and a restless intelligence did not fit her for a position whose prime requisite was conformity to someone else's taste and whims. . . . We get a picture of a young woman already prematurely grave and almost self-consciously moralistic and philosophical."[18] What we get is a picture of her *rage*.

Whatever the true inner cause of it, a gravely moralizing propensity was in fact increasingly characteristic of writers as a group. More and more they saw themselves as rescuers of the national values and spiritual leaders of the whole Third Estate. Marx once suggested that the makers of revolutions, fixing their attention on domination from above, often see only that one basic social division and thus consider themselves to be but leaders of "the whole mass of society confronting the single ruling class." Undoubtedly this is true, but there are signs that the artist-intellectual's mounting frustration was also inspired in part by a growing concern for the spiritual integrity, the Englishness, of his own ill-defined class—a class he was, however, *learning* now to define, by moral oppositions to aristocratic influence, as the truly legitimate leader of the people. It was in 1766 that Oliver Goldsmith presented "the middle order" of society as "the true preserver of freedom" and the true repository of "all the arts, wisdom, and virtues of society"—as the spearhead, that is, of the Third Estate, of Fielding's 'Nobody,' of Marx's 'whole of society' opposed to the one clearly defined 'class'; yet he also presented the middle class as absolutely besieged by the aristocracy, threatened by the "Cartesian vortices" of "great men."[19]

It was, as we saw earlier, just at this time that the floodgates of tourism were beginning to open. Cosmopolitan aesthetic betrayals, personal slights, social cronyism and occupational discrimination were galling enough, but the whole cultural mongrelization of the middle and lower ranks, a development seemingly threatened by the tremendous rush of continental tourism, was evidently the last straw in exciting the nationalist writers into a generalized anti-aristocratic campaign. The periodicals and travel literature of the sixties and seventies saw an increasingly fervent debate over the value and effects of such foreign exposure, while the light literature of the period discloses more generalized fears over the problem of the frenchification of 'our youth,' a problem deeply entangled, as in the materials examined earlier, with related alarms over the whole contemporary growth of 'luxury' and 'modern morality'—that is, over the lavish, excessive, bizarre and imitative modes of behavior being elaborated during this period, the 'showing the spirit of an heir' discussed by Habakkuk, the 'ridiculous excesses' discerned by Marshall, Stone, and others.

To the irritable, suspicious, self-conscious, and moralizing intellectual, all the evils of the day seemed increasingly interconnected as the emanations of a corrupt, self-seeking, and culturally alien upper class. The pattern of literary attack, typically voiced by the urban intellectual in the guise of a rural sage, can be examined in fictional harangues such as that in Henry Mackenzie's *Man of Feeling* (1771), in which the line of condemnation can be observed to run in just a page or two through all the compass points of the expanding mythology, from the prevalence of false social ideals to the whole accursed system of Fashion, to the problem of the education of youth, to the foreign pollution of English taste and spirit, to the deplorable effects in general of luxury and the pursuit of pleasure, and at last—a point increasingly emphasized—to the widening gulf between the "votaries" of "thoughtless dissipation" and the interests of "the people": "With the administration of such men the people can never be satisfied." The sense of internal social division along cultural lines was growing, with a spirit of increasingly militant defiance on the more popular side accompanying and helping to provoke one of increasingly exaggerated contempt on the other; and among intellectual products one may note a progressive interweaving of nativist with primitivist motifs from the fifties, when writers deplored the "pestilential" spread of luxury "through the nation," down into the seventies, when xenophobic poetry on "these Injur'd Isles" sought salvation in the embrace of rude "Nature" and in release "from foreign Commerce, Confidence, and Gold,/From foreign Arts—from all that's foreign."[20]

The erupting social anger of the seventies, with its increasingly vigorous insistence on the need to shun every influence given off by the World, may be discerned in innumerable writers. Here is a blast from the minor poet John Langhorne:

> Foregone the social, hospitable Days,
> When wise Vales echoed with their Owner's Praise,
> Of all that *ancient Consequence* bereft,
> What has the *modern Man of Fashion* left?
>   Does He, perchance, to rural Scenes repair,
> And 'waste his sweetness' on the essenc'd Air?
> Ah! gently lave the feeble Frame he brings,
> Ye scouring Seas! and ye sulphureous Springs! . . .
>   O from each Title Folly ever took,
> Blood! Maccarone! Cicisbeo! [gigolo] or Rook! [crooked gambler]
> From each low Passion, from each low Resort,
> The thieving Alley, nay, the righteous Court,
> From BERTIE'S, ALMACK'S, ARTHUR'S, and the Nest

Where JUDAH'S Ferrets earth with Charles [Fox] unblest;—
From these and all the Garbage of the great,
At Honour's, Freedom's, Virtue's Call—retreat![21]

4. IMAGINATIVE LITERATURE BY THE EIGHTIES: SANDFORDS VS. MERTONS

Perhaps the best way to sum up the impact of all this propaganda by the eighties, and to display many of its chief characteristics by that period, is to analyze some of the imaginative literature of that decade. Take Thomas Day's extremely popular novel, *Sandford and Merton,* published in three parts from 1783 to 1789. Day's life experiences, like those of Wollstonecraft, Smollett, and others, illustrate many ways in which prevailing attractions to the *mode* were likely to sting the sensitive middle-class writer into anti-aristocratic propaganda. Born in 1748, an awkward and ungainly man, the son of a customs officer, Day spent much of his later adolescence in search of a romantic partner. When at last in Lichfield at the age of twenty-three he discovered, or thought he did, such a partner in Elizabeth Sneyd—the lovely daughter of a major, well read, full of wit and gaiety, and very up-to-date—he discovered also that happiness would depend on conforming strictly to the hypnotic model of the man of fashion. For when he attempted to dominate and counter-hypnotize her with his tirades against fine people, fine titles, fine clothes, and "the empire of fashion," she roundly told him off, crying that she "could not be satisfied with the abhorrence, which upon all occasions he expressed, of accomplishments which he had not been able to attain."[22]

There went his high horse; and there surely was the romantic crack of doom for many another bourgeois lover. One is only too greatly reminded in Day's personal experience of the disadvantages of Fielding's Horatio, whose 'sighs and tears, love and tenderness' had counted so little with Leonora against the formidable 'French-English' Bellarmine's 'gaiety and gallantry.' But Thomas Day was not ready to give up. He resolved to do his best, and the decision is instructive. With drums rolling he climbed aloft to the cultural trapeze that would take him direct to the too un-Elizabethan bosom of Elizabeth Sneyd. "With the bright eyes of Elizabeth before him," as his biographer relates, he betook himself to France. He meant to acquire all the graces. With characteristic intensity he undertook to polish himself. He had his work cut out for him. Dancing masters and fencing masters labored over him for weeks. For many hours a day he practiced under his French riding masters the curvet, the volte, the demi-volte, the croupade and the capriole. He hired Monsieur Huise to straighten his knock-knees in a horrid bracelike contraption made of boards and screws, and for days on end "endured tortures, pent up in the stocks 'with a book in his hand and contempt in his heart.'"[23] At last he was ready. Arrayed in splendid clothes, powdered, scented and bewigged, instructed in the graces, displaying his French, pointing his toes, he sailed home with his heart full of hope.

Alas, the frog prince was only froggier. "When Elizabeth saw him, she tittered." He had abandoned simplicity but fallen wide of savoir-faire. Elizabeth rejected him and the romance ended miserably. "He had made a fool of himself, and it had been brought home to him in a cruel way."[24] The whole humiliating experience helped to shape and intensify his fictionalized attack on 'the World' in his immensely popular novel of the eighties, which rigidly contrasted the idealized simplicity, morality, intelligence and patriotism of an upstanding rural English community to the immorality, superficiality and viciousness emanating from the 'polished' and frenchified Great.

Sandford and Merton's plot is quite simple, a mere device by which Day lured into his moral world the book's many readers—and there were armies of them, for this novel was not only one of the most popular books of the decade but, for young people, of the entire succeeding century.[25] Its theme is emblematically foretold near the beginning when arrogant young Tommy Merton, the son of rich and fashionable parents, is saved from a serpent which has partly coiled itself around him. His rescuer is Harry Sandford, the son of a simple farmer. The story then works back and forth across this dividing line until at last, and despite various backslidings, young Tommy, helped by virtuous Harry and also lectured to death by the tirelessly moralizing Reverend Barlow (a rural sage, Day's alter ego), emancipates himself forever from all the evil influences to which he had once thought himself happily born—that is, from the noxious effects of Fashion in all its guises.

i. two Englands

From beginning to end the book presents in radical contrast to each other two co-existing worlds of value, two entire systems not only of morality but of manners, tastes, pastimes, impulses and ambitions, which in turn are no less unremittingly identified with social position, that of the Quality on the one hand, that of the non-Quality on the other. What we have are two sociomoral worlds, different as castles from cottages yet occupying the same landscape, the England of the 1780s; the one maintaining an unjustified hold over the other by dint of wealth, snobbery, and mindless social imitation of its specious charms, even while the latter is presented as the home of all true superiority in Day's single-minded, rigidly organizing, and transvaluing moral vision.

One of the things most noteworthy about Day's attitude is the completeness, the comprehensiveness of this transvaluing moral vision, which confidently takes in, colors, then installs in its proper place in the dualistic landscape every object and act of contemporary life. Everything is clothed in signifiers, everything is brought into sociomoral focus, everything figures in one great, sustained, simple, repetitive commentary; a circumstance which, if it helps to explain the book's later popularity as an educational tool, also suggests something about the coherence and maturity of Day's worldview in this decade of the eighties.

The book is itself a prolonged 'howl of execration.' Day divides all society into two groups, persons of fashion and everyone else. This invidious dualism, like many others in the novel, is conveyed in a great variety of ways, with inset stories and allegories, by means of symbols, through Day's narrative observations, and through the speeches and actions of his characters. We are told that young Tommy "thought he had a right to command everybody that was not dressed as fine as himself." His mother coldly observes that the young ploughboy who has just rescued her own child is tainted by that "certain grossness and indelicacy in his ideas, which distinguish the children of the lower and middling classes of people from those of persons of fashion." The fashionable hags clustered at the Merton estate are made to echo the same idea, knitting their brows at poor Harry's awkwardness and fussily observing that "it was not proper to introduce such vulgar people to the sons of persons of fashion." The same point, the Quality's arrogant exclusiveness, is reinforced from the other direction. Harry privately reflects that the people at the Mertons' estate "seemed to consider themselves, and a few of their acquaintance, as the only beings of any consequence in the world." Day, stepping forth as narrator, amplifies this and simultaneously throws all other class distinctions into the shade with such observations as that the virtuous Miss Simmons, an orphaned child of gentry stock, had certain disabilities (she could not speak French, and was ignorant of foreign music) "which disqualified her almost as much as Harry for fashionable life." The Reverend Barlow, addressing Tommy's father, declares that "Gentlemen in your situation in life are accustomed to divide the world into two general classes; those that are persons of fashion, and those that are not. The first class contains everything that is valuable in life; . . . the second comprehends the great body of mankind, who, under the general name of the Vulgar, are represented as being only objects of contempt and disgust, and scarcely worthy to be put on a footing with the very beasts that contribute to the pleasure and convenience of their superiors." Mr. Merton himself, the novel's only Beau Monder with any semblance of real virtue (and this figures less as a concession to aristocratic goodness than as something indispensable to the novel's machinery, which requires that Tommy's education be entrusted to the leather-lunged Barlow) concedes that there is "too much truth" in this characterization.[26]

Everything separating the two classes is subtly harped upon. The novel gives the sensitive underdog's view of the dichotomous social relations of the 1780s—a dualistic pattern which, as we saw earlier, was sharp enough in reality to strike the notice of foreign visitors like Archenholz. The arrogance of the fashionable, their looks of "consummate impudence," their "insufferable contempt" for those beneath them, receive much rancorous attention. Their behavior combines a "hypocritical civility" learned partly from Lord Chesterfield—Chesterfield's "opinions are now considered as the oracles of polite life," and there is no difference between a lord and a Macaroni ("a lord, or a macaroni, as I think you call them")—with much cruelty and indifference spiced with "jests and sneers," "contemptuous sneers." (It was "so provoking to be laughed at!")[27] The earthly ambitions of the fashionable, "those who engross the riches and advantages of this world," were all superficial and detestable. "Their whole happiness consists in idleness and finery"; "pleasure and sensuality" were their only objects, and uselessness was the effect: "it is the first qualification of a gentleman never to do anything useful"; "the rich do nothing and produce nothing, and the poor everything that is really useful"; "those who are vain of being gentlemen can do nothing useful or ingenious."[28] The implications of this were very grave, not only regarding the political and military affairs of the nation ("You cannot imagine, that men fit to command an army, or to give laws to a state, were ever formed by an idle and effeminate education"), not only with reference to the wholesale destruction of resources ("the great object of all their knowledge and education, was only to waste, to consume, to destroy, to dissipate, what was produced by others"), but also with regard to the moral servitude and dependence gradually produced by all this: "This inability to assist either themselves or others, seemed to be a *merit* upon which every one valued himself extremely: so that an individual who could not exist without having two attendants to wait upon him, was superior to him that had only one; but was obliged in turn to yield to another who required four."[29]

ii. education and advancement in genteel appearances

As this suggests, the novel launches a sustained attack upon the education of the fashionable. Upon the stage which Day sets for them, their *"politeness"* and *"superiority"* amount to nothing more than the cultivation of appearances, the mastery of approved social poses, an attitude of arrogance, and a simulation of cosmopolitan sophistication—"nothing," as Day succinctly puts it, "but dress, walking with their toes out, staring modest people out of countenance, and jabbering a few words of a foreign language." Precious to all this was the "importation of foreign manners," the "smuggling" of "foreign graces." Miss Matilda Compton, a pattern of fashion, "talks French even better than she does English," while the father of another smart young lady "gives half-a-guinea a time to a little Frenchman, who teaches her to jump and caper about the room."[30] Though Day nods in the direction of humane values transcending national boundaries, briefly praising "the common friend of all the species" and at one point even criticizing "the false antipathies which so many nations entertain against the diet as well as manners of each other" (he thus acquits himself of a bigoted kinship with the unreasoning mob), he is no less the literary nativist beneath it. He has no intention of foregoing the advantages afforded him by tucking "French trimmings" like semaphores into the buttonholes of the great, for these were the hallmark of that internal moral disunity which so concerned him, and which he saw as the source of selfish ambitions growing at the expense of the public good.

Despite his small demurrals he might have taken as his own motto the words he puts into the mouth of a humble sailor: "I have fought many a battle with the French, to defend poor old England."[31]

The whole education of the fashionable, not merely the overtly 'foreign' part of it, was a systematic training in "artificial graces," the acquisition of a perfected taste for "fraud and insincerity." Yet this, as Day lamented, was the key to success in contemporary society, in which personal advancement and a simulated worldliness went hand in hand. Thus young Tommy, according to the odious Mrs. Compton, should be schooled not under Barlow but "in some polite seminary where he might acquire a knowledge of the world, and make genteel connexions. This will be always the greatest advantage to a young gentlemen, and will prove of the most essential service to him in life. For though a person has all the merit in the world; without such acquaintance it will never push him forward, or enable him to make a figure."[32]

iii. splendid vices over real merit

In Day's cosmology it was this blind pursuit of genteel appearances and hence 'connexions' that provided the bonds of the entire social world, the chains by which the Fashionable bound to themselves in submission and potential moral corruption the whole pitiful world of mere ordinary people. Of course this is a persistent theme in all the literature we have studied. And as with the earlier authors we examined, this blind pursuit was the real target behind Day's attack on 'fine clothes,' for these symbolized the mindless attachment to appearances and hence to the social authority of the Quality. Day hardly bothers to conceal his contempt for this authority. He really approves, despite the lip-service he insincerely pays to the idea of social hierarchy, of the violence wrought by two urchins upon a boy so finely dressed that he "looked like a Frenchman." But clothes were only the most obvious aspect of the central social problem, the attachment to genteel appearances. The problem was as difficult as it was important. Day concedes, even as he laments, the difficulty of resisting the impressions of the great, the difficulty of distinguishing between seductive appearances and real virtue: "To be armed against the prejudices of the world, and to distinguish real merit from the splendid vices which pass current in what is called society, is one of the most difficult of human sciences." In his next sentence, knowing a little as we do of his own past, we may detect a bitter reflection upon both his own conduct and the lamentable glitter of Elizabeth Sneyd: "Nor do I know a single character, however excellent, that would not candidly confess he has often made a wrong election, and paid that homage to a brilliant outside, which is only due to real merit."[33]

Fashionable appearances were a trap and an insidious substitute for morality. In the world of the Mertons, "the omission of every duty towards our fellow-creatures, was not only excused, but even to a certain degree admired, provided it was joined with a certain fashionable appearance; while the most perfect probity, or integrity, was mentioned with coldness or disgust, and frequently with open ridicule, if unconnected with a brilliant appearance." In such an appalling condition of society, so dependent upon mere appearances, upon seeing and being seen, it was no wonder that "many people," unable to distinguish true from specious quality, "content themselves with aping what they can pick up in the dress, or gestures, or cant expressions of the higher classes."[34]

iv. imitativeness

Looking over his shoulder we thus see why Day hates every sign of imitation, 'aping,' as a pattern of behavior. It was the lever by which the Fashionable maintained their ascendancy, and the moral undoing of everyone else. To be impressed was to be oppressed. Hence beneath the attack on fashionable education and manners we find a central moral attack on imitative behavior itself. It is Tommy's poisonous "taste for imitation," acquired in the company of the fashionable, which leads him into backslidings from the redemptive harangues of Barlow. Tommy's model here is the revolting Master Mash (an ancestor of Thomas Hughes's 'Flashman'), the villain of the tale and the very personification of imitativeness. Day carefully builds up Mash's simian caricature. He tells the reader that Mash, "though destitute of either wit or genius, had a great taste for mimicry," at the same time preparing his symbolic identification with "the imitative animal," the monkey—already identified through apes with social imitation, through baboons with Frenchmen, and, as noted earlier, with the devil as well—by including a discourse upon the imitative and mischievous traits of monkeys in general, a short inset tale exemplifying these traits through a certain "monkey that resided in a gentleman's family," several small touches suggesting the resemblances between the "slender, emaciated figures" and "grimaces" of monkeys and "young gentlemen," and at last a stout farmer's outward perception of Mash as "dressed so much like a monkey or a barber."[35]

With this in the background, Day then leads his readers into the novel's chief passage of dramatic conflict. What he presents is an archetypal battle arising from virtuous Harry's instinctive resistance to Mash's imitativeness. Mash, "the biggest and strongest boy in the whole company" as well as the most arrogant and violent, first attempts to engineer Harry's social humiliation by meanly tricking him ("practicing the sublime science of imposing upon unwary simplicity") into attempting to dance the minuet at the Mertons' ball. "Harry imitated as well as he was able," but of course fell all over himself and his partner—it is the only occasion in the novel in which good Harry can be seen to imitate anyone. A few pages later, Mash contrives still another social humiliation for Harry, again at the expense of the virtuous Miss Simmons (who this time gets her dress spoiled instead of her feet trodden). Thus the tension builds. A few pages after that, Mash, after insulting Harry as "a spy and an informer" and a "dirty little blackguard" because he refuses to cover up the other boys'

misdeeds by lying, escalates the violence into a fistfight, the central enactment of the simultaneously social and moral opposition so doggedly detailed throughout the book. One may well imagine the joy and even the
sense of personal triumph which must have overcome thousands of humble and now forgotten English youngsters as they read of the "cool, un-
yielding courage" of little Harry as he faced the abominable Mash and at
last "by one successful blow levelled him with the ground."[36]

v. Harry's character and world

Young Harry is of course the central figure in Day's demi-world of
virtue. He is both the focus of personal identification for the male reader
(as Miss Simmons is for females) and the living exemplification of those
values which for Day were no less the real substance of Harry's world
than arrogance, artificiality, mimicry, and uselessness were the moral realities of Mash's. In the many passing references to Harry's character and
actions we find what Day regards as the constituents of "*real* superiority
and excellence," the characterological foundations of real merit. These
characteristics should be carefully noted, as we shall refer to them again
later when speculating on the National Identity. Day dwells upon the "innocence" of Harry's character, his "openness of temper." He never tires
of praising and illustrating Harry's "honesty," his inability to "tell an un-
truth." He treats him as the embodiment of practical intelligence, possessing "an understanding naturally strong." He lauds Harry's "firmness," his
"firm tone of voice," "steady countenance," and "bravery." And he holds
up for admiration Harry's love of work and, through it, of independence—"I hope I shall soon be big enough to go to plough, and get my
own living; and then I shall want nobody to wait upon me."[37]

Harry's father, cut from the same cloth, "a plain, honest farmer" of
"coarse, but strong morality," the head of "a whole family of innocent
people," doubles with Barlow and several others to provide the symbolic
linkage between Harry and the extended national community; and then
in addition, through such devices as the elder Sandford's reminiscences
on his own youth ("and that is near forty years ago"), a pattern of historical linkage is articulated, running from the much glorified community of
yore to today's near "ruin of all the nation" through the "mad" pursuit of
"*gentility.*"[38] Harry's world, its moral, social and historical features thus
skilfully drawn, is then further detailed by setting it amongst a grouping
of well-chosen colored mirrors—a neat tactical variation on 'the dumb
rhetoric of the scenery' so often employed in this subterranean style of
propaganda. Day portrays Harry's virtuous world by means of many devices: by including a variety of exotic parables, historic tales, and sidelong
observations on how a nation of free men may turn into one of slaves, "a
nation of monkeys"; by presenting many extended anthropological reflections upon the virtues of rude native societies, the "savage grandeur of
man in his most simple state" (there is much emphasis here on the
positive relationships between virtue, homespun education, patriotism,

ancestor-worship, martial exploits, and liberty); and, finally, by threading through his text a pattern of cross-referenced generalizations on how "the barbarians are a great deal wiser than young gentlemen," on how "great virtues and good dispositions may sometimes be found in cottages, while they are totally wanting among the great," etc.[39]

vi. progress of the virtuous oppressed

Day thus presents, as beneath the ascendancy of the vicious and exploitative Fashionable, the Virtuous Oppressed. The view is warm and panoramic. It is as though Fielding in his fictional tale of 1742 had projected poor Horatio as a full-fledged character into the glittering world of the beguiling Bellarmine (Mash) and the beguiled Leonora (Tommy), rather than leaving him a small part on the edge of it; or as though the Britannia of the 1750s, though still shown as manacled and abused by her oppressors, were now pictured as surrounded and encouraged by a large family of sturdy supporters. Of course the great central myth is still there. In *Sandford and Merton* we find the same basic network of ideas as was detailed earlier, the same archetypal story of alien pollution told by the English storyteller to the English about themselves. There is the same dream logic of belief, a pattern of half-truths linked together through socio-moral personifications and symbolic contrasts, a dynamic gaining its energy from fears of the seduction of 'unwary simplicity,' the whole working by indirection as an allegorical representation—a simplified explanation—of existence as it was experienced in the 1780s.

Yet the central myth is harder to detect in *Sandford and Merton* because it is no longer presented through simple fables about visibly frenchified half-breeds and virtuous Englishmen but rather through an enormous metasocial and metahistorical commentary in which its basic logic has been expanded to include (and hence for readers schooled in this myth, as so many were by the 1780s, to explain) a whole world of supposedly contingent details. Of course there is nothing strange in this, considered as a fact of mythic evolution; every collective myth, every historical and racial 'big lie,' originates in smaller lies and patterns of overlapping equivocations such as those we found earlier in Hogarth's pictures and Foote's plays. But the significant thing about this tableau from the 1780s is its very comprehensiveness, the fact that Day includes an organized and coherent picture of the manners, virtues, historical descent, and anthropological affiliations of the Ineligible. In other respects the novel's philosophical content is not greatly different from that of Brown's *Estimate,* written a generation earlier (1757–58). Both authors take much the same attitude toward France: both were educated men, neither was a raw and simple Gallophobe by any means, both exhibit a certain wary appreciation of France even while abhorring and attacking French cultural influence in England. Day's mind, like the mentality of his country by the eighties, is divided. He self-consciously accepts the merits of cosmopolitanism as an intellectual and philanthropic stance, but at the same time he is much less guarded than Brown in expressing hatred towards the anti-national and Francophiliac elite in charge of his own country. Both authors exhibit the same intense hostility to the fashionable world; in both, Hogarth's 'war against connoisseurship' has spread into an obsessive desire, as Day indirectly acknowledges, to "wage war with most of the polite and modern accomplishments." There is a passion to bring the rich man much "nearer to an equality with his fellow-creatures," a thirst for "bringing the two classes nearer together"—not by striking compromises between them but rather by pulling down the pretensions and poisonous influence of the great. And it is fundamentally the same dread of universal corruption that leads Day, as it had led Brown nearly thirty years earlier, to hope for "some legislator" who could draw up a "code," some "general rules of conduct," by which all could live in harmonious equality.[40]

But Day's perspective is in some ways so much more highly evolved than Brown's and so much more popular in its basic assumptions that one may sense a qualitative change here, an alteration not to be explained solely by reference to the different positions and outlooks of these two authors as individuals. Essentially what we have before us is the temporal evolution and philosophic expansion of the basic ideology, and the progress of the cultural drift with which it was connected. The key development is the idealization of the English people in the mass. What is important to realize is the fact that Day no longer identifies the strength of the English nation in any sense whatsoever with the ruling class, Brown's 'higher Ranks in Life,' 'those who *lead* the People.' The strength of Day's nation is the strength of the virtuous and allied people themselves, shunning, opposing and rejecting the influence of the Great, just as Harry rejects Mash, his father rejects the money proffered by Mr. Merton, and young Tommy at last rejects forever his tonnish friends. Day dissects the vices of the fashionable with quite as much relish and disgust as Brown had done, but he also devotes a very great deal of effort to portraying the superiority of the virtuous, something which Brown had completely omitted and the other propagandists at mid-century had often neglected, thanks less to their amity towards the Quality than to their ambiguity about the bumpkin *Volk*—an attitude which, needless to say, they faintly shared with the arrogant World, and which hence to that extent dulled their attacks upon it.

Day's loving and idealizing (if nonetheless paternalistic) attitude toward the English masses also helps to explain the difference in tone between these two authors. Both were tremendously angry men, but in Day's book there is a new suggestion of self-confidence and strength. Brown's book drags clanking chains of anguish and despair, while Day's ends with the trumpets of virtue aloft. The difference between Brown and Day is a little like that between the frenzied patriarch of an apocalyptic sect and the calm, smooth-shaven pastor of an established congregation, one eye sternly fixed on missionary endeavor, the other on the coming of the Promised Land. It is as though Day himself were becoming the 'legislator' for whom both Brown and he yearned, and his audience the thirsting and grateful recipients of that 'code' which both authors saw as vital to the salvation of their 'despairing nation.'

5. THE SCHOLARLY REVOLUTION

Behind this, and allied to it, was another great pattern of intellectual transformation. It is important to see that many differences between Brown's book and Day's are attributable also to the immense scholarly revolution that took place between the 1740s and the 1790s. This event has received little attention because we have not possessed the tools by which to understand it. Just the right perspective, however, was laid down long ago in a little-noticed observation by Leslie Stephen, the great Victorian critic. He remarked that what was in actual fact a "natural" and "spontaneous" (though sophisticated, witty and "correct") literature of Augustan Neoclassicism was, over time, gradually transmogrified "by whole systems of equivocations" into something that could be denounced as "'artificial'!", and divined at the heart of this process a sense that Englishmen "ought not quite to accept the yoke of the French Academy. . . . The sturdy Briton would not be seduced to the foreign model. . . . This points to the process by which the Wit becomes 'artificial.'"[41] Here was one of those flashes of insight found in thinkers of true genius, an instinctive decipherment of the whole literary revolution.

'Stirrings' is the name given by Minogue to the initial phase of nationalist activity. This, he explains, characterizes a period in which the country's intellectuals, becoming aware of their culture as a victim of oppression, begin to reject foreign ideas and grope around for a distinctive national cultural identity. Kohn, pursuing the same idea, remarks that during the eighteenth century in central Europe "the intellectuals extolled the beauty of their own language and literature in contrast to the French." In English literature, as we noted earlier, the whole era from Dryden's time to Johnson's was a period when, according to Clark, "everyone was aping French fashions."[42] It was this French cultural supremacy, the despotism of French taste no less in literature than in so many other fields over which "connoisseurship" reigned, which provided the baseline of many European nationalist movements; and it has only been the illusion of English uniqueness which has concealed the significance of this for English literary development.

In fact the signs of an ascending anti-French literary nationalism are only too plentiful once one begins to look for them. Many documents of so-called pre-romanticism must be re-examined in this light. Take Richard Hurd's influential *Letters on Chivalry and Romance* (1762), which literary analysts have always regarded as an important landmark in the transition from neo-classic to romantic aesthetic values. Hurd's treatise may indeed be read in this traditional light, for its tendency is to vindicate and then extol the 'Gothic' and 'romantic' characteristics of medieval and Renaissance poetry, characteristics which Hurd's contemporaries in 1762 were still much inclined to despise and condemn. But to observe only this and to overlook the many thrusts against "modern taste" which mark Hurd's treatise is to miss the deeper dimension of his argument, for in fact its aesthetic topsails are borne along by pulsating engines of anti-French rhetoric whose tendency is to vindicate the "sublimity" of Spenser, Shakespeare, and Milton by chopping up the resistive influence of French aesthetic standards. To examine this text of 1762 is to see a striking resemblance between Hurd's aesthetic argument, John Brown's diatribes of only a few years earlier, and the half-stated cultural and moral propaganda which we have already found embedded in the graphic art and fiction of the 1750s. Hurd's treatise is peppered with sidelong hits at "the *French* criticism," the "French wits" and their ubiquitous followers "the fastidious *moderns*," "the more *fashionable* sort of critics," among whom Hurd includes a number of his own English predecessors such as Davenant, Shaftesbury and Addison, "Rymer, and the rest of that School" with their "flimsy" and "canting" essays, and other "philosophic moderns" who "have gone too far, in their perpetual ridicule and contempt" of the alleged "barbarities" of Gothic Romance. "The French criticism," he complains, has gained sway over "the rest of Europe. This dextrous people have found means to lead the taste, as well as set the fashions, of their neighbours." Whether this arose from French "national envy" or from some aspiration to "a sort of supremacy in Letters," "whatever their inducements were, they succeeded but too well in their attempt." The aesthetic defeat of Imagination, of the "marvelous," the "romantic," the "Gothic," was the result; and unhappily this was also the defeat of *English* genius. The supreme irony in all this, Hurd wants to suggest (in 1762 he must still simulate cosmopolitan universalism and urbanity), is the palpable inferiority of the French themselves in the realm of truly sublime poetic creation; their very language, he absurdly declares, though "fit for business and conversation," is "absolutely unsuited to the genius of the greater poetry."[43]

This was not, as one of the great earlier writers on pre-romantic literary evolution (Summers) might have put it, a "mystical escape" from "the problems of the hour." It was a taking the bull by the horns. One cannot agree with those analysts, treading the traditional pathways of explanation, who tell us that "by the middle of the eighteenth century" the "new tendencies" of English Romanticism "were no more than tendencies, tentatives [*sic*] reaching out without conscious program—other than the desire to make poetry more noble by making it more philosophical—and without conscious rebellion against the tyranny of tradition that had operated so long."[44] Fiddlesticks. These ideas are residues of the myth, *which we see here being established* by Hurd, that English literature, being innately superior to French, had never really stood in any relation of subservience to it and had evolved quite independently under its own nobly philosophic imperatives, its own ethereal causalities. This notion, if one actually looks closely at the living and breathing writers of the 1750s and 1760s, evaporates into thin air. Hurd's treatise should be regarded as a document of English literary nationalism, one of many that progressively broke the hold of French aesthetics and simultaneously built up a new and distinctively English aesthetic philosophy. It was no coincidence that 'pre-romanticism' and the English nationalist movement rose simultaneously in time, from the second quarter of the century, or that the famous 'precursors of romanticism,' authors like James Thomson and Joseph Warton, inveighed so often against the "corrupting arts" of the "circling junto of the great," with the dreadful result "(which Heaven avert!)" that "Britannia's well-fought laurels yield/to slily conquering Gaul."[45] Similar sentiments are to be found in virtually all the major and minor poets of the mid- and later eighteenth century, from Shenstone, Chatterton, and Smart onwards.

i. an age of collectors

We see then that an aesthetic revolution—not merely an evolution—was beginning; that this was a time in English literature of vigorous anti-French cultural 'Stirrings,' marked by efforts to rejuvenate, glorify and assign formal definition to the qualities of native art. Now what else should we think about the literature of this period? Another distinction often made about the initial phase of nationalist activity is that its cultural products tend to divide into two characteristic groupings, one primitivistic, the other scholarly. Smith, working at a very high level of generalization, writes as follows:

> The cultural dimension of nationalist movements has two aspects: a populist and Rousseauan nostalgia for the simplicity and sturdiness of agricultural life, which embodies in pristine form the essence and inner virtue of the community, uncontaminated by urban luxury and corruption; and an academic, scholarly component, which is not only useful in undergirding the historic claims of the movement before the bar of world opinion and sceptical authorities, but can also provide the whole nationalist enterprise with a legitimacy based on scholarly research. . . .Hence the proliferation of historical, philological, ethnological, socio-demographic, art-historical, musicological, and other forms of historicist enquiries, and the appeal of nationalism for those engaged in such investigations.[46]

In the next chapter we must return to a fuller consideration of the first of these two important points, the poetic and fictional search for the 'inner virtue of the community.' But here the thing to grasp is that the phase of 'Stirrings' makes itself felt not only in an elaboration of a supposedly distinctive national aesthetic philosophy ('English Romanticism') but also by a sudden upsurge in scholarly activity, particularly in a rapid proliferation of linguistic, philological and ethnic researches, the intense investigation and writing of history, especially literary history, the composition of national dictionaries and encyclopedias, the founding of national academies of art and music, and so on. The whole outpouring is essentially ethnic in its central concerns, antiquarian and critical in content, educational in its contemporary impact, and ideological in its overall significance.

Here again the literary researchers, should they cast these new nets, will find many an empirical fish to Frye. The literary age, often found (and left) dull by many young scholars slogging away on the approved academic treadmills (Pocock's 'Humanism' having furnished the latest of these), was in fact one of the most extraordinarily diverse, innovative and seminal periods in the whole history of English scholarship. It was a period of extraordinary and unprecedented activity in the collection, study and promotion of everything pertaining to the national cultural heritage. Namier blandly wrote that this was "an eclectic and inquisitive age," an "age of collectors, with a passion for accumulating no matter what—books, prints, manuscripts, shells, pictures, old coins, or currency of the realm."[47] This may have been (as he thought) an expression of the "materialism" of that age, but that was hardly the quiddity of it. Just consider the magnificent cultural flowering of the period 1750–80. The chartering of the Society of Antiquaries (1751), Johnson's preparation of a dictionary of the English language (1755), the opening of the British Museum (1759), the preparation of the *Biographia Britannica* (1747–66), the production of the first edition of the *Encyclopedia Britannica* (1768–71), the establishment of innumerable societies for 'the Encouragement of the Arts,' the writing for the first time of the histories of English painting (1762–80), music (1776–89), and poetry (1744–81), the founding of the Royal Academy (1768) and the establishment at last of an English school of painting—these were but a few manifestations of the tremendous surge of activity in this area, a tremendous expansion of national self-study, 'consciousness-raising,' and self-promotion.

This extraordinary vigor, as we saw before, should be traced not to ghostly anticipations of Wordsworth but to a new and more aggressive attitude of cultural competition with the French—who, leaders of Europe in many of these spheres, were of course already well supplied with their universally admired dictionaries, encyclopedias, academies, and so on. Samuel Johnson, like Hurd a dean of this scholarly awakening, reveals a basic motivation common to many English intellectuals in the preface to his *Dictionary* (1755). Here we find just the same pattern of exaggerated fears, warnings, and neurotic assertions as that which we discovered in other writings of about the same date—Foote's plays, for example. It is worth recalling, as a point aside, that Johnson as he wrote this preface was still filled with those tangled emotions toward his fickle patron the Earl of Chesterfield which we noticed earlier. Observing that "it is incident to words, as to their authors, to degenerate from their ancestors, and to change their manners when they change their country," he warns with what might be deliberate ambiguity against "the folly of naturalizing useless foreigners to the injury of the natives," and then a bit later begins to unbutton his philological paranoia in the nervous assertion that "our language, for almost a century, has, by the concurrence of many causes, been gradually departing from its original *Teutonick* character, and deviating towards a *Gallick* structure and phraseology, from which it ought to be our endeavour to recal it." Then a little later, cautioning against the "mixture of two languages" which must inevitably arise from international literary intercourse, and against the judging of educational accomplishment by mere proficiency in non-native languages (this from him who had wanted to boast himself *le vainquer du vainquer de la terre!*), he lets tumble out his crazy fear that the frenchification of the English language, "if it be suffered to proceed, will reduce us to babble a dialect of *France*." Upon which he then majestically gathers himself up, and with a defiant flourish dedicates his book to England. We can sense here—it is a vital point of psychology to which we must return later—how closely and self-pityingly he identifies his own underrated and overworked self with the undervalued language and literature of his country. His dedication serves as both a vindication of England and a discreet throwing of his own worth (intimately connected now with England's—the two fortify each other) into the face of all detractors:

> I have devoted this book, the labour of years, to the honour of my country, that we may no longer yield the palm of philology, without a contest, to the nations of the continent. The chief glory of every people arises from its authours: whether I shall add any thing by my writings to the reputation of *English* literature, must be left to time: much of my life has been lost under the pressures of disease . . . much has always been spent in provision for the day that was passing over me; but I shall not think my employment useless or ignoble, if by my assistance foreign nations, and distant ages, gain access to the propagators of knowledge, and understand the teachers of truth; if my labours afford light to the repositories of science, and add celebrity to *Bacon,* to *Hooker,* to *Milton,* and to *Boyle.*[48]

Yes, that was the pantheon of 'Eng. Lit.' in 1755. Most of its greatness was yet to come; a reminder which helps to explain why the French were, at that time, so widely deferred to. But a new spirit of resistance was afoot, and the ideas expressed in this dedication were becoming increasingly widespread in the fifties. Similar sentiments, indeed similar words, appeared in the first charter (1755) drawn up by a committee of British artists urging support for the establishment of a Royal Academy: "We voluntarily yield the palm to every petty state that has produced a painter . . . one would think England the only country in the world incapable of producing one . . . as if the air and soil that gave birth to a Shakespeare and a Bacon, a Milton and a Newton, could be deficient in any species of excellence whatsoever."[49]

ii. the revival of native literature

No less symptomatic of the new cultural nationalism was the central emphasis in so much of this scholarly activity on the native languages and literary traditions of the British Isles, an emphasis which naturally expressed itself, just as it was to do later in Germany, in the careful preservation and study, and increasingly the imitation, of earlier 'literary remains.' Butt and Carnall comment on what they call "the peculiar character of the 1760s," describing this as a decade "particularly marked by the unusual range of scholarly study of earlier literature, and the reflection of this in the imaginative literature." Much of this activity, they say, "must necessarily remain an obscure and confusing subject." Perhaps so, but the rise of English nationalism goes far to explain it. As Minogue observes, the drive of nationalist cultural activity is "to discover a past which will support the aspiration of the present."[50]

Some day the literary analysts, working with new compasses, will map all this territory afresh. The odds are good that they will find that a powerful urge to vindicate, revive, and glorify the native culture runs right through the eighteenth-century antiquarian tradition, from the preface to Ramsay's *Evergreen* (1724—a fitting literary analogue to Hogarth's *Masquerades and Operas,* produced in the same year), which argues in favor of poetry neither "pilfered" nor trimmed with "foreign embroidery" nor "spoiled in transportation from abroad," down through the epoch-making collections and critical evaluations of the 1760s and 1770s—Thomas Percy's monumental *Reliques of Ancient English Poetry* (1765), for example, whose influence extended even to Germany (where, as Bernbaum casually observes, it "gave a basis for the theories of Herder"), as well as the seminal literary histories of Samuel Johnson (*Lives of the Poets,* 1779–81), and Thomas Warton (*History of English Poetry,* 1774–81). Characteristically, Warton's treatise opens with irritable complaints about the extent to which "our Saxon ancestors," not only after the Norman Conquest but for hundreds of years earlier during the age of Frankish ascendancy in Europe, rendered "absolute and voluntary submission" to the cultural "yoke" of France. "It was no difficult task," he growled, "for the Norman lords to banish that language, of which the natives" were already "absurdly ashamed." Behind this lay the same promptings of cultural resentment and national self-assertion which had moved other scholars like Johnson and Hurd, and which among imaginative writers inspired the unfortunate poet Christopher Smart (deranged like so many others) to pray (1763) that "the ENGLISH TONGUE"—then internationally a poor second to French—should become "the language of the WEST."[51]

iii. the rise of nationalist historiography

The new interest in the native language and literature—the clearest manifestations, of course, of the national 'genius,' the national 'soul,' the 'spirit of the people'—was but one branch of a much more pervasive though equally symptomatic revival of national historical studies in general. "It is history," writes Smith, "and history alone, which can furnish the bases of ethnic identity and the psychic reassurance of communal security that goes with it." The application of historical methods to the study of literature was itself a great innovation: according to Miller, more was accomplished in the subjection of literary criticism to historical modes of thinking during the two decades from 1750 to 1770 "than had been done in the whole one hundred and eighty years before." But this was only one aspect of the surge of historical interest. Peardon, tracing what he unambiguously calls "the rise of nationalist history" in the writings of "a new group" of historians who made their appearance in the early reign of George III (Catharine Macaulay, John Millar, John Whitaker, John Pinkerton, Robert Macfarlane, and others), examines the many signs of this "new nationalism," calling particular attention to the new "expression of patriotic sentiment in historical writing," the new "consciousness of nationality," and the remarkably intense "interest in race and national origins."[52]

This last, he believes, was the result of converging interests in linguistic origins and ethnic moral characteristics. Typically its product was a great deal of vague and complicated writing, some of it simply pseudoscholarly flummery, on what the new historians were apt to call the origins and 'Genius of the People.' One of the most interesting of the group was John Pinkerton, who busied himself with attacks on "the deplorably low state of the study of English history" (he attributed this to insufficient support by the upper classes and to the fashionable attraction to non-British languages and histories), and called for establishment of an Academy of National History, the inauguration of British historical studies in the universities, the founding of public libraries, and so on, much of this to be supported by "liberal subsidies from the rich." He contributed to the new historiography a pugnacious *Dissertation on the Origin of the Scythians or Goths* (1787), which, like other contemporary works, for example Whitaker's *Genuine History of the Britons asserted* (1772), extolled in opposition to various critics the qualities and heritage of the 'native stock.' Pinkerton blasted those who had "exerted every art to calumniate our Gothic ancestors"; "the name of Goths, the sacred name of our forefathers," he cried, "is an object of detestation." Yet the Goths were in fact the parent race of all the great peoples in history! No Celtic people, without infusions of Gothic blood (such as had occurred in the British Isles), was capable of the slightest degree of true civilization. So much for those who had scoffed at Britain's illustrious ancestors and pretended "to show Gaul the parent country of modern nations in Europe, and thus to support the French dream of universal monarchy"![53]

iv. the 'rampant' racialism of 1760–89

The expansion of linguistic, literary and historical research was bringing also, as in the books of Pinkerton and Whitaker, an intensification of thought about communal racial origins. Indeed this emerged as a logical necessity in the context of researches like those of Hurd, Johnson and Warton, researches which (as the reader must have noticed in our samplings) assumed a basic contrast between that which was 'French,' 'Gallick,' and 'Norman' on the one side, and that which was 'Gothic,' 'Teutonick,' and 'Anglo-Saxon' on the other. Kedourie writes that the spread of communal racial ideas is a sure sign of that development of a 'comprehensive doctrine' which is one of the earmarks of nationalism. Indeed the expansion of racial and genealogical discussion was an integral aspect of the whole effort to clarify, vindicate, and extol the forgotten and unknown sources of the national character. It was no accident that 'John Bull,' himself largely an invention of the 1750s (though with roots earlier), was already by the sixties acquiring definition in English periodical literature as "a very worthy, plain, honest old gentleman, of Saxon descent."[54]

Of course the implications of this for the analysis of English literature have not yet been worked out. Several modern authors have, with varying degrees of success, attempted to disentangle some of the threads of what amounted to an extraordinary outburst of racial discussion during the later eighteenth century, but a very great deal of research, based on principles developed outside the study of literature itself, needs to be done. We do have materials enough to piece together a rude theory which might serve till something more sophisticated can be devised. It is obvious, first, that the Teutonizing and Saxonizing—in its largest sense, the Gothic—revival of this period was the creation of literary men. Second, this trend was not only flourishing but even "rampant" by the 1760s (as MacDougall has written). Third, as Kliger found, this 'gothicising' tendency was not by any means limited to aesthetic discussion, but also intimately connected with social and political debate. Fourth, it cannot be doubted that in politics this racial mythologizing was instrumental in the projection of democratic (anti-'Norman') political ideas during the period 1760–90 (a point to which we shall return later). A fifth point helps to bring all this together: for as Poliakov argues, the later eighteenth century witnessed in virtually every major European country an intense if covert 'Controversy About the Two Races' which contemporaries visualized as inhabiting that country, a controversy in which the political facts of aristocratic domination and popular subordination were debated in terms simultaneously moral, cultural, and racial. Poliakov observes that "class was coupled with 'race', that is to say, with a culture; or, to put it more exactly, at the root of this class confrontation there was a cultural confrontation which was perceived as a conflict between different bloods." In each country, in other words, aristocratic ascendancy was on the one side justified, and on the other attacked, by tracing it to ancient invasion and the conquest of one race by another, a conquest both physical and cultural. Thus the Abbé Sieyès in his famous *Qu'est-ce que le Tiers État?* (January 1789) presented the complaints of 'the people' in the newly developed rhetoric of Gallo-Roman (popular) versus Frankish (aristocratic) genealogical descent, culture, and legitimacy:

> Why should [the Third Estate] not relegate to the forests of Franconia all those families which persist in the foolhardy pretence of being descended from the race of conquerors and of having succeeded to the rights of conquest? The Nation, thus purged, would, I believe, be able to console itself by the thought that it was constituted of the descendants of the Gauls and the Romans only. In truth, if one insists on distinguishing one manner of birth

from another, might we not persuade our luckless fellow-citizens that the descent which they derive from the Gauls or the Romans is at least as worthy as that which they might have received from the Cimbri, the Welsche and other savages who emerged from the swamps and forests of ancient Germany?[55]

This passage has received too little attention from a scholarly world still bemused by what it imagines to have been the 'sublime cosmopolitanism' of the French Revolution—another idea to reconsider later. So common was the tendency to picture political events in racial terms that in 1793 Catherine the Great remarked: "Do you not see what is happening in France? The Gauls are driving out the Franks."[56]

We thus have a general context in which to view the evolution of English racial discussion during the literary period 1740–89. On the one hand, a myth of genealogical descent was being elaborated; a myth which traced the 'truly' English community (or British—a point insisted upon by some contemporary ethnologists) back to the humble Saxons (a branch of the hitherto despised 'Goths,' a shorthand term for all the barbarian tribes which had defeated Rome), and, through this Germanic group (some authors maintained also that the ancient Britons were 'originally' Germanic, contrasting them with the Celts of Gaul), back to an assortment of glorious Biblical and Homeric ancestors. Year by year the vision of a 'truly' English or British racial community with a common past and a common moral, social, cultural and political makeup was pieced together from a maze of scholarly and pseudoscholarly research, and then fitted with tremendous emotional appeal by associating it with the idealized moral qualities of the Saxon ancestors (of which more in Chapter Six). The political implication, of course, was that the innate moral superiority, historic precedence in the British Isles, and Germanic institutional inheritance of 'the people' entitled them to a much larger share of legitimacy and power than they were currently suffered to enjoy by their ('Gallick,' Norman, French) oppressors. As one radical writer declared in 1771, "Whatever is of Saxon establishment is truly constitutional, but whatever is Norman is heterogeneous to it, and partakes of a tyrannical spirit."[57]

This same quotation nicely reveals the other side of the process as well, the effort to tear down the cultural pretensions and ultimately the suggested genealogical (hence social) superiority of the national elite. Shklar, an authority on genealogical myths, has written on the dual functions of 'Subversive Genealogies.' Such genealogies, she observes, "can serve as readily to destroy as to enhance claims to social supremacy." The elite was full of Francophiles like Chesterfield who sneered (as we caught him doing earlier) at the rise of bourgeois travel as 'a second incursion of Goths and Vandals' upon the Continent, and it teemed with Beau Monders who scornfully defined 'Gothic' (as a writer for the *World* did) as "the privilege of playing the fool, and of making [oneself] ridiculous in whatever way he pleases." To them the gothicizing tendency, like the so-called vogue of sensibility, was vulgar and bourgeois. But, on the other hand, waves of writers like Hurd and Pinkerton were now rising up to pronounce themselves 'Gothic' and proud of it. "The term 'Gothic,'" says Kliger, "appears on both sides of an antithesis; that is to say, it is used in praise or in censure." And it was the vulgar gothicizers, not the sneering anti-Goths, who were winning the day: "We may conclude that Englishmen gave to the Gothic faith the assent of all their faculties, imaginative and logical. . . . Gothicism was a basic concept, developing in the fiber of the nation."[58] More simply, Saxon racial myth figured importantly in the expansion of the nationalist ideology. It provided a broad bottom on which to build the sense of nationality and citizenship.

6. THE NEW ETHNIC CONSCIOUSNESS

Many other distinctions could be made about the nationalistic character of literary and cultural activity during this 'Age of Energy' (as some analysts have called it).[59] There are entire realms of activity to reconsider—the field of popular music, for example, which during this period saw not only the creation of the great British national anthems but the production, as Greene notes, of more popular British music that is still current than probably any other era.[60] But the central fact, no matter which way we look at all this activity, is that English consciousness was increasingly pervaded by a sense of ethnic identity. This had been awakened by 'disparagements' and 'humiliations' suffered earlier, it was intensified by a belligerent if somewhat defensive artistic and moral response to these, and it was solidified in the realm of deeply held beliefs by the spread not only of a new nationalistic moral and civic philosophy (as in Brown's *Estimate*) but by the progress in the sixties and seventies of innumerable new historical, linguistic, aesthetic, literary and racial researches into the Elizabethan, 'Gothic' and 'Saxon' past. And this, of course, provides the key to the problem of literary evolution raised earlier in this chapter. It was this latter development, this scholarly renaissance of the third quarter of the century, that stood between Brown's *Estimate* in the 1750s and Day's *Sandford and Merton* in the 1780s, providing the latter many of the materials so skilfully woven into its message of folkish virtue and solidarity, and conditioning the minds of readers to accept, as many of them would not have done in the 1750s, its essentially dualistic, melodramatic, and radically democratic vision of reality.

Equally obvious is the fact that this heightened sense of ethnicity, of 'we-group' identity, was held in place by a sharp though naturally distorted and increasingly generalized conception of what was 'French.' Undoubtedly the internal prejudices and ethnic diversity of the British Isles helped to foster this; it is an old tactic to unite in-groups by anathematizing out-groups. The 'French' or 'Normans' furnished a useful hate-object even to rival schools of Anglomaniacs and Celtomaniacs, and, there are reasons to believe, may have helped them to resolve their differences. But that point is too small to bother with here. The brute fact is that the sense of collective identity was held in place, whether in consciousness of the past or of the present, whether in the realm of manners or in those of literature or politics or war, by a mortar of anti-French propaganda, a cement of 'we-they' oppositions. The 'they' of this formulation were the French themselves and the domestic elite, the Ton, corrupted by tastes, manners and morality supposedly originating in France. The propaganda was composed in about equal parts from fear and admiration, envy and disgust, and laid on with diminishing inhibitions by neurotic and self-asserting literary men, increasingly fed up with the catholic tastes of the Quality and inclined to look upon England's own leaders as culturally, politically and racially tinged by excessive association with the Great Satanic enemy, 'slily conquering Gaul.'

All of which is only to say that the growing cultural and social dualism described earlier, with its Francophilism on the one side and its 'howl of execration' on the other, was working its way through and electrically charging the whole world of English letters. This antagonism was the secret source of at least six of every ten volts of that mysterious 'Energy' in contemporary literature. The very texts themselves—the writings of Hurd, Johnson, Thomson, Pinkerton, the Warton brothers, etc.—proclaim their origins in the anxieties, humiliations, provocations and self-assertions which we considered earlier. The rancorous complaints against French aesthetic dominance, the anxious feelings about the deficiencies of English art and scholarship, the neurotic and even paranoid fears over the creeping disintegration of national cultural identity, the medley of undertones directed at the great, rich and fashionable in England, the passionate and assertive claims for the future greatness of the art, language and literature of the English race, the personal identification with this cause and the investment of tremendous labor towards its fulfillment—it would be hard to find an order of proofs more telling than this.

7. PRE-ROMANTICISM R.I.P.

What then of 'pre-romanticism'? Because the contemporary ambivalence was not only aesthetic but moral and social, reflecting an historic confrontation between the claims and values of the 'eligibles' and those of everyone else, between everything signified by 'Fashion' and everything signified by 'Merit,' it would be naive to continue to think that 'pre-romanticism'—the increasing primitivism of contemporary literature, its tendency to exalt the humble and low-born, etc.—was the result simply or even primarily of aesthetic trends (the 'Rise of Feeling,' 'Growth of Sensibility,' 'Growing Popularity of Loco-Descriptive Poetry,' 'Influence of Rousseau,' etc.). Such concepts, though not without meaning, lack power. It is better to reverse the emphasis altogether. Without denying the operation of purely literary trends and influences, it would be much more reasonable to say that the increasing primitivism of contemporary literature was the natural consequence of rising anti-aristocratic feeling and the propagation, very often through the convenient and historically appropriate device of anti-French oppositions, of a supposedly English system of morality and aesthetics, a system with distinct social as well as national orientations, calculated to confront French supremacy, abase the frenchified great, and glorify the British many as the 'true' source of national virtue. Of course this is not to deny that a far-reaching intellectual and aesthetic revolution was under way by the mid-eighteenth century, a revolution which favored the emotional, oracular, pastoral, primitive, and subjective elements which we discern at the end of the century in 'Romanticism.' Far from it. It is, instead, only to urge that the aesthetic revolution, like the later one in Germany which it greatly helped to inspire (conventional interpretation has confused the true order and sequence of Anglo-German intellectual influence), was an integral part of a still larger *nationalist* revolution whose mainspring lay not in mere aesthetic causalities but in the human discontents of the alienated and frustrated intellectual, 'casting around for a cultural identity' with one hand held up against French cultural domination and the other frantically leafing through the 'buried' literary past.

The shape of contemporary literature was dictated not by a spirit of pure aesthetic theorizing in a germless philosophical laboratory but instead by the passionate feelings of frustrated men and women in an age of torn attachments and uncertain identity. Lipking intuitively captures its central feature when he suggests that the sudden outpouring of literary history and criticism was related to an unusual sentiment of patriotism— not an ordinary patriotism but something peculiarly thirsting, insistent, demanding, and intimately involved with the whole contemporary idea of the nation. Referring to the first great histories of English poetry in the late seventies, he writes that "the public demanded" such surveys, that "Warton and Johnson responded to a national desire for an evaluation of what English poets had achieved," adding that "England expected" a "glorious national poetic pantheon" and that *English literary history itself was thus shaped at the outset* "by the need for a definition of the superiority of the national character."[61] In this small unnoticed fact we behold the mythic origins of our own modern academic understanding. Eng. Lit., as a critical discipline, grew out of passionate nationalistic claims which may still distort our vision in untold ways.

W.Hogarth inv.^t et del.

C.Grignion sculp.

Et spes & ratio Studiorum in Cæsare tantum.

Published according to Act of Parliament May 7.1761.

Juv.

9. 1761, after Hogarth. Britannia nourishes the stunted and parched national
arts. This print, which served as frontispiece to a catalogue sold to benefit
impoverished artists, reflects their hope for a new prosperity under young King
George III. Compare Plate 6, shown earlier (p. 62), which appeared in the same
catalogue.

CHAPTER SIX

The Moral Elevation of the English National Identity

No distant clime shall servile airs impart,
Or form these limbs with pliant ease to play;
Trembling I view the Gaul's illusive art,
That steals my lov'd rusticity away.
                                        —SHENSTONE

Every thing we have done is in the style of hostility to France, as a nation.
                                        —BURKE

EVERY NATIONALIST MOVEMENT, according to the experts, involves a search for the 'essence and inner virtue of the community'—a quest, that is, for the National Identity. Of all aspects of nationalist intellectual activity, this is the one most central and most important. Hence for the historian trying to decipher this multifarious activity, this Identity, if he can make it out, furnishes a Rosetta stone, for *it* is the nebulous essence round which all else revolves. One could never, on a mere printed page, picture in anything like all its rich historic detail the great and always subtly shifting concept of the English National Identity. But one might perhaps take a stab at outlining its chief features in the age of its emergence, and at explaining its extraordinary importance to the nationalist movement's success.

1. CONCEPTS OF NATIONAL IDENTITY OR CHARACTER

National Characters do exist, whether or not we are able to describe them fairly; scholars, journalists, diplomats and filmmakers, not to mention joke writers, work meaningfully with concepts of them all the time. A concept of national character may be thought of as a stereotype, an image of what are felt to be the distinguishing characteristics of a national community of people—a personality, in other words. But the thing itself, National Identity, is really much more complex than a stereotype or cartoonist's rendering—a scowling John Bull, an openhanded Uncle Sam, an indignant Marianne rallying the people—because of its psychological, educational and historic dimensions. That is, National Identity *is* the thing imperfectly represented in caricature, a quintessence, the distinctive pattern of traits more or less commonly shared by all members of a culture, hence a pattern of enculturation, hence a common history.

This helps to explain why the quest for national identity was histor-

ically delayed until the eighteenth century. The very notion of a 'character' common to all nationals could not easily have dawned in earlier ages
marked by tremendous internal diversities of speech, religion and culture.
And then France's cultural domination of Europe furnished the spur, for
non-French intellectuals would not otherwise have bothered with their
nations' supposed identities save in the conditions of cultural disorienta-
tion and identity crisis which this brought on. In turn, this explains why
the English National Identity was a product formed in an anti-French
mold, and why in the Victorian Age it bore all over it the residual marks
of this foundry work. The National Identity had become increasingly definite and glorious in the English mind just as the vision of the French
Character had become more abhorrent, for the one myth was projected
against the other, the self-glorifying national abstraction against the horrid foreign counter-abstraction. Houghton brilliantly hits the mark with
his suggestion, thrown out as a mere aside in one of his voluminous foot-
notes, that the supposed greatness of the Victorian character rested on
comparisons with "what existed in France."[1] Here is the key to the Victorians' visceral revulsion against everything 'French,' for each Englishman's self-concept, partly shaped in this national mold (this
conception of what it meant to be English), was partly formed then from
this earlier anti-French foundry work. To be truly English was to live up
to a stereotype generated in anti-Frenchness.

This points again to the all-important role of the literati in shaping
nationalist ideology. For the concept of national identity, though presented as a finished product to *der Volk* as if it were a simple distillation of
characteristics deeply embedded in all true countrymen, is originally simply an artistic projection, an image deliberately fashioned by a single
group in the age of 'Stirrings' and national awakening. Qualities *chosen* by
frustrated intellectuals are projected as *national* traits. As Meinecke
quaintly puts it,

> Within the nation itself different concepts of the nation come into conflict
> with each other, and each of them alone claims to represent the nation truly
> and properly. . . . Part of the nation unselfconsciously and sincerely regards
> itself as the core and essence of the entire nation . . . the ideal image of the
> nation is always the mirror of what stirs in individual souls.[2]

This passage, it will be seen, carries us a step further. The image of the
national group is not only a partial image, moulded by intellectuals, but
very largely a *mirror* image of those intellectuals as they saw themselves
and wished themselves to be. The tendency is apparent in many movements besides the German. The early poets of New Zealand took up "the
burden of [New Zealand's] national identity . . . not out of patriotic piety,
but out of [their] own search for self-definition." Rankling under the public neglect of their poetry, attacking their country's cultural bondage to
England and America, relating their own literary insignificance to New
Zealand's, and reaching out to local landscape, wildlife, and native myths,
these alienated writers took up a twofold "self-definition of a poet" and

quest for "a distinctive mode of national poetry," a simultaneous "definition of self and country" which ultimately resulted, of course, in a vindication and glorification of both.[3] This was the classic pattern, an independent retracing of the pathway taken first in eighteenth-century England: the bardic anxiety and suffering, the obsession with problems of identity, the revolt against imitation, the sharpening eye for local scenery, the wrapping of the solitary self in martyr's robes of collective suffering and redemption, these have all since become familiar marks of nationalist literary development.

We see then that the national image is an idealized projection of traits selected by writers in their interconnected effort to reject the alien culture and thus 'find' both their own culture and themselves, to *identify* the basic qualities of the national soul (especially manifest in the national literary heritage) and *realize* these in their own works of art. The projected identity of the entire group is thus in its origins the product of an inward literary quest which is simultaneously psychological, cultural, and historical; it is the product of a confused and introspective search by the anxious, unhappy, sensitive and intellectual few to establish ('discover') a pattern of values by which everyone, and preeminently themselves, may attain identity, hence autonomy, freedom and power.

This helps to explain how the concept of national identity, once it is widely distributed throughout the nation, functions not only as a *description* but, in view of the prestige it fraudulently enjoys as the archetype of all national character, as a *mythic ideal* of personal and collective redemption (or regeneration, as the nationalist mentality would have it). "The nation is invoked," explains Talmon, "as vessel of redemption for the individual no less than for society." The propagandist—to peep behind the curtain at him—in effect beckons everyone to follow him in *realizing* the national character. Hence it is no wonder that English literary historians, discovering an increasing frequency of "communal personifications" in eighteenth-century poetry, characterize the whole poetic evolution as one that began (in the Augustan Age) with the poet as anonymous speaker and ended with him playing (in the Romantic Age) the communal utopian guru, "a prophet whose myth," as Siskin puts it, "is not of actual community but of what community might be." Butt observes that "a lost and irrecoverable Eden" is the underlying theme of much later eighteenth-century poetry, while Frye similarly writes that the centrally defining feature of Romantic poetry proper (circa 1790–1820) is a "redemption myth," a myth of the "recovery of original identity."[4] Again we see the earmarks of the maturing nationalist movement.

Of much more importance to political and social historians, however, is the popular impact of this activity, the fact that the concept of national identity, once it has gained credibility with the nation at large, becomes an object of mass personal identification, hence an extremely powerful vehicle of moral change and social transformation. In essence it becomes a 'role model' for the whole community. Like some secular Benedictine Rule, the National Identity shapes character and thus history. Meinecke

caught the passion in this process as he outlined Germany's critical transition from the eighteenth century to the nineteenth. This represented, he
wrote, a process of mass consciousness-raising in which the "ideal and
abstract concept of the national personality" became merged with "the
individual personality and its sphere of life" in such a way as to furnish
"the common factor in these individual wills," in this way bringing individuals to a consciousness of the nation's potential greatness and flooding
them with "an intense longing for national realization," a longing that "is
not satisfied until everything is nationalized that is at all capable of nationalization."[5] What this means (to de-Hegelianize it a bit) is simply that
the individual identifies himself with what he has been taught to believe is
the Character of his nation, that through this he instills in himself traits
which he then shares with others similarly sensitized, and also that
through this identification he acquires passionate motivations joining his
own personal endeavors to a dream of national fulfillment.

We come then to the processes of popular education. The concept of
national identity is propagated not only in poetry—though this medium,
uniquely given to symbolic representation, is often of major importance—
but in an immense variety of literary, artistic and educational processes.
For example, Barzun shows how its elaboration entails the launching of
an age of national literary hero-worship in which the great authors of the
past—masters of the native tongue, hence specially attuned, it is believed,
to the national spirit—are revived, reappraised, and then presented as
"great figures which common opinion regards as embodying the soul or
spirit of a given people." The Geniuses and Heroes of the past are made
into exemplars of the National Identity, personifications of the National
Character. We note that here too the reign of George III strikingly con-
forms to the blueprint of nationalist take-off: this period marked the
ushering in of a new age of hero-worship which carried far into the nineteenth century and which saw not only the revival of national authors
such as Shakespeare and Milton, and the renewed glorification of other
ancestral figures such as Hampden and Sydney as new "patriot-symbols,"
but the continuous creation of new English heroes in such figures as Samuel Johnson and the Duke of Wellington—both distinguished in battles
against the French—in a process with very far-reaching effects. Charles
Churchill's 'Rosciad' (1761), which attacked the excessive admiration of
foreign models and together elevated "SHAKESPEARE and JOHNSON"
in the "patriot hope" to "make England great in Letters as in Arms,"
typified the beginnings of this multifarious process. The outcome in the
nineteenth century, promoted by several generations of increasingly insular and dogmatic propaganda in the works of such writers as Wordsworth, Hazlitt, and Carlyle, was typified in Macaulay's ridiculous but only
too characteristic assertion (1833) that the "higher use" of French literature was to publicize the profundity of Britain's: "The literature of
France has been to ours what Aaron was to Moses, the expositor of great
truths which would else have perished. . . . The great discoveries . . . are

ours . . . we found truth, but we did not impart it. France has been the interpreter between England and mankind."[6]

In sum, the innermost intellectual activity of the age of 'Stirrings' is the elaboration of an abstract National Character, a moral, intellectual and aesthetic personality with supposedly national traits. It is this extremely important creation which we must attempt to investigate here, this stylized phenomenon elaborated over and over in countless ways, not only through the representation of bygone Geniuses and Heroes but through pseudoscholarly study of the virtuous Ancient Race, invidious contrasts with symbolic Enemies, the iconographic delineation of the national personality in popular engravings and prints, and the representation of national virtues through the unending parade of virtuous characters in fictional, poetic and dramatic arts.

It is this mythic creation which stands as the central object of individual identifications with the group, the historic group with its glorious (though, it is alleged, forgotten and betrayed) past, its present claims upon individual volition, its mission toward future power and freedom. The National Identity derives its central functional importance in the dynamics of nationalism from the fact that it helps to overcome inherited particularistic loyalties (such as religious, political, and regional ones), replacing these with a mythic ideal of character which functions then to promote a real national community worthy of it—as Smith puts it, "to create the 'new man', healthy, vigorous and free." Moreover it is a mere truism of academic observation that the emergent national ideal, no matter in which country it is created and no matter what its specific attributes, is everywhere credited with general qualities of innocent simplicity and deep emotional responsiveness—moral qualities, essentially leveling ones, with built-in biases against existing manners and systems of education. The concept of national identity, a creation of frustrated writers, is an archetype of simple morality and humble social class; it subtly conveys not only the supposedly distinctive moral virtues of the citizen but the moral fraternity of all the nation's countrymen downtrodden and oppressed. John Bright's belief (1858) that "the nation in every country dwells in the cottage"[7] had a long and complicated history behind it, enacted no less in Bright's own Rochdale than in Berlin and Dublin and Auckland.

2. THE RISE OF 'SINCERITY'

The English quest for National Identity began around 1750 and was substantially complete by 1830. What evidently happened was that the eighteenth-century literary concept of the 'Noble Savage,' originally used as a stalking-horse in the man-in-general social criticism of the early Enlightenment, was gradually nationalized and parochialized by the literati and hence made the noble bearer of values supposedly distinctively English. 'Sincerity' was the name given to this manufactured national ideal.

Literary scholars have glimpsed aspects of this momentous work without fully appreciating its tremendous significance. Guilhamet begins his excellent book on what he calls 'The Sincere Ideal' in English poetics with the statement that "shortly after 1750 in England the curious notion that poetry ought to be written with a personal sincerity began to afflict the common reader, poets, and even critics, on a relatively wide scale." Noting that this was linked to the resurrection of the great authors of the past—Shakespeare, Spenser, Chaucer, Milton—he points to the peculiar tendency to praise these authors not so much for their works as for *a morality* supposedly common to them—"not for their achievements in drama or epic, but for their spontaneity or originality"—that is, for the virtue of 'Sincerity,' which connoted a certain untutored purity of both moral intention and artistic expression. He finds that this Sincerity was increasingly treated in the latter half of the century as a distinctively English possession, "worn as the badge of a superior culture." "England is associated with every sincere and genuine emotion, while France receives . . . castigation for servility and guile. . . . Indeed, France and her allies are military and moral threats to all the virtues which compose the sincere ideal."[8]

Others, working further down the line, encounter the same phenomenon. McKillop describes the rise of "an archetype of simple virtue which was widely accepted and richly elaborated," finding this to have been generated in the growth of artistic feelings of "local attachment"—of an aesthetic nativism like that of the New Zealanders mentioned earlier. Fairchild takes it into the next century, suggesting that by the Romantic Era this archetype had become "the embodiment of a creed"—the heroic personification, then, of an ideology. Trilling, writing on the Victorians, maintains that by the mid-nineteenth century Sincerity was looked upon as "the English trait" par excellence. "The trait on which the English most prided themselves" was "their sincerity, by which they meant their single-minded relation to things, to each other, and to themselves." Both at home and abroad "there was widespread belief that England produced a moral type which made it unique among nations." Ralph Waldo Emerson expressed the general view:

> Emerson had no doubt that sincerity was the defining quality of the English character. In his *English Traits*, published in 1856, he recurs to it frequently and with vivacious admiration. Sincerity, he says, is the basis of the English national moral style. 'We will not have to do with a man in a mask,' he conceives the English to be saying. 'Let us know the truth. Draw a straight line, hit whom and where it will.' The English, Emerson tells us, are blunt in expressing what they think and they expect others to be no less so; their confidence in each other makes them unique among nations: 'English believes in English. The French feel the moral superiority of this probity.' And Emerson goes on to say that the superiority is not merely moral; the practical power of the English 'rests on their national sincerity'.[9]

What all this really means is that 'Sincerity' *was* the English National Identity, the specific pattern of values articulated at the heart of the whole ideological movement. What the literary scholars have detected is a tightly linked network of values which were firmly believed to be uniquely English, a pattern which was articulated in the later eighteenth century, amplified in the early nineteenth, and passed on to the Victorian Age as a sort of comprehensive code which affected not only the individual's image of himself but the attitudes and ethical relations of the English people in the mass both toward each other and toward the peoples of other nations.

It is no wonder that the literary scholars, sensing the tremendous importance of this 'Sincerity' but unequipped to deal with it as a mainspring of English cultural development, cast hints in that direction. Trilling, though he never mentions nationalism, writes that the Englishman's submission to the code of Sincerity led him towards "an uncompromising commitment to duty, a continuous concentration of the personal energies upon some impersonal end, the subordination of the self to some general good"—words strikingly reminiscent of George Eliot's encomium, quoted earlier, on how English 'national consciousness' affected each individual. Guilhamet comes still closer, at one point even suggesting that "the development of sincerity as an ideal and the intensification of British nationalism and imperialism were concurrent and complementary." He returns to this in his conclusion: "When I claim that sincerity and British nationalism were concurrent ideals, I assume that something as pervasive as a strong nationalism must have a coherent set of ideals to sustain it. Sincerity, in various forms, had such a sustaining effect."[10] This was a remarkable stroke for one chiefly engaged in scouting the pathways of odes, sonnets, and ballads.

3. What Did 'Sincerity' Mean?

Let us attempt to define the elements of this ambiguous concept—"the disparate elements," as Guilhamet calls them, of this Sincerity which (so he states in his conclusion) "remains by its very nature shifting and indefinable."[11] We cannot hope to complete the job in this book, but we can make a start at least by considering some five specific virtues which the propagandists clearly had in mind when elaborating the Sincerity of the English National Character.

i. innocence

Sincerity meant, first of all, artlessness, or innocence. The word sincere derives from the Latin *sincerus* and in its earliest English usages meant clean, sound, or pure. In early times it was applied more to things than to persons; a sincere wine was one that had not been adulterated. By Shakespeare's time it was applied to moral character as well, connoting an absence of dissimulation or pretence. Sincerity as a trait of character was thus a certain purity, an absence of artfulness or deception. But by the beginning of the nineteenth century the term suggested something larger than that, a virtue at the head of all the others, a moral innocence without which no other virtue could exist. "Sincerity," wrote William Godwin, "once introduced into the manners of mankind, would necessarily bring every other virtue in its train." George Walker wrote in a sermon of 1808 that sincerity "is not so much a distinct virtue of itself, as a general quality which gives a stamp, a value, and a very being to all the virtues."[12]

ii. honesty

Sincerity referred not only to moral character, the purity of the native self, but to the self's utterances; it referred to the self as subject as well as object. It referred to the voice of the self, and, as Trilling nicely puts it, to the degree of "congruence between avowal and natural feeling." In short, the word sincere meant 'honest' or 'truth-telling' or 'serious' in addition to 'pure' and 'innocent.' Wordsworth's conception of sincerity comprised both of these aspects in the ideas of "veracity, earnestness, integrity." Carlyle had in mind the latter, the expressive and subjective quality, when he wrote that "the excellence of Burns is . . . his *Sincerity,* his indisputable air of Truth. . . . The passion that is traced before us has glowed in a living heart."[13]

iii. originality

Sincerity also meant a certain gift of inspired creativity; of genius, or spontaneous originality. Guilhamet, as noted earlier, believes that the chief cause of the remarkably sudden rise of sincerity as an ideal was the importance it acquired in aesthetic discussion from around the middle of the eighteenth century on. In this context the word 'sincere' meant 'natural,' 'spontaneous,' and 'original'; terms which, of course, were directed against literary art, particularly poetry, that was condemned as 'contrived,' 'artful,' 'imitative.' Guilhamet rightly notes that sincerity figured here as both an ideal and a polemical battering ram against the caricatured "anti-ideal" of Gallic neoclassicism; earlier we noted Leslie Stephen's shrewd observations on the same process. It was thanks to this that Wordsworth, by the beginning of the nineteenth century, was able to think of sincere poetry as expressive of creative originality, "the spontaneous overflow of powerful feelings." As the result of decades of critical discussion—for there was much to be said in favor of learned imitation in the classical style, and against giving full rein to the untutored voice of the self—a revolution in English aesthetics was accomplished, by which sincerity, meaning originality as well as purity and honesty, became "the *sine qua non,*" as Abrams puts it, "of excellence in poetry."[14] We may note that in this process the literati gradually elevated a concept which not only flattered English authors immensely but excluded 'imitative' and 'artful' France from all possibility of literary (not to mention moral) greatness. It was this same overblown concept which Macaulay treated as a received truth in the 1830s when he vaunted English profundity and complacently described French literature as a water boy called to carry this to mankind.

iv. frankness

The moral, expressive and aesthetic aspects of sincerity implied a certain distinctive quality in manners, namely a frankness and courageous forthrightness of address. Sterne taught that we learn "by observing the address and arts of man to conceive what *is sincere*." Godwin wrote that "Sincerity, a generous and intrepid frankness, will still be found to occupy perhaps the first place in the catalogue of human virtues." The same suggestion of a characteristic manner appears in this from Carlyle: "Let a man but speak forth with genuine earnestness the thought, the emotion, the actual condition of his own heart."[15] The pure moral state of the heart is not only expressed honestly and spontaneously but *spoken forth* frankly to the world.

Now it should be noted that frankness may act as a powerful solvent upon social conventions. An assertive frankness, hostile to formalities, will often have the effect of leveling social interaction and reducing much of it to the plane of egalitarian exchange. The eighteenth-century writers understood this well enough, and many of them shared a growing taste for direct expression 'from the heart.' "I hate formality and compliments," wrote Wollstonecraft, for these had "nothing to say to the heart." English sincerity, 'a generous and intrepid frankness' speaking *to* the heart (the Sincerity) of the other party, could only work like acid upon the ornate system of 'politeness,' i.e., of heirarchy-supporting manners, which, as we have noted, was still being extended in the fifties and sixties even while the ethic of sincerity was being generated against it. Of course the brew was strengthened by maintaining that the one was intrinsically 'French,' the other 'English.' Foote makes one of his characters comment approvingly on the forthright speech of another: "Spoke with the sincerity of a Briton." To this he contrasts the insincere behavior of the frenchified Buck on preparing to receive his former English friends: "They say, forms keep fools at a distance. I'll receive 'em *en cérémonie*."[16]

v. moral independence

Sincerity meant, in addition, a personal style of moral independence and self-reliance. As the frank manner associated with it implies, sincerity meant a certain directness not only of speech and address but of opinion and action, logically based on a conception of behavior consistently related to inward standards of purity and honesty. Richard Hurd, in an essay of 1759, makes one of his characters follow the "road of Sincerity. . . . I, in the simplicity of my heart . . . resolving, as I did, to hold my principles, and follow my judgment, I fell into . . . unhappy circumstances."[17] A truly sincere man was morally independent, unafraid to oppose the opinions, styles, ceremonies and inhibitions imposed by society if these did not square with his inner sense of what was right. The sincere man always preferred what was *right* to what was *approved* when the two were at odds.

There was thus a certain rude iconoclasm implicit in the sincere style, a certain assertive consciousness of the independence of the self in the face of received rules and opinions. The sincerer writers of the early eighteenth century, working in an age still hostile to such subjective values (which at that time were regarded as impertinent and antisocial), often experienced their own sincerity as a social liability. Jonathan Richardson wrote: "We talk and look as if sincere,/But woe be to us if we are." Edward Young complained that "The world's all face; the man who shows his heart/Is hooted for his nudities, and scorn'd." A cultural turning point at mid-century may perhaps be inferred from a letter of 1751 in which the poet William Shenstone described to an acquaintance an embarrassing social encounter which, he wrote, "threw me under a Necessity of offending either against the *Rules* of Politeness, or (what are more sacred with me) the *Laws* of Sincerity." Shenstone decided to act by reference to himself, rejecting conventional courtesy and the forms of the world on the strength of what he felt to be a superior mandate from within. Following the guide of Sincerity, he acted independently. One of the things that may have emboldened him to do so was the fact that this was the decade of the 1750s in which the novelist Samuel Richardson was also preaching the virtues of the sincere man who "lives to himself, and to his own heart, rather than to the opinion of the world." At the same time, Richardson's Swiss admirer, Rousseau, was extolling the same moral independence in the noble savage: "The savage lives within himself," Rousseau approvingly wrote in his *Second Discourse* (1754); "the sociable man knows how to live only in the opinion of others, and it is, so to speak, from their judgment alone that he draws the sentiment of his own being."[18]

Among literary men the challenge to 'live to oneself, and to one's own heart' was sharpened in the third quarter of the century by the gathering revolt against aesthetic conventions and rules, a revolt which, as Guilhamet describes it, the poet experienced as a "conflict between the formal qualities of poetry and the 'real' self of the poet." Early symptoms of this revolt may be discerned in another of Shenstone's letters (1748) in which the poet defends his writing on "so *low* a subject" as the village schoolmistress, yet sheepishly explains how he sought to escape ridicule for doing so "by *pretending to simper* all the time I was writing." True poetic creativity, it was increasingly believed, emerged from the unmasking of personal feelings; it emerged from a conscious nurturing of the moral and intellectual independence of the artist. The task of the poet, as Thomas Gray began to see it, was "to cultivate the native flowers of the soul, & not introduce the exoticks of another climate." But rules and conventions were themselves 'exoticks,' and hence Gray was led to the still more radical assertion that "rules are but chains, good for little, except when one can break through them."[19]

Thus there was spreading a subversive idea, in its implications not limited to aesthetic philosophy, that conventions were by their very nature chains upon sincerity, chains upon the heart. John More, a minor critic, wrote approvingly in 1777 that "all moderation is at an end, whenever the heart breaks loose." Cowper nourished a conception of spiritual independence (sincerity) so radical that he saw every species of literary imitation as a form of servility: "Imitation, even of the best models, is my aversion; it is servile and mechanical." It was this same sincerity, not as innocence, honesty, originality, or frankness, but as spiritual independence, to which Wordsworth appealed at the end of the century when he enjoined the reader of *Lyrical Ballads* to "decide by his own feelings genuinely, and not by reflection upon what will probably be the judgment of others." It was this same quality which George Walker had in mind when in 1808 he characterized "the sincere man" as one "who has a constant sense of what is decent, right and just, and in all the delicate actions of his life scorns on whatever account to turn aside from his upright path."[20] In this confident dogmatism one may measure something of the remarkable success in English opinion of the ideal of sincerity since those decades much earlier when a sincere man was 'hooted for his nudities, and scorn'd.'

4. SINCERITY PERSONIFIED

By this time the reader will have noted that these five characteristics—innocence, honesty, originality, frankness, and moral self-reliance—constitute not only a psychological profile but the outlines of an heroic personality. What we have here, in silhouette, is the National Identity itself, a mythic collective personality with distinct ethnic and social referents. The above 'English traits,' so often discussed *as* traits in aesthetic and moral writings, were frequently *personified* in more popular channels of expression—poetic, fictional, dramatic, iconographic, and so on. In fact we have encountered this mythic personification many times already in this book without taking notice of it. It makes its appearance through the innocence, gravity, plainness and impulsive righteousness of Fielding's 'poor Horatio'—that is, through the representation of poor Horatio himself, Horatio with tags of Englishness all over him, as a personality. It manifests itself through the forthrightness and moral independence of Smollett's Stentor Stile, the beef-eating scourge of his 'bedizened and bedaubed and transmogrified' countrymen in Paris. It was etched and re-etched into the public mind through prints, criticism, historiography, and the dramatic arts: through the innocence, virtue and honesty of Britannia; through the wonderful primitive sincerity, honesty and boldness of the ancient Britons and Goths (so foully oppressed by the Normans); through the innocence, indignation and forthright action of Foote's Lucinda, and the 'ancient roughness' and 'native spirit,' the 'native plainness, and honest hearts' of those ancestral Britannic forebears whom Foote summoned to stand beside her in scornful rejection of the manifold insincerity attributed to France: 'Trulls, toupées, trinkets, bags, brocades, and lace; A flaunting form, and a fictitious face.'

Many other representations could be listed. David Garrick had the same mythic personality in mind when he contrasted the truly "superior beings" of yesteryear to those alien lordships of his own time—"They bore a race of mortals stout and bony,/And never heard the name of Macaroni." Hurd's essay of 1759 projects an entire pattern of 'Sincere' personality in which the key traits are simplicity, honesty, plain dealing, and courageous independence, as opposed to malicious hypocrisy, sycophancy, dissimulation, and *"accommodation"* (i.e., the spirit of worldly "INSINCERITY"). In poetry, Shenstone had the same mythic personality in mind when he vaunted (as he so often did) the "lov'd rusticity" of early England and the much-to-be-admired qualities of "our bold fathers," every one of them a paragon of sincere virtue. In actual fact, as Shenstone reluctantly acknowledged, this race of paragons painted their bottoms with berry juice, wore beads round their necks, and openly indulged in acts of fishing, using artificial lures; but apart from these sorry practices of deception they were ever so sincere in every way. "Sincere themselves, ah too secure to find/The common bosom, like their own, sincere!"[21]

As to the novel of the later eighteenth century, the sincere type abounds in it. Primrose, Goldsmith's vicar of Wakefield, is an early example. A later one is Day's Harry Sandford, whose key traits of personality—innocence, honesty, natural genius, firmness, and love of independence—were detailed earlier (Chapter Five). The novels of Henry Brooke, Frances Sheridan, Richard Cumberland, and S. J. Pratt project much the same stereotype. The hero of Smollett's last and most popular novel, *The Expedition of Humphry Clinker* (1771), is a very fair representation of it.

Having considered Smollett's outlook some twenty years earlier in *Ferdinand Count Fathom* (1753), let us glance briefly at the new plebeian hero in his hands. Clinker is a man of "great simplicity of heart," "simplicity of character," says Smollett: just the man, we see, to confront the present age which has "degenerated to a total extinction of honesty and candour," an age in which "the human soul will be generally found most defective in the article of candour" (sincerity): "we are all a pack of venal and corrupted rascals," cries the despairing Bramble (Smollett's alter ego), "so lost to all sense of honesty, and all tenderness of character, that, in a little time, I am fully persuaded, nothing will be infamous but virtue and public-spirit." But Clinker is our man. Though he is poor and awkward, Bramble takes him on as servant. He soon discovers that Clinker is not only pure but uniquely gifted—"Clinker, who is a surprising compound of genius and simplicity"; in his own way a baby Shakespeare. (Macaulay's race of brainy immortals heaves one inch more into view.) Clinker is so infectiously pure of heart that by his example he becomes "a reformer in the family," ready "to preach and to teach" beyond the family as well. He is, like Harry Sandford, pure, honest, an original genius, forthright, and morally independent; and of course he is ever humbly devoted to the sincere ideal. After he discovers that he is the natural son of Bramble, he adjures his betrothed, the equally simple Win Jenkins, to remind him, if he should ever become proud, of his lowly origins, "nursed in a parish workhouse, and bred in a smithy."[22]

The mythic personality is developed not only positively through such materials but also negatively, through anti-French contrasts. Clinker's rival, not for the hand of Jenkins but for her virginity, is the crafty and altogether frenchified English valet, Dutton, "an exceeding cox-comb, fresh from his travels. . . . The fellow wears a solitaire, uses paint, and takes rappee with all the grimace of a French marquis." Smollett tips his hand, showing the mechanics of his symbolism, as he introduces Dutton: "If I am not much deceived by appearance, he is, in all respects, the very contrast of Humphry Clinker."[23]

Dutton, like Day's abominable Mash, is the anti-type of the true Briton. He is the embodiment of Insincerity—of impurity, falseness, imitativeness, obsequiousness, and moral vassalage to Fashion. This established, the man—"the traitor," as Smollett artfully calls him, always working the subterranean levers of association—then half-seduces poor vain Win out of her own character (every instrument of this conquest bears the stamp 'Made in Paris') and thus (again the serpentine imagery of seduction) "imperceptibly wound himself into her good graces." But the Britannic Clinker at last gives his anti-ideal a proper cudgeling and drives him out of the story, much as Lismahago, another of Smollett's primitive originals (a Scotsman), later settles a very similar clash in values by tremendous violence upon the French valet of Oxmington (a cowardly and insolent English lord), and as Bramble himself (a Welshman) conducts a wholesale "reformation" of the life of Baynard, ruined by his relatives who figure in precisely the same way as symbolic Anglo-French aliens.[24]

A large-scale projection of the same basic polarity in values, crystallized so neatly in oppositions between sincere Britons and frenchified 'traitors,' forms the larger structure of the novel itself, which through Bramble's excursions permits Smollett to descant on virtually every aspect of "this degenerate age" of 1771, this "vile world of fraud and sophistication" in which everyone is so mindlessly "infected" with the "rage of displaying their importanece"—"the whole nation seems to be running out of their wits"; an age of "false taste, false appetite, false wants," taking its lead from the "monster Bath" and from that "misshapen and monstrous capital," London, where ladies of "the *bon ton*" reigned, where that "ridiculous ape," that "ape in politics" the Duke of Newcastle held his levees, and where "every clerk, apprentice, and even waiter" assumed "the air and apparel of a petit maître." Against all this, the virginal Clinker shines as the representative of true native virtue. At the novel's end he marries Jenkins in a group wedding which symbolically links all the sympathetic characters, English, Scotch and Welsh, in ceremonies "according to the antient Britons."[25] Smollett's last work was thus a benedictory farewell to all his British countrymen. In it he not only pounded away, as before, at the Quality and at Fashion, but hailed that extended world of the *Volk* which in following decades writers like Day and Cowper, Burns and Blake and Wordsworth, were to treat more appreciatively even than he.

Perhaps one may be permitted to digress just a little further in this discussion of the National Identity's elaboration and transmission. It is

instructive to note that very much the same framework of characterizations and symbolic oppositions holds together Fanny Burney's very popular *Evelina* (1778). The point is significant in itself, as it helps to show
again the great breadth of the intellectual movement with with which we
are dealing here. *Clinker* was the last work of a cantankerous, funny,
coarse, opinionated, Scotch sailor-surgeon and man of letters; it was published in the year of his death. *Evelina* was the first novel of a young,
demure, and comfortably situated daughter of a noted London musicologist, a woman moreover who doted on that "Pythagoras," Dr.
Johnson, whom Smollett so scornfully lampooned in *Clinker*. Burney is
noted for her portrayals of London society, Smollett for his caricatures of
eccentrics met along the road. In all outward respects this pair had little
in common. Indeed it may also be mentioned that neither of these bore
much outward resemblance to the authors of some of the other works we
have touched upon—the bantering and wisecracking Foote, the severe
Day, the lovable Goldsmith, the antiquarian and scholarly Hurd, the with-
drawn and aesthetic Shenstone, slave to his gardens in Shropshire. And
all of these were second-rank authors, with the exceptions of Smollett and
Goldsmith—hardly considered to be of the same 'circle.' But it is not at all
a literary circle that we are considering, not even a 'school' or extended
group, but rather the great mass of contemporary intellectuals, sharing by
the seventies both a general state of consciousness and an increasingly
comprehensive yet focused system of ideas; even though, as is natural,
with significant differences in approach, emphasis, and tone.

How small these were may be studied by a comparative reading of
Evelina. Considered as an instrument in the molding of cultural values,
the book's mechanisms are all familiar already. Here beneath the text of
action and incident is the familiar subtext of nationalist ideology, a structure consisting basically of two opposed networks of national-social-moral
valuation, each identified with the various characters by a multiplicity of
family-linked cultural cues ('the dumb rhetoric of the scenery'); dual networks of value which, as activated in the evolution of the plot, involve the
emotions of the English reader in the perilous vicissitudes and at last the
final triumph of what is English-sincere-good over its enemy, what is
frenchified-insincere-corrupting.

The chief object of identification is the heroine, Evelina. She is, like
Clinker, the very personification of Sincerity. She is "young, artless, and
inexperienced," the "offspring of Nature, and of Nature in her simplest
attire," of "obscure birth" but "with a virtuous mind, a cultivated understanding," significantly no less capable of "fortitude and firmness" than of
"gentleness and modesty"; the very enactment and human realization of
"artless openness," "ingenuous simplicity," the "guileless and innocent
soul," incessantly praised by her humble and virtuous gaurdian, Villars
(Burney's rural sage), for "thy singleness of heart, thy guileless sincerity!"[26]

And what does this virtuous ingénue discover in the nation's capital
and in its watering places? "What a world is this we live in! how corrupt!

how degenerate!" And what is the source of this? Paris looms as a mysterious power that holds Evelina and even England itself in its grip. On the first level, it is the source of sin, danger and anxiety: it is the site of the events leading to the tragic ruin of Evelina's mother, it is the permanent residence of her profligate and francophile father, Belmont, it is the place where the ultimate decision about her fortune and identity as Belmont's daughter will be decided, and it is the adopted residence of her dreadful maternal grandmother Madame Duval, a combative Francophile ("it was difficult to discover whether she was an English or a French woman") who maneuvers to get Evelina into her clutches so as to take her back to Paris and revamp her education (overthrow her guileless English sincerity, which to Duval is her *"bumpkinish air"*), and thus make of her a "woman of fashion," a horrid "woman of quality" just like herself.[27] Thus Paris figures in the heroine's life as the oozing spring of a strange but lethal charm, especially deadly to 'persons of fashion,' which has captivated, addicted, and destroyed or made cultural turncoats of her own English relatives, and which threatens her too with a fate worse than death, namely the erasure of her sincere English identity and transformation into that transvestic condition of frenchified Qualityhood which was the dreaded bugbear of the English literary mind.

On the other level, much as in Smollett's *Clinker,* we find an enormous backdrop cut from the same cloth, implying the same threat not to Evelina (England personified) but to the moral fabric of the nation itself. The two key figures here are Mirvan, a sea captain and pattern John Bull who has a fixed hatred of "whatever is not English," and the supercilious and lecherous Lovel, his complete antithesis, the pattern London man of fashion, a leering and sneering clotheshorse who is pleased to "lead the *ton* in the *beau monde."* Through Mirvan's incessant denunciations of the frenchification of English society the contemporary reader was educated to fear how all-consuming this process had supposedly been during his lifetime. Mirvan's uncontrollable agitation on this subject informs his every word and deed, establishing throughout the book a line of ferociously nativist opinion. London is a disgusting nest of denatured Englishmen so appalling that "I knew no more what to do with myself, than if my ship's company had been metamorphosed into Frenchmen. . . . I'm almost as much ashamed of my countrymen, as if I was a Frenchman, and I believe in my heart there i'n't a pin to chuse between them; and, before long, we shall hear the very sailors talking that lingo, and see never a swabber without a bag and a sword."[28]

The English Quality were supposedly behind all this. The idea is registered in many ways, most frequently in Mirvan's explicit identifications of this class with the French (and of both of them with monkeys and the devil) in the course of his unending attacks on Madame Duval ("Go to the devil together, for that's the fittest voyage for the French and the quality . . . you and the quality may have the devil all to yourselves"); and, similarly, in his attacks on Lovel, whom, like Madame Duval, he insults throughout the book, then bloodily assaults in its climactic scene. This important scene, rather like Clinker's fight with Dutton and even more like Harry's with Mash, turns symbolically on the supposed resemblance between the man of fashion and the monkey—"*Monseer* Longtail," a monkey "full-dressed and extravagantly *à-la-mode*." "Odds my life," declares Mirvan, "if it was n't for this here tail, you wouldn't know one from t'other."[29] To study only this one scene identifying Lovel with his simian "twin-brother" is to see how extraordinarily useful to the nationalist philosophy was the symbol of the ape, which at one stroke greatly simplified the task, logically always the toughest even in the dream logic of the nationalist argument, of pinning the English man of quality both to France as his spiritual homeland and to imitativeness (Insincerity) as his fatal flaw.

But the reader may ask whether *Evelina*, considered as propaganda, can really be said to have recommended the unreservedly anti-French and anti-aristocratic hostility so consistently advanced through the attitudes of Mirvan. A distinction does need to be drawn, but it is only one of degree. It is true that Evelina does eventually marry an English nobleman, one who in fact at one isolated point evinces what Burney very guardedly calls "his approbation" of Paris.[30] Burney's point of view is neither so unqualifiedly gallophobic as Smollett's nor so idealistically democratic as Day's. She distances herself somewhat from the former by treating Dubois (the novel's only real Frenchman) with mild sympathy; and she shows herself a bit of a snob through Evelina's reactions to the vulgar Branghton family and through other small touches.

But this, though it shows that Burney was not wholly immune from either the lingering Francocentric cosmopolitanism of the age or the snobbery of the middle classes, is rather beside the point. Neither Smollett nor Day was totally immune from these influences either. The point is not that Burney utterly loathed the French themselves (indeed she later, in 1793, married a French refugee), but that she instructed her readers in detestation of the Quality. The point is not that the book preaches beneath its surface a flaming democratic nationalism but that it preaches something just a little short of that and logically as well as historically anterior to it, a leveling contempt for the abilities, tastes and morality of the rulers of England as an *alien class*, together with the legendary account of the dreadful cultural crisis into which this class had supposedly led the country. A careful reading of this work of 1778 leaves little doubt that Burney, though a sophisticated twenty-five-year-old Londoner when she wrote it, herself believed in the horrible, creeping frenchification of English life which the apoplectic Mirvan decries, and that she saw this primarily as the work of a viciously self-seeking, arrogant, and frenchified 'race' of English aristocrats.

Particularly significant here is the language surrounding Lord Orville, the unbelievable man-of-marble paragon whom Evelina at last marries. Burney distinguishes him sharply from his family, friends, and all the rest of the misnamed Quality, preening themselves as Lovel does upon their superior style of life—"our customs, our manners, and *les etiquettes de nous autres."* When Evelina falls in love with him she sees him (the italics are in the original) as "a *being superior to his race*," and when she misunderstands him she decides that his actions have "levelled him with the rest of his imperfect race."[31] Through her reactions to this selfish, cold, libertine, gambling, frivolous, French-spouting, and above all arrogant 'race,' a powerful attack is mounted, more subtle but no less persistent than that of the bellicose Mirvan, upon the alien beings at the top.

And then of course, to return to the original point, the sincere character of Evelina herself, like those of Clinker and Sandford, is a standing reproach to this alien 'race.' One sees Burney expressing her own feelings as well as shaping the social resentments of her readers through the heroine's accounts of her dealings with the Ton: "Altogether, I feel extremely uncomfortable in finding myself considered in a light very inferior to the rest of the company"; "I knew not, till now, how requisite are birth and fortune to the attainment of respect and civility."[32]

But we have little space here for further illustrations; the imaginative literature of the seventies and eighties simply teems with personifications of English Sincerity. Indeed Guilhamet at one point rightly observes that "sincerity and its related virtues" constituted "an ideal of behavior, complex and coherent," and at another he characterizes it as "a complex self-righteousness similar to that of the Puritans"—a *personality*, that is, which is precisely the point that needs to be understood here.[33] Sincerity meant not just a single trait nor even just a collection of them but a composite personality which supposedly was 'given' in the nation's past and which allegedly still belonged in some immanent way to its simpler inhabitants.

5. Countercultural Revolution

How then did this myth function in the culturally divided reign of George III? The answer is that it functioned as the shaping agent of a rapidly spreading counterculture guided by the intellectuals. On the one hand, as the reader will have noted, Sincerity represented not only a positive ideal but a rejection of everything meant by its opposite. Much of the evidence discussed earlier reveals this duality; Hurd's essay of 1759, contrasting 'SINCERITY' with 'INSINCERITY' as two opposed systems, illustrates the point. The whole literature of sincerity may be thought of as a continuous polemic against what was felt to be the manifold insincerity of the age: pollution of moral character, dishonesty in expression, imitativeness, sycophancy, and toadeating '*accommodation*,' as Hurd contemptuously put it, in all the 'Commerce of the World.' The besetting moral evil of the time was seen as *falsity*—that predominance of 'face' over 'heart' decried by Young, that 'total extinction of honesty and candour' denounced by Smollet, that horrifying excess of 'guile' and 'deceit' and 'dissimulation' whose condemnation figures so centrally throughout the literature of the period.

To the literary analysts this obsession with falsity has presented a very great mystery. But this is only natural, since the problem is not really one of literary interpretation but of historical psychology, dependent there-fore upon historical interpretation. What it boils down to is this, that what was felt to be the root moral evil of the age was the near universality of 'mimicry'—of pretence and dissimulation and purely imitative behavior. The attack on falsity bespoke an angry consciousness of the *fictitiousness of the social self*.

Now we all know that such a consciousness may exist in other climes than later eighteenth-century Europe. Such a consciousness is to some extent simply a fact of life in highly organized societies, a result of the circumstance that man, to succeed, must adopt many imitative poses even while realizing that *he* is not *this*, not what he pretends to be. To Lord Chesterfield, who believed that politeness was primarily the art of adapt-ing oneself to one's company, such behavior was the essence of good man-ners: "When you go into good company (by good company is meant the people of the first fashion of the place) observe carefully their turn, their manners, their address; and conform your own to them"; "a man of the world must, like the Cameleon, be able to take every different hue; which is . . . but a necessary complaisance; for it relates only to manners and not to morals." Such was the eighteenth-century code of politeness, and the code too of 'eligibility'—"the Chesterfieldian code of success," as one of the earl's biographers remarks.[34]

But of course the same behavior may be seen in a very different light, as 'soulless' duplicity and opportunism. Which of us living even now, two hundred years later in a far more egalitarian age, does not know some-one—a barber perhaps or a car salesman, or the fruit-and-vegetable man at the market—who by his deferential 'complaisance,' his flattery and syc-ophancy, seems to be the very negation of an independent being? Does he not experience a certain contradiction between this outer self, this social behavior which he enacts, and his own inner being? Which of us indeed has never known in his own mind the tension between these two selves, the pure inner one (which seems to us, as it were, given in Nature) with its integrity and independence, and the social outer one (given, it seems, by Society), 'bedaubed and bedizened' in layers of fictitiousness, tricked out to scale the cliffs of 'eligibility'?

But this imitativeness or insincerity or 'other-directedness' or excessive conformity or socially imposed dishonesty, whatever one cares to call it, was in some very special way felt by contemporaries to be the fundamen-tal moral ailment of their time. What is, to most of us in our permissive and individualistic age, only a matter of casual observation and private feeling, was in that age a subject of the deepest emotional concern and public outcry. How to explain this?

The English ideologue, as we noted, saw this falsity, this 'modern mo-rality,' as the result of alien influence. Unable to view it in grand historical perspective (as we are able to) as the last moulting of feudal society nearly overcome by commercial wealth, he reached out, just as we often do when confronted by the unintelligible, to his myths, and interpreted it as the creeping frenchification of English morality. Alarmed by the seeming disintegration of English life, he fished up explanations from the tangled inheritance of half-truths and myths by which people always try to make sense of changes too large for contemporary understanding. And were these not, all around him, French clothes, French accents, French manners and pretensions? Were these not French frills upon his own head and feet, and French contraptions upon his own aching natural knees? England's problems were France's fault.

We, however, know better. From our vantage point we can see that behind this 'Frenchness,' and indeed largely responsible for it, were, as has been shown throughout this book, profound historic realities which really had very little to do with the foreigner. The contemporary falsity or fictitiousness, the Insincerity condemned by the intellectuals, should actually be seen as the adaptive social ethics of an oligarchical society pushed by historical forces ever more towards the brink of excess; it was the mark of an unprecedented historical crisis dating from about 1750. What happened was that the walls of 'eligibility' were suddenly tilting more steeply, while those attempting to clamber up them were multiplying faster than ever. Mindless imitation and runaway conformity—again we recall the plaintive squeals of all those men 'from Wapping to Westminster' struggling about in their banyans in 1785—were the natural expression in social behavior of an oligarchic culture such as that matured in Britain by the middle of the century. As we saw earlier, the elite, threatened from below, increasingly resisted social mixing and instead sought to restrict power, opportunities and rewards to itself, and as part of this attempted in every way to underscore its own cultural supremacy. This in turn (since rewards, opportunities and 'eligibility' were limited) had the effect of setting off the craze of imitation.

It was this which, by filling the intellectuals with a growing consciousness of their own and of society's imposed hypocrisy, tripped off the thirst for honesty—for sincerity. Exactly the same thing was happening in France. Trilling comments that in France a burning concern for sincerity in the sense of personal authenticity, of a rejection of the fictitious selves imposed by organized social life, linked the writings of such authors as Rousseau and Diderot into an ethic which at last embraced Robespierre and the other zealots of the French Revolution in what Albert Mathiez called a "subjugating" and "profound sincerity," and Hannah Arendt, looking at it from the other side, called a compelling mission "to tear the mask of hypocrisy off the face of French society."[35] Exactly the same sense of inauthenticity, of moral self-betrayal and hence psychic self-contradiction even to the point of 'rage,' of schizophrenic madness, afflicted the English—some of them. A rising, a 'subjugating' ethic of sincerity figured in *both* France and England as the cultural response to an historic crisis essentially economic and social in origin.

Therefore, to consider the whole matter in its proper context as actually a great historical problem of European dimensions, the cult of Sincerity was triggered by the clash, in its intensity and popular breadth totally unprecedented in European history, between the rising claims of the increasingly prosperous and ambitious middle orders, and the anti-thetical efforts by the European elites to reassert their threatened domi-nance by underlining their cultural superiority, the uniqueness of their 'style of life'; an effort which in its outlandish affronts to common sen-sibility, its rapid drift towards an affected and globe-trotting cos-mopolitanism, and its inevitable tendency to 'infect' the 'whole nation' with the 'rage of displaying their importance'—' the whole nation seems to be running out of its wits'—an effort which, in its many 'ridiculous' and even 'bizarre' excesses, had the *unintended* effect of *overstraining* that very network of social imitation which was in each country the fundamental support of this continued aristocratic dominance, indeed its only ultimate guarantee. Social inferiors, confused by the outlandish drift of those very forms which hitherto had kept them more or less in attitudes of admiring submission, increasingly experienced the deferential behavior due to su-periors as a split between the integrity of the private or 'natural' self and the fictitiousness of the social self, the self in its increasingly gaudy and even elephantine dress of roles, conventions, disguises and conformities, straining ever towards that 'eligibility' claimed and infuriatingly monopo-lized by 'the circle of the people of Fascination.' It was at this point that the artist-intellectual, by turns confused, humiliated, depressed and en-raged by this very real cultural and psychological crisis, and certainly its most sensitive observer and *public interpreter*, stepped forth 'with a book in his hand and contempt in his heart' to articulate the yearnings that were felt by all sensible people beneath the one clearly perceived 'class' at the top. It was just here that, reading the cultural chaos as the result of alien influence and seeking his own 'natural' self in the midst of it, he began to invent and attribute to the folkish ancestors those very qualities which seemed most deficient in his own age (and in himself too, as was sug-gested in our examination of his neuroses), thus laying the groundwork for a revolution in values which would soon transform the history of Eu-rope, indeed the world.

Thus came the elaboration of National Identity. But why was this so very important? How did its elaboration meet and resolve this tremen-dous historic crisis? Look at it this way. Before the rise of nationalism, aristocrats were ordinarily the chief living exemplars of all that was Best: the class of 'superior men' who ran things was (as we saw in Chapter Two) regarded as the very personification of cultural value, of *Value-in-General*, 'world' value admitted throughout space and time, and it was through descending layers of social emulation that these superior men continued their ascendancy. But what if it were to be increasingly asserted, and be-fore long increasingly believed, that there was no true value at all but *local* value? This would put the 'superior men' at a great disadvantage by dis-crediting the cultural base of their authority (the Grand World Opera House in which they enacted their 'theater of greatness'), casting doubt on their loyalty to the group, erecting an alternative pattern of value—*our* Value—for all to admire and imitate, and resetting the stage in a brand new Opera House (call it Podsnap Hall) for the rise of an alternative elite better able to exemplify that pattern.

That is pretty much what happened in England. To consider it again in its psychological aspect, the acceptance of English Sincerity worked like the finding of a successful psychotherapy by a divided personality. We noted a profound tension, historically conditioned, between two aspects of the self, one given by Society and requiring conformity to standards endorsed by the World, the other given by private self-consciousness and prodded by a rebellious awareness of hypocrisy, of social make-believe and the abandonment of personal judgment and common sense. Sincerity stepped forth as a ministering angel to this inner psychic tension, on the one side facilitating rejection of the 'worldly' and 'Chesterfieldian' rules of society, on the other permitting, nay encouraging the individual to define himself against the newly minted pattern which—wondrous turning-point in history!—he was able to regard as *his own*—'his' by virtue of *national moral inheritance,* an inheritance which supposedly had been *bequeathed* to *him* by the brave Goths and Shakespeare and all his other illustrious ancestors in their state of 'natural simplicity' (hence ultimately bequeathed to him by God as well). *His* ancestry, *his* inheritance, was now a treasure above that of any mere Man of Quality—*denatured* by cosmopolitan taste, *disqualified* for cultural leadership by too many rutting expeditions to Paris and slimy platefuls of Neapolitan pasta. In sum, the rising prestige of the nation provided to the humble individual not only the 'role model' but the moral backing and social courage required to emancipate himself from Fashion and assert himself confidently as an individual of worth in his own right.

Naturally it was the artist-intellectual himself who first felt this call, his impulse being not only social but aesthetic and professional. For without sincerity, so it was increasingly believed, there could be no true originality, no 'genius'; and the merger of ideal with personality, or rather the integration of personality around the ideal, could probably be traced from the days of Shenstone (whose "life was an attempt to exemplify the sincere ideal") and Day (so terribly severe in his adherence to sincerity) down to those of Wordsworth, Blake (who regarded himself "as the rough honest character . . . called upon to . . . overcome the smooth rogueries of Jacob-like deceivers"), and Carlyle: "Sincerity was the chief measure of his hero, whether in the avatar of prophet, priest, or poet."[36]

Shenstone's turning from the 'Rules of Politeness' to the 'Laws of Sincerity' was paradigmatic. He became more confidently 'himself' just as he became more confidently 'English.' As the decades passed, each person faced essentially the same alternatives and made his own choice, a choice (to put it more sharply and abstractly, of course, than it was actually likely to be experienced) as to whether he would be governed by the rules of the World or by those supposedly inherited 'laws' of Englishness, inherited through the concept of national identity. We noted that Day, rejected by Elizabeth Sneyd, made a similar choice, in his own way swearing off *'pretending to simper.'* In short, then, for the individual the acceptance of Sincerity functioned as psychic therapy, a sort of 'conversion experience,' the dramatic resolution of a problem of torn identity and, behind that, of torn moral, intellectual and social allegiances. The age of cosmopolitanism was dying, and for unimportant people, indeed everyone but the Great, the promotion of the National Character was simultaneously a clarification and promotion of personal character. It was this which Meinecke attempted to capture in his idea of the 'merging' of 'the individual personality and its sphere of life' with the 'ideal and abstract concept of the national personality.'

But this points to a larger cultural and educational process in which the masses in their turn were also called upon to exemplify the national virtues, a process whose reality and power we seem entitled to infer from the broad historic realization of 'the Sincere Ideal' by mid-Victorian times. We cannot trace that gigantic process here, but there is one sort of evidence for it in the literature we have already studied. Much of this literature furnished for everyone exposed to it a comprehensive guide to sincere personal behavior, a textbook on what Day described as that 'difficult science' of distinguishing 'true' from 'artificial' superiority; a science which he then advanced throughout *Sandford and Merton* by teaching the 'truly English' attitude on clothes, music, dancing, manners, education, entertainments, foreign languages, and many other things. In effect, what he was doing here was developing within the nationalist ideology the specific rules which, when absorbed by his readers, would create among them precisely that same sort of 'we-consciousness,' that definite cultural style, facilitating in-group self-awareness and excluding 'truly' inferior outsiders (the Quality and those who aped them), which we detected earlier as marking off those very people at the top of the social scale, the Quality, from these very 'bumpkins,' 'Goths,' and 'barbarians' below. Just as cosmopolitanism provided the trump cards of status, solidarity and exclusion for the Ton, so the cultural style of English Sincerity, evident in attitude, manners, clothes, and tastes, emerged to perform the same function for their increasingly self-conscious and self-righteous opponents.

Thus considering English nationalism again as a social movement, we see that Sincerity functioned as nothing less than the vehicle of what was to become a profound social revolution, increasingly powerful as it gained supporters through processes of education and conversion like those suggested above. Its popular inculcation undermined the existing (Chesterfieldian) pattern of social interaction and the brand of polite and imitative ('insincere') morality which this favored, simultaneously building up in its place a countercultural morality promoting the integrity and assertive independence of the individual. Sincerity depicted the whole external system of valuation as 'false,' as 'artificial'; at the same time it asserted the legitimacy of a new *national* system based on far more egalitarian standards completely unrelated to the main existing indicators of status ('connoisseurship,' wealth, family ancestry, 'connexions,' etc.), standards based instead on attributes supposedly implanted in all the English or British people (innocence, honesty, frankness, originality, moral independence).

Sincerity thus revolutionized the social ethics inherited from the aristocratic past and laid the moral foundations of democracy. It struck at the social order, brought the great into disrepute, exalted the insignificant, and legitimized an overhaul by the patriotic bourgeoisie of the whole system of social authority. By the 1830s it had established a powerful alternative social code of its own, one which was to attain such dominance by the mid-Victorian age, and to impose such an extraordinarily powerful social discipline—surely unmatched by any other modern democracy, perhaps even any modern state save Germany and Japan in the 1930s—as to call down upon itself a characteristic if only partly effective counterattack a century after its rise: "The first duty in life," cried Oscar Wilde, "is to be as artificial as possible"; "man is least himself when he talks in his own person. Give him a mask and he will tell you the truth."[37]

6. THE ENGLISH NATIONAL IDENTITY ON THE EVE OF THE FRENCH REVOLUTION

By 1789 the concept of English National Identity was well established. Much had changed during the lifetime of Samuel Johnson, who entered print in the 1730s as an anonymous translator of French literature, and was laid to rest in 1784 as "the first literary character of a great nation."[38] We saw the concept of the national character emerging in the fifties amidst the cries of Johnson and Foote and others that 'we have lost all our ancient characteristic, and are become a bundle of contradictions.' A generation later, in the tide of the literary revolution, its outlines were clear enough for it to be an object of veneration and dogmatic assertion.

It would be hard to find a handier guide to this development than John Andrews's *Comparative View of the French and English Nations* (1785). The book's tendency may be judged from its portrayal of French vanity. The great besetting evil of French civilization was "the preposterous desire most individuals are tormented with to figure above their condition," a desire which led the Frenchman "to lay out almost all he is worth" for expensive apparel and other trinkets "in order to make a parade among his acquaintance." But this French evil was infectious: "of late years we have experienced a tincture of the same infatuation . . . it cannot be dissembled that they have imitators in other nations, and even among us." The disgusting "influence of Fashion over the French—their excessive admiration of exterior accomplishments" was something to be publicized in much detail. "Few individuals in France live for themselves, and can be said to follow the bent of their own inclinations." This imitative conformity was "as essential a difference as any subsisting in the character of the French, when compared with that of the English: no people acting more from pure, native, unrestrained impulse than we do, without inquiring about the ways of others; and no nation, on the other hand, more tamely submitting to the guidance of the mode, in every respect, than the French."[39]

Here was the forked tongue of Sincerity. But many of Andrews's comments reveal the continuing turmoil in domestic opinion over the meaning of Frenchness and the value to be attached to it. There was much misunderstanding on this subject just now. The French themselves, "undervaluing and insulting their neighbours," were "so given to arrogate an universal superiority over all nations . . . they would inculcate every where the persuasion that they . . . prescribe the laws of wit, elegance, taste, and knowledge, wherever they can be said to flourish." Unfortunately there were also many Britons "so enamoured of France and its inhabitants, as to forget the superior ties that bind them to their own nation," and so "profuse in its praises, as to prefer it to their own, even in those things wherein its inferiority is apparent." There were "numbers of our countrymen" who were "so far frenchified" as to endorse these French claims. Yet there were now such tidal waves of "national antipathy" developing, such a "torrent of contagious prejudice" flowing up in each country against the other, "that a considerable part of society is in the dark, respecting the real character of two nations, whose fame and proximity should render them no strangers to each other."[40]

Hence the timely importance of such a work as this, a book to help every modest Englishman, and some not so modest, attain a proper view. Did not the author condemn "a wanton, absurd hatred" between nations, invoke the "laws of humanity," and solicit faith in his own "impartiality" on at last half a dozen of his 488 pages? Was he not intimately conversant with how the French, all thirty millions of them, thought, felt, and behaved at all times? Did he not give them their due? Their gaiety, politeness, education, literature, the attention they paid to women, and especially the superior respect they paid to literary men, all received praise, though often backhanded. But (warming to the task) "the errors, faults, and vices of a people, ought, indeed, never to be spared."[41]

The protracted discussions which fill the book make it clear that the French Character was the very antithesis of the English. The French were *impure* in moral character: "gallantry" was "a field wherein a Frenchman delights to expatiate," while France was "indisputably the native soil" of such impurity, its spirit being in turn "successfully propagated through many parts of Europe." The French were *dishonest:* they had an "exaggerating humour" which "urges them into the most impudent fictions." They were *not morally serious:* there was "a levity of temper that appears to be inseparable from most of them." They were *not frank and forthright:* "the art of varnishing himself is another peculiarity in a Frenchman," and even their language, the reflection of their character, was full of "hints and circumlocutions," exactly "like a person of an artful, insinuating address." Such people could lay little claim to true *originality*, "the French being notoriously more solicitous than any other people, to tread in the steps of the fashionable world." No wonder they had no taste for *personal independence:* witness "the profound submission" with which they bore "the heavy yoke of bondage."[42]

Running through all this (and much more to the same effect) are the two familiar strains of marginal notation on England, the one debunking, the other romanticizing. The one batters away at the Great, subtly identified as 'so enamoured of France as to forget the ties binding them to their own nation.' England, through her greater wealth, had perhaps "a greater abundance [than France] of those whom opulence infatuates and renders supercilious and insolent"; England's "grandees," like France's, were "continually immersed in intrigues of state"; "many of our English gentlemen" were filled with that impure spirit of gallantry "propagated" from France; English "pettifoggery" was also of French origin, for "as the Normans are supposed to be the most litigious of all the inhabitants of France, it is not improbable their ancestors first brought the spirit of legal altercation into this land." The same line of comment includes criticism of "that regular system of corruption which has nearly subverted the constitution" and of those "basest instances of infidelity and treason to this nation" which were to be detected amongst trusted holders of power. "What a constitution is ours?" demands Andrews; "or rather what an infamous representation is made of it, by those whose interest requires that we should not deviate from the absurd and pernicious track we have so long adhered to with the most despicable punctiliousness and servility?"[43]

The other line of comment works by contrast to, rather than comparison with, everything 'French.' Here the text reveals the characteristic adjustment of social reference-point from England's grandees to everyone else, a folkish mass led by the writer himself. Many phrases, like brushstrokes in pointilist art, serve to build up the myth of the national identity: "We serious, grave Englishmen"; the "blunt, unceremonious disposition" of the English; "the native manliness of our disposition"; "the boldness of our disposition, and the unrestraint we profess in the manifestation of our thoughts"; the English language, "like a plain, blunt man, avoids prolixity, and comes to the point at once"; "our more solid way of thinking"; "few of their writers are as profound as ours"; "this nation," with its "character . . . of sense, courage, and genius"; "the superior excellence of the English workmen in their respective branches, comparatively to those in France"; that "passion for independence . . . so conspicuous in the natives of this island"; "that national freedom and felicity which were the objects of our ancestors"; the "republican principles" [*sic*] of "our government"; the wonderful "courage and resolution in the inhabitants of this island."[44]

Thus Andrews, where he is not knocking down France or firing oblique salvos at the Quality, may be seen setting up the ideal superiority over both of the English National Character. The growing boastfulness of the eighties may be savored in this extract:

> The English are, perhaps, the only people at present whose propensity to exalt themselves above others, falls but little short of that of the French; but even they are not so universal in their claims to unrivalled excellence, being willing enough to allow their neighbours to surpass them in many respects. Neither should it be omitted, that the English are above dissembling the high opinion they entertain of themselves. They aver their sentiments with

candour and downrightness, while the French, with a pretended solicitude that renders them peculiarly ridiculous, often affect to conceal that deep-rooted belief of their unlimited super-eminence, which is, nevertheless, perpetually betraying itself in their words and actions.[45]

And so on he went, through all his impure, less than honest, unoriginal, unprofound, but perhaps only unintentionally deceptive opus. It was in this way that the bourgeois opinion-makers, working across the whole broad front of literature and 'equivocating' their way down the decades, gradually appropriated to England all the fine values implied in Sincerity, and denied them to their neighbors across the Channel.

This, notwithstanding the injustice of it, was a fact of great importance. For as any educator knows, people acquire qualities that are continually ascribed to them. Whether England's ancestors had really been more sincere than France's—surely a debatable proposition, and the propagandists, by the way, had a devilish time explaining away Shakespeare's levity—is unimportant. It is not even important, though it is amusing, that British ideologues apparently borrowed some of their ideas of sincerity from French writers of the early eighteenth century.[46] What is important is the fact that by the 1780s the British people were indoctrinated in the *belief* that they and their ancestors uniquely exemplified these values. For what distinguishes a spiritually mobilized group from a mere community of people living side by side is a difference in self-awareness, a difference in conceptual organization around a more or less clear and inspiring idea of the collective self; in this case, of the Sincerity of the True Briton.

7. SOME EFFECTS OF THE NATIONAL MYTH

The literati thus promoted the rise of that great mythic conception of the National Character which, so it would appear, has had so many profound and lasting effects. A number of these have already been discussed, but a few more deserve attention in view of their importance.

i. rise of the man of letters

Certainly one effect which should be clear at this point is that the myth permitted the intelligentsia to cast itself in the role of defender of 'true' native culture while attacking and discrediting its supposedly 'alien' manifestations—a cardinal feature, of course, of nationalist activity in any country, and its greatest strategic advantage. The nationalist myth, which sharply opposed what was 'truly' English to what in fact existed, permitted the intelligentsia to initiate a class struggle against a caricatured elite and its moral infrastructure, under the guise of an international struggle. In turn, to see this should facilitate a clearer understanding of what has been described as 'the rise of the man of letters' in the later Georgian and early

Victorian eras. The critical point for literary professionals came in about the seventies as this group rapidly grew in numbers and as its members created a cultural and intellectual style which originally belonged mostly only to themselves, or rather to an idealized vision of themselves. This worked for them in many ways, but what is particularly significant to note here is the fact that it bolstered their self-confidence and strengthened their claim to public importance by spreading an ideology which uniquely extolled writers as spiritual exemplars—'heroes'—and hence mentors.

One effect of this was to give them the fortitude required to be truly iconoclastic and original as writers; English nationalism and Romantic literary originality were very intimately linked. But another effect more significant historically was to give them a strong power base in an ideological crusade which, though originally cultural and moral in purpose, was inevitably political in implication. The political side of it, as we shall see in the next chapter, had taken very definite shape by the 1780s, though it was to be altered by the repression of the nineties. But despite this the stage was set for the next phase of the movement (circa 1795–1825), when much of the remaining work could be carried out by a new generation of bards and evangelizers, working under the greatly strengthened pretext of France-proofing the whole country.

ii. attitudinal transformation and industrial revolution

There are signs also that the propagation of the National Identity played a very significant role in the contemporary economic take-off. The theorists of nationalism, as noted earlier, see many important connections between the growth of nationalist ideology and that very complex process known as 'modernization.' Unless they are wrong, then we have already a presumptive case in favor of reorienting our understanding of England's sudden dash into industrialism.

As Mathias affirms, the Industrial Revolution began "between the 1740's and the 1780's." Its attitudinal side is that which remains most baffling to historical investigators. One cannot read about its origins without being struck by the thinness of the discussions of attitudinal change: we are given the pieces of economic endeavor but not the endeavorers, the parts of the economic vehicle but not the drivers. The economic historians recognize the seriousness of the problem. Hartwell laments that there has been "insufficient research" on "the bases of belief, and on the relations between belief and action, especially economic action." Quoting other experts on the need to understand basic motivational changes both "in the minds of men" and "in personality between generations," he confesses that "we know precious little" about these subjects, little about "the development of the social environment" which somehow produced the "necessary attributes" of personality favoring economic change. He thinks a solution might emerge from a deeper understanding of contemporary social history: "European and English history must be re-examined . . . so that the . . . role of social change can be integrated into our explanations of economic growth."[47] We thus observe that economic history, like literary, awaits a revised treatment of social development.

Perhaps some questions might help to jog the thinking processes. What was the international economic situation, and the psychology produced by it? Was not the economic situation similar to, indeed merely symptomatic of, the cultural situation which we have already studied? Crouzet, comparing the economic growth of England with that of France, shows that the French growth rate between 1715 and 1780 was just as rapid as the English. In fact, during the middle third of the century the French were shutting England out of Europe's markets, contributing to a dramatic fall in Europe's share of England's total exports (from 80 percent to less than 50 percent). Crouzet states that French growth after 1730 "was general and quite fast. English industrial growth at this period was somewhat sluggish." The same thing is observed by Deane, who begins her account of the Industrial Revolution with the statement that "the British economy of the mid eighteenth century" was "poor" and "relatively stagnant," with "the mass of the people [living] close to economic disaster."[48]

Yet it was England, not France, which now began to experience a tremendous surge in her economic life. Is this not astonishing? What *were* the 'changes in the minds of men' and 'in personality between generations' which account for it? What was the "change in the mind of the representative producer" sought by Deane and the others?[49] Have we not, earlier in this chapter, documented such changes at this very moment in English history? Perhaps then some economic historian, reflecting on these, will some day write a history predicated on the idea that England's economic miracle was stimulated in much the same way as her literary miracle, and by the same cultural dynamics; that *the psychological mainspring of 'Romanticism' was that of the Industrial Revolution as well*. The key, of course, would lie in a comparison between writers and industrialists, a comparison like that briefly pursued earlier here (Chapter Five), in connection with middle-class attitudes toward patronage and Fashion. Think, if you will, of the contemporary writer not as a propagandist but simply as a representative producer, a worker. Perhaps the preface of Johnson's dictionary (1755), in which the alarmed and paranoid English worker may be seen attempting to confront French excellence, and through his own productive efforts to overcome it, should be set up for the contemplation of all students of this period, not just literary ones? For what we have is a man toiling languidly at first for the approval of Lord Chesterfield, and then, humiliated and angry, with tremendous energy for himself and the glory of his country. For Johnson, the promotion of English productivity was inseparably connected with the assertion of his own identity and worth. Perhaps in the same way, English industrialism in general was stimulated by primal anti-French fears and by a vigorously self-evaluative and then competitive response to these, a response which in some way evolved between the 'stagnant' and self-doubting forties and fifties (when, as we recall, English playwrights complained that the cachet of foreign wares was so great that English goods had to be 'smuggled thro' the street'), and the boastfully self-assertive eighties, when writers such as Andrews were so apt to trumpet the excellence of English 'genius' no less in manufactures than in the realms of thought and literature. Was it England's 'social harmony' and 'social mobility' which powered the Industrial Revolution, or was it not actually the reverse? Anxiety, we know, tends to stimulate self-evaluation and innovation in any field. Our analyses of the rise of English industrial supremacy should give more attention then to the fact that at this stage in history, industrial supremacy meant *English bourgeois supremacy over France*—a circumstance too much neglected among the many familiar 'factors' of 'industrial take-off.'

It seems certain that England's literary and economic revolutions were both stimulated by common psychological dynamics shaped in the same historical situation. But, further, it seems equally likely that these two revolutions, once begun, fed each other. What, for example, were the likely effects upon an industrialist of the new gospel of the national identity? We cannot doubt that he was directly exposed to it. Indeed it was their zeal for learning which specially marked such men out as industrial pioneers.[50] What then were the nationalist literature's effects upon them? It is possible to imagine many, but let us concentrate on just one. Samuel Johnson in 1783, in a phrase often cited by economic writers, exclaimed that "the age is running mad after innovation; all the business of the world is to be done in a new way." The great unsolved problem is why this innovation began. Deane writes that the official records of inventors' patents suggest that something quite extraordinary in the way of innovation was beginning to occur in the 1760s. What was the cause of this extraordinary technological outburst of the third quarter of the century? To many experts this is, as Crouzet puts it, "the heart of the matter: Britain was the place where all the basic inventions which created modern industry . . . were made, perfected and introduced into industry. . . . England experienced a real outburst of inventiveness." This "is the basic fact . . . which we must . . . try to explain."[51]

We already have, right here in hand, the material from which to shape an explanation. The nationalist literature promoted that 'frank' rejection of hand-me-down attitudes which was so vital to the acceptance and implementation of new technical ideas. Think of inventiveness as these literate industrializers were incessantly urged to do. If the glorious folkish ancestors were truly original and bold, then was there any answering boldness and originality today? Was there not indeed a tremendous compulsion to become more boldly original oneself? To do so was to *become more English!* Consider the lesson taught by ethnic revivals in our own day, in which every assertion of ethnic pride is accompanied by exaggerated claims as to the inventiveness of the ethnic forebears, and by the erection of heroic 'role models' to look up to. Was this not happening in England at this very moment, in the fifties and sixties? The country's real ancestors may never have served her so well as the newly exhumed and cosmeticized Saxons and Shakespeare and Milton and all the other mythical paragons of English Sincerity did, leaning on the mind of invention in every field and helping to turn the downright mediocrity of the 1750s into the wondrous achievements so apparent a century later.

Think of it. There, hung up in the national portrait gallery, was English 'Genius.' "Have I a genius for anything?" It was young Jeremy Bentham, born in 1748, who asked himself this question in precisely these words—deciding, of course, that his own 'genius' lay in legislation. But the same question must have formed in the mind of anyone who could read. Literary historians have produced no satisfactory explanation of the remarkable number of essays on 'Genius' and 'Originality' that began to appear in the fifties. But one expert remarks insightfully that the inspiration communicated in these "must make every reader feel that he or she too is an original genius . . . the effect is almost intoxicating." Englishmen were repeatedly told that genius was "not as uncommon as one might suppose," and that the essential thing was for each person to permit his own "to develop uninhibitedly." Typical was Edward Young's commandment (1759) to "dive deep into thy bosom . . . excite and cherish every spark of intellectual light and heat, however smothered under former negligence . . . [and] let thy genius rise."[52]

How would this have affected a man like James Watt? Born in 1736, Watt was just now in his mid-twenties. In fact it was just a little later, in 1764, that he began tinkering with a model of Newcomen's antique steam engine. It is instructive to recall, as a reminder of the traditionally anti-innovative climate still prevailing, that it was in this same year, the year of Hogarth's unhappy demise also, that John Kay, perhaps the greatest English inventor of the preceding generation, died in poverty and obscurity (in Paris, in fact). Now Watt was an avid reader of every sort of literature. John Robison, who knew him well, remarked that "no matter in what line—Languages—Antiquity—Natural History—nay Poetry, Criticism, and works of Taste . . . he was at home, and a ready Instructor." Among his friends were John Millar, one of the 'new nationalist historians,' and Thomas Day. Like them he was a man of remarkable determination, severe morality, and outspoken candor; his associates described "the naive simplicity and Candor of Mr Watts Character." He was also, as we noted in Chapter Five, a man of great 'sensitiveness on questions of class-feeling and priority'; late in life, after achieving fame, he refused a baronetcy. Further, his biographers say that throughout his life he was troubled by headaches and psychological depression. He entertained a particular hostility towards the aristocratic Henry Cavendish, whom he suspected, together with Lavoisier in Paris, of having stolen some of his scientific ideas. It is also recorded that he believed the English House of Commons "possessed" by the "devil." Such was the man whose statue was to be placed in Westminster Abbey in the 1820s, and whom Wordsworth was to salute as perhaps the most extraordinary genius his country ever produced.[53]

Now there is, to be sure, little way of knowing with absolute certainty whether young Watt consciously nourished in himself an ideal of 'native genius' as he labored for five years over the flues and cylinders of New-comen's machine, deriving inspiration from it till at last he patented a better one (1769). But we do have one of his letters, reminiscent of Johnson's preface of 1755, which certainly suggests that Scotland at least figured powerfully as both motive and object of his endeavors in revolutionizing steam power: "If I merit it some of my countrymen, inspired by the *Amor Patriae* may say: '*Hoc a Scoto factum fuit*'" (This was made by a Scot).[54]

It would seem that the main system of motivation was a little different from those prevalent today. A tennis enthusiast might say that it was more like that of the Davis Cup than of Wimbledon, more perfectly associating personal achievement with national. Suppose then that some future researcher, working through the materials of Watt's life, were able to show that the inventor was indeed powerfully influenced by the Sincere Ideal. Would he not then hold a key to the most stubbornly insoluble problem of the Industrial Revolution? The economic historians themselves say that the problem is one not of technology but of culture, and, within that, of psychology. Crouzet, lamenting that "it will never be fully explained why England had so many great inventors in the eighteenth century," writes that "all the historian can hope for is to understand the environment." Mathias sums the problem up in a noteworthy declaration. Surveying the comparative readiness of France and England for industrialism in the eighteenth century, he writes:

> France had as impressive a record of scientific advance, of high standards of mechanical contrivance . . . as England. Much greater positive, deliberate help was given by government to acquiring new industrial skills in France. . . . Some key inventions, known for many decades, were not actively diffused in the [English] economy until the later eighteenth century, time-lags which suggest that the acquisition of new technical knowledge was not a prime determinant of timing in the development of many new techniques. And if it was just the *natural genius of the English people* to do these things, there is *an onus of proof on explaining just why that genius saw fit to wait until the mid-eighteenth century to throw away its disguise.* . . .[55]

For future historians, that onus may seem less burdensome than it did when Mathias wrote this.

iii. early myth-making and later scholarship

It is quite possible that nationalist mythology has also prejudiced our own view of the past. Its inculcation, based so largely on discrediting everything French, has distorted our view of eighteenth-century England, and probably of France as well. Take the example suggested by Andrews's *Comparative View*. How would the uninitiated researcher interpret this document, this seemingly rather innocuous, and, considering its deceptive appeals to objectivity, straightforward discussion of the two countries facing the English Channel? In all probability he would incline to see in it simply a confirmation of his own learned assumptions about the legend-ary 'differentness' of English and French manners and institutions in that period. He would have little clue to it as part of an immense corpus of propaganda, an evolving mythology subtly supported by virtually every branch of contemporary literature.

Taking the English nationalist myth at face value, as the truth rather than as the expression of men feverishly priding themselves upon just those qualities which many of them desperately feared they were nearly without—innocence, honesty, frankness, originality, and independence—we unconsciously assimilate our scholarly studies of eighteenth-century institutions to this myth, and then unconsciously validate it again by ap-plauding the fruits in the nineteenth century of its tremendous impact upon the national mind during the interval. We never see the thing itself, much less the process by which it was formed. We never see how the paranoid anxiety and cultural despair of the 1750s helped to foster the sweeping and self-serving prevarications and idealizations of the 1780s, and how these served as the basis of the triumphant dogmatism of the Carlyles and Macaulays of the age to come. Thus—to trace misunder-standing backwards—it never occurs to us that the great results in the nineteenth century might never have been achieved but for the tremen-dous dynamism generated in the National Identity, and that this itself would never have arisen if English character, 'genius,' institutions, social mobility, art, and the rest had been half so unique, half so unlike the patterns in France, as what the propagandists engaged in magnifying these differences represented them to be. To Andrews, and to many oth-ers like him, the similarities between France and England seemed so great that it was felt necessary to invent and project ideational differences to conceal and eradicate them. Yet these propagandists, these early na-tionalists, are today's 'primary sources,' their words often uncritically ac-cepted as the basic data of historical understanding. In fact we accept them the more uncritically because without the 'differences' which were their stock-in-trade we have no theory nearly powerful enough to explain the priority of industrialism in England, rather than in France! It should be pointed out that Crouzet, who has made a study of these supposed Anglo-French differences and of the modern economic historiography projected from them, firmly rejects many of them as non-existent, as mythical.[56] The crux of the matter is that Andrews and his many friends were at that very moment in history *creating* the attitudinal differences which we now *assume*. But if the early mythmakers—many of them found-ers of our modern scholarship—made fools of us, they made believers of their own people, and that was what counted. That was what they had set out to do in the first place, to eradicate French influence and remold the National Character.

iv. the creed of 'One Nation'

The growth of Sincerity implied a profound moral, psychological and social revolution through the reorientation of personal consciousness and behavior. The personal adoption of Sincerity was an adoption of strenuous individualism, of what some writers called 'self-regarding' behavior. Thus the ethic of Sincerity, taken to its limits, implied that intense individualism but also that collective moral anarchy which was in fact present in both the writings and the behavior of the Romantic Age, the period from the 1790s to the 1820s. Sincerity was a strenuous call to the independence of the individual, and as such it promoted a revolution against the status quo.

But there was another side to it, one which promoted a new conformity. The revolution was self-limiting. Sincerity, as we have seen, was not only a revolutionary ideal but a powerful affirmation of what was held to be the philosophical essence of the English nation at large, its identity, the *National Character*. Thus the final success of the revolution pointed not to anarchical individualism but to fraternal solidarity: the more it succeeded, the more each individual supposedly found his true character in the primal moral essence of the nation, the values ascribed to the group as a whole; and, by the same logic, the nation itself achieved gradual realization not merely as an ideal but as a community of like-minded men and women, a living community of sincere English wills. As Guilhamet observes of the poets in his study, sincerity was something to be attained not only through the perfection of the individual self (the realization in each self of the national ideal), but more largely through a collective realization somewhere in the future of "a state singularly uncorrupt," an "almost prelapsarian condition" of society;[57] that is, according to our interpretation, of a national paradise, a New Jerusalem, in which all Englishmen, assertive, morally independent, and free in their own selves, would by virtue of this very fact be united with each other in a common invisible bond, a common consciousness of ethnic identity and selfhood as a national community.

Thus the ideal of Sincerity was both a revolutionary personal ideal and an eschatological communal doctrine of the secular utopia to be realized through the fulfillment of the One Nation. It was, just as the experts on nationalism believe to be true of nationalist ideologies in general, an ideal both revolutionary and reintegrative. It combined an *injunction* to personal independence with an utopian *promise* of fraternal solidarity which, it was vaguely assumed, would arise from the progressive realization throughout the land and in every heart of the distinctive, underlying collective self of England. English nationalism thus beautifully resolved the problem of the One and the Many, the most ancient and fundamental problem of political science: the freedom of the individual was reconciled with the welfare of the group through the metaphysics of national realization. (The same metaphysics figured at the heart of the new English economic theory, which future historians may indeed some day interpret as simply a natural unconscious projection, in the economic realm, of the basic bourgeois nationalist ideology.)

But ideals, by their very nature, are never fully realized. The great struggle for One Nation against the suggestedly alien elite, and within that a multiplicity of lesser struggles involving the same basic assumption and working through changing adaptations of the same rhetorical strategy, continued into the nineteenth century. And it should come as no surprise that there were more arrivistes in this period who, as Girouard has shown, discreetly changed their names to give themselves a quality, a Norman French panache, which it was impossible to buy or earn. In the evolving elite and in the snobbery that persistently clung to it there were always fresh targets of concern, and the battle for One Nation could very probably be traced down through the rhetoric of the generations, down through the Disraelis and Gladstones, the Baldwins and Attlees, even the Thatchers and Benns of today. It was only yesterday that one of Mr. Benn's followers, adapting old ideas to new realities, attempted to dust off the Tories by declaring "that today's Norman Yoke upon us was the occupation of this island by American troops."[58]

And yet in one sense the great initial battle was won by the mid-Victorian age, when not only the middle classes but also the children of the elite and even the 'respectable' portion of the working classes shared to a remarkable degree, a degree without parallel in English history, a common code of behavior, that famous 'Code' which G.M. Young and so many later historians have discerned at the base of Victorianism;[59] that code so often traced, in the absence of a better theory, to the workings of Evangelical religious faith. Truly it is a measure of the great extent to which the country at large had accepted and realized the National Identity by 1860 that a close observer such as Emerson could attest both the strenuous individualism of the English character and the communal solidarity which was believed to result from this: 'English believes in English.' It was in this age, after a century of maturation, that the national ideal came perhaps as close as it ever would to earthly fulfillment.

10. 1768. A radical print in two parts, which (above) prophetically represents the tension between England and her American colonies as a mutilated and destitute Britannia, slipped from her global position, her ships for sale, and (below) treats this as the triumph of Britain's internal and external enemies, typified by Bute and Louis XV: the former stabs Britannia in the back with one hand and with the other exposes "her Weakness" to Spain's thrusts, while the French monarch stabs her in the eye, clasps America to himself, and crows that now he will be "King of de whole World." Meanwhile a Dutchman steals away English commerce.

CHAPTER SEVEN

The Launching of English Radicalism in the Age of George III

The age of virtuous politics is past, and we are deep in that of cold pretence. Patriots are grown too shrewd to be sincere, and we too wise to trust them.

—COWPER

WHAT WAS the political effect of the developments we have studied? To understand this rightly we should turn again, before plunging into the details of English political history, to survey the political characteristics of nationalist movements in general. It is, first of all, well to keep in mind a fact sometimes forgotten by political historians, namely that nationalism is something larger than mere politics, that it *enters* the political domain from a sphere outside it. Nationalism is a phenomenon of feeling and consciousness, an intellectual phenomenon, which originates in certain stressful cultural and psychological conditions, which typically manifests itself in literature, which may very well spawn a social movement, which not infrequently spills over into politics as well, but which nevertheless aspires to a state of affairs so idyllic as to make politics, literature, and social movement irrelevant.[1] That is, its ultimate goals, like its roots, are cultural and psychological: its goals are personal wholeness and fraternal solidarity within a completely united and free community, a real community of the future to match the mythical one of the past.

It is because the nationalist utopia lies in a realm above mere politics that nationalism often cuts across traditional party alignments. And for the same reason, the political strategies employed to realize it may vary widely, depending on local circumstances, from left-wing emancipation movements to right-wing authoritarian ones. Washington, Hitler, and Ho Chi Minh were all nationalists. There is (as we are reminded in studying Rousseau's concept of 'general will') no single exclusive route to the utopian objective, the individual's attainment of a sense of being a full member of a freely self-determining community whose will is identical to his own.

Thus each specific nationalist movement's political agenda is largely determined by three circumstances, two of them 'given,' the third quite variable. On the one side we have what may be regarded as two universal constants: the nationalist's resentment of an entire pattern of existing arrangements, usually political as well as cultural and social, which he experiences as alien to the true spirit of his community; and, in consequence, his desire to revamp this and secure the results in institutions reflecting this idealized spirit. And then thirdly we have the specific 'group situation,' the local circumstances within which he must conduct his struggles.

It is the perception of patterns among these 'group situations' which has led modern experts to set up typologies of nationalist development. Smith's three main classifications furnish a handy reference-point. 'Secession' nationalism, as he calls it, describes the dynamics of historic movements (Polish, Czech, Armenian, etc.) typically originating within ethnically diverse empires. Here the ethnic group, first awakened by the growth of cultural nationalism and hence sensing itself to be a prisoner in the larger unit, seeks to 'secede' and then establish a free state fully coextensive with itself, at the same time expelling or forcibly homogenizing aliens within the new national boundaries. 'Renewal' nationalism, a second major type, describes movements (French, Persian, Chinese, Cambodian, etc.) within ethnic polities which at least nominally run their own affairs, though "the rulers are regarded as collaborators with encroaching aliens," or even as themselves "aliens, though they share their culture (or a version of it)" with their countrymen. Here, since there is no need for an initial war of secession, political activity is trained directly on the radical rejuvenation of existing institutions and their perfection as instruments of the culturally unique and free community; the nationalist movement takes political shape (as Minogue writes) as "a direct enemy of conservative politics," "a force which seeks a radical transformation of politics." Thirdly, there is 'Territorial' nationalism, the sort, for example, which has animated many African states since World War II. Such movements, lacking much cultural homogeneity beyond that imposed by former colonial masters, attempt to erect the new political state upon a heightened consciousness of the national territory itself and its physical boundaries. In this classification there is no cultural "dog" beginning "to wag its political tail," but the reverse: one of the ethnic or cultural subgroups commonly takes the lead in such a movement, and thus winds up creating the new institutions in more or less its own cultural image.[2]

Neither England nor Britain, as we saw earlier, figures in the experts' thinking about nationalism. Smith reluctantly accepts the supposition that England somehow attained nationhood without it, and hence suggests a special non-nationalist category to contain what is fancied to be the English road of development, an exception to all the known rules.[3] In fact, however, English nationalism was certainly of the 'Renewal' type and some day will doubtless be looked upon as a purer example of this even than French (which now figures as the classic case); whilst *British* nationalism will surely be regarded as an enlargement of English into a larger 'Territorial' variety coming upon the heels of the English movement. That is, what began and flourished in England as a 'Renewal' movement took on some of the features of a 'Territorial' one within the British Isles (and beyond, as the cultural imperialism of the Victorians would seem to suggest). This movement, far from being non-existent, was probably the earliest and strongest on earth, and one of the most successful.

The typical progression is from vague cultural 'Stirrings' to full-blown populist political activity—'the Struggle for Independence,' as Minogue calls this second typical stage. Nationalism ordinarily manifests itself first in a two-sided cultural activity, a reaction against what is felt to be an alien cultural domination, together with a quest for the National Identity. But the demand for cultural autonomy, since it recognizes no limits, leads inevitably to political demands. To preach the uniqueness of Czech culture, for example, was implicitly to call for cultural autonomy under the Czechs, but this in turn implied questioning the political supremacy of the Hapsburg Emperor, and beyond that the legitimacy of any government not based upon the mythic strength of the Czech personality—that is, upon the contemporary embodiment of the National Identity, the Czech people themselves in the mass. The populist politics of nationalism are thus implicit in its cultural origins and its ideal of total cultural freedom from alien domination. Though nationalist thinkers may be slow to see this (they typically think at first of 'the people' as a cultural entity rather than as a political unit with political rights), the only certain guarantee of spiritual liberation lies in the sovereignty of the people themselves.[4]

Thus the growth of collective self-consciousness promotes the shaping of a program for popular sovereignty. Cultural nationalism strengthens the sense of community, while this in turn sharpens awareness and hence criticism of the actual state structure which allegedly obstructs the communal will and corrupts the agencies through which it should be expressed—the schools, the churches, the bars of justice, the boards of civil administration, etc. Growing criticism of the political establishment provokes official resistance and repression, which then only help to confirm suspicion that the state is in anti-national hands.

Paralleling this evolution, and linked with it, an intellectual process begins in which the inherited symbols of collective unity and political sovereignty undergo subtle internal transformation with the passage of time. Unaltered, the old symbols will no longer suffice, for at the end of the evolutionary process the basis of political legitimacy is (as was just suggested in the Czech example) no longer the inherited political state or ruling class but rather the immanent ideal of the National Identity, the mythic personality bequeathed by the national ancestors and supposedly inherited by every native child. In the final analysis it is *personality* rather than property or inherited rights which becomes the new source of political legitimacy, and while this does not necessarily point to republicanism or parliamentary democracy (for history demonstrates that a single leader or group may, for a time at least, enjoy the full confidence of the masses as their authentic spiritual representative), neither will it sanction political leaders unable to present themselves convincingly as metaphysical bits of this divine national essence, the National Character.

Much of this may be glimpsed in the development of French nationalism, supposedly the prototype of all nationalist movements. In the early eighteenth century the French monarchy was still the chief symbol of the French nation, of its unity, territorial integrity, and political sovereignty. But adjustments began as the century passed and as conflicts deepened within French society. It was the 1750s, a decade of war, that saw new intellectual distinctions being made between the monarchical state (the government) and the nation. In 1755 an obscure cleric named G. F. Coyer, condemning his more sophisticated contemporaries, began to preach that no love was so pure as that felt for the nation, and that this embraced both the state and all orders of society. Amidst the growth of French cultural nationalism (of which there were many manifestations in the sixties and seventies), a new political attitude, a "new patriotism," as Kohn calls it, was coming into existence, pairing together the king and the whole French people as the proper objects of patriotic feeling.[5]

But advanced opinion was already moving beyond this. It was at about this time that Rousseau, totally rejecting the embodiment of the nation in the monarchy or ruling class, completed the intellectual transition by firmly identifying the nation with the people themselves, and both of these with an ideal of communal morality and fraternity. Meanwhile Rousseau's friend, Mably, together with younger writers such as Sieyès, undertook what amounted to the racial repudiation of the French upper classes in a strain of ethnohistorical propaganda contrasting the domineering Franks with the downtrodden Gauls. The French state, according to this, was in fact simply the perpetuation of ancient force and fraud, an usurpation of the original rights of the French people; who, it was said, had before the Frankish conquest elected their kings and participated actively in popular assemblies. It was in this radicalized context that Sieyès, in his famous pamphlet of 1789, attacked the privileges of the 'Frankish' upper classes, suggesting that they should return to the German woods from which they had supposedly come, and advanced the claims of the Third Estate as the true French nation, defining 'nation' not as the encyclopedists had done earlier, not as a 'quantity of people' living in 'obedience' to a government, but as "a *body of associates* living under one common law and *represented by* the same legislature." Here at last 'the nation' and the whole 'associated' people were one; political power was theoretically derived from mere membership in the *ethnie*, the ethnohistorical community. The revolutionary Declaration of the Rights of Man and the Citizen (August 1789) legally confirmed the same point, which has since become the foundation of modern democratic political faith.[6]

1. Four Typical Phases of Growth

Another thing illustrated in the French progression is the fact that nationalism, once intruding itself into politics, typically advances through several political phases. The first is that which is least understood, chiefly because too many analysts wrongly think of nationalism as something 'imported' rather than incubated within. The key development in this first phase is the emergence of nationalistic political ideas. There are signs that prolonged patriotic excitement often plays midwife to this emergence, as it apparently did in France in the 1750s; that an intensified patriotism promotes the politicization of nationalism. Of course we must remember that eighteenth-century nationalists did not recognize themselves as such but rather as 'patriots' (the term 'nationalism' was not even coined till the late 1790s); it is for us, studying historical patterns in retrospect, to make appropriate distinctions between the two tendencies and think out their interrelationship.

We recall that patriotism, as noted earlier, is a very old and essentially conservative and defensive sentiment, a strong attachment to the established symbols of state power, especially in a context of international rivalry: "Patriotism is largely conservative in its operation."[7] Nationalism, on the other hand, is a much more all-consuming sentiment, attached to symbols of the people and the collective personality, and inclined towards radical innovation. The only thing deeply in common between the two sentiments is a passionate desire to defend what are regarded as national values. And this is evidently the link by which the one may assist the birth of the other.

But under what circumstances will this occur? If Kiernan is right in believing that nationalism undergoes a long phase of preparatory development, Smith is probably no less correct in maintaining that a sudden upsurge accompanies its actual birth as a recognizable political phenomenon. At some point or another, one must believe, a decisive historical moment is reached. Is it during the excitements of war? Handman contends that such a transformation only occurs in conditions of sustained "provocation" by some very powerful antagonistic group, conditions in which the individual's "concern with the life and honor of the group" becomes deeply, even obsessively, agitated. Chadwick agrees, maintaining that the transformation requires "the stimulus of a powerful antagonistic force, either within the same country or beyond, but not too far beyond, its borders."[8] What this suggests is that political nationalism is typically born in a time of war, especially when the enemy is believed to haunt the fatherland as well as direct the armies of the foreigner; that is, when cultural nationalism, built up from its cultural conspiracy theory and spread by alienated intellectuals, is already present. Political nationalism, one might say, begins its hatch from cultural nationalism in an atmosphere conditioned by war, heightened patriotism, and suspected antinational conspiracy by real or make-believe aliens, an atmosphere highly favorable to wider public acceptance of the subversive ideas of the alienated few.

Of course the time must be ripe for extended struggles against the domestic upper classes, the true ulterior object, in many cases, of nationalist complaint. For though political nationalism may make its first appearance during war against the foreigner, at bottom it nevertheless represents, as all the specialists agree, a domestic struggle rather than truly a foreign one; "a condition of civil war," as Minogue characterizes it, "and often . . . a civil war in which little notice is actually taken of the outside aggressor." Nationalist movements, writes Kedourie, "are ostensibly directed against the foreigner, the outsider, but they are also the manifestation of a species of civil strife" which erupts in a time of "powerful social strains" when communal institutions are weak. "The masses," according to Kiernan, when they are "sufficiently aroused to turn against foreign domination," are "apt to be in a mood to turn against their own parasites as well—'the Eaters', as they were expressively called in Burma."[9]

To sum up, then, what typically occurs during the first political phase of an expanding nationalist movement is that the emotional arousal and patriotism generated during wartime furnish a powerful reservoir of sentiment, and that, when underlying conditions are ripe, and when there are reasons to suspect influential domestic groups of disloyalty, this patriotic sentiment may become transformed into nationalism in the minds of those individuals and social classes specially prepared to accept it. Of course one will not find the chief power-holders adopting this deeply subversive ideology, or regarding themselves as members of an anti-national conspiracy; nor, on the other hand, would one look to the illiterate masses as primary bearers of truly nationalistic ideas. Hence the first stage of activity must be one of considerable confusion, with the old patriotism continuing alongside the new nationalism and even contradicting it— "Patriotism and nationalism may work against one another," as Minogue remarks;[10] and yet in the realm of intellectual development, the first tentative steps (as in abbé Coyer) toward the expansion and redefinition of the idea of the political nation.

The later phases have received more attention. Of course all these phases overlap each other in reality, and it must be remembered too that the nationalist movement does not develop in a vacuum, but rather in a flux of allied events and tendencies. For instance, in the cultural realm the growing romanticization of 'the people' has the effect of increasingly enhancing the worth of every person and thus of lending weight to arguments in favor of more fully representative political institutions. On the other hand, as was suggested earlier, official resistance to nationalist activities may help to spur the movement on by creating excitement as well as public confrontations and martyrs, in events which then are likely to be read as further corroboration of the nationalists' claims.

But if we leave such influences aside and simply concentrate on the evolution of the political movement itself, the distinguishing mark of its second phase is the emergence of leaders and groups of activists— "agents" and "agencies," as Argyle calls them.[11] Generals, admirals, popular politicians, holy men, even princes and kings, have led many nationalist movements, and the influence of the 'charismatic hero-leader' is often very important. But more important still are the second-rank activists who articulate the nationalist political demands, disseminate propaganda, found political organizations, and seek to mobilize opinion hostile to the political establishment. This group of more or less full-time 'agents,' typically quite small in number, constitutes the real heart of the political movement, and furnishes its continuity over what may be decades of struggle.

The typical 'agent,' says Smith, is bourgeois, educated, often a professional man, not infrequently an intellectual, who experiences with particular keenness the "frustration . . . and impaired mobility, both political and social," imposed upon him by a snobbish and exclusive elite. He may come from the geographic periphery of his country, and hence doubly feel himself an outsider. His emerging political ideas, says Minogue, "often related to allegations of neglect or discrimination (or both) on the part of successive administrations," constitute a rejection of what he sees as the private interests dominating the state, in the name of interests broadly and passionately identified with the whole public, 'the people,' i.e. the nation. For him the *national* interest becomes the great touchstone of political value, and through this attachment he is led into what Kedourie calls "a new style of politics"—self-righteous, uncompromising, and ever prone to view politics "as a fight for principles, not the endless composition of claims in conflict." Often his great idée fixe becomes the purification of politics by the removal of some horrid alien influence, some pervasive evil from which he tends to derive all others. In his efforts to organize 'agencies' of communication and political action he reaches out to respectable social groups such as the gentry and, even more, to urban commercial groups whose interests are particularly well served by the progress of nationalism; but it is the 'petty bourgeoisie' of small traders, artisans, teachers, and so on, those "irregulars of history," who respond most passionately to the movement, thanks to its promise of personal attachment to the great new *corpus mysticum* of the nation. The movement is least congenial to the social ranks at the top and bottom of society.[12]

The agent's political arguments may take many forms, but usually central to them is the recommendation of political innovations by reference to ancestral precedents, supposedly dredged up from history but often quite imaginary in content. The nationalist's real attitude to the past is complex. He must cherish ancestral characteristics as marks of national identity, yet he must also reject much of the past because it holds progress in chains. His political demands, though deceptively backward-looking, are revolutionary, for he seeks an immediate and total overthrow of the existing political system.

The specific character of nationalist political demands depends on local institutions, the long-range goal of communal self-determination, and, inevitably, the special interests of the agents themselves. The movement aims at collective independence and self-government, but it also aims at power for itself, power for the intelligentsia and the (typically, bourgeois) social groups near its own core. Nationalism's unusually plastic ideology constitutes a false simplification of class society into a community of ethnic neighbors united against rich, oppressive, wire-pulling aliens (or surrogate aliens), and it is this which helps to explain its extraordinary appeal, its cross-class attraction and its ability to unify societies much better than other ideologies, socialism for example. But it is the nationalist agents themselves who decide who 'the People' effectively are; it is *their* agendas which dictate proximate political objectives and the acceptability of those political changes which actually occur. Sieyès was not a democrat, and the constitution of the First French Republic stopped far short of universal manhood suffrage. The nationalists themselves, despite their holistic ideology, decide when the political emancipation of 'the people' has been accomplished.

Ordinarily this occurs after a third, climactic phase of development which has been dubbed 'Mustering the People.' At some point, in response to events, the nationalist movement spills into the streets. The larger community, sensitized to its supposed 'ancient rights' by the nationalist agencies, awakens to political action in its own behalf. The movement 'goes public' in overt political demonstrations which then have the important added effect of strengthening the extended community's awareness of itself as a political force. Such demonstrations, augmented by the proliferation of other mass events—public festivals, theatrical performances, the funerals of leading patriots—constitute a new political fact of much importance, regardless of any immediate political results attributable to them. For in them the community gathers, in effect, to worship itself, not the king, not the nation's military power, not even its heroes of yore. The crowd becomes a congregation celebrating itself in a secular liturgy, democratically participating in the newly articulated myths and symbols of the whole community. The irony is that although such rites tend to reinforce the new idea of popular sovereignty, they may in fact act to forestall the growth of constitutional democracy by providing an emotionally satisfying alternative to it. Emotional fraternity and equality in the mass, together with a sense of national self-determination on the international stage, may help to divert and sidetrack the democratic impulses implicit in nationalist ideology. The new "liturgy of nationalism" may become a substitute for meaningful participation in parliamentary government.[13]

How then does one judge the political success of any particular nationalist movement? At first glance the answer would appear to be fairly simple: by measuring political results against the goal of national liberation (or renewal) and communal self-determination. But these are vague standards, and the analytical problem is further complicated by the fact that nationalist movements may rise, reach an apparent climax, subside, and then rise again some decades down the road, inspired by some new (or revived) anti-national menace. 'Renewal' movements are especially prone to such recurrences, but in fact every variety of nationalism, simply because nationalist goals are impossible to realize fully, is likely to experience the reopening at some point of political issues which earlier were treated as closed. And analysis of such subsequent revivals is the more difficult because after the first great waves of activity, nationalist rhetoric, so powerful in its appeal, is likely to be found on the lips of every political speaker, including those most desirous of stamping out nationalism. Nationalist rhetoric, like that of socialism, presents a bag of tools and disguises in which all may rummage. It may be borrowed by the enemies of nationalism, just as nationalist festivals may be co-opted—such was the case in Germany in the later nineteenth century—by the enemies, not the friends, of the people. In official hands, nationalism may degenerate or regress into a mere unthinking conservative patriotism—'State Patriotism,' as Smith calls it.[14]

And yet despite such complicating factors, the success of nationalist movements may be meaningfully judged by the extent to which they attain a fourth and final phase of development, the phase of 'Consolidation and Normalization.' Simply to reach this phase is some measure of a movement's power, for many fall short of it. The key point is that the community now seems to witness its own triumph over the enemies of communal self-determination. In 'Secession' movements this historic moment is particularly easy to mark, for there it involves a visible transfer of power and the replacement of old flags and symbols by new ones identified with 'the people.' In 'Renewal' movements this triumph is apt to occur less spectacularly, but in either case its hallmark is the climactic casting-down and replacement of political aliens, or what Smith calls the "nationalisation of personnel, sometimes involving expulsion."[15]

It is at this point, this first moment, as it were, of 'independence,' that the importance of the popular hero-leader becomes fully apparent. "How can we imagine the United States without the figure of George Washington, Venezuela without Bolívar, Ireland without De Valera, or India without Nehru"?[16] The hero of independence, on attaining power, represents in his own person the overthrow of alien influences. As a man of outstanding personal qualities who displays his identification with the people in his dress, manners, and actions, he represents to all who see him the long-awaited merger between national identity and political power. He personifies both nation and state, and thus seems to exemplify in his own person the political triumph of the people over their enemies.

But this is not the only reason why the emergence of "this single figure of outstanding qualities" is held to be of such "crucial significance in the formation of nationhood" (Calvert). For it is under his authority, while he acts as both symbol and interpreter of the popular will, that the new or 'renewed' system of political legitimacy, geared to what are now habitually invoked as the interests of the whole community, becomes institutionalized. It is during his administration that the people, for years now accustomed to view themselves as a 'race of heroes,' begin to undertake in the hard light of day and often with some disillusionment their new duties as citizens of the rejuvenated nation-state. The leader's mission of 'Normalization' may thus prove difficult in the end, and it is small wonder, given nationalism's unleashing of tremendous forces in the economic and social spheres, that the new leadership may welcome another long symbolic re-enactment of the original 'Struggle for Independence' as a device for ruling and homogenizing the population. "Here," as Minogue comments, "is the reason why the day after independence, leaders of new states are to be found proclaiming that the struggle has not ended, but has only entered a new phase." The phase of 'Normalization' may thus serve as a jumping-off point either for some era of conservative 'State Patriotism' or for some later nationalist resurrection employing devices borrowed from the first. But it should be noted that 'Normalization' is most successful, and thus most complete, in those nations which acquire great international prestige, "world approval and respectability," in the aftermath of the initial nationalist struggle.[17]

2. THE ENGLISH 'GROUP SITUATION' AND THE NEW POLITICS OF THE FIFTIES

We come then to the specific political character and evolution of the English movement. The English nationalist movement, like many others, was essentially cultural in origin, a cultural and ideological growth without any clear political purpose at all at its beginning. As was suggested earlier in the examination of Hogarth, there are good reasons to believe that it began as a drive to overthrow and expel the prevailing Continental and especially French cultural hegemony, a system of international cultural influence; a system, however, which, precisely because men will assume superiority over others on grounds of culture, gradually involved Hogarth and many who followed him in an expanding crusade with moral and social as well as cultural objectives. It was because English political institutions worked as such institutions usually do, to inhibit such crusades and preserve the superiority of those who oppose them, that the nationalist movement was gradually drawn into politics.

There was a counterpoint between the growth of cultural self-consciousness, the course of domestic and foreign events, and the stimulation of nationalist political activity. This activity was naturally shaped in the 'group situation,' of which an important component was the system of 'Whig Ascendancy' created by Sir Robert Walpole in the earlier part of the century and managed by his protégés the Pelham brothers in the forties and fifties. These wealthy landlords and their friends in the 'Great Revolution-Principle Families' saw themselves as patriots in the traditional sense, conservators of the Hanoverian Succession, the liberties of 1689, and parliamentary supremacy. When they thought of the English nation they thought of Parliament, and when they thought of national freedom they simply thought of their own continued parliamentary dominance. By exploiting anti-Jacobite fears against toryism and by careful attention to appointments, patronage, and elections, they built up the machinery by which they kept the Stuarts off the throne, their own ministries in power, and their supporters happily 'eligible'; while at the same time they wooed 'country' (independent and Tory) opinion and sought to ensure general satisfaction through policies aimed at peace abroad, domestic prosperity, and financial stability. They cut taxes, welcomed foreign capital into the country, consolidated the national debt, reduced military expenditures, cultivated friendly relations with France, subsidized France's rivals, and pursued a defensive policy in foreign affairs, designed to uphold Hanover's safety and the balance of power.

But by mid-century the cautious policies and oligarchical style of this Walpoleian 'old corps' were being outrun by an important segment of public opinion. There are many signs that nationalist perspectives, nourished in the deepening cultural and social irritations which we studied earlier, were now beginning to filter directly into political attitudes. Outwardly the cry was for a purer politics at home and a more aggressive spirit in foreign affairs. A new 'patriotic' politics was emerging, even though in some respects there was little new in it. It was already an established ploy for opposition politicians to portray themselves as 'true patriots,' determined to rescue the crown from evil ministers and to restore the balance of the constitution which these men were supposedly upsetting for their own personal advantage. Walpole himself as a young man had played the part, raising cries against 'placemen' and the 'slavery' supposedly contemplated by the king's ministers, while later in the 1730s Bolingbroke and others had raised the same cries against him, denouncing his 'system' and adding that it was only through nonpartisan politics, patriotic service to the crown, that the general welfare could be served.

What was really new about the patriotic politics of the fifties was not its condemnations of 'corruption' and 'faction' nor even its vitriolic denunciation of ministerial dithering in foreign affairs. What was new was its remarkably strident insistence that the road to national greatness was the global expansion of British trade and the total destruction of that French economic and military power which, like French culture, was now flourishing everywhere; and, secondly, its deepening suggestion, which we noted earlier in contemporary prints, John Brown's *Estimate,* and other sources, that England's vital affairs were in the hands of hardened Francophiles, addicted by both taste and fashion to the superiority of the national enemy. Here at high noon of that cosmopolitan century was 'the stimulus of a powerful antagonistic force, either within the same country or beyond, but not too far beyond, its borders.' What was even more strikingly novel about the new patriotism was the fact that it actually took power for a short time under William Pitt, and thus became the cry not of disappointed factions but of the king's own ministry.

Pitt was the first 'charismatic hero-leader' of this nationalism beginning its hatch into English political life, its political mentor in the same way that Hogarth, Brown and Johnson guided it into art, philosophy and scholarship. The disastrous opening events of the Seven Years' War brought him to this high place in history while arousing those sentiments of 'agitating concern with the life and honor of the group' which often accompany the onset of nationalist political activity. The global struggle opened with repeated humiliations of British military forces by the French. The British were massacred on the Ohio River and in Calcutta, overrun in western New England, Minorca, and Hanover, and threatened by a Channel invasion. Pitt was given power in the midst of these events (November 1756) but received little support from the old corps, jealous of his popularity and wary of the threat this implied to the political system; despite the menaces of France he was soon forced from office. Then an extraordinary thing happened as London and a dozen other cities expressed the public's fury by conferring their freedoms upon him and otherwise defiantly parading their support of 'the Great Commoner.' In a faint but unmistakable alignment, Pitt and the cities faced off against the oligarchy and the French.

Pitt was already a uniquely popular figure by this time. Before the war he had distinguished himself by his blistering attacks on ministerial subordination of British to Hanoverian interests, and, when serving the Pelham administrations, by his many talents and his refusal on moral grounds to milk the public funds in his care. Like other father-figures of nationalism he cultivated an image of himself as a selfless patriot, a lonely leader without a following in a jungle of anti-national bosses and hirelings. Naturally he was, like every ambitious politician of his day, a Whig, but his true attitude toward whiggism foreshadowed the toryism of Disraeli, to whom the Whigs were "that 'anti-national party' . . . the enemy of all great national institutions." He repeatedly condemned what he called the narrow spirit of "old corps connexion," which "rendered national union on revolution principles [of 1689] impossible."[18] His failure to achieve cabinet rank before 1756 was seen by the public, especially his ardent commercial followers in London, as the result of his incorruptibility and of sinister maneuverings against him. He fed this with skillful insinuations and an epigrammatic eloquence which has delighted many biographers. The old corps, he said, were "united only in corrupt and arbitrary measures"; the German princelings whom England subsidized were traitors, and ministers who favored them were guilty of "renouncing the English nation"; in the crisis of the Seven Years' War only he could "save this country"; his fitness to lead rested not on boroughmongering but on spontaneous popularity—"It is the people who sent me here"; England's fundamental problem, the fact that "in every quarter of the world we are inferior to France," was due to defective morale, and its solution was to break England's spiritual submission to France and liberate her inner greatness: "I want to call England out of that enervated state into which twenty thousand men from France can shake her."

Buoyed up by public support, Pitt took charge again in 1757 and it was under his leadership that the miraculous victories of the next few years occurred. These go far to explain the tremendous new popularity he attained, but there was something more to it. Historians have sensed that there was something noumenal and irrational beneath Pitt's popularity; they have called it 'enigmatic'—that is, inexplicable in conventional historical terms.[19] It would be more descriptive to call it emblematic, for Pitt did indeed trade upon something not reckoned on before, namely the swelling undercurrent of nationalist sentiment. He was a political stand-in for the cultural dream come true, the dream of *national renewal*. He figured as the unexpected realization in politics of the mythic triumph of Britannia, a fulfillment of the myth of national oppression, liberation and redemption. He was 'poor Horatio' released and rampant, the very personification of English moral superiority, sweeping the French and the French-English junto of appeasers and oligarchs before him. There was indeed more to his popularity than would appear to conventional exam-

ination. To many contemporaries he seemed to represent the national
ancestry's answer to the predicted moral crisis of oligarchy, a sudden,
unexpected restoration of those ancient British virtues which were just
now beginning to be hawked under the name of 'Sincerity.' And by his
example he seemed to infuse the same spirit into others. Hints of all this
appear in the phrases by which the City of London saluted him in 1760 as
'THE MAN WHO BY THE STRENGTH OF HIS GENIUS AND THE
STEADFASTNESS OF HIS MIND AND A CERTAIN HAPPY CON-
TAGION OF HIS PROBITY AND SPIRIT RECOVERED, AUG-
MENTED AND SECURED THE BRITISH EMPIRE IN ASIA, AFRICA
AND AMERICA AND RESTORED THE ANCIENT REPUTATION
AND INFLUENCE OF THIS COUNTRY AMONGST THE NATIONS
OF EUROPE.'[20]

A graph of nationalist morale in the 1750s, were we to construct one,
would thus show a state of gloom at the early part of the decade, a sudden descent to new levels of fear and frustration near the middle of it
(compounded now from political as well as cultural causes), and then a
remarkable escalation to unimagined heights of euphoria at its end, regis-
tering not only the successes of Pitt and of British arms but the enactment
of a morality play beneath the surface of things. This happiness, the euphoria, the sense of miraculous liberation from an alien grasp, was then
heightened even more by the death of the unattractive George II and the
coronation of his virtuous grandson in 1760.

George III was the first English king in the age of nationalism, and he
not only sensed the fact but welcomed it. To the people, the country's
political leadership now seemed under the joint control of not one but
two great and 'sincere' national heroes. George was no less ostentatiously
proud of his British heritage than Pitt, and even more irrationally mis-
trustful and belligerently inclined toward the 'circling Junto' of oligarchs
who, he imagined (for he too shared the patriot's nightmare), sought to
'storm his Closet' and make him their prisoner. The young king, untar-
nished by politics, shone forth as another national liberator, potentially
more effective even than Pitt in giving lung to 'the Voice of an abused
People' (as John Brown had put it a year or so earlier), in becoming the
leader of a projected crusade against what Brown had decried as the
ruinous selfishness, disloyalty and un-English influences of the *'leading
People.'* 'Britannia Redux,' the figured backdrop of illusions behind the
stage of politics, now seemed to present two heroic rescuers arm in arm.

3. JOHN WILKES AND THE TUMULTS OF THE SIXTIES

It was too good to be true, and many new 'betrayals' and disillusionments
were to be the price of a deeper and more definite political movement;
the English 'Struggle for Independence' was not to enter its second phase
till the later sixties. For the truth, of course, is that neither Pitt nor the
king was the fleshly incarnation of the National Identity, and, further,
that beyond a sufficiency of military power, the true interests of the Brit-

ish nation were something upon which even advanced 'patriots' might disagree. In 1760 Pitt wanted war, personal control, and small measures to dilute the oligarchy's power, while George wanted peace, personal control, and a much more thorough destruction of the oligarchical manipulation of politics and the oligarchical spirit in public life. Both were, just as the 'sincere' stereotypic National Identity wanted them to be, aggressive and obstinate, and this also pointed to a collision. It is clear that from the first day of the new reign, when Pitt brazenly forced the young king to revise his characterization of the "bloody" war to "expensive but just and necessary," patriotic hopes focusing on a lasting union between king, minister, and people would soon be disappointed.

George was concerned about the war's huge cost. Responding to complaints about the land tax, moved by a larger and indeed more truly national constituency than Pitt, convinced that Britain's overseas acquisitions were more than satisfactory, and increasingly persuaded that Pitt like all the other politicians (except his own 'dearest friend' Lord Bute) wanted to reduce him to "a state of bondage," he determined to make peace at almost any price. Pitt, on the other hand, supported by West Indian merchants, the London crowd, and a miscellany of 'country' patriots, would be satisfied with nothing less than the complete destruction of French colonial power. The upshot was his resignation in October 1761. His supporters saw this as the result of pro-French sympathy at work in the political elite. Openly voicing the preconceptions we have studied, they darkly insinuated "that a French-influenced faction was behind the opposition to Pitt's policies," attributing his fall to the "malice of the 'frenchified faction'."[21]

These suspicions seemed more deeply confirmed by subsequent events. Pitt, it turned out, had been right in predicting the war's continuation, and the government's rejection of his advice proved costly. On the other hand, the colonial war, still conducted on his plans despite his absence, continued to prosper amazingly, with many new Bourbon possessions falling into British hands. Small wonder that the Peace of Paris (March, 1763), negotiated by the Duke of Bedford—one of the most notorious appeasers and Francophiles of the day—and piloted through Parliament by Bute and the unsavory Henry Fox (another notorious Francophile, Pitt's sworn enemy and in many ways his moral anti-type), was execrated by the Pittites as a disgraceful sell-out. This seemed particularly true of the valuable conquests of the Caribbean, which were indeed most generously returned to the Bourbons. There was also the fact that by their perfidious treatment of Prussia the ministry had forfeited any future help on the Continent against France, and thus condemned Britain to international isolation even while Choiseul, the French minister, was dedicating himself to revenge and the rebuilding of French power. Pitt denounced the treaty for three hours in the House of Commons, lacing his speech with suggestions of ministerial treachery and national surrender, concluding that "we retain nothing, although we have conquered everything." He continued for many years afterwards to treat "the entire overthrow of the French system" as the imperative mission of English policy.[22]

The psychology of the Pittites in 1763 thus resembled that of many German nationalists in the radical summer of 1919. A long and dreadfully expensive war had ended with the nation in possession of enormous territorial gains, which then evaporated in the hands of despised politicians returning from Paris with a few scraps of paper. Somewhere there was an international 'system' at work, and England's governors were in it. Under the circumstances, the intense suspicions of sinister influences and alien conspiracies which already haunted the nationalist mind could only be further intensified; and moreover it was just at this time, as we recall, that the floodgates to Calais were opening for the greatest wave of touring in the nation's history and the further supposed de-nationalization of England's privileged youth. We must continue to bear in mind the important fact that in English social belief the sixties and seventies were a time of obsessive worry over national decline, and particularly of profound and not totally unjustified fears over the frenchification of young Englishmen. Undoubtedly France's invisible political influence was the more widely credited because of this highly visible social influence over the nation's elite.

But then Britain did retain many of her conquests, and emerged in 1763 as the leading colonial power on earth. Here, in nationalist thinking, was not a contradiction (for illusions obey no logic) but an object lesson. To the 'agitated' patriot this figured as proof of what England could do when led by ministers who truly expressed the national will—by ministers who "*dare* to do justice to their country," as one journalist termed it,[23] putting words to the unresting suspicion.

The Pittities, propelled for nearly a decade through all the registers of political emotion, thus found themselves plunged back into bitter frustration in 1763. When Hogarth died in 1764 he sank beneath a load of political unhappiness as well as cultural torments and professional humiliations. The same was true of the expiring John Brown, with his revivalist philosophy (distinctly Pittite in political implication) of national renewal and purification under a popular government led by 'SOME GREAT MINISTER.' At least the Pittites were endowed now with a new awareness of each other and of what they might accomplish. Their Pittism, however, was a far stronger force than attachment to Pitt or to any other man selected to represent it in politics. It is a measure of the intensity and blind momentum of this emotion that when Pitt resigned in 1761 and accepted a peerage for his wife and a large state pension, he was furiously reviled as a false patriot by many who only days earlier had idolized him, his effigy being burnt in the City and his wife vilified as Lady Cheat'em.

And this was only a mild instance of the anti-aristocratic political violence which increasingly marked the sixties—another sign of the political impact of the propaganda we studied earlier. Bute and Bedford were hissed and pelted in the streets, while for more than a year the treaty negotiations were denounced in furious language and in "an Inundation of such Infamous, obscene and Shocking Prints as were never before known in England." In 1765 London weavers marched on the House of Lords after it approved free trade in French silks, and, convinced that secret agreements existed between Frenchmen and the ministry, provoked riots which almost brought the ministry down. Three years later there were still more riots particularly directed against the property of the rich and fashionable. "'Tis a time of most licentious and plentiful abuse of all persons of eminence," complained the Earl of Malmesbury; "the discontent . . . grows more and more universally."[24]

And so patriotic sentiment in the mid-sixties, though wildly 'agitated' and suspiciously trained on 'all persons of eminence,' was without a positive political focus. Its political philosophy was immature, its figureheads half broken. Pitt, though not without lingering popularity and a patriotic charisma which even the king continued to feel, was seen in a more critical light. George, the would-be 'patriot king,' lost some popularity through his handling of the conclusion of the war, and even more through his bull-headed reliance upon Bute, who, as a Scotsman, further inflamed the feelings of nativists obsessed with the betrayal of England (either directly by the Scots, or, and this suspicion rested on live memories, indirectly by France working though Scotland). The weakening of George's popularity increased with the John Wilkes affair in 1763, in which Wilkes was hounded down for having publicly suggested, among other things, that Bute had secured the ratification of the Peace of Paris through bribery of the House of Commons. Wilkes's martyrdom carried the wartime excitement into the postwar era, figuring notionally as continuing proof of an alien conspiracy at work in the political state, implicating even the king in this conspiracy, and thus widening even further the perceived gap between state and nation.

Absurdly enough, it was the old corps which now attempted to don the mantle of National Deliverer. Historians understand that beneath the shuffle of contemporary politics the king's most obdurate and permanent opposition was that posed by this broad "aristocratic clique," inspired by a "feeling of caste."[25] The same group was, of course, the prime target of the hostile propaganda detailed throughout this book. If George had been as lax and pleasure-loving as Louis XV, or as incompetent as Louis XVI, the rising tide of anti-aristocratic feeling might well have borne him down just as a similar hostility ultimately did the Bourbons, in the wake of an anti-aristocratic political revolution. But George, psychologically fortified, was more determined than they to counter the aristocracy, and in fact more successful at it. The immediate effect of his efforts however (again much as in France) was to breathe new life into his old corps by permitting them too to pose, however ridiculously in the sharpening gaze of their many critics, as still another rescuer of national 'liberty.' While the country inched toward an entire new politics, based on new principles of legitimacy being prepared in the cultural renaissance now in full swing, the Whig magnates snatched up their wooden swords for what they saw as a repeat performance of the parlor drama of 1688, a clash between tyranny and 'men of weight and substance.'

The battle was first joined in 1762 when the Duke of Newcastle, the aged leader of the old corps, having been repeatedly affronted by Bute and the king, resigned. Then instead of being recalled, as he imagined he would be, his many followers, the 'Pelhamite Innocents,' great lords as well as the humblest functionaries, were brutally purged from office. The king now thought himself happily rid of the tyrannical and corrupting influences of the 'Great Revolution-Principle Families.' With their political dominance broken he could proceed, in what he unvaryingly called "these very licentious days," to the purification and unification of all his people under his own pure, honest, frank, original, independent, and unambiguously British leadership. "Men of less principle and honesty than I pretend to may look on public measures and opinions as a game, I always act from conviction. . . It has ever been a certain position with me that firmness is the characteristic of an Englishman. . . I begin to see that I shall soon have enfused some of that spirit which I thank Heaven ever attends me."[26] The Britannic reign of virtue, long awaited by king and suffering people, would begin.

The un-Britannic oppressors, however—the Revolution Families—saw things very differently. Of course they were no more un-British than un-German were Germany's small population of German Jews during the Weimar years (a mere one percent), whom, within the 'group situation,' they subliminally resembled in their unwanted notional role, their elaborately rigged epiphenomenal mission as rich, wire-pulling alien oppressors. The great Whigs, as we saw earlier, had their own distinctive notions of themselves and of the national danger, and as a group they were still far the most powerful men in the land, thanks to their acres and continuing social ascendancy. And thus the Revolution Families, having come to think of high office as a 'predestinated' birthright and of themselves as representing both the purest Whig principles and the preponderance of 'natural weight' in the country, began to entertain visions of a reviving royal despotism. Was not the king surrounding himself with Tories as Lords and Grooms of the Bedchamber? Was not Bute a Stuart, and were not he and the king setting up, behind the old Tory smokescreen of 'measures not men,' a new 'system of favouritism' by which they intended to destroy all connections and reduce all politicians to dependence on the crown?

In truth the king's tactics were only those perfected already by the Whigs themselves, but such suspicions came easily to the old corps grandees, a group which included the richest men in the land and which boasted the superiority of its ancestry and social credentials over all others, including those of the royal House of Brunswick. Very few of these magnates, in point of fact, were of 'revolution lineage,' the greatest of them being, as the king's friends derisively pointed out, descendants of the Stuarts, their bastards, their courtiers and agents.[27] But the bedrock

of politics is self-serving delusions, and the magnates were no less attached to theirs than the king to his, and the arriving nationalist 'agents'
to theirs. And so still another illusion of conspiracy began to flourish.
However mutually incompatible, such illusions continued to spread con-
tagiously through the political groupings, the exaggerated fear of conspiracies naturally provoking reactions which themselves were seen as
conspiratorial.

It was thus against disturbing signs of 'Tory' conspiracy in the background that the old corps began to piece together its own 'confederacy.'
The large group of disgruntled and proud politicians ranged around
Newcastle and Rockingham (Newcastle's successor as leader of the old
corps) began to spread the idea that the king had 'designs on the constitution,' and to evolve what was then the heretical idea that consistent political opposition by an antiministerial 'party' (meaning themselves) was in
the best interests of 'the people.' According to Charles Fox, a later recruit
to the Newcastle-Rockingham group, politicians out of office should unite
in consistent and principled opposition to ministerial policy, and, when
invited into office, should exercise solidarity amongst themselves and a
monopoly over all important royal appointments; in sum, they should
either oppose the king or dominate him (as they had done in the past),
but they should do it all according to 'principle,' the only reliable basis for
continuous political organization. "We and *we only*," wrote Rockingham,
were oppositionists "on system and principle." It was this novel view of
'party,' this self-serving though cosmeticized version of what was still
widely mistrusted as aristocratic 'faction,' which, more than any other
political idea they held, distinguished the 'grand Whigs' of the Newcastle-
Rockingham school from all other politicians in the eyes of contemporaries, and particularly sharpened the contrast between them and the
other main group fallen from royal favor, Pitt and his small band of parliamentary followers. For Pitt, though he continued to profess respect for
the moguls and promised to base any ministry of his on their support, in
fact opposed government by 'party' no less earnestly than King George
himself, and repeatedly vowed that "he would never force himself upon
the King" nor climb to office as a member of a "cabal."[28]

The old corps 'cabal,' its tonnish young men thirsting for office, looked
for an opportunity to strike back and avenge the purge of 1762. It was
the government's arrest, by means of a single 'general warrant,' of the
impertinent Wilkes and four dozen others (1763), which gave the Rockinghams their first golden opportunity to align themselves with 'liberty'
and paint the king's friends as agents of despotism. While the aged Duke
of Newcastle persuaded himself that the arrests symbolized "the end of
Charles the Second's reign coming on very fast," younger members of his
connection, bestirring themselves from their haunts in 'the circle of Fascination,' paraded to visit Wilkes in the Tower, trumpeted the case for
freedom of the press and free speech for members of Parliament, and
looked on encouragingly (though with secret apprehension) as crowds of
Londoners, still driven by wartime excitement and anger over the Trea-

son of Paris, took to the streets in support of 'Wilkes and Liberty.'[29]

This was only the beginning of the Rockinghams' novel flirtations with 'the people' in their long and badly fought match with George III. Even while themselves briefly in office (1765–66) they supported the first truly national petitioning campaign of the age, an extraparliamentary agitation designed to strengthen their hand in forcing the repeal of the American Stamp Act. George succeeded in ridding himself of 'King Rockingham' soon afterwards and tried out a ministry recommended by the City of London, a nonpartisan ministry under Pitt (who forfeited still more of his popular appeal on becoming Earl of Chatham in 1766); but this ministry too, though emphatically supported by the king in his war against 'those confederacies of great lords,' failed in consequence of Chatham's ill health. The Rockinghams discovered another chance in 1769. At this great historic juncture they thought they saw in the petitioning tactic a means of throwing out the king's ministers, forcing a dissolution of Parliament, and bringing themselves to power on a huge tide of public opinion. They were very wrong in their estimations, and the fact provides another striking proof of how remote they had grown from common sentiments despite the artificial bond newly created by George's supposed tyranny. It was not their professions of liberty so much as the French lace on their coats and the macaroni on their butter plates which impressed the suspicious men who watched them. *They* were the cabalistical bugbear of nearly everyone else (save the network of Dissenters who habitually supported them).

The tumults of the later sixties did not arise solely from the Middlesex elections of 1768–69, for there was a continuous history of popular unrest and rioting in this decade. Nor was Wilkes, the central figure in these elections, the real cause of the political emotions which swirled through them: he was instead the object selected to personify and represent those emotions, just as the king and Pitt had similarly been selected earlier in the decade. The emotions, implanted in many ordinary people through innumerable experiences both public and private, and further agitated in them very deliberately by many propagandists in many different ways, arose from much deeper sources. Wilkes, though himself indeed one of the finest of these propagandists, should be looked upon as the third political recipient of those passionate feelings of cultural resentment, social and political exclusion, psychological alienation, historical *angst,* and ancestral self-glorification whose formation we have studied, and it seems impossible to appreciate his full significance except against this complicated background. In a way he was like a magnet dropped into the iron filings of nationalist sentiment. At a time when political feelings were high but politics in disarray, and the energies of political affiliation diverted from ordinary channels by the unattractiveness of the politicians and the incoherence of the two parties in transition, he gave a renewed and very sharp political focus to the struggle for freedom from what seemed an un-Britannic way of life, imposed by the poisonous aliens at the top. Though Pitt had once performed this role, his transformation into

Chatham left the people with no hero so appealing as Wilkes. But then because Wilkes increasingly waved the flag of 'the people,' they, in championing his political cause, were learning to champion their own.

The 'condition of civil war' (Minogue) was about to bear fruit. As Professor Brewer has admirably shown, the Wilkesite commotions assisted the spread of a nationwide network of anti-establishment feeling, symbolism, and ceremony, all revolving round the defense of 'English Liberty.' The tumults of 1768–71 gave still more focus and tremendous new intensity to the generalized passions and unrest which had stirred the country since the beginning of the Seven Years' War, assisting their spread both geographically and socially, and funneling them into a radical political program. Familiar is the story of Wilkes's return to England from his exile on the Continent and his victorious parliamentary candidacy for the small, urbanized county of Middlesex in March, 1768 (his 'courtier' opponent unsuccessfully blasting him as an iniquitous "French Renegade").[30] After this there followed his arrest, imprisonment, and expulsion from Parliament on charges dating from his earlier scrape with 'despotism.' There were weeks of nearly continuous rioting. The climax came amid great clamor in Wilkes's thrice-repeated re-election and expulsion from the House of Commons (February–April, 1769), followed by his replacement by George III's hand-picked candidate, Henry Luttrell, whom he had beaten by a margin of nearly 1,200 votes to 300. The central point that emerged in all this commotion, with its violence, military repression, petitions, lawsuits, and pamphleteering, was the fact that a majority of the House of Commons, encouraged by a vindictive king and his patronage-wielding ministers, was capable of setting aside the rights of the Middlesex electors. By implication, the rights of every elector in the country, indeed the British Empire, were insecure in the face of royal displeasure and a corrupted political system. The crisis of the constitution, long predicted by the intellectuals, had arrived. Even the king, in whom so much hope for 'national renewal' had been vested, now seemed almost as corrupting as the oligarchs he had displaced.

The Whigs in opposition fed the Wilkesite clamor and tried to ride it into office. Chatham, struggling to regain popularity as tribune of the people, delivered philippics denouncing the corrupting power of royal influence, and publicly chided the Rockinghams, the only parliamentary group numerically capable of standing up to the king, towards an agitation more popular than any they had known.[31] The Rockinghams, not to be out-Whigged, maneuvered to strengthen their hand by taking over the huge extraparliamentary petitioning campaign they found leaping up around them. Rockingham imposed himself on the debates of the enraged Middlesex freeholders and himself drafted the first of these petitions (April 1769), at the same time taking care to limit the freeholders' grievances to the injustice of Luttrell's acceptance into the House of Commons, not the much more explosive issue of the rottenness of the representative system itself. National freedom to the Rockinghams still meant the supremacy of a parliament run by themselves, not the representation of the sovereign people in a purified House of Commons. They were in the position of buccaneers attacking a rotting hulk which they wanted not to sink but to refit for another splendid season on the high seas; their wealth, grace, and social authority made them think their intentions might go unnoticed. If they had spent more time reading, and less in gaming and traveling, they might have noticed other pirates on the horizon.

4. THE EMERGENCE OF AGENTS AND AGENCIES

The movement was now entering its second phase. 'Agents' of the second rank were emerging, beginning to articulate a coherent political philosophy with clear political demands, and to organize agitation through associations reaching well beyond the metropolis. The uproar of 1768–71 was by no means confined to London and nearby Middlesex: the government received dozens of Wilkesite petitions from almost twenty counties and a dozen towns and cities, signed by a quarter of the total voting population; and this was but a sign of the excitement reaching well below the 'respectable' political classes, down into the unenfranchised. More and more people were reacting to the political drama, learning to identify with political aspirations, and, guided by the literati, to contemplate their rights to political participation not merely as property holders but as 'free-born Englishmen,' descendants of the fabled ancient community. While the king and the politicians looked back to 1689 for the symbols of national liberty, the arriving nationalist 'agents,' defining the nation differently, looked much further back for theirs and imagined they found them in the happy days before the Norman Conquest. The urge grew to unite and 'recover' these fictitious ancestral liberties.

It was thus by no mere coincidence that the first 'agency' was founded by a man almost as noted today for his pioneering philology as for his radical politics. The Society of the Supporters of the Bill of Rights (1769), the first organization to attempt the unification of all patriots in a nationwide political network, was launched by key figures in the Wilkesite agitation, led by John Horne (afterwards known as Horne Tooke). Horne, providentially named, was the trumpet of the movement, its first mouthpiece outside the political establishment and its indefatigable organizer. He founded both of its original political agencies, the Bill of Rights society and the Constitutional Society (1771), which in turn was the parent of the radically democratic Society for Constitutional Information (1780); he was a founder of this also.

He was the pattern 'agent.' Born in Westminster in 1736, he grew up amongst small traders; his father ran a poultry shop, and two of his brothers became tradesmen. At school he came to feel both intellectual superiority and social inferiority to many of his classmates: on being asked by "the sons of people of distinction" about his father's "rank and condition," the ten-year-old boy, making play on the Levant trade, cleverly passed himself off as the son of "an eminent Turkey merchant!" The father sent him to Cambridge (where he graduated with honors in 1758), then pushed him into the Church, buying him a living at New Brentford in Middlesex, only a few miles from London. He liked teaching but did not take his clerical duties very seriously; his Christianity, Hazlitt said later, was almost non-existent. But it should be noted that he was nonetheless a loyal Anglican; he disliked the anti-episcopal outlook of Dissent, and detested Catholicism not only because it was "superstitious" and opposed to "human freedom" but because "he abhorred the idea of a connexion with, and a reliance on, a foreign jurisdiction, as this seemed to trench on the independence of his native country."[32]

It was at about this time that Horne began to indulge those new interests in 'the genius of the English language' which he shared with so many contemporaries, and which were to earn him his honored title of 'The Grammarian,' the first philologist to examine the Gothic and Saxon roots of the English tongue. In his interests and achievements one sees a parallel with those of James Watt, also born in 1736; both were twenty-four at the accession of George III, and there are signs that both were deeply influenced by the cultural revival then in motion. It is certain that the new motivations carried Horne well beyond literature. On political questions he displayed "a degree of zeal" which, as even his fond biographer admits, amounted to "political fanaticism." His biographer speculates on the source of this, finding it in an amorphous conspiracy theory—another reminder of Watt, who saw Parliament as 'possessed' by 'the devil.' All his life, we are told, Horne was actuated by a profound "suspicion, however strange and unaccountable it may appear," that "a regular plot was actually formed" for the destruction of the English constitution. "He burned with impatience to support its tottering fabric."[33]

This meant that in the early sixties he burned with admiration for Pitt. His biographer admirably catches the depth and nature of this enthusiasm: "The image of Mr. Pitt seemed to have haunted his dreams." In fact Horne always trusted the Pitts, father and son, more than any other politicians; a sentiment he shared, as we shall see, with all the other early 'agents.' But such passionate feelings were not easily contained, and before long they found a second object in Wilkes. Wilkes in 1765 was forty years old, Horne twenty-nine; the younger man's identification with the older is obvious in his first political effusions. Having written a song celebrating Wilkes's liberation from the Tower, Horne now anonymously penned a flaming 'Petition of an Englishman' (1765) in which he courted the martyrdom already suffered by his hero, challenging the government to track him down, squeeze out his eyes, cut off his tongue, and throw him into the frenchified stocks (the "Croix de St. Pillory") they were preparing for all the English sons of liberty. "No! Wilkes, thou art not alone—we are all OUT-lawed." He welcomed his fate: "My heart in its first pantings beat to LIBERTY . . . and even in death I will not be divided from her."[34]

Such was the uncalm heart with which the radical parson greeted his idol's return to England in 1768 and his parliamentary candidacy as a freeholder of Middlesex. Horne himself was now a Middlesex freeholder; it would be hard to invent a better illustration than he affords of the interconnectedness of leading elements of the Third Estate, the links between ambitious merchants, disgruntled freeholders, alienated men of letters, and the political volatility current among them all. Horne threw himself into the elections and was indeed more prominent in them than Wilkes, who spent much of this time in jail. He canvassed the county, instigated prosecutions against soldiers responsible for the deaths of Wilkesites, and made speeches so wild as to suggest that he would gladly dip his hands in the tyrants' blood—he said that "in a cause so just and so holy, he would dye his black coat red!" In fact he managed, in the course of these years, to insult, cross swords with, or fight a lawsuit against nearly everyone in the political elite, from Bedford, Grafton, and Mansfield on down. As he saw it, the whole political establishment was involved in the disenfranchisement of the people.[35]

Horne is believed to have penned not only Middlesex's second petition (Rockingham's was quite unacceptable to one of his outlook), but, through his expanding influence in the City, London's two petitions to the king as well. Though couched in terms of submission, these were in fact threatening lectures, and it is no wonder that George pronounced them "disrespectful to him, injurious to his parliament, and irreconcilable to the principles of the constitution." The petitions stated bluntly that it was "morally demonstable" that the men in "the present house of commons do not represent the people." They complained of "our invaded birthrights" and held up "secret and visible machinations" as the cause of the nation's woes. There was a "secret and malign influence" at work in every successive government, and it was lodged not only near the throne but in the House of Commons. The people, sustained by their ancestors, would reclaim their lost liberty: "As it was gained by the stern virtue of our ancestors, by the virtue of their descendants it shall be preserved."[36]

Horne's 'agency' of 1769 was a new type of machine in English politics, and it ran on much richer fuel than whiggism and toryism; powered by nationalistic passions, it turned English politics toward democracy. Though initially set up simply to relieve Wilkes's debts, the Bill of Rights Society soon became an extraparliamentary pressure group drawing together in a single force the resentments and resources of many hitherto scattered individuals. While the parliamentary opposition organized petitions whose aim was to bring about a dissolution and new elections, Horne and his friends went much further. They appended to their petitions long lists of grievances and began to evolve what has been called "a kind of charter of Radical demands," which by 1771 included the impeachment of Wilkes's persecutors, the passage of laws against political bribery, the exclusion of placemen and pensioners from the House of Commons, the repeal of many taxes recently imposed on the Americans, and, most important, the institution of annual parliaments and the promotion of "a full and equal representation of the people in parliament." They sought to impose these demands upon Parliament by circulating a pledge to support only those parliamentary candidates who expressly agreed to work towards their enactment.[37]

The demands went so far that Wilkes, who still had parliamentary aspirations, was reluctant to endorse them, and this provoked a schism in which many of the more earnest radicals followed Horne into his new Constitutional Society (1771). The plain truth is that Wilkes—'no Wilkite,' as he said, and only 'a patriot by accident'—was even less the hoped-for National Redeemer than Pitt or the king. The nationalists had been able to conceal this from themselves so long as he remained a martyr in jail, but when he was released in April 1770, opinion began to outrun him just as it had the other midwife-figureheads. Wilkes was a political opportunist and free-spending rake who too obviously aped the Ton he was expected to drive from the temple. Rockingham rightly favored him over Horne, believing that he (as Rockingham put it privately) "would be easier to manage." Indeed Horne had warned Wilkes, his former idol, against his acceptance of secret subsidies from Rockingham and his lavish style of life, expressing "both his own and the public dissatisfaction at the laced liveries and French domestics of a person supported by the bounty of others," that is, by the contributors to the Bill of Rights Society. It was hard for Wilkes to sustain the image of the 'sincere patriot' in his smart new Kensington home and expensive scarlet suits—adorned with "the most fashionable gold buttons," sent to him from his beloved Paris by Baron Holbach.[38] When he selfishly objected to the Society's financial assistance to certain printers struggling over the public reporting of parliamentary debates, Horne angrily seceded from the organization, taking with him many of its more influential members, and founded the Constitutional Society.

The name was not carelessly chosen. Horne, an educated man and a passionate patriot, now attached himself to something that would never betray him—that is, to the Constitution, popularly (in fact, as we shall see, ancestrally) interpreted. This was really the last inevitable step in his emancipation from the personalized politics of a dying age and his acceptance of a mythic ideal as the foundation of political faith. He would rally the people and teach them their constitutional rights. At the same time, the philologist in him would teach them a greater love and clearer understanding of the language in which those rights were supposedly enshrined.

The political drift of the sixties thus resembled that in France, where the ideal of that decade, the 'king united with his subjects,' was slowly giving way to another centered much more substantially on the will of the whole associated people. The people themselves, as an abstract idea, were becoming the object of political allegiance through the activities of 'agents' (who appeared earlier in England than across the Channel) and the assistance of the intellectual revolution in the background (which was earlier and stronger in the British Isles than in France or anywhere else). Political loyalty was being transferred to the idealized moral entity of the nation, just as, in literature, the 'frequency of communal personifications' and the elaboration of 'an archetype of simple virtue' registered other facets of the same great cultural drift, the key international event in the age of the democratic *nationalist* revolutions.

i. radical ideology and Saxon legitimacy

Here is the place to pause for an examination of the political ideology of Horne and his friends. It is no exaggeration to say that this has confused many later writers on English political history. At the heart of the whole interpretative problem is the need to account for the fact that, as Brewer explains, the radicalism emerging late in that decade constituted "a qualitative shift in the argument about reform,"[39] a major change in the nature of left-wing ideas and demands. The central problem that has long occupied political historians thus bears a striking resemblance to those facing economic and literary historians as well, for all three disciplines detect momentous but not very easily explainable new departures centered in the 1760s.

It was the more or less simultaneous impact of nationalism on all the spheres of life which accounts for this. The sixties saw the first fruits of the movement in many fields, politics included. A whole generation of people, educated in nationalist perspectives, was now reaching maturity. We saw that Horne was exactly the same age as Watt; in fact he was also a member of the same 'generational cohort' as the other best-known radicals of the coming age: he was born in 1736; John Jebb was also born in 1736, while John Cartwright and Christopher Wyvill were both born in 1740. All four came of age during the Seven Years' War, and, like their new king (born in 1737), were in their vigorous early twenties in 1760. With the Reverend John Brown they shared similar fears about a huge, dark plot against the 'tottering fabric' of their country, and a similar 'fanaticism' in their determination to fight it. And they were fortified in this by a shared historical philosophy, largely developed during the third quarter of the century.

This philosophy, contemptuously tossed aside by many historians as irrelevant baggage aboard the radical program, was in fact the foundation of their whole political ideology. Few investigators have noticed that Horne, Cartwright and Jebb were not only agitators but historical folklorists of one sort or another. What was distinctively new about their radicalism was the fact that they demanded a novel solution to the ills of English political life, namely the expansion and democratization of the franchise. But they genuinely saw this not as a novelty but instead as a *restoration* of liberties stolen from the people already; they saw themselves not as 'radicals' (a label applied later) but as restorers, reformers. Their political demands were projected from a distinct and (though they did not recognize this themselves) substantially new conception of the English Constitution which had its foundations in the new, folkish, ethnohistorical ideology of English cultural nationalism. With William Cobbett, the great moralist-historian-agitator who followed them, they might have declared,

with none of some academicians' modern, post-Marxian sense of the con-
tradictoriness of this, "We want *great alteration,* but we want *nothing
new.*"[40]

Wanting 'great alterations' toward democracy, they persuaded themselves that this had been a fixture of English antiquity. Again we are reminded of how political nationalism waits upon the 'Stirrings' of cultural
nationalism, needing its elaboration of pseudohistorical ideas as a runner
for its demands. Some historians have indeed noticed, apparently without
suspecting the ideological significance of this, that "the 1760s were
marked, on both sides of the Channel, by a universal eagerness to re-
discover and idealize ancient constitutions." The truth is that the ethnohistorical ideas of Horne and his friends, far from signalling a "quite
extraordinary naivety,"[41] far from being the ridiculous antiquarianism
which conventional scholarship imagines them to have been, were nothing
less than the pivot on which the radicals attempted to overturn and de-
mocratize the whole political structure they confronted. Like all nationalists they posited an egalitarian paradise in the past, demanded that
this be 'recovered' in the present, and held the current system up to it as
damning proof of modern corruption, unconstitutionality and il-
legitimacy.

But their historiographical problem was a delicate one, like that of a
surgeon probing life-sustaining tissues. Their immediate concern was to
vindicate civil liberties, and this meant upholding the Bill of Rights
against the crown. But the long-range task was to shift the whole basis of
contemporary politics, and to do so in such a way as to escape falling into
the arms of a revived old corps whiggism, marching behind that same Bill
of Rights and the other shibboleths of 1689. What the radicals wanted was
to go forward toward democracy, not backward toward some newly legiti-
mated compact between crown and oligarchy. This meant that in their
appeal to the historical foundations of national 'liberty' they had to acknowledge but at the same time overleap the aristocratic settlement of
1689, playing down the Glorious Revolution as the touchstone of national
liberties, instead reaching much further back to the nebulous and ill-doc-
umented golden age of the Saxon common man, the age before the coming of the Normans and the establishment of the feudal system. It was no
accident that the evolving literature of cultural nationalism provided exactly the sort of historical backing they needed, for many of them helped
to write it. A whole generation of radical nationalists began to invoke the
mythological history of Saxon freedom and Norman oppression in its
efforts to de-legitimate contemporary government and stimulate people
to 'repossess' their stolen rights.

The reader will recall that the outlines of this process, considered as
part of English literary development, were sketched in Chapter Five,
where we abstractly contemplated the rise of the 'new nationalist historiography.' In the early seventies, the period with which we are now concerned, this process was bearing fruit in a number of very craftily written

historical treatises. The most influential of these was Obadiah Hulme's *Historical Essay on the English Constitution* (1771).

Hulme's book is a powerful polemic, resting on and drawing all its authority from a mountain of historical and pseudohistorical fact. He brandishes his historian's credentials at the beginning, explaining that he has "carefully examined the foundation upon which the constitution was established in England, by our Saxon forefathers."[42] His whole text is designed to leave no doubt that the English constitution *was* that Saxon constitution, nothing more nor less, and therefore that every current political institution which differed from it—that is, from what he said it was—represented a vile usurpation of the rights of the English people.

He painted a most attractive picture of it. Nature, Reason, History, and God had all smiled on the happy Saxons. Many of their records were lost and evil oppressors had destroyed others, but thanks to historical research the constitution could be reconstructed. "If ever God Almighty did concern himself about forming a government" he had surely guided the Saxons in theirs, for the Saxon constitution ingeniously preserved "the natural rights of mankind," man's "natural right" to liberty, within a framework of political society. Doubtless many Indian tribes, even today, could "naturally fall into our way of government, upon the Saxon principles, with a very little instruction." This imperishable constitution breathed the spirit of liberty and equality: "They considered every man alike, as he came from the hands of his maker . . . whether he were rich or poor." There were no hereditary royal or noble distinctions among the sincere makers of the English constitution, and their entire structure of government, from tithing to shire to parliament (witenagemot) to the elective crown itself, was one of ladders of election, always uniting the whole from the bottom up. These ladders were renewed annually: "They never gave up their natural liberty, or delegated their power, of making laws, to any man, for a longer time than one year." Power, when exercised beyond strict limits, would corrupt anyone, and the wise Saxons realized this; hence every year the whole structure of government was renewed by a flurry of electing, so that only the wise and virtuous became leaders. Annual elections by the whole people were the very "quintessence, the life and soul of their constitution; and the basis of the whole fabrick of their government." Alfred the Great, "a prince of the most exalted merit, that ever graced the English throne, from that day to this," united the country and hence "the constitution of this country, became finally established, as a great nation." England, a folkish commonwealth surmounted by kings elected for life, was made.[43]

Then after six hundred idyllic years came the Norman Conquest, the Great Divide in the nation's history. It was not really a conquest but a betrayal by the priesthood. (The text is fiercely anticlerical.) "William the bastard, duke of Normandy . . . put an end to the Saxon mode of government," and there followed seven hundred and five years of fraud and unconstitutional government, right down to the date of writing. But the ancient constitution was not totally lost; it was "only buried under the rubbish collected by time, and new establishments." Hulme judges everything after 1066, every reign, act, charter, decree, and petition, by the degree to which it *restored* the constitution. Thus in the reign of Stephen, "wars prevented any further progress, during this reign, in restoring to the people their elective rights." Constitutional time stopped in 1066; political history afterwards was the story of "every further attempt, of the people, to recover either their civil or religious liberty."[44]

The English did reclaim some of their idyllic inheritance by two processes, either by purchasing back bits of it or by favoring this or that branch of the usurpers in return for constitutional restorations. Magna Carta was a case in point, a partial restoration. (By constantly contrasting "the English" with the Norman establishment Hulme manages to make this look like a purely native effort.) After lauding the reinstitution of the witenagemot in 1218 (the beginning of Parliament), he then skips lightly over the later Middle Ages and the Reformation (glancing darkly at the growth of rotten boroughs), and comes straight to 1625.

His attitude toward Charles I is unsympathetic, but he is no friend to Charles's enemies. The parliamentary politicians were little better than the tyrannical king, for with their Act of 1641 instituting the Long Parliament they launched the process under which modern parliaments, pretending to champion the people's rights against the crown, in fact absorbed these stolen rights themselves and began fleecing the people under their own pretended authority. The politicians wished to "change the mode of government, of this kingdom, into, what they called, a COMMONWEALTH; but, in reality, to vest the power in themselves, destroy the regal authority and enslave the people."[45] It is important to observe that Hulme was decidedly a monarchist, no 'Commonwealthman' nor sympathizer with republicanism in an anti-monarchical sense.

The "rebel parliament" gave way to Charles II's "pensioned parliament." Charles saw that he could maintain his tyranny by sharing the spoils with a venal House of Commons, and thus began the loathesome tendency which now in the eighteenth century constituted the greatest obstacle to constitutional reclamation. The inglorious Revolution of 1688 opened the door by sanctioning the merely "frequent" (not annual) summoning of Parliament. Greedy politicians soon afterwards imposed their odious Qualification Act of 1711 and Septennial Act of 1716, excluding all but the landed rich from the House of Commons and authorizing their oppression for as many as seven years at a stretch. So now at last the sacred annual "elective power of the people," this "first principle of our constitution," the people's "constitutional right of inheritance," was withheld from them by their own pretended delegates![46]

Thus armed, Hulme hits the beach; he arrives at his own historical period and heads straight for the enemy's armory, its treasurehouse of constitutional legitimacy. Contemptuously he remarks upon "what a slippery foundation the first principle of the constitution now stands, upon this REVOLUTIONAL ground; where the parliament have vested themselves with a power, to restrain the annual exercise of the elective power of the people, by acts of parliament." It was as plain as anything in Euclid that no such power existed. The whole authority of the men in the House of Commons lay in a delegated trust to protect the rights of the people who sent them there, and this trust was written in history. These men were "no longer the representatives of the people, than they were constitutionally so, that is, for one year." They possessed no constitutional right to alter the conditions under which they held office, for otherwise the whole logic of delegated authority was absurd. "The house of commons are, constitutionally, a body of men merely passive, with regard to their creation, duration, and dissolution." Nor could they pretend that they had ever been given the power to restrict electoral rights, for the "elective power of the people" was clearly "their constitutional right of inheritance." It followed inescapably that any parliament erected on electoral restrictions was erected on usurpation—on "acts of power, and not acts of law." The real intent of the men in power was to "rob the people of their rights" while throwing sand into their eyes with "false, fraudulent, and delusive" arguments concealing the constitutional iniquity of what they did. Contemporary government was based on power and fraud, not the constitution. To think otherwise was to imagine that there was no permanence whatsoever to the constitution, nothing that outlived the legislative performances of these usurpers who had stolen and bought their way into office. Upon such reasoning "our constitution may be one thing to-day, and another thing to-morrow." Upon such reasoning the usurpers could so drastically restrict electoral rights as to permit only themselves to vote, whereupon they would not only do all the representing but all the selecting! Then their false pretensions to legitimacy would be fully unmasked, for when that day arrived "they would elect one another, and then the aristocracy would completely throw off all disguise."[47]

Having bored these deep holes in the enemy's pretensions to legitimacy, the mythmongering historian then goes on to lay his charges and light the fuses; that is, to incite rage against the holders of this illegitimate power. Hulme's treatment of the great landlords is absolutely scorching. Detailing the economic and social depredation carried out under their unconstitutional authority, he repeatedly denounces them as a small, arrogant, and infinitely greedy "class," "all men of one interest," "a down right rank aristocracy, of the rich in land," whose selfishness, as displayed in their crass manipulations of the game laws, the corn laws, land taxes and window taxes, the taxes on malt, soap, and other 'necessaries,' rivalled that of any tyrants in history. Their vile traffic in offices, pensions and contracts, their gigantic engrossment of the land, their underhanded bounties to themselves from the Treasury and the mouths of the poor, their legislative spoliation of the middle and lower classes, all this was conducted in defiance of the sacred constitution of the land, whose first principle (as he repeats over and over) was that parliaments were to be elected annually by every taxpayer, every man who "paid his shot and bore his lot." None of this disgusting traffic would occur if the English constitution were truly in force, for "no corruption can stick upon a body of men, that is continually changing."[48]

The people had lost almost everything dear to them: "their constitutional, and natural liberty; their birthright, and inheritance, derived from God and nature!" More than this, they had "lost the distinguishing character, of Englishmen!" They had to repossess all this, "and that quickly too, or they will be lost for ever." But how to do it? Would some great leader rise to help them? "Much has been said, and much has been writ about patriotick kings, and patriotick ministers, but give me leave to tell, the good people of England, that it is all PATRIOTICK NONSENSE." The days of paternalism under some longed-for Messiah were ending: the people had to look to themselves. "Let the people only contemplate, their own strength, dignity, and importance." Then they would not be deflected by the tricks of politicians, whose game had always been to divide and thus divert them from their common interests and rights: "Thus the people of England have been spending their strength, and fury upon one another, about whigs and tories; high-church and low-church; conformists, and non-conformists; and such-like things of no more import, to the happiness, and well-being, of this nation, than long men, or short men; or fat men, and lean men."[49]

The true repository of faith was the people themselves, *all* the people. The people must turn to each other, rejecting the dominion of party prejudice and traditional alignment: "Let us then fling away all animosity, and tear from our hearts all party, names of discord, and evil distinction; and unite, heart and hand, as one man, from the east to the west, and from the north to the south, and recover, by our union, what we have lost, by our divisions." The way to obtain redress was by *popular national union;* "by associating together, in order to form a new chain of union and strength." A nationwide network of political associations, linked by correspondence, should be established, its head in London, its base in every parish and every market-town. The whole associated mass would throw its weight behind a detailed plan to demand annual elections throughout the island of Great Britain. Under this plan, parliamentary elections would be by secret ballot; electoral qualifications would be simple, uniform, and very democratic, as they had been in Saxon times; in the counties, every freeholder would vote; decayed borough electorates would be reconstituted and enlarged from the inhabitants surrounding each borough, and in every borough and town "every resident inhabitant, that pays his shot, and bears his lot, should be entitled to his election, for a member of parliament." Until all this occurred, the national network of political associations should force a rejection of every placeman, pensioner or contractor who solicited their votes, and bind every parliamentary candidate, in writing, to move and vote for annual parliaments and the repeal of all laws restricting the franchise. Only thus would the constitution be *restored* and the oppressors routed from their seats of power.[50]

There was something more to be noticed about these oppressors. Not only was the 'burial' of the constitution outrageous, but it was kept in its grave by men who, though wearing the sheep's clothing of English constitutionalism, cared nothing for their country. We have encountered this same idea in other intellectual settings (in fact we earlier examined it in another publication of the same year, Smollett's *Humphry Clinker*). The enforcing mechanism at work in Hulme's text is that same half-conscious imperative, that same unspoken but persistently hinted premise, which we have found operating in many other contexts, namely that what Englishmen must reject and overthrow is something *alien,* something *un-English,* something more or less reminiscently *French.* On the one hand, Hulme's repeated characterizations of "these qualified engrossers" as a single "class" of aristocratic landlords, "one class of men," "five or six hundred rich and powerful men," underline their social and political separateness from the rest of the nation. On the other, memories of their supposed descent from the predatory Norman aristocracy reinforce notions of them as ethnic aliens. There was not an un-hereditary Saxon *ealdorman* or *thane* among them. Hulme slyly marks the un-English titles, territorial names, and hereditary powers of the "new order of men, with new authority, derived from the [Norman] king." He approvingly quotes an "old author" who lauds "OUR GOOD OLD LAWS" and prays to be defended from "a foreign yoke, and domestic slavery." He sharpens the point with jabs at the (French) morality and life-style of the Quality—his sarcastic suggestion, for example, that they might well pass a parliamentary act requiring everyone but themselves to eat "horse-beans, pease, and potatoes; and that none but themselves, their wives and children, with their whores, pimps, and parasites, should [be] allowed to eat wheat." It was to give prominence to the understood connection between French characteristics and the yoke fixed upon England that Hulme sententiously presented, as though it were a rule of thumb by which to detect the real enemies of the constitution, his distinction between Saxon and Norman principles of government: "Whatever is of Saxon establishment, is truly constitutional; but whatever is Norman, is heterogeneous to it, and partakes of a tyrannical spirit."[51]

ii. the Norman Yoke

Let us stand back now to contemplate all this from a much more abstract point of view. What we have here is an expression of the theory of the 'Norman Yoke,' described some years ago by Christopher Hill, England's greatest student of the seventeenth century, in a brilliant essay occasionally cited but in fact very poorly digested by many writers on the eighteenth century. This theory, according to Hill, is perhaps the oldest political idea in English history, a mythical but (unlike most other early radical ideas) "entirely secular" conception, a primitive, dualistic "class theory of politics" with a long history running right down to the present century. The theory probably began or at least acquired a certain empirical basis in the facts of the Norman Conquest. It evidently passed down orally as a fragmentary memory till the sixteenth century, at which

time it was enlarged and afterwards converted into a virtual "political philosophy" by the Levellers and Diggers of the seventeenth century. What
happened to it after this, and why, is a little uncertain; Hill modestly
disclaims specialized knowledge of these later periods. For some unclear
reason the theory saw an extraordinary revival from about 1770, one
which saw a tremendous widening of its acceptance and influence. It began to take on, as it had not done during the religious and anti-royalist
struggles of the seventeenth century, a cult of King Alfred as Saxon hero
and law-giver. A symptomatic event, says Hill, was the publication of the
very *Essay* we have been examining here, Hulme's treatise on the English
Constitution. This work, he says, seems to have had "a remarkable
vogue," its basic ideas being stated over and over by many contemporary
and later radicals, including Catherine Macaulay, James Burgh, Cartwright, Granville Sharp, Paine, the Society for Constitutional Information, the London Corresponding Society, Spence, Carlile, Cobbett,
Hetherington, the Chartists, etc. In the nineteenth century it became a
pillar of Victorian historiography.[52]

The theory's main ideas were very simple: Saxon Englishmen had governed themselves, the Normans took this away and imposed a lasting tyranny of alien kings and landlords, the people remembered their lost
liberties and kept struggling to recover them. Thus according to this theory, England was "a nation in captivity and vassalage to a foreign power
and an alien aristocracy." The theory

> united the Third Estate against Crown, Church, and landlords, branding
> them as hereditary enemies of the people. It suggested that the ruling class
> is alien to the interests of the majority of the population. Even if they no
> longer speak French, whether or not they are of Norman descent, the upper
> classes are isolated from the life of the working population . . . The nation is
> the people.[53]

The theory thus constituted a powerful political "counter-authority" to
the men in power. It was "dynamite" because men believing in it "fought
for the liberties of *England*, for the birthrights of *Englishmen*."[54]

The importance of Hill's study to our own should now be obvious: his
essay is a magnificent pioneering investigation of English nationalism.
The fact that he did not see this himself is but further testimony to the
extraordinary blind spot that exists in English historiography on this subject, for of course the 'theory of the Norman Yoke' is *the theory of the
English nation*! It is the local variant of the nationalist mythology that exists, however deeply buried now in our own time, in virtually every modern state (a mythology, we might note, which nativists and troubled
intellectuals may revive as circumstances may seem to require). It is the
story of the nation's divine origin in the past, the foreign devil's machinations against it, the alien encroachments and oppressions hanging over it
in the present, its urgent obligation to renew and return to itself. It is
easier to see all this when we work, as we have been doing here, from
terms of reference much wider than those presented in English political

history, terms drawn from the contemplation of nationalism in the age of the Enlightenment. And of course the theory of the Norman Yoke is more than a 'political philosophy,' even in the widest sense; it is a comprehensive ideology of emancipation.

There is one further point to add to Hill's very important observations. He generally treats the Norman Yoke as a political *concept,* passed down in books and picked up by the radicals of the later eighteenth century. But it was more than that to them, and they experienced it in a much more intimate way. There are many signs that this old nativist idea rose naturally in their minds as a convincing picture of reality, a reality to which they thought themselves eyewitnesses. To put it another way, Hill's essay, because he does not venture into social or literary history, never conveys an idea of the enemy they thought they saw in their midst. His essay unveils a parade of would-be Anglo-Saxons decrying the Norman Yoke, yet he never asks who the Normans *were;* he never casts his eye on 'the French.' We never get a view of the immediacy and objective relevance of these anti-'Norman' fulminations; the 'theory' is treated too much in historiographical and political contexts, as a controversy over 1066 and its implications. We never glimpse the England of the seventies with its Chesterfields and Foxes in their French suits and feathered hats, or poor Thomas Day pointing his toes and groaning in M. Huise's contraption, or the pretty social climbers twittering their mangled French at the theatre and calling their countrymen 'animals' and 'canaille,' affecting to despise everything English as proof of their own superiority and 'eligibility.' But it was the perception of all this, something grounded less in books than in the vivid daily testimony of the five senses, which gave such extraordinary power to the new anti-Norman campaign, the campaign of *national renewal* in the climactic last decades of enlightened cosmopolitanism.

iii. the American Saxon Revolution and the politicians

The seventies saw an accentuation of almost all the political tendencies we have examined thus far. King George, still jockeying against the circling oligarchs, became enmeshed in the very system of management which it had been his dream to see destroyed. He did find a reliable prime minister in Lord North (1770), who, putting together a coalition of placemen, independents, and the remains of several small factions, built up a large parliamentary majority. The ministry, though denounced as corrupt, was probably no more so than Newcastle's and Rockingham's had been.[55] Parrying criticism and receiving much support in the country, North devoted himself to policies of moderation, attempting to avoid confrontations with the hotheads in America.

The 'drunken ragamuffins' (as he privately called them) were in a righteous uproar about a few paltry taxes, but the real source of irritation was the ideological filter through which they read the actions of successive ministries. Professor Bailyn, the American historian, has likened the colonial situation to a ticking bomb. There was a "peculiar configuration of ideas" in America, together with a deep-seated conspiracy theory which worked as detonator to set them off. And what were these ideas? They were not, as has too carelessly been assumed by authors unacquainted with the American pamphlet literature, the "natural rights philosophy" of Locke and the early Enlightenment (though after the rebellion began, these rather hastily conned "abstract universals of natural rights" were held up before world opinion in justification of the act). The real basis of American revolutionary ideology, says Bailyn, was the imported body of English radical literature, particularly that which was produced in the decade 1765–75—that is, as we have seen here, in the swelling tide of English nationalism.[56]

This was a very important discovery. Now we are in a position to see that what it really means is that American nationalism was, at the time of its origin, essentially just an offshoot of English. Bailyn, forging like Hill through the academic bulrushes, happened upon another of the many geologic outcroppings of English nationalism, so well hidden from traditional scrutiny. The key element in American revolutionary ideology, he says, was a strange historical mythology: "The view most characteristic of the Revolutionary pamphleteers," he writes, "postulated an ideal constitution based on an elected assembly in Saxon England, destroyed by the conquest, regained with modifications in the course of centuries of struggle that culminated in the Glorious Revolution, and that was once again challenged by the corruption of eighteenth-century politics." The detonator to the American revolutionary mentality was an amorphous "fear of a comprehensive conspiracy against liberty throughout the English-speaking world," the sign of this conspiracy being a growing and multifarious corruption. In England these ideas, the American historian believes (he draws on the conventional historiography), apparently "had relatively little political influence"; they were apparently the ideas of "the Cassandras of the age . . . enemies of complacence in one of the most complacent eras in England's history [*sic*]." But in America "they were immensely popular and influential. There, an altered condition of life made what in England were considered to be extreme, dislocating ideas sound like simple statements of fact."[57]

Here is a vivid example of how the fond misrepresentation of English 'social harmony' has prevented our seeing larger unities in the history of Western Civilization. At some point in the future, however, the synthetic view will surely be that the American revolutionaries, idealizing their country as a lonely outpost of Saxon independence in an increasingly corrupted world (and no doubt seeing themselves, just as English nationalists did, as 'sincere' Saxon rustics—a point which will have to be investigated by American literary historians), read the government's actions just as their English confreres did, not so much by objective analysis as against a lamplit scenario of creeping ruination and enslavement; though with these differences, that they, looking at things far away and taking the English propagandists more literally, felt themselves even more defenseless against all this corruption and enslavement, yet also in a better position to sever themselves cleanly from it.

To many textbook writers, rhapsodizing on the American Revolution as a struggle to secure the 'universal rights of man,' it might come as a rude surprise to learn that Thomas Jefferson "painstakingly collected every scrap of evidence to reconstruct the history of his 'Saxon ancestors,'" believing Saxon England to have epitomized his conception of liberty.[58] We cannot dwell on this here, but it seems certain that the study of English nationalism will throw new light on the American revolution and the ideology of American nationalism (a topic hardly more studied than English, and certainly deserving, in our own dangerous age, of systematic investigation);[59] and then further, since the French Revolution was affected by both American and English influences, very probably on it as well, helping to dispel certain stubbornly persistent misconceptions (many planted by Edmund Burke) about the supposedly 'abstract' and 'universal' ideology of the French revolutionaries.

Some day, when we understand more about the historic genesis of nationalism, it may even be discovered that there was a peculiar triangular relationship between England, America, and France, in which the patriots in each locale saw their own upper class as the agent of one of the others. The difference between the three groups of patriots was perhaps not so much one of ideas as of 'group situation' and hence of the foreign devil, the particular bugbear, elaborated to carry the propaganda of national renewal. American patriots were afraid of enslavement by a conspiracy centered in England, whereas the English were afraid of one centered in France; while French patriots, hearing the English upper class denounced ever more loudly by English and American radicals, looked with increasing trepidation upon the Anglophilism of their own elite, ostentatiously displayed even amidst the moral decay and fiscal ruin of the 1780s.

So far, at least, as England was concerned, the international situation encouraged the growth of these suspicions. England's international position in the sixties and seventies was one of growing impotence, while France's was one of growing strength and self-confidence till the mideighties. English worries over the pervasive influence of the 'French system' hampered imaginative policy toward America, and suspicions began to grow that the American leaders were playing into French hands. After the rebellion began, a conviction arose that Washington and other American leaders were secretly in the pay of the French court.[60] It is hardly surprising that with France's entry into the war in 1778, and with successive English disasters and even another invasion scare (like the one of 1756) in 1779, the extreme paranoia of the Seven Years' War leapt up again. Its renewed intensity and belligerent irrationality are conveyed in Burney's *Evelina* (1778), full of Captain Mirvan's apoplectic vociferations against France, French influence in England, and the Francophile tendencies of 'the Quality.'

The reader may recall that in this novel, Lovel, the Francophile man-about-town, is made a symbol of the 'race' of English noblemen. Besides the social animosity in this there was also the growing political unpopularity of the great landed families by the later seventies, a circumstance reflected with special clarity in the declining fortunes of the Rockinghams. In fact their extreme unpopularity was one of the main props of North's government: though the late seventies saw growing disapproval of the war against the Americans, there was less reluctance to press blindly on with it than to help George's enemies into power. Naturally the Rockinghams, even though conservatively opposed to popular movements, embraced the American cause as part of their opposition to the king (intellectually assimilating the American Revolution not to 'Saxonism' but to the Glorious Revolution and Lockeian theory). But this apparent disloyalty played right into North's hands, allowing him to accuse them of the treason they were suspected of anyway. Samuel Johnson, always anti-Whig, spoke for many onlookers. When asked what the oppositionists meant by their attacks on North, he replied: "They mean, Sir, rebellion—they mean in spite to destroy that country which they are not permitted to govern."[61]

The suggestion of treason became still more damaging after France entered the war in 1778. Now the Whig grandees were accomplices not only to rebellion but to the French plot to dismember the Empire; they were secret coordinators of all the threats to England. Their habit of running off to Paris at every opportunity did not help their image. And now there were specific cases in which army and naval officers with Opposition connections refused to serve their country, and such incidents, widely publicized, only blackened it more. In 1780 Charles Fox contemptuously summed up the public attitude toward him and the Rockinghams. They were "described as a faction of the most obnoxious kind: a faction who were enemies to the welfare of their country. At one time they were called Americans, at another time Frenchmen, at another time Spaniards, and now the phrase was that they were Dutchmen. In short, they were at all times any thing but Englishmen!"[62] He hit the nail on the head.

Not much happier during this decade were the Chathamites (as we must now call the ennobled Pitt and his followers). They were still the favored party of the discontented middle classes, the best vehicle within the establishment of the nationalist aspirations growing outside it, but their lack of numbers and of a large landed interest made them dependent on the very 'faction' that they, in common with the king, really wanted to displace, the Rockinghams. And so although Chatham in 1770 began to talk of the need for some constitutional change, he soon grew mealy-mouthed again, concerned about Rockingham's support and the need to preserve unity within the Opposition. Nor could he and his helper, Shelburne, look to the king for support, for Chatham had forfeited George's confidence earlier and continued to offend him by taking a negative but vacillating position on the American issue.

Here an internal contradiction ran through the thinking of all the nationalists, both the few and rather cautious ones in Parliament, the

Chathamites, and the boldest ones outside it—"the Horne set," as Christie calls them.[63] The difficulty was that although all these men opposed making war on the Americans, they were equally horrified at the thought of American independence. They saw the colonists as part of the mystical fraternity of all Englishmen, and they also feared that American independence spelled disaster for the empire and still greater impotence against France. Thus Chatham and many who thought like him contradicted themselves repeatedly, advancing hairsplitting arguments which even they themselves did not understand, attacking English imperial authority with one breath and then supporting it with another. Chatham died in 1778 after a final speech calling for vigorous prosecution of the war to keep the colonies in the empire. The same contradiction appears in Hulme's book, which first blasts Parliament's authority, then instructs the American 'brethren' to help purify and then obey it.[64]

iv. the radicals in the seventies

As to these extraparliamentary radicals, their history in this decade was one of modest gains, followed by stagnation during the American war. Although they expanded activities in the midlands, their most effective work was done in the metropolitan area. They subsidized several newspapers and won a victory when the printing of parliamentary debates became accepted (1771). At the same time, however, the dispute between Horne and Wilkes broke out into a long and mutually damaging correspondence in the newspapers which had the effect of embarrassing the nascent political movement and providing much amusement to all its opponents.

It is instructive to read the record of this, for it furnishes a guide to the inner disunity of the Left, divided between old-style elitist rabble-rousing and new-style nationalist radicalism. Two points are especially revealing, the attitude toward the Rockinghams, and that toward the political education of 'the people.' Wilkes (and the anonymous 'Junius,' who entered on his side) saw the Rockinghams as (in Wilkes's words) "the most *virtuous* of all the late administrations," noble foes of royal tyranny, and assailed Horne for his detestation of them. The Rockinghams, wrote Wilkes damningly, were *"the men you most hate."* He was right. Horne did hate them and deplored the fact that it was only through them that the Chathamites might ever gain power. The party of reform, insofar as one existed at all, was a captive of the party of oligarchy and pseudopatriotic obfuscation. Nothing of genuine value could be expected from the Rockinghams, "whose little politics," Horne scornfully wrote, were "confined to the making of matches, and extending their family connexions, and who think they gain more by procuring one additional vote to their party in the house of commons, than by adding their landed property and feeble character to the abilities of a *Chatham,* or the confidence of [the] public." The Rockinghams were devoted only to themselves, and their vaunted patriotism of 1689, which supported only the civil but not the political rights of the citizen, was merely a cloak. And it was they who lurked behind Wilkes and Junius, subsidizing their appeals not to the spirit of Englishmen but to the mindlessness of the crowd, all in order "to keep up a clamour against the *persons* of the ministry," without "a *material* change of measures, and without any security for a tottering constitution."[65]

So intense was Horne's feeling against the moguls that his opponents, perhaps truly misunderstanding the new political outlook which it represented, attempted to twist it into a self-interested desertion of the public cause. The haughty Junius, his page dripping with condescension, insinuated that the Rev. Horne now favored corruption and despotism in a personal quest for a bishopric! Horne counterattacked, ripping up Junius as a "pander of corruption" for his apologetic treatment of rotten boroughs, and reiterating his own well-known abhorrence of the North ministry's measures. He candidly stated, however, that to him it was no embarrassment to say that his own attachment to the king was "more zealous and sincere" than that of any politician; and it was a nice question, whether North's boroughmongering was really more pernicious than the hidden designs and insincere patriotism of the grandees and their literary running-dogs: "The *cause of the country*," in the view of the latter, was "merely to vex the king; and any rascal [meaning Wilkes] is to be supported in any roguery, provided he can only thereby plant *a thorn in the king's side.*— This is the very extremity of faction, and the last degree of political wickedness."[66]

Beneath this squabble we may discern the inner alignment between Horne, Chatham, and the king, a convergence of attitudes and purposes which in the eighties was to come together triumphantly in an anti-aristocratic union between the Crown, the younger Pitt, and the radical nationalists. But this was formed not merely from opposition to the grandees but also from an elevated and optimistic idea of the character of the British people. In Horne's eyes, Wilkes's true colors were shown in his aping of the great, his moral insincerity, and the speciousness of his appeals to the "uninformed simpletons" who doted on him, calling their voice "the *voice of God*." Because the only true hope for improvement lay in "the common sense of the public," the people should be spoken to sincerely and honestly. To flatter them—to resort to insincerity—was only to betray them in the end, for the credulity thus fed would inevitably be exploited by dishonest men for their destruction. And it was wrong anyway to teach them, as Wilkes did, to seek the restoration of their rights "as a favour from any set of men," for this would only sustain the evil old processes by which these might be stolen away again. The people, in the end, could look only to themselves.[67]

Despite the unpleasantness caused by this wrangling on the Left (necessary, of course, to the democratization of 'patriot' politics), the radicals were able to register a small victory in the election of 1774. The campaign to elect M.P.'s favorable to reform helped to produce about a dozen such men in Parliament—still a very tiny group, of course, in a House of 558. Wilkes was among them, and he was more serious now in his radicalism, partly thanks to Horne's admonitions and to competition with him. In 1776 he became the first man to propose in Parliament the drastic reform of the franchise, so as to permit even "the meanest mechanic, the poorest peasant and day labourer" to vote: an English parliament should "speak the free, unbiassed sense of the body of the English people and of every man among us." That he began with panegyrics on the state of representation in ancient times is but one sign of the fact that the rhetoric of 'Saxon' freedom was spreading. There were early instances of its being used in the Middlesex furor of 1768–69, and Chatham showed his drift into it in declaring that "no privileges were concessions from the Crown, but derived to us of the Rights of our Saxon Ancestors."[68]

This spread of radical ideology was furthered by the publication of other radical works, widely read, such as Burgh's *Political Disquisitions* (1774-75) and Cartwright's *Take Your Choice!* (1776). Historians on the lookout for the ever-mysterious source of English radicalism have suggested that works such as these "may be said to represent expressions of the Commonwealth tradition," but this is misleading, for most of them introduced constitutional ideas that were substantially new in the late 1760s. Horne's biographer found the key distinction long ago when he observed (in 1813) that "the idea of amending, by restoring the constitution to its first principles, is of no very remote origin, having been first conceived within the last half century." The great rallying cry of the seventeenth century, he pointed out, was not for more popular representation but for more frequent and freer parliamentary meetings as a bulwark against royal tyranny and political intimidation.[69]

What is most interesting about Burgh is not his ideology, with which we are already familiar, but the way in which his personal evolution reflects the whole drift of the nationalist movement. He, like Smollett, was a Scotch immigrant and older than the other men we have considered in this chapter. He arrived in London in the early 1740s and soon developed an intense British patriotism and a suspicion of those responsible for anti-Scottish prejudice in England, seeing them as conscious or unconscious agents of France. Considering himself "a moralist in Babylon" and thirsting, like John Brown, for a general reformation of *"sentiments* and *manners,"* he began a career of philosophical castle-building. In the fifties he saw the only possible hope for national purification in a grand national association of virtuous aristocrats. But as this wildly unrealistic proposal came to nothing, he spent the early '60s writing out lengthy private instructions for young George III, explaining how to unify and cleanse the people. The king made no reply, and this approach proved equally fruitless. Gradually, as Burgh's biographer explains—catching here the essential drift of the whole movement—the "moralist in Babylon" became "the moralist politicized." Upbraiding the public for "courting the yoke and bowing their necks to a set of encroaching grandees," Burgh went on to propose, in the more plebeian cultural atmosphere of the seventies, a "GRAND NATIONAL ASSOCIATION FOR RESTORING THE CONSTITUTION," a panacea much like Hulme's. His influential *Political Dis-*

quisitions was packed with moral, social and ethnohistorical materials of the sort we have studied, and with vitriolic attacks on the aristocracy. The book was full, as Butterfield has pointed out, of "quasi-revolutionary implications" of concerted political and even military action. "Ten millions of people," wrote Burgh threateningly, "are not to sit still and see a villainous junto overthrow their liberties."[70]

It was the legendary Major John Cartwright who carried the nationalist argument to its logical conclusion in his famous manifesto *Take Your Choice!*, a work which thus naturally stood for generations as the classic radical statement; and of course it was Cartwright himself, not Paine or some other republican dreamer, who became (as Samuel Bamford recalled in 1839) "our venerable political Father." Symptomatically, Cartwright's book contains many arresting thoughts about patriotism. The true patriot was a man obsessed with devotion to his nation: "The love of his country he finds the ruling passion of his soul; and he knows that the duties of patriotism, the aggregate of all the minor social duties, cannot cease but with his vital breath."[71]

Following the path of Hulme and Burgh, Cartwright rehearses the familiar pseudohistory, holding up the supposed *"antient practice of the constitution"* to show that the current system of representation "hath no foundation" and hence "ought instantly to be abolished." Though not without hope for King George (praised on some of his personal qualities), Cartwright sweepingly tars the parliamentary politicians as traitors, "treacherous agents," prepared to "sell their country," ready "to destroy their country," subscribers to doctrines of *"treason to our country."* Constitutional restoration really depended on the people: "Trust not, I say, in princes nor in ministers; but trust in *yourselves,* and in representatives chosen by *yourselves* alone!"[72] The admirable Burgh had shown the way by recommending a Grand National Association for Restoring the Constitution. Such a body would possess tremendous power, for there was virtually nothing which could not be done by "an associated nation." Such an entity could "level a throne with the earth, and trample authority in the dust. And it can do these things of *right.*" The people were sovereign; united, they were omnipotent. And the time of reckoning was at hand; the "character of the nation" would soon become clear. It would soon be determined whether the English people would resume their "ancient sterling spirit" and throw off the yoke of their oppressors (Lord Chesterfield is made to personify the type), or, as there was too much reason to fear, exhibit themselves as the product of "imported" values, "the cringing servility, together with the frivolous fopperies and loose principles, of Italy and France." "Blush, Englishmen, blush, if there be a spark of manhood left in your composition! And, when ridiculed with the title of free men, hide your ignominious heads!"[73]

The one point upon which Burgh had been too cautious, Cartwright believed, was the obligation to restore a uniform and *universal* franchise. The earlier propagandists, following Locke, had vested the franchise in the possession of property of one sort or another; but this was an error.

Every Englishman, even the poorest peasant in the land, had "by birthright a property in the English constitution," one which gave him an inalienable electoral right. The right to vote was guaranteed in both the divine moral law of nature "and the express doctrine of [the English] constitution in particular" (in its ideal form a replica of the divine law), to which every Englishman was an heir by simple birthright. The right to vote was implanted in the personality of every man who shared in the national character. *"Personality,"* Cartwright insisted, "is the *sole* foundation of the *right* of being *represented*."[74] Here at last was the doctrine of egalitarian suffrage which now underlies electoral rights in virtually every modern democratic state; a doctrine first suggested, it may be true, in the nationless universalism of the early Enlightenment, the age of Locke and Pope and Voltaire, but as a matter of historical fact bequeathed to us by Cartwright and the other pioneers of nationalism, men of the late eighteenth century.

Despite the important intellectual consolidation represented by these books, and the promising signs of popular support shown in the elections of 1774, the later seventies was nonetheless a time of bitter frustration for the radical movement. A major sticking point was the hopelessness of accomplishing anything without the strong backing of the recognized political groups; and as we have seen, the Rockinghams were unsympathetic to reform, the Chathamites powerless without the Rockinghams, and the king, struggling against both and then their American friends as well, in no mood for political alterations.

The predictable course of development was thus sidetracked for a time. At first the colonial difficulties naturally strengthened the nationalists' hand, giving weight to their claim that a system of slavery was being drawn over all the English people. Horne, speaking about the colonists in the late sixties, declared that "our cause is one—our enemies are the same." The same radical sympathy continued in the early seventies, even though general opinion was beginning to harden against the unruly Bostonians. When violence broke out in early 1775, Horne sprang up in an attempt to channel anger against the government, not the English brethren across the water. In a meeting of the Constitutional Society he carried a motion raising a subscription for the relief of the families "of our beloved American fellow-subjects, who, faithful to the character of *Englishmen,* preferring death to slavery, were, for that reason only, inhumanly murdered by the king's troops at or near Lexington and Concord." These words landed him behind bars for a year, after a farcical trial for seditious libel; he was evidently the only Englishman so punished for opposing the war.[75]

Despite the radicals, general opinion was beginning to flow still more strongly in favor of symbols of authority, not of the extended family of Englishmen. The king received many loyal addresses supporting his coercive efforts, even from communities which might have been thought pro-American. Perhaps the best way to explain what happened is to say that the mindless conservative old-style patriotism of the many, always lively in wartime, was beginning to come down like a tidal wave on the new-style radical patriotism (nationalism) of the thoughtful few, sympathizers with the rebels, attackers of the political system, disgusted critics of the whole social system, prophets of collective doom. The radicals, bitter at this turn of opinion, were compelled to ask themselves deeper questions about what kind of a people the English were: "Is this the people," Cartwright morosely asked, "who are so fond of liberty? No; we have always mistaken them; they are selfish, arbitrary, and tyrannical. . . . 'Tis really strange, the national character of Englishmen should have been so much mistaken!"[76]

When the Americans were officially declared rebels in August 1775, the radicals' isolation became even more complete. Nor were they themselves firm any longer in their pro-American views. Even in the early seventies there had been murmurings in radical circles that the Americans ought to pay their taxes, and that if America deserved justice, England deserved obedience. Thomas Day, just now beginning to involve himself in radical political activity (in 1780 he would become a founder and propagandist for the Society of Constitutional Information), sniffed at the Declaration of Independence and sarcastically reflected on the hypocrisy of the American planters waving their speeches of liberty in one hand and their whips in the other. The radical mind, idealizing all the English common folk, regarded America as part of the English nation, and was unable to take American independence seriously till the battle of Saratoga (1777), which suggested that things might ultimately go that way. Radicalism then slumped into a gloomy quiescence, punctuated by denunciations of the government for having lost the colonies through pervasive corruption and the failure to reform the system of representation in time.[77]

The war thus temporarily derailed what would otherwise have been a more normal course of political development. By isolating and further calling into question the loyalty of the great Whigs it did assist the larger anti-aristocratic realignment taking place from the 1750s. But it also served to call into question the radicals' loyalty for the first time. It dealt a blow to the momentum of the movement, gathering power for nearly two decades: it alienated the radicals from their natural constituency, the mass of ordinary Englishmen; it set them against the king, who, to a point at least, would have been their supporter; and it brought them closer to both parliamentary groups critical of the war, not only their natural friends the Chathamites but their natural enemies the Rockinghams, by 1780 making them reluctant war brides of the very men they 'most hated.' And, finally, the war also divided them in their own minds, draining their vigor and blunting the dogmatic sharpness of perspective which was one of their assets. As we have seen, their own opinions were disturbed and ambiguous on the American question. They were monarchists and imperialists, while the seceding Americans were fast becoming republican anti-imperialists. Hence they clung to a confused hope that the Americans might be kept within the empire by a scheme of imperial federation and perhaps simultaneous political reform. Even at war's end they dreamt that America might still tarry, if not within a reorganized empire, then in a commercial union with the mother country.

Thus Cartwright's activities in the later seventies were nicely characteristic. He divided his time between helping to train the Nottingham militia against the threat of French invasion, meditating the organization of a radically democratic reform society, and concocting last-ditch schemes for reconciliation with the Americans. He handed the king an address pleading for a comprehensive solution to both the American problem and the problem of corruption at home: the government should proclaim peace, bring the troops home, declare a day of national fasting and humiliation, then call a general election which would be guided by a royal proclamation supporting a restoration of the constitution in all its purity; upon which the next Parliament would give the Americans legislative independence within a renovated empire, and the Americans, having taken note of the change of heart in England, would gladly take their new place as members of "the grand British league and confederation."[78]

But of course it was too late for all this. Cartwright's friend, Horne, was also engaged in a characteristically radical pursuit in the later seventies, though better suited to reality. At his sentencing he had cried that he "had an employment, which would confine him in his room, longer than their lordships would dare to confine him!" After his release he helped to produce a gigantic book of *Facts: Addressed . . . to All the Subjects of Great Britain* (1780), replete with the usual references to "our ancestors" on the one hand and the "three or four hundred mercenaries, in the two houses," on the other, calculated to prove that the war was crippling the country and that the corruption of the political system had reached a stage of crisis: "We are now arrived at a period when either corruption must be thoroughly purged from the Senate, or the nation is finally and irrecoverably undone."[79]

5. Mustering the People

Horne and his friends were more correct now than ever in their apocalyptic warnings. The stormy events of 1779–84 did constitute, as has been suggested by a few historians (much criticized by their disbelieving colleagues), 'England's French Revolution,' though in a manner and with an outcome which evades understanding save when seen in the context of nationalist political development.

It was the war's staggering expense and growing futility which brought radicalism out of the doldrums in 1779. Middlesex, bellwether of radical activity, was where it first began to revive, the immediate cause being a by-election in which the North government disqualified a popular candidate on a technicality. The radicals seized upon this as a further example of tyranny, and, hoping to rouse other counties as they had done a decade earlier, drafted a petition to the House of Commons.[80]

More important than this however was the fact that the Middlesex free-holders also approved a resolution that "for the purpose of preserving the independence of this county a general meeting of the freeholders be held monthly during the sitting of Parliament." They decided, in effect, to set up a standing committee to act as a guardian of electoral liberties and local watchdog of the whole political system. The body met for the first time in December, and at this remarkable meeting was presented a still more remarkable proposal by John Jebb, an 'agent' no less zealous for change than his friends Horne and Cartwright. He proposed the creation of similar standing bodies throughout the nation and the establishment of a national supercommittee to be drawn proportionally from their memberships; that is, he proposed a national organization which would in fact constitute a morally superior and democratically more representative body than Parliament itself. What he called for was nothing less than an 'anti-Parliament,' a 'National Assembly' (both terms were applied to the scheme by excited contemporaries); an extraparliamentary shadow government which could even be called upon, if circumstances required, to supersede the House of Commons. Members of Parliament, he declared, were to be looked upon as mere "proxies" whose voice "must be regarded as annihilated when the voice of the Principal shall be thus distinctly heard." The "solemn hour" would soon arrive when the true delegates of the nation would "sit in awful judgment upon the traiterous invaders of their rights."[81]

i. 'association'

Nothing could have been more inevitable than the surfacing, sooner or later, of this very radical proposal. Black, the historian of what has been rather nebulously called 'associationism,' intuitively captured this inevitability when he wrote that "the nation was maturing more rapidly than the professional politicians, and the nation was beginning to speak."[82] The political aim of nationalism, as we have noted, is to establish a government with which each member of the community may positively identify himself, finding his own character and will directly reflected in its. One path to this lies in the empowering of the 'charismatic hero-leader' who seems to personify in his own character the will and personality of 'the people'; and for a short while, around 1760, Pitt's government had seemed to fill the bill. But as the movement's difficulties multiplied and its ideology evolved, it seemed increasingly evident that the only reliable sanction for truly popular government lay in a far more arduous reformation of the whole electoral system, one which would give meaning to popular sovereignty not just through lucky chances and symbolic identifications with political figureheads, but solidly through an entire restoration of the mythic system of self-government. Down to the mid-seventies the only means by which this might be accomplished were agitation, petitioning, and the imposition of binding instructions upon parliamentary candidates. But these were weak tools. There was no way to force Parliament to act upon any petition, nor was there any way to compel the politicians, most of whom were seen accurately enough as trimmers and artful deceivers, to honor election pledges even if they made them (and most refused to do so).

All this lay in the background in 1779. Inevitably then there emerged the idea of a nationwide association which would not only bring pressure to bear locally but which also, with its headquarters in London, would continuously oversee, morally intimidate, and so coerce Parliament to exhume the glorious Saxon constitution. 'National association' was the natural consequence in political thought of the idea of popular solidarity advanced in English cultural nationalism, and it thus naturally came to the fore in the unfolding logic of the reform campaign. Horne and his friends had invented its basic machinery in 1769, Hulme in 1771 had proposed using it for constitutional restoration, Burgh and Cartwright had begun to treat it as a panacea a few years later. And there were also the object lessons of the American Stamp Act Congress, the Irish Association, the Continental Congress, and the Irish Volunteers, all of which represented quasi-national pressure groups. As Pares remarks, "In America and Ireland the established representative institutions of the country were so obviously controlled or frustrated by the British Government that nationalism could only take extra-official forms."[83] The same remark applies to Britain itself.

The nationalist agents yearned to build around themselves a mass movement, to 'muster the people' in an organization with authority and permanence equal to the enormous task cut out for them. And so even while Middlesex sent out a call for a national reformers' conference to meet in London, similar ideas were brewing elsewhere, most notably in Yorkshire, where the Reverend Christopher Wyvill was also beginning at this very moment to plot both a nationwide petitioning campaign and a supporting 'association' of very much the same type. He too was prodded by the cost of the war and the many immediate discontents of the late seventies, but, like the others, he was more profoundly 'agitated' by what he saw as the interconnected moral and political corruption dragging his country down to ruin. The twofold object of his activities, he later explained, was "the restoration of national morals" and "the preservation of our Constitution on its genuine principles . . . almost lost under the immense accumulation of abuses."[84]

Yorkshire, however, was not Middlesex, and Wyvill was forced to work in an environment much more heavily influenced by the great Whig magnates, indeed by Rockingham himself, who dominated Yorkshire's politics. Mistrusting the magnates but knowing the futility of acting without them, he began to weave his political strategy. He planned it in such a way as to conceal his twofold desire for fundamental alterations and a nationwide anti-parliamentary Association (though he did insist, with characteristic radical suspiciousness, that no M.P. should be a member of his organization). His professed aim was an attack by petition, calculated to be popular also with the squirearchy groaning under heavy wartime taxation, on that expensive 'corruption' which the Rockinghams identified with royal political patronage; that is, on that one species of waste and political manipulation which they themselves bitterly resented, and which, even despite their encrusted conservatism and their hopes to dominate some future ministry, they were prepared to see abolished.

This was a shrewd strategem. The magnates, seeing in Wyvill's plan another opportunity to pour the winds of popular discontent into their own drooping sails, rapidly drew up a Wyvillian plan of 'economical' reform to present in Parliament, and simultaneously turned their great regional influence to the creation of a petitioning campaign which crossed the lines of many counties; but which left in many of them, as Wyvill had slyly intended, standing structures of 'association and correspondence' whose devotion to whiggism was far less certain than to the principles of 'the ancient constitution' as expounded in the propaganda of the seventies. Before long, notes Butterfield, these committees began arrogating to themselves "the power to speak as the authentic voice of the people of England . . . streaming up, so to speak, from a hundred sources in town and country."[85]

Thus arrived the clamorous spring of 1780. In Parliament the Rockinghams especially hoped to capitalize upon the war-weariness slowly festering among the independent county M.P.'s, who until this time had persistently supported North in preference to any 'junto' run by the Great. But again they were disappointed. Nearly all they could wring from the nation's distress and the racket of petitioning was the trivial parliamentary resolution of April 6 that royal influence was a menace which should be diminished. Meanwhile the national supercommittee of Association—"Mr. Wyvill's congress," as the king warily called it—was meeting nearby. The discontented hoped for miracles while the satisfied nervously denounced it as a disruption of national unity during wartime and a Trojan Horse of the Opposition.

At this extraordinary Assembly of March 1780 there was a great sense of fraternity and a desire to cooperate in the forging of a united program, and some historians, partly because the radical ideology is so badly misunderstood, have made too much of differences between what they call the 'metropolitan radicals' on the one hand and the 'county reformers' on the other. Certain differences did exist. The urban delegates generally preferred a program calling for annual parliaments, the abolition of rotten boroughs, and a broad extension of the franchise, whereas the country delegates, though strong on the first two points, were attached to the idea of providing parliamentary seats for 100 more 'independent' county M.P.'s. These differences reflected the differing personal interests and strategic calculations prevailing in urban and rural England, and also the gross relative under-representation of the county freeholders, but they signified no truly important divergence in ideological orientation amongst the radicals. We encounter here the convenient 'plasticity' of nationalist ideology. The desire of all the radicals was the 'renewal' of the political system through the reinstitution of the ancient constitution, but no one, not even the mythmongering ideologues who incessantly talked about it, knew what the ancient constitution really was.

Therefore some were free to believe, in accordance with much of the fictional as well as pseudohistorical literature of the movement, that the rural gentleman was the purest and most authentic embodiment of the ancient national character, and that he would be, in Parliament, the surest guarantor of authentically representative government—a belief sustained also in the more conventional political faith, which held that the county M.P. was the salt of the constitution. At the other end of this mini-spectrum, made up from personal interests, calculations of political success, and purely speculative historical distinctions, were those few who had already come to believe, with Cartwright, that the fundamental building-block of political independence was the personality of each and every Englishman; a belief which pointed not so much to more 'independents' in the House of Commons as to a simple widening of the franchise. Cartwright, however, who like Jebb and many other 'metropolitan' radicals had roots in the country, and who like Horne still retained a belief in the property qualification for membership in the House of Commons, was prepared to compromise, and at length the conference produced a program which urged the restoration of annual parliaments, the authorization of 100 new county members, and a national Plan of Association. What the delegates really wanted, besides that united front between themselves and the 'parliament-men' which the war had helped create and which now seemed vital to any hope of success, was a purified national government responsive to themselves, the intelligent and respectable men of the propertied middle classes; and that is just what they proposed.

But several months later, by the late summer of 1780, these grand projects lay in ruins, while the general election of September registered new gains for Lord North. The meteoric movement of 1779–80 had crashed—temporarily. In fact it had suffered from a succession of blows. Most important was that dealt by the Rockinghams, who first assisted the Association Movement, then reversed themselves (April 1780) when they saw that they could neither limit it to their popgun war of economical retrenchment nor curtail its dangerous tendency to subvert the whole system by which M.P.'s were chosen. From its very inception they had worked to dominate it, first by presuming to define its objectives, second by attempting to take over its leadership and cast its limelight upon themselves, which they nearly accomplished through Fox's pseudoradical posturings in Parliament and the Westminster Committee of Correspondence (Wyvill had been forced to back down on his ban against parliament-men), and third by imposing conditions on its program, as Rockingham did when he induced the unhappy Wyvill, at the close of the March meeting, to switch one of his demands from annual to triennial parliaments. When the Rockinghams found that they could not control it by any of these methods they simply pulled the rug from under it in the counties, withholding their support from its operations and hence destroying its authority to speak for the nation—that is, for anyone but the earnest radicals who constituted its bare organizational structure.

Of course the radicals were bitter, even though experience had taught them to expect little else. The forced friendship was totally unnatural, and some called for its immediate dissolution. Wyvill, though still convinced of its necessity, sadly reflected that "the assistance of the Great Whig Aristocracy . . . was not to be expected" in any truly significant reform. Jebb inveighed against the way the Rockinghams had manipulated the whole movement only to support their economical tinkerings, while Day lashed them as false friends to liberty, cried that he had "never yet heard of an aristocracy . . . that was not the universal tyrant and inquisitor of the species," and incited his Essex audiences to "rise up with the irresistible force of a well-disciplined army." And it was not only the radicals who were dismayed: Shelburne was equally incensed at the spectacle of Rockingham, "the head of the whigs, as he styles himself . . . obstinately stopping the free course of popular spirit, which alone can ever oppose the court."[86]

ii. "Sincerity in Politics"

Thus 'associationism' stumbled in the late spring of 1780, a victim to the contradictory ambitions of the two groups which had brought it into being; or to put it another way, a victim to what Veitch rightly called "something disingenuous" in the whole conduct of Rockingham and his followers throughout this crisis.[87] Now this was a matter of more importance than might appear to conventional examination. We have already studied the cultural background of this period and found at work a growing and increasingly obsessional thirst for 'sincerity,' not only as a people's standard of morality but behind this as something much more, a mark of participation in the English National Identity. This moral and social evolution, this phenomenal growth of the cult of Sincerity between the fifties and nineties, had a conditioning influence on politics just as it did on everything else; here was an important factor in 'the structure of politics' not counted by Namier.

Politics took place in a current of moral evolution whose effect was to elevate gradually, year by year, the symbolic importance and hence political value of sincerity as a facet of political style. In 1780 the public was far less tolerant than it had been in 1760 of duplicity and hypocrisy in English politicians. The critical transition between moral styles had come in the seventies, when playwrights such as Goldsmith and Sheridan alternated uncertainly between the older, essentially aristocratic social ideal of witty and insouciant urbanity, and the new bourgeois code of sincerity—of 'English' purity, honesty, frankness, originality, independence. The tempo of moral change increased still more in the later seventies under the strain of the American war and the influence of prolonged struggle in the name of 'principles.' In 1776 Lord North had laughed away Wilkes's proposal for parliamentary reform with tactics of scoffing 'jocularity' (the radicals never forgave him for it), but this was no longer possible in the eighties, when every idea touching 'the people' demanded a sincere and even reverential handling—or a convincing appearance of it. A modern pollster, examining the complicated politics of the early eighties, might say that there had emerged by this period a highly evocative and even potentially explosive 'sincerity issue' beneath the surface of political activity, and that it was critically important for every politician who valued his future to 'get on the right side' of this issue, so deeply grounded now in people's basic feelings about themselves, the moral identity of their nation, and the personal qualities necessary to any man or body of men worthy of representing and leading it. The 'sincerity issue,' our pollster might point out, was not one simply of a leader's personal integrity but rather a much larger one of moral symbolism, and beyond that of his fidelity to the National Character, the key underlying question in the politics of this entire age.

Suspicions about the un-English insincerity of Parliament as a whole stood behind the impulse to create a National Assembly uncontaminated by parliament-men, and there can be little doubt that the imputation of insincerity rested more or less heavily on all members of the political establishment. The Speaker of the House of Commons discreetly addressed himself to it when he cautioned the House (March 13, 1780) that debate over the Rockinghams' economical measures was delaying a consideration of the popular petitions which were now pouring in: "The House," he warned, "should proceed to consider them with all imaginable dispatch and alacrity, to avoid every thing which might give a reason to doubt their sincerity." And indeed such doubts weighed with special heaviness on the Rockinghams and their followers. Throughout this tense period there ran a theme of snide accusation directed at their motives and at the ridiculous anomaly of the aristocracy pretending to embrace the aspirations of the people. Repeatedly it was said that economic distress was due less to taxes than to the exorbitant rents of the mighty landlords; that the Whig oligarchs, when in power, had been more corrupt and incompetent than ministers under royal influence; that the Rockinghams' economical reform measures revealed a characteristic tenderness towards their own sinecures, which they proposed to continue for the lives of existing holders even while 'invading' the king's private finances; that the failure of these same reforms in Parliament was due in no small measure to their own indifference and irresponsibility, when many of them, during a critical week in April, abandoned politics in favor of the Newmarket races; and that their flirtation with the Association Movement, even though half-hearted, constituted an attempt to transfer "the sovereignty from the senate to private cabals and self-created assemblies."[88]

These insinuations tended to concentrate on the most prominent of the Rockingham band, Charles Fox, who, having been bred a placeman and having earlier earned a reputation as a slashing anti-radical (the London mobs had mauled him a decade earlier for his attacks on Wilkes and his unpopular stand on the printer's case), was now in his turn attempting to play the rabble-rousing tribune. By 1780 he had professedly become an extreme reformer, the chief parliament-man to walk out of the governing class and embrace the associationists. The Rockinghams' parliamentary foes could not have wished for a plumper target for their insinuations of aristocratic insincerity. Even his name gave them a weapon, and at every step they made much of his extreme notoriety as a gambler, womanizer, and corrupter of aristocratic youth (it was even widely believed that he had corrupted the Prince of Wales), his descent from the half-French Charles II (something he shared, as contemporaries well knew, with Richmond, Grafton, and other members of the Whig elite), his ill-gotten wealth from his infamous father, Lord Holland, his unpatriotic rejoicings at British humiliations during the continuing war, and so on. Stung by these reproaches—attempting, we might say, to get on the right side of the sincerity issue—he struck back at his parliamentary critics, dwelling particularly on the hypocrisy of those county M.P.'s (angrily defended by North as "a set of men as respectable as any in that House") who, he charged, cared only to adopt the appearance, but not the principles, of sincere reformers like himself. Ironically it was he who flung down the ultimate challenge of the day. It was Fox who, in the House of Commons (February 1780), called for a public test of the sincerity of all the politicians:

> We say to the ministry, you misapply the public money; nay, you do worse, you apply it to bad purposes: ministry say to us, You want our places; and thus the charge of corruption is given and retorted. Come now, let us see whose child corruption is; opposition are willing, are desirous, that it should be sacrificed; ministry have often made similar professions; *the time is come to prove the sincerity of both;* see who will now acknowledge; see who will father this dear but denied child, corruption![89]

Fox and the Whigs often repeated this challenge while they remained out of office. It is amusing to see them carelessly helping to prepare the tremendous explosion which before long was to blow them into the political wilderness for half a century to come. For their chance was coming. Soon they would be permitted to show just how Sincere they really were.

iii. the Gordon Riots

The dénoument was conditioned by other events which we have little space to consider. One was the Gordon Riots of June 1780, which racked London for more than a week and left hundreds dead. This event is usually regarded as sui generis, unrelated to the radical movement; but the distinction seems very doubtful when we reflect that George Gordon's Protestant Association was consciously created as a popular counterforce against what was felt to be the un-English conduct of the upper classes in Parliament. Many English radicals, like those in America, considered the Quebec Act of 1774, which gave sanction to the institutions of the French Canadians and hence established 'French Laws' within the English-speaking community, to be one of the sinister expressions of anti-national influence at work in the political establishment. Then in 1778, the very year that France joined the Americans in making war on England, a Catholic

Relief Bill, relaxing the anti-Catholic oaths required of British soldiers, sailed through both houses of Parliament, almost as if in defiance of the nativist prejudices welling up from below. This bill reflected, among other things, the sophisticated and cosmopolitan values still prevailing at the upper reaches of English society. Wilkes and the London Common Council inveighed against it, while Frederick Bull, a prominent radical and a friend of both Wilkes and Gordon, in early June 1780 darkly warned the House of Commons against "the late toleration of Popery" in which he discerned "a deep laid ministerial plan to undermine the liberties of the people." Were an historian to analyze the Gordon episode with such indications as these in mind, it might seem less bizarre that Gordon, an unbalanced M.P. who considered George III "papistical" and who detested the cosmopolitan Rockinghams even more, should have organized the anti-parliamentary agitation which chanced to run amok just a few days later, meeting little initial resistance from sympathetic London magistrates and significantly turning its wrath as much against wealthy sophisticates living in Westminster as against the Catholic laborers of the poorer districts.[90]

The Gordon Riots reflected the sharpening contradiction in values between the continuing (in some respects even deliberately accentuated) cosmopolitanism of the Quality and the aggressive nationalism emerging in opposition to it. Butterfield, though he never mentions nationalism in discussing these events, shows an intuitive sense for them by writing allusively against the background of Nazism. The very unanimity of the English governing class, he observes, in passing "one of their most enlightened acts of leadership," the Catholic Relief Bill, "proved to be a pitfall, offending not only rational prejudice, but deep dark passions, strange as Nazi hatreds, and as baffling as anti-semitism"; and he then goes on to suggest a likeness between Gordon, "the idol of the masses in a time of hysteria," and Adolf Hitler. But despite these and other hints, Butterfield resists his own suggestion (again we note the inhibitive power of the Forbidden Idea) and concludes vaguely that all the extraparliamentary agitations of this period may have represented "part of the growing pains of a new type of state necessitated by the increase in population, the great agglomerations in towns, and the changes in the technique of life itself."[91]

The riots, a violent lower-class manifestation of the same mentality which was driving the radical movement, had the effect of scaring the radicals away from tactics dangerous to public order. For all their paranoid fears they were men of intellect and at least moderate property, whose aims lay far from burning down London or looting the Bank of England. So while they did not, after the riots, abandon their idea of National Association, they became more sensitive to the need to keep their movement 'legal and constitutional,' and found themselves under a continuing obligation to select their leaders from the corrupted world of 'parliament-men.'

iv. Pitt the younger, the radicals, and the mounting crisis

This continued dependence did not mean impotence, however. Indeed the movement had come far since its incubation under Pitt. It had tremendously expanded in numbers, respectability, intellectual substance, apocalyptic forebodings, and 'restorative' zeal. Its ideology of supposedly unique English values and historical decline had been articulated and circulated in many works of propaganda, its basic political objectives had been thought out and announced even in Parliament, its demands were now supported by a small group of men in the House of Commons, a growing body of dedicated agents had long fought for and exhibited its ideals to the wider public, and, thanks to the Association Movement, there now existed not just in the metropolis but in many parts of the country a cellular organization of radical activists and sympathizers. Many intellectuals had joined the movement, and with the founding in 1780 of the Society for Constitutional Information (SCI), it virtually began its own publishing industry, churning out great quantities of propaganda which was circulated to every corner of the land. The radicals experienced defeat in 1780 but they too, like the Rockinghams, were readying themselves for future opportunities, always broadening their base and incessantly preaching (as the SCI proclaimed in its manifesto) "to the COMMONALTY AT LARGE a knowledge of their lost rights." The foreign visitor C. P. Moritz left testimony to their propaganda's impact when he marvelled in 1782 at "how the lowliest carter shows an interest in public affairs; how the smallest children enter into the spirit of the nation; how everyone feels himself to be a man and an Englishman—as good as his king and his king's minister."[92]

This captured not only the political excitement but also the pugnacious anti-elitism of 1782. The national psychology as a whole was now riper than ever for drastic changes. The mood was bitter, irrational, and more volatile than at any time since 1763. France was about to impose a treaty more humiliating than the one twenty years earlier; the war had been lost, the empire 'dismembered,' and Britain disgraced as a great international power; even Ireland seemed close to secession. Dissatisfaction with the nation's governance was now nearly universal. North's ministry, having disintegrated after the surrender at Yorktown (1781), collapsed in March 1782, the despairing king raving that those who demanded an end to the war had "lost the feelings of Englishmen."[93] Forced to choose his new ministers from the two groups uncontaminated by his war policy, he had turned to Shelburne, and, with great bitterness, to Rockingham, his enemy for twenty years. Morosely he found himself at last required to submit to 'the great party,' the party of the Whig moguls, of 'connexion' and 'faction.'

Of course the Rockinghams were far from seeing themselves in the same light. Preening themselves now, as Foord remarks, on "their sincerity and consistency"—one notes this concern running through all the rhetoric of this period—they saw in their own triumph a vindication of their uncompromising doctrine of 'party,' and, naturally, a happy restoration of truly constitutional government, established again upon a 'Revolution footing.' The nation, as they narrowly defined it, was returning to safe hands. As one of their tracts asserted, control was now at last restored to those who were "most worthy of the confidence of Parliament," men who possessed "great personal weight of character and fortune" and "the hereditary purity of those principles and virtues which saved the country in 1688."[94] In this we note that even at this late date they still defined political legitimacy and national sovereignty by standards long since abandoned by the radicals. Rejoicing nonetheless in their own virtues, and feeling morally exonerated in the nation's humiliation, the Rockinghams sat down to work. To please the watchful nation and gratify themselves they fired a few rounds with their economical popgun, their attack on the structure of royal 'influence.' And then, exhausted with reforming, they stopped dead in their tracks.

William Pitt the younger, who in 1781 had entered Parliament alongside Shelburne and the other Chathamites, wanted to go much further. He called, in a long speech packed with the ideas of Hulme, Burgh, and Cartwright, for a parliamentary inquiry into the whole structure of representation (May 1782). The constitution should be reformed to its ancient state, in which the representation of the people had been "equal, easy, practicable, and complete." Sir George Savile, the respected Yorkshire M.P. who in 1780 had cut his ties with Rockingham ("Now I am returned by my constituents"), seconded the motion with an interesting remark which again reflects the shadowy suspicions always felt towards the great Whigs: the Rockingham-dominated House, he said, "might as well call itself the representative of France as of the people of England."[95] But the Rockinghams cared little for the views of their critics, and they had had enough reform. In fact, led now by Fox, they peevishly departed from the infant ministry which they had not been wholly permitted to dominate, enraged that the king, upon Rockingham's sudden death (July 1782), had given the premiership to Shelburne, not to one of them. Again they fumed against what they imagined to be a Tory plot between a pliant minister and the obstinate king, who was indeed more crazily obsessed now than ever with visions of enslavement to them. While Shelburne defended George's right to choose his own ministers (for otherwise, as he famously said, "the monarchical part of the constitution would be absorbed by the aristocracy, and the famed constitution of England would be no more"), Fox determined to storm the government again and teach them both a lesson.

But meanwhile Pitt's speech had set off another great popular agitation. The defeat of his motion led to the celebrated Thatched House Tavern resolutions of May 1782, in which he and the leaders of the SCI decided to unleash still another nationwide reform campaign. The nationalist movement was now gaining strength with every day that passed. In literature we have already seen the remarkable new vigor and confidence expressed in the eighties, while much the same was true of the realm of economic 'take-off'—Cartwright's younger brother Edmund, incidentally, was now inventing his power loom and wool-carding machine. And in politics there was again at long last a genuine patriot in charge of government. Shelburne was one of the few noblemen—contemporaries were able to count no more than eight or nine in the whole country—who supported parliamentary reform. For years he had worked with the radical intellectuals, proven his willingness to support fundamental alterations, and done his best to find an accommodation with the Americans. Now he was prime minister; and Pitt, Chancellor of the Exchequer, was his chief spokesman in the House of Commons. The arrival of the younger Pitt, as Veitch observed, "meant an immense accession of strength to the reforming party." Pitt's later admirer, Rosebery, captured the drama of the event:

> In their despair, men looked round for a saviour of society, who should cast the money-changers out of the temple of Government, and restore to Britain . . . a decent and honourable existence. At this moment, there appeared before them a young university student; rich with lofty eloquence and heir to an immortal name; untainted in character, spotless in life. . . . To a jaded and humiliated generation the son of Chatham came as a new hope and a possible revelation.[96]

Though melodramatic, this really does capture the spirit of Pitt's reception outside the political establishment. To the reform crusade he brought not only the great name and retrospective glamor of 'the Great Commoner'—and this meant much in the embittered and highly volatile postwar atmosphere—but also, for such a young man, an impressive record of his own. At the age of only twenty he had worked in the Association Movement, and he continued to sit at Cartwright's knee, solicit Wyvill's advice, and pour out his ideas to Horne, a close associate. In Parliament he called for thoroughgoing reform; and since becoming the ministry's chief spokesman in the House, he was the object of burning hopes that the administration might actually do what a truly national government ought to do. The radical intellectuals doted on him as they had on his father earlier, and there are signs that they already saw in his youthful innocence, frankness, and attachment to 'English' principles another personification of 'poor Horatio,' the now well-established stereotype of the virtuous nation itself. Horne lauded "his talents, his candour, his ingenuousness," and augured wonderful results from his efforts. Wyvill, equally infatuated, conferred upon him the ultimate seal of approval: "As to Mr. Pitt's sincerity it is unquestionable."[97]

With the times so propitious, the latter part of 1782 saw another great wave of extraparliamentary activity, the radicals blanketing the country with propaganda and organizing another petitioning drive. Horne believed, as he excitedly declared in a pamphlet, that England was "on the eve of a peaceful revolution, more important than any which has happened since the settlement of our Saxon ancestors in this country." The radicals and their growing body of supporters thought they saw their millennium approaching. They anticipated much from Pitt, and some even at this late date still vainly believed Fox to be (as Wyvill hopefully wrote in August) "a cordial friend to . . . the cause of the people." By early 1783 the House of Commons was deluged with scores of petitions. Pitt prepared his strategy for a second parliamentary struggle. His proposals called for a disenfranchisement of rotten boroughs and an addition of M. P.'s to represent both London and the counties. From all the petitions, says Veitch, there came "one unanimous complaint" that in spite of "the original excellence of the Constitution," the "House of Commons no longer spoke the voice of the people of England."[98]

v. the Fox–North coalition

And then, from out of the blue, came the thunderbolt of the Fox-North coalition, which destroyed Shelburne's ministry (February 1783), buried the petitioning campaign, and installed in office together as friendly allies the two leaders of the day who, in addition to their now manifest opposition to organic reform, seemed most to represent totally contradictory sets of principles. Few events in English history have caused such a sensation as this unexpected union between North, the ex-premier, and Fox, formerly his loudest critic. One must leave England and the eighteenth century to find a parallel for it. Its effect was like that created by the Nazi-Soviet Pact of August 1939, when Hitler and Stalin, after years of mutual denunciation, joined to carve up Poland. The radicals were aghast at its cynicism; this was not what they had meant by 'association.' Typical was the blast which Wyvill inserted in the *York Chronicle*: If Fox and his adherents imagined that the English people still credited their friendly professions, then "THEY ARE DECEIVED AND THE PEOPLE OF ENGLAND ARE NOT." To Horne the coalition represented two factions "greedily and infamously united" to "overpower both king and people."[99]

The coalition, because it involved a large majority of the parliament-men, seemed to prove the radicals' declamations against political corruption and national degeneracy more conclusively than anything yet put on paper. Observers everywhere were stunned at the cynical collaboration of the parliamentary chiefs and appalled at the morality of their 'myrmidons,' who could so easily set aside all the principles which had formerly divided them, and who seemed to show by their conduct that they had either been raised on another planet—or country, and there was something to that—or that they simply cared nothing for the values of England. Here, in the face of decades of talk about English Sincerity, some of it even their own, Fox and North publicly convicted themselves of the worst moral, social and political sin one could commit in 1783, the sin of Duplicity Without Limit—of total Insincerity.

Foord expresses his feeling that "the unfavourable reaction to the coalition . . . was derived from an ethical rather than a Constitutional code." He is absolutely right: the code was that of Sincerity. The violent reaction to the coalition was along moral lines, not constitutional or political ones. And this explains why at last the nation, like a crystal struck by a hammer, divided along the moral fault-line deepening since George III first took the throne, with the king, Pitt, the radicals, and now the vast bulk of the people on one side, and the aristocracy and their henchmen—'an insolent aristocratical band,' as they were called—on the other. The confrontation, as Cannon observes, produced "the most acute political convulsion since the Revolution of 1688. Contemporaries talked of the possibility of civil war." A firestorm of indignation rose from every quarter against the parliament-men, the illegitimate oppressors, "the enemies of the nation," as Horne, with his usual vehemence, termed them. Cannon proposes that one may see in this confrontation "an English counterpart of the rivalry between monarchs and nobility that was so marked a feature of the European scene at this time."[100]

And then instead of dousing the conflagration, the Foxites, confident that they now controlled the only opinions that really mattered, those of a majority of parliament-men, heaped fuel upon it with their India Bill (November 1783). Here is still another sign of the remarkable insensitivity, betokening remarkable arrogance and exclusiveness, of the men who traveled in Fox's set. Of course they judged themselves, as we have often noted, very differently and according to their own standards of value—essentially cosmopolitan standards, worthy ones indeed, which acted to immunize them, as Fox himself suggested in 1782, against "any local prejudices whatever." The Foxites continued to think of themselves, and of the political institutions they claimed by hereditary right, as existing on an almost olympian plane above common opinion, and, so far as the House was concerned, persuaded themselves that they could secure its control by the same old methods used before the age of popular awakening. Fox may have conceived the India Bill as an instrument for reforming the system of Indian government; but the details of the plan would have seemed, even to a less suspicious public, to lead to the channeling into his hands of such a vast store of patronage that he and his 'confederacy' might establish their predominance in the House of Commons forever. And that is just the way it was perceived, as the contrivance of a political conspiracy intending to make Fox an entrenched 'dictator' over the king and everyone else. A decade later the historian William Belsham wrote that the India Bill "was almost universally condemned as a measure in the highest degree arbitrary and oppressive, and with consummate artifice calculated to perpetuate the power of an administration who were the objects of the national detestation."[101] All Fox's earlier preoccupation with curbing the influence of corruption now seemed exposed as insincere demagoguery. In the Commons, Pitt heaped scorn on the coalition. In the countryside there were tremendous new outcries of condemnation, fueled also by Fox's totally disrespectful attitude toward the king and toward his prerogatives in the choosing of ministers.

6. CONSOLIDATION AND NORMALIZATION

In the midst of this extraordinary crisis King George again proved himself a better judge of his people's attitudes than the 'insolent aristocratical band.' Seeing and of course sharing the public resentment at the ministry which had forced itself upon him, he determined to discard it by methods more truly unconstitutional than any he had yet been guilty of. In December 1783 he personally engineered the defeat of the India Bill and abruptly dismissed Fox and North, in spite of their very large parliamentary majority. He then installed the younger Pitt, the 'schoolboy Minister,' and upheld him for several months against a hostile Parliament still controlled by the coalition leaders, who naturally persisted in believing that anyone attempting to govern without them had departed from his senses. But feeling in the country was violently against them. Hundreds of frenzied addresses of support reached the king, while in London Pitt was feverishly lauded and voted the Freedom of the City for his role in "supporting the legal prerogative of the Crown and the constitutional rights of the people."[102]

The young prime minister, though greatly outnumbered in the House, was not intimidated by Fox's vociferations and votes of censure. "His coolness and courage were admirable," writes Brooke; "had he faltered or taken fright, all would have been lost." He made it clear, says Watson, that his was "not a government of flippant gamblers" but "a serious attempt to establish a stable system on the basis of the patriotic concensus of opinion." He was both a reformer and a 'king's friend,' his face set against faction, corruption, and servile adherence to the views of any great man. In Parliament he defended himself boldly against Fox and struck back through his actions as well. When the sinecure post of the Clerkship of the Pells, worth £3,000 a year, fell vacant in January 1784, he proved his attitude toward 'jobs' by giving it away, even though precedent would have supported his taking it himself, and, notes his biographer, "in view of his poverty his friends urged him to do so." The refusal was an act of 'Sincerity.' It was an act of purity, honesty, frankness, moral independence, and even, in the contemporary political environment, of some originality; and of course it contrasted strikingly with the morality of Fox's India Bill. The refusal was an act like those of the Sandfords in the novel which Thomas Day was now writing, a refusal to participate in the profits and, by implication, the whole system of corruption and degeneracy. And in a political leader the same gesture was, as one admiring radical prophesied, "the act of a man, who feels that he stands upon a high eminence, in the eyes of that country, which he is destined to govern."[103] This was a very fair piece of political punditry.

i. excommunication of the Foxites

In March 1784 the king dissolved Parliament and, in effect, referred the crisis to public opinion in a general election. What he wanted was

clear to everyone, for the election took place amid "one of the most exten-
sive publicity campaigns of the eighteenth century." What the king
wanted was popular approval of his recent use of the prerogative, electoral backing for Pitt's ministry, and a convincing repudiation of 'King
Fox' and the coalitionists. He succeeded beyond his wildest dreams: the
coalitionists, denounced from the housetops and vilified on every street
corner, were flattened. The *Annual Register* gave the verdict: "So complete
a rout of what was looked upon as one of the strongest and most powerful parties that ever existed in Great Britain, is scarcely to be credited."
One hundred and sixty of Fox's supporters—many of them henceforth
termed 'Fox's Martyrs'—were either defeated or frightened out of running. Their defeat reached even into their safest constituencies, their rotten boroughs and hereditary electoral preserves. Fox himself won so
narrowly in Westminster (where Horne and Jebb helped to lead the campaign against him) that the election was challenged and he had to retreat
to a friend's pocket borough for the Orkney and Shetland Islands.
Horne's attitude to the election was epitomized in a pamphlet he wrote
afterwards, 'Two Pair of Portraits,' where he contrasted in tabular fashion
all the virtues of the Pitts, father and son, with the vices of their inveterate
lifelong enemies, the Foxes.[104]

The Foxites were not only conquered and overwhelmed, but banished.
M. D. George calls it their "proscription," but Foord finds the *mot just:*
they were "excommunicated." The election of 1784, as contemporaries
were to remember for decades afterwards, was the great turning point in
the electoral history of the Whigs. They were consigned to the outer
darkness, doomed to wander for political eternities as the 'damned souls,'
the "*âmes damnées* of Mr. Fox." In the 1790s their Francophile internationalism helped to ensure that they would stay there for still more eternities. The Whig Party did not take power again for half a century, not till
1830, and even then this was perhaps due less to popular confidence in
the Whigs than to their enemies' forfeiture of confidence, their 'Tory
populism of the eighteenth century' (as Plumb shrewdly characterized it)
having largely congealed into a reactionary landed conservatism as obnoxious to national sentiment as 'Revolution-Principle' whiggism had been
earlier.[105]

Many postmortems have been done on the election of 1784, and historians have taxed their ingenuity to explain its spectacular results. But the
unalterable fact, acknowledged by nearly every writer, is that the fundamental issue, the one that affected contemporaries far more than any
other, was simply the moral contrast between Pitt and Fox. Cannon is
typical in writing that "it is hardly possible to exaggerate the extent to
which the anti-coalition campaign was based upon the new minister's reputation for purity and integrity," and that this in turn "would have been
less decisive had it not contrasted so pointedly with the public image of
his main rival." M. D. George shows how the contrast between the two
leaders ran through the events preceding the election: "Fox's rapid loss of
popularity, while that of Pitt as rapidly progressed, increased the drama

of the conflict. He [Fox] was now only in derision 'the man of the people,' and this, together with the support given to Pitt by the radicals, reformers and 'dissenting interest' left the oligarchical element in the Whig party starkly apparent." Pitt's biographer believes that "in so many ways, he [Pitt] was the antithesis of Fox," while Fox's takes a very similar attitude.[106]

Yet the historians feel a little uncertain about resting too much on this explanation because they think the moral contrast between two men, even two opposed political leaders, simply too insignificant to explain the electoral landslide in a political world which we have been trained to believe was dominated by jobbing and 'fixing things.' But the obvious explanation is nonetheless the right one. Of course it is vital to understand how this moral contrast worked in the framework of contemporary values. Historians may dwell very instructively upon systems of bribery and favoritism, and they may elucidate the intricacies of local politics, but still they will not get political history right till they get the ideals, the propaganda, the delusions and the mass perceptions right. The importance of symbols in the intellectual and political life of mankind is too obvious to require argument, and equally obvious is the fact that such symbols often work by antithesis. It is no less plain that many people today, even in highly developed nations, see their political leaders as personifications, living symbols, of whole interrelated systems of ideas and value, and that in earlier times people were even more prone to do so in the absence of advanced education and communications. The key to the election of 1784 is the fact that Pitt was perceived as the embodiment of the English National Character, while Fox was perceived as its antithesis.

Pitt was bathed in the glow of Sincerity, the 'reputation for purity and integrity,' as Cannon calls it, while Fox was the evil incarnation of Insincerity and hence (as Belsham recalled in 1796) the foremost 'object of the national detestation.' This symbolic dualism in contemporary thought and literature—it was the dualism of Horne's 'Two Pair of Portraits'—pervaded the political environment from the time that the younger Pitt first stepped on the political stage, if not indeed from years earlier when the two men's fathers had vied for attention. Foord, as we saw earlier, divined that public opinion toward the Fox-North coalition of 1783 was guided by some undefined 'ethical code,' a code connected with ideas of sincerity, hypocrisy, and the national good. He was right, and exactly the same thing guided opinion toward Pitt and Fox a year later. This 'code' was the code of Sincerity which we attempted to dissect in Chapter Six, the 'Sincere Ideal' which stood at the heart of the nationalist ideology and performed so many important functions in it. It was this which provided the great balance scales in which the politics of the eighties were anxiously weighed, no less than literature, art, manners, and all the other manifestations of national culture. The election took place in a mental environment conditioned by the dualistic influences which we have found in the nationalist ideology, with Pitt and Fox standing as figurative representations of the two normative patterns projected in it, the system of Sincerity and its foil, the anti-ideal of Insincerity. And of course we must try to keep in mind too the whole excited emotional context, not only in 1784 but throughout the two preceding decades. Ironically it was Namier himself who, writing in 1933 on Nazi Germany and seeking historical parallels from French, Irish, and South African history, postulated that "the rise of a pathological nationalism . . . after a national defeat seems a recurrent phenomenon" in history.[107]

Small wonder that Fox was buried in vilification. He was quite astonished at "the amazing abuse which is heaped upon me," but rightly attributed the electoral defeat to "popular frenzy."[108] Though he was, as his friends attested, the most charming and generous man in his circle, he was the national scapegoat outside it, the symbolic representative not only of his political 'confederacy' but of 'a class.' The election gave people throughout the kingdom, non-electors as well as electors, a once-in-a-lifetime opportunity to express themselves directly on Fox and Pitt, or rather on their public images, on everything they were believed to stand for. The election was thus a real-life enactment of the figurative combat which had now been enacted so many times in the nationalist literature. It was sincere Harry Sandford beating the stuffing out of the insufferable Master Mash, Humphry Clinker destroying the odious and frenchified Dutton, Captain Mirvan bloodying the nose of the arrogant Lovel; it was the humble Saxons below, throwing out the evil Normans above. It was, no matter what else has been discovered about it, mere comic-strip drama, acted out on the high stage of politics, with what seemed the nation's liberty and destiny at stake. A vote against Fox was a vote for the National Identity and National Independence, and a vote for Pitt was the elector's affirmation of his own morality and identity as a true Englishman. Here was a significant early instance, long before today's 'image-oriented' politics, of how popular moral identification, through the leader, with the subliminal image of National Character, would become the hidden fulcrum of modern politics.

ii. the people's Will

The 1784 election was the climax of the English nationalist 'Struggle for Independence.' As Pares remarks, the event "was, for that generation, a decisive battle." It marked "an epoch," says Rosebery, "in English politics. It was hailed by the nation as a new departure." Of course it was not a bloody event like the French Revolution, nor an unsuccessful campaign like the Corsican struggle for independence, nor anything so spectacular as, say, Colombia's war to free itself from Spain, nor anything so agonizingly prolonged through decades of revolt and submission as, for example, the Italian, Irish, Serbian, or Polish independence movements. This was the fifty years' climax of a distinctly eighteenth-century nationalist movement, generated in the international environment of the second and third quarters of the century and conditioned in the specifically English 'group situation.' It resembled the American movement more than any other, though of course the latter ultimately gravitated to 'secession' and found its 'renewal' there. The excommunication of the Foxites in 1784 was the expulsion, symbolic but nonetheless emotionally satisfying and politically effective, of England's alien oppressors, the equivalent of the American republic's banishment of the Tory Loyalists; and Pitt was England's George Washington, the national saviour destined to lead the country for the rest of his life. Here was the leader, the newspapers exulted (1784), who would work in the people's cause "with all the zeal of *an honest man* and *a sincere patriot.*" Borne into power, as contemporaries said, "on the shoulders of the people," he was the 'charismatic hero-leader' chosen to preside over the phase of 'consolidation and normalization.' It was because he represented the long-sought union between Power and People that his real strength lay in his 'charisma,' in an irrational network of psychological identifications between the people, himself, and the romanticized ideal of the National Identity. Many historians have sensed this without knowing quite how to express it. Watson observes that Pitt's political strength was always peculiarly dependent upon popular confidence in his character: Pitt's strength "was always subject," he writes, "to the qualification that he must remain true to the picture of himself accepted by the country"—that is, to the stereotyped image of the National Character which he was believed, more than any other public man, to personify.[109]

We have no more space here for discussion of politics after the election of 1784, or of important related issues such as the breakup and reformation of political parties under the impact of the nationalist movement. It surely seems likely, in view of continuing uncertainty over "the character of middle-of-the-road Toryism, or whatever it was that the Younger Pitt and Lord Liverpool espoused,"[110] that analysis of the history of the Tory party would benefit from a deeper understanding of what political nationalism means. It seems likely too that some of the theorizing about 'English Deference' might require rethinking. But really the possibilities for new research and interpretation seem almost endless, and we have reached a stopping-point adequate to the present purpose.

It must suffice to point out in conclusion that Pitt's triumph in 1784 was in many ways the fulfillment of the preceding generation's political hopes. "He became the symbol of 'good government' far removed from the bumbling inefficiency of the king's 'favorites' of the 1760s and 1770s and from the excesses of the Foxites who seemed to place their own narrow interests ahead of the country's." He brought calm after three decades of instability and national crisis, and he was the author of reforming policies, strongly supported by the generality of the people, designed to purify the institutions of government and liberate the economic and moral power of the middle classes. He was a superb administrative reformer, streamlining the organs of government, eliminating sinecures, reducing opportunities for corruption, reforming and simplifying the tax structure, stabilizing finances, strengthening and purifying the civil service. He reformed the government of India, supported the abolition of the slave trade, and gave a cautious hand to his friend Wilberforce's projects for the reformation of morality. He presided over the economic acceleration of the later eighties and, following the new economic ideas of Adam Smith, negotiated in 1786 a commercial treaty with France which greatly assisted England's economic re-invasion of the Continent. (It would appear that the treaty also helped to quicken nationalist feeling in France: "Many Frenchmen came bitterly to accuse the British of having outwitted them in order to exploit them.")[111]

There remains only the question of parliamentary reform. The issue is not insignificant, but we are now in a position to see that it was less important than many experts have assumed. Although, in the view of scholars who have examined the matter, Pitt's administrative reforms in fact eliminated corruption and political manipulation more effectively than parliamentary reform as it was then conceived could have done, Pitt nevertheless remained committed to this important radical objective, and in late 1784, "all afire with enthusiasm," persuaded his radical supporters to begin another national agitation. Wyvill spoke for all the agents when he stated his conviction (December 1784) that Pitt was determined "to put forth his whole power and credit, *as a man* and *as a minister, honestly* and *boldly* to carry a plan of reform, by which our liberties will be placed on a footing of permanent security."[112]

But the House defeated his plan in 1785. A number of circumstances were responsible for this, including the king's reluctant attitude and the malicious action of the Foxites, but the most important factor was simply the apathy of both the radicals and the general public. Some historians have seen in this, the fact that parliamentary reform languished under a minister prepared to support it wholeheartedly, a 'paradox,'[113] but actually it was just the reverse. The simple fact, however regrettable, is that people do not chase hard after solutions except when chased hard by their problems. The sudden lethargy of the radicals is not paradoxical when we take into account the true aim of nationalist political agitation. Its primary purpose, evident from the great days of the elder Pitt, had been to usher in, if need be to force upon the political establishment, a government truly felt to represent the English people. But that is exactly what the younger Pitt's government was, a government with enormous popular support, felt to express the people's will and character. What was the urgency then in campaigning further for shorter parliaments and a wider franchise? These were but means to an end now realized; at most they were tools for a more protracted job which could be left to the future. The task of putting liberty on 'a footing of permanent security' was a luxury which could wait. And was there not heartening evidence now that the 'renewed' Englishman of the future would be equal to the task when the necessity presented itself? Taking everything into account, there were enormously stronger grounds now than at any time in memory for pride in the national character and confidence that England's government truly belonged to her people.

Thus it would be a great mistake, looking at things from the perspective of 1785, to imagine that the radical movement had failed. It is because it did not fail that agitation subsided so rapidly. Continued agitation might only have given another handle to the people's enemies, the Foxites; but the main point is that the movement subsided not from considerations of expediency, certainly not from repression, but from joy and satisfaction. The radicals were delighted. Thanks to the happy turn of events and their own prodigious labors—reshaping the whole public attitude toward the national past, the constitution, political legitimacy, and fundamental rights of representation—public opinion had, in many respects, caught up with them, and for a while they became invisible in the general euphoria. Jebb, when he died in 1786, was happy; Day, when he died in 1789, was content. In that same year Cartwright, who was not easily fooled, still firmly believed that Pitt might do "somewhat great and good" in the way of parliamentary reform. Horne similarly "remained firm in his attachment to Mr. Pitt," in 1788 joining the prime minister and others to found the Constitutional Club, whose motto was 'King and Constitution.'[114]

In this we may see strikingly symbolized the fact that patriotism, which nearly always till 1784 had been the earmark of anti-ministerial politics, was now being assimilated to the support of the king and his prime minister. This is a sign of the 'consolidation' of the people's triumph, the institutionalization of the nationalist takeover under an English king, prime minister, and parliamentary majority. Symptomatically also, the later eighties saw the beginnings, in many public ceremonies, rites, and festivals, of a cult of George III which was to grow continuously afterwards. The 'liturgy of nationalism' was being developed. At the same time, Pitt was beginning the transformation of the national ruling class, breaking the exclusive connection between the peerage and the greater landlords, and at the same time expanding the peerage from an English to a British base, including eminent Scots and Irish: "Between 1780 and 1830, a group which was almost exclusively English became a genuine U.K. peerage."[115] In these and in many other interesting respects, 'Normalization' had begun.

7. Radicalism, the Historians, and the 'Atlantic Revolution'

This chapter is too long already, and this is not, in any case, the place for complicated historiographical discussion. But perhaps there is just room for one or two brief comments on how this chapter fits in with existing ideas about eighteenth-century radicalism. Professional historians, acquainted with specialized literature, will already have seen by themselves how this interpretation seeks to incorporate earlier ones.[116] The radical movement, according to our vision of it, arose naturally by itself from English historical development in the eighteenth century, it concerned itself deeply with moral and social issues and was by no means exclusively devoted to political reforms, it was fully self-propelling and required no extra inspiration from America or France (though assuredly it received such influences), it was quite compatible both with monarchism and with a revitalized Anglicanism, and intellectually its roots lay more in the new cultural, historical, antiquarian and ethnic concerns of the mid-eighteenth century than in seventeenth-century intellectual inheritances, whether 'Commonwealth,' 'country,' Lockeian, or simply whiggish. This is certainly not to deny that such inheritances found their way into it, but only to urge that none were as important as has been thought. Broadly speaking, during the age of George III the Left actually embraced two distinguishable bodies of political doctrine, the one Liberal—i.e., whiggish, universalist, and tied to 1689 (a doctrine of civil liberties, private property, and the limitation of state power, favored both by the Whig élite and by many of their Dissenting supporters), and the other Radical—i.e., much newer and more democratic but also tied to ideas of moral coercion, social discipline, and collective uniformity profoundly abhorrent to the Whig spirit. In sum, the old Lockeian and universalist liberalism of the seventeenth century (the basic Whig-Commonwealthman tradition) was now joined, but in some respects vigorously contradicted, by a new populist radicalism (*remotely* traceable also, it is true, to earlier ideas, as Hill's essay shows), and this ambivalence on the Left underlay much of the political complexity of the period 1760–1825. Of course the French Revolution, as we shall see more largely in the next chapter, greatly complicated things still more. The supposed 'abstract universalism' of the French Revolution, much exaggerated by Burke, its first prominent English interpreter, and then dumped like tar over Paine and other prominent writers of the Commonwealth tradition, has helped to confuse our modern perceptions. It has led some observers to regard the ineffectual, dissenting, cosmopolitan and quasi-republican liberal protests of Priestley, Price and Paine as peculiarly 'modern,' 'germane,' and 'truly radical,' while at the same time to discount as non-radical, antiquarian, and 'naive' the great popular grassroots movement guided by Horne and Cartwright and their successors—that is, the mainstream movement of English popular reform, the same which found its way into both Chartism and middle-class Radicalism. It is largely due to this same visual distortion, which could scarcely have survived long had historians viewed English history in the light of nationalist development elsewhere, that Horne, Cartwright, Cobbett and their followers have often been very incorrectly characterized as conservatives, even as strange antediluvian reactionaries. Professor Butterfield stands virtually alone as the one commentator to see that these angry agitators "pulled out of early history the shapes they had manufactured in their wishful thinking, and furnished their generation with just the type of anachronism that it required."[117]

But the general reader will probably be more interested to consider the fundamental relationship between this radicalism and that which emerged in several other countries in the later eighteenth century. Some prominent French and American historians have found a high and useful vantage point from which to contemplate this in the idea of an entire pan-Atlantic 'Age of Democratic Revolution' stretching from roughly the 1770s to the 1830s. Many years have passed now since Professor Palmer, rightly dissatisfied with the tendency to study national histories in isolation from each other, undertook to argue that 'Atlantic civilization,' European civilization on both sides of the Atlantic, was swept in the three or four decades after 1763 "by a single revolutionary movement, which manifested itself in different ways and with varying success in different countries, yet in all of them showed similar objectives and principles." This sweeping interpretative idea has found very few English supporters save Jarrett, whose fine comparative study of English and French politics during the period 1759–89 shows how very similar were the problems of the two countries, yet how enveloped in mutual suspicion their peoples were: "It was," he penetratingly observes, "this paradoxical polarity between the two most powerful countries in the world that lay at the root of the 'Age of Revolution' of the late eighteenth century."[118] Apart from this, however, many other historians, bemused by the mythical 'social harmony' and too often led by conventional precepts to treat the English radicals as complacent non-radical reactionaries, have resisted the effort to draw England into the larger picture and have thus set up a formidable barrier to more general acceptance of the thesis.

But there is, it is true, another barrier as well, raised by Palmer himself in his rather too hasty assumption that it was "the *philosophe* literature . . . the literature of the Enlightenment" which promoted "the universal impulse to liberty" which supposedly united all the various radical movements.[119] Frankly it is rather surprising, in view of the outcomes of all those radical movements, to see that so little consideration has been given to the possibility that they were promoted by *nationalist,* rather than enlightened and cosmopolitan, ideas.[120] One of the better critiques of the Palmer thesis was written by Goodwin, whose discussion makes it clear that two principal difficulties discouraging acceptance of that thesis are, first, English historians' encrusted disbelief that a truly radical political movement existed in England in the seventies and eighties, and, second, an inability to reconcile unmistakable diversities of local radical ideology (the 'Saxon' ideas of the Americans, for instance) with the universal *scholarly assumption,* completely unquestioned, held by both proponents as well as critics of the Palmer thesis, that it could only have been *cosmopolitan* ideology which united radicals everywhere and furnished the 'like-mindedness' which drew them into radical activities.[121]

The reader will see how the present chapter fits into this larger controversy. If its interpretation of English history is at all correct, then the Palmer thesis, substantially modified, would seem to receive important new support. For our study helps to dispose of both the objections mentioned above. First, England *did* witness a truly radical political movement, one which (as Butterfield and Cannon, careful students of it, also believe) came close to revolutionary violence in the period 1779–84 and which only drew decisively back from it as a result of Pitt's triumph and Fox's overthrow in 1784. And as to the second objection, this too should vanish in the recognition, assisted by a new understanding of English radicalism, that what constituted the like-mindedness of radicals across the western world, from Bogotá and Boston to Madrid and Berlin, was not the cosmopolitanism which they all inherited from the increasingly remote past, the age of Newton and Locke and Voltaire, but rather the *nationalist* ideologies, structurally similar yet individually varied according to 'group situation,' which were generated in their countries as these sought identity and power in an international community nourished in secular ideas and ripe for fundamental modernization.[122] It was not cosmopolitan political ideas but nationalist ones which were spreading like wildfire in the second half of the eighteenth century.

Of course this points also to a need for revisions in the general theory of nationalism. Two findings which seem particularly noteworthy are the fact that this phenomenon was born nearly half a century before the experts have thought it was, and also that it flourished first in that one country where, according to present theory, it never really existed at all. Plamenatz was some decades off the mark when he endorsed the general view "that there was little or none of it [nationalism] in the West before the end of the eighteenth century," but he was, on the other hand, absolutely right when he urged that nationalism "is to be found only among peoples who are, or are coming to be, sharers in an international culture whose goals are worldly. Nationalism is confined to peoples who, despite their rivalries and the cultural differences between them, already belong to, or are being drawn into, a family of nations which all aspire to make progress in roughly the same directions."[123] Here is the true key to the Age of Democratic Revolution. In its philosophical soul, this Age was not the realization but the repudiation of cosmopolitan ideals; it was the beginning of the new era of democratic nationalism. It was not so much 'the rights of man' as the rights of Englishmen, Frenchmen, and other nationals, that was to bring whole peoples into the streets.

What then, it may be asked, of cosmopolitan idealism? One can only speculate on its subsequent history, a subject far removed from our own study. The ideal of universal liberty and brotherhood, partly handed down to us by the ancients, partly a dream of Voltaire and the eighteenth-century philosophers, partly a guise of aristocratic power in a remarkably fraternal era, an appeal later of revolutionaries desperately seeking foreign assistance, a thing of little popular attraction and unhappily of little historic reality beyond a small number of mere phrases and paper proclamations, seems to have passed down into the nineteenth century in much the same condition it had usually held before that, namely as an educators' fiction (though enhanced by the few universal notes of the American and French Revolutions), a fiction functionally similar to the dangerously powerful new nationalist myths of the modern era but deliberately trained against them, a shibboleth taken up not only by Marxists and international trade unionists but by anti-nationalist intellectuals of every stripe, a myth about something supposedly realized or half realized late in the eighteenth century, then pointed to over and over by caring men and women trying to tame and elevate this hating and warring world.

11. 1817, Williams. An attack on the 'Apostacy' of the Lake Poets. Southey, like
Wordsworth and Coleridge, was, as Hazlitt remarked, a former 'Ultra-Jacobin'
turned 'Ultra-Royalist.' Here, crowned with laurels (he was appointed poet
laureate in 1813), and with his government pension nearby, he sits astride the
official butt of sack, which gushes 'Adulation,' 'Sycophancy,' 'Servility,' etc. The
Devil holds up a wreath of nettles.

CHAPTER EIGHT

The Long Revolution, 1789–1830

I held forth to a working man . . . on the established text, reform was
revolution . . . I said, 'Why, look at the revolutions in foreign countries,
meaning of course France and Belgium. The man looked hard at me and
said . . . 'Damn all foreign countries, what has old England to do with
foreign countries'; This is not the only time that I have received an impor-
tant lesson from a humble source.

—GLADSTONE

B Y 1789 the making of English nationalism was over. All its ideological
elements were in place, its cultural realization was well under way.
The following half-century, the period 1790–1840, saw the natural unfolding of much of its moral, social, aesthetic, political and intellectual
program into the realities of Victorian Britain.

'1789,' however, with all its resplendent historical symbolism, partly
obstructs the view of this larger and longer evolution. 1789 is an important marker in English as well as French and European history, but in
some ways it has been assigned too much importance. The diverse English
reactions to the revolution in France, and then the gravitation into still
another prolonged Anglo-French war, lasting a quarter of a century down
to 1815, are seen as marking out fundamental new patterns, 'modern'
patterns, in English history and culture, in some instances too sharply
distinguished from 'traditional' tendencies existing before 1789.

It is true that there were many interesting developments during this
quarter-century. Thus some modern authors have devoted themselves to
studying the tremendous anti-French reaction of the nineties and the sup-
pression of English radicalism, others to the remarkable takeoff of the
Methodist and Evangelical movements, others to wartime economic production, the beginnings of factory development, the rise of industrial unrest, and the formation of a working-class 'consciousness,' still others to
the remarkable efflorescence, apparently in two successive waves, of what
is regarded as a single literary movement called English Romanticism, and
yet others to new intellectual currents such as Political Economy and Util-
itarianism. The whole period 1789–1830 was indeed one of tremendous
energy and remarkably diverse activity, much of this profoundly influenced by a newly heightened consciousness of the threat posed by England's resurgent and dangerous neighbor across the Channel.

It is hardly surprising then that this exciting period has attracted probably more scholarly attention than any other in English history, and that
so many academicians have devised so many theories to explain its lines of
development. Unfortunately, however, despite the fun and usefulness of
this, the net result has been to complicate almost beyond belief the gen-

eral picture of the period, especially as regards the basic ideas that guided contemporaries through it. The general interpretative situation has not changed much since the time some years ago when Professor Webb observed that "the treacherous morass of early nineteenth-century intellectual life offers one of the greatest challenges to historians of Britain today."[1] But the noteworthy thing about our theory of English nationalism is that its introduction into the picture, instead of further complicating matters, provides a powerful central idea, magnetized, as it were, in the natural flow of the preceding fifty years, around which we may attempt to group and hence understand more clearly many puzzling aspects of that dynamic age. Of course a detailed re-examination of that period can hardly be accomplished in the few pages remaining here. The purpose of this concluding chapter is simply to show in a summary way, building on numerous suggestions earlier, the continuing advance, even in that notorious 'morass' of the Romantic Age, of the English nationalist movement. For despite setbacks and various changes in cast, costume and script, the movement itself in all its reality and power did advance steadily through that period, progressing on a broad front beneath the many confusing surfaces of things. There, unseen beneath the glitter of '1789,' was one of the great ongoing realities of the Georgian Age of English History, a nation-building movement fully existent in 1788, and triumphant by the Victorian era despite a spirited aristocratic and anti-nationalist counterattack centered in the two decades 1800–20.[2]

1. THE POLITICAL CONTINUITY OF THE MOVEMENT

Apart from the blinding effect of '1789,' another reason why the nationalist movement has escaped notice is the fact that, owing to its marked success by the late 1780s, its conservative opponents were by then beginning to appropriate some of its ideas and rhetoric in attempts to assimilate its popularity to their own antithetical ambitions. Such a fate has, of course, greeted every successful radical idea in history, from ancient Christianity to modern Marxism. Sooner or later, conservatives appropriate the popular elements of such ideologies and turn them to their own uses. A noteworthy instance of this intellectual shoplifting is presented by Burke's famous *Reflections on the Revolution in France* (1790), which some authors now wrongly treat as the original source of organicist English political and social theory. The truth is that Burke, defending the upper classes against a much exaggerated 'French' radical threat, in fact borrowed his organicist ideas from the English radical writings of the pre–1789 period. The idea of a native social compact, enshrined in history and passed down as an inalienable inheritance through the generations, was scarcely original with him; indeed many of his most 'metaphysical' phrases of 1790 might easily have been lifted straight from earlier texts by Cartwright,[3] though in Burke's hands the purpose was not, of course, to extend liberty but to restrict it. His purpose was not to demand a resumption of ancient rights but instead to check such demands by identifying them with supposedly 'abstract' and 'foreign' impulses. With Burke the theory of the English Nation was adapted, for the first time in its long history, to the cause of aristocratic ascendancy and social conservatism. Burke aimed to hijack and remold the mythology which had always constituted the radicals' most powerful argument for democratic change.

Naturally they scorned the attempt, and the fundamental continuity after 1789 of the pre–1789 movement is nowhere more clearly revealed than in the stubborn persistence with which they clung to and, year after year, reasserted (much to the dismay of some left-leaning historians today) their 'Saxon' ideology of the 'free-born Englishman'—essentially populist, monarchist, anti-aristocratic, anti-foreign, anti-republican, wedded to the myth of the Norman Yoke and of an egalitarian social compact in the halcyon pre-Norman days of King Alfred, framed on a dualistic social theory pitting 'People' against tyrannical usurpers. The continuity of the movement is manifest also in their continuing reform proposals and political tactics. Although the movement was thrown badly onto the defensive during the 1790s, so that its first political priority necessarily became again (as in the mid 1760s) the *defense of civil liberties*—the only point, as we saw before, on which radicals and Whig grandees (and Dissenting intellectuals as well) might heartily concur and enter into alliance—its positive program, so far as it was strong enough to sustain one at all, was also exactly the same as it had been before 1789: a demand for annual parliaments and manhood suffrage. The radicals' ultimate *tactic*, implied in their creed, also remained the same—the convening of a super-convention, a grand national anti-parliamentary assembly of popular delegates; something which they attempted several times in the tumultuous nineties, and then again, despite legislation prohibiting it, in the stormy postwar period (1817). Even their personnel, their key 'agents,' remained the same: Horne, though now in his late fifties, was one of the most active radical organizers of the nineties, reactivating the SCI in 1791, helping to found the London Corresponding Society (LCS) in 1792, and running for Parliament on radical platforms in 1790, 1796, and 1801; while Cartwright, equally active during the nineties, became the prime radical organizer after Horne's death (1812), founding the first of the new radical Hampden Clubs that year, barnstorming the country and founding dozens of other such clubs during the next five years, then calling and taking the chair at the first national meeting of club delegates in 1817. The younger radical leaders—Hardy, Gerrald, Thelwall, Burdett, Hunt, Cobbett, Hone, Bamford—were disciples of these two great political warhorses, bred in the same stable, sharing their 'antiquarian' cultural and linguistic interests (on which several of them, following Horne, published books), priding themselves equally on their mythical British political heritage and no less bent on 'restoring' it; and even the most hotheaded and extreme of the postwar left-wingers, deluded into harebrained insurrections and desperate plots by spies sent out by the Tory government, differed from these others not in ideas but simply in their greater willingness to put to the test the 'English right of revolution.' It is but symptomatic that the Cato Street Conspirators, the saddest and most desperate bunch of them all, went to their deaths proclaiming themselves proud 'sons of ancient Britons.' And finally, also throughout this period from beginning to end, the 'sincere' moral ideas of the English nationalists, strenuously advanced in a myriad of ways—most notably through the extremely popular writings of Cobbett but also, for example, through the sober standards of conduct propagated in numerous workingmen's lodges and trades unions—helped to create even among the industrious poor that distinctively nineteenth-century English culture of moral sobriety, individual independence and collective fellowship which in 1750 had been mostly just a dream in the minds of a few middle-class literary malcontents, but which by 1850 had become the bedrock of national feeling, thanks to the ideal of English National Identity and to the many propagandists who inculcated it.

But why then was the movement, in its *political* aspect, such a failure? If it endured all these hard and unpredictable years, and even in some important ways flourished, then why were not Manhood Suffrage and Annual Parliaments written into the statute book by at least 1825? The answer is that during much of this time it was stalled under a wave of repression—the suspensions of Habeas Corpus; the legislative acts banning local, regional, and national associations; the strict rules against correspondence, political assemblies, and demonstrations; the imposition of tough new standards of blasphemy, treason, and sedition; the heavy taxes on reading material and the banning of books; the use of paid police informers and agents provocateurs against supposedly conspiring traitors; the treason trials. The movement, in other words, was sidetracked by new legal inhibitions mostly imposed in the nineties and then periodically renewed and added to as late as 1819, and hence for the same reason it lacked coherence, central leadership, and a national structure. English nationalism, considered solely in its political department, was much stronger in the 1780s than it was to be again till 1831, at which time there were indeed renewed hopes that Manhood Suffrage and Annual Parliaments might actually be 'restored' at last.

But there was, it is true, an issue of popularity involved here too. Besides official repression, there was also a heavy moral loss sustained in the 1790s. The nationalist political movement temporarily lost the tactical advantage which had nearly always in the past constituted its greatest potential strength, its *anti-Frenchness*. Indeed in this respect the pre–1789 situation was temporarily reversed in the nineties, and the movement lay paralyzed for more than a decade (circa 1790–1805) under exactly the same slur it had formerly cast against its upper-class opponents, namely that its motivations and actions were insidiously 'French' in origin. In the nineties the movement lost its claim to defend England and hence its claim to popularity; and instead it was again reduced, somewhat as it had been during the period 1779–82, to the position of being a hated cult of supposed anti-English traitors, friends of France and of French ways.

Of course it was nothing of the sort, but Tom Paine and his Americanophile and Francophile friends left it open to that imputation. After the fall of the Bastille the sudden prominence on the Left of a band of rationalist intellectuals, formerly pro-American and now, it seemed, enthusiastically pro-French—Deists, unitarians, crypto-republicans, bourgeois universalist *philosophes* like Price and Priestley, Wollstonecraft and Paine and Godwin, all connected with Dissent—gave a handle to the movement's upper-class enemies such as they had never had before, and they pressed their advantage to the hilt. Paine, back from America, contemptuously replying in his *Rights of Man* (1791–92) to Burke's newfangled ancestor-worshipping conservatism, did not even bother to conceal his impatience with the monarchism of the radicals or their infatuation with the ancient constitution; and this, together with his pro-French apologetics and sardonic anticlericalism (revealed more largely in his *Age of Reason*, 1793), plunged the whole reform movement into a deepening unpopularity which Horne and Cartwright and their disciples were powerless to throw off, despite their efforts to hold it clear of 'Paineism' and 'Jacobinism.' It can hardly be thought surprising, in view of all we have studied so far, that many of these radicals increasingly shared the anti-French feeling of *der Volk*. Some of the leaders of the LCS, even while their own government was rounding them up in the late nineties, wanted to join the Volunteers against a dreaded French invasion. Cartwright, as we saw, had felt the same impulses twenty years earlier during the invasion scare of 1779, though it should be remembered that he was none the less radical for all that.

Thus the English reformers of 1790–92, hailing the French ones, dropped their favorite weapon the tar brush, and when they looked for it again were appalled to discover that it had been snatched up by their enemies for use against themselves. By 1793, when war broke out between the two countries, the radicals had already begun to be beaten up, denounced, imprisoned, tried, transported, and executed as traitors, agents of France. The loyalist reaction was very deep, and, though orchestrated by the rich, it embraced all classes. Everything English was now suspiciously evaluated in the light of its possible relationship to French Jacobinism. 'French principles' became a technical term in the English courts, signifying criminal activity. As the reactionary mood of the nineties hardened, the whole country reverberated with the loyalist battle-cry of 'Church and King' and with incessant warnings against an imagined French-inspired rising of English artisans and laborers. Anti-French propaganda of every sort spewed from English pens, presses and pulpits.

Here too, of course, in this torrent of anti-French propaganda, unprecedented in volume, we see many continuing patterns from the pre-1789 period. Before 1789, as we saw earlier, the 'French Character' was treated as the reverse of the English and made its ideological foil. The French, as described by Andrews in 1785, were impure, dishonest, dissembling, imitative, and servile; the stereotypical Frenchman was an artful conniver, somehow monkeylike in his airs, dress, and manners, devilishly angling to seduce John Bull and his virtuous daughter; and this 'French' symbolism was polemically tied to the English Quality like a can to a dog's tail. After 1789, during the nineties, many of these same elements remained central in anti-Jacobin propaganda, but there, not surprisingly, this propaganda was instead very largely channeled against English radical intellectuals and working people, not the English upper class. Particularly interesting is the new, much enhanced role of the monkey (still a symbol of the Frenchman), which after 1789 became transformed into a destructive, King Kong-like ape, often surrounded by scenes of havoc, decapitation, and war; while Voltaire, the most famous of the French philosophers and always the supreme representative of French literary genius, now achieved new prominence as the supposedly conspiring mastermind of universal atheism and pan-European revolution. Representative of this whole anti-Jacobin pattern was a political print from 1803, 'The Arms of France,' which features a guillotine dripping with blood (the French 'Constitution'), whose twin supports are a rampant tiger holding a tricolor flag inscribed *Desolation,* and a grinning ape in a tricolor sash and bonnet rouge trimmed with bells like a jester's cap, holding its own tricolor flag, *Atheism;* the ape is seated on two thick volumes inscribed *Voltaire* and *Rosseau* [*sic*], while dangling beneath these is a pamphlet, *Tom Paine.* Incessantly hammered into the English public mind during the nineties, these sensational anti-Jacobin ideas affected attitudes towards English radicalism for many decades to come. In the 1819 Westminster election, for example, anti-radical prints routinely smeared Horne's disciple Sir Francis Burdett by associating him with the familiar figure of the French ape carrying a standard of 'Radical Reform.' Similarly, the "indiscriminate abuse" of Voltaire, according to Campbell, the distinguished Victorian barrister, remained "in England the test of orthodoxy and loyalty" as late as 1850.[4]

Thus the English radicals, those few of them with any heart left for politics at the end of the nineties, had a hard row to hoe. Political reform was now completely out of the question; the fight for civil liberties, for the mere right to speak and write, was all that was left to them, and so they worked again in tandem with the patrician Foxites of the Opposition, even though the latter were no more seriously committed now to constitutional alteration than they had ever been. The whole country was in the grip of a feverish 'Church and King' reaction.

But the reader may ask whether this prolonged condition of nervous agitation and superheated patriotism was really likely, in the long run, to serve the interests of anyone in the upper classes. Would it not instead ultimately feed the propaganda of the bourgeois intellectuals, always in the past the authentic spokesman and defenders of 'the People'? The more clear-sighted radicals saw that it would. One of them, James Watt's son, noting that reactionary loyalists had self-interestedly stirred up the lower classes with patriotic alarms, shrewdly predicted in 1793 that "the day will come when they shall curse the senseless cry of Church & King &

feel their own weapons turned upon themselves." He was absolutely right. The end of that decade saw what was perceived at the time as the "nationalization of liberty-politics at home";[5] the alarms against English Jacobinism and Paineism sounded increasingly hollow in the ears even of those who rang them. By 1805, with the French Republic abolished, Napoleon pursuing a European empire, and Lord Nelson the hero of the hour, the French peril could no longer in any logical sense be laid at the door of anti-government critics like Cartwright and Burdett. Indeed the shoe was now almost back on the other foot again, and zealous patriots like Cobbett, unimpeachably anti-French, began arraigning the government for neglecting military preparedness, abusing England's fighting men, overtaxing the people, and mismanaging the war. The humiliating Convention of Cintra (1808) and military disasters of 1809 only added grist to their mills. By 1812 there was a revival and new proliferation of anti-government 'agents and agencies,' and four years later, after the war, there began a mounting cycle of protests and popular demonstrations reminiscent of those that had followed the American war earlier. The crass upper-class self-interest evident in the Corn Laws of 1815, the renewed suspension of Habeas Corpus and the government's imposition of what the radicals vilified as 'continental despotism,' the ministry's 'un-English' use of spies and provocateurs, and finally the reckless use of lethal force against unarmed 'free-born Englishmen' on St. Peter's Field, Manchester (1819), all served as proofs to nationalist agitators who now again, dressed anew in the battle garb of John Bull, were able to stigmatize their highborn governors as enemies of the English nation despite the ape cartoons and 'Jacobin' counter-stigmas directed against themselves. The groundswell of anti-government outrage and popular feeling after this 'Peterloo Massacre' of 1819 was so great that despite the prosperity of the twenties and other counter-influences (the differences now increasingly apparent between middle and working classes, for example), a united 'English People' stood ready again in 1831 to demand from its oppressors the 'Saxon rights' invented for them some sixty years earlier by Horne and Hulme.

2. EVANGELICAL ANTI-CONSPIRACY

Thus the long military and ideological struggle against France, like the earlier one against the American rebels, though it had the effect of temporarily derailing the nationalist movement, failed to deflect it from its deeply laid course. Again we are reminded that there is nothing so powerful as an idea whose time has come. But the clearest proof of this lies not in the history of politics at all but rather in that of religion, where again we are able to discern a key turning point just near the year 1800. The basic pattern was exactly the same as in politics, a heavy swing forward of the pendulum just after a terrified embrace with reaction. Indeed in this realm, much more speedily and forcibly than in that of politics, the day suddenly dawned when the hysterical anti-French loyalists were forced to 'curse the senseless cry of Church & King, & feel their own weapons turned upon themselves.'

It was the Low Church zealots of the Church of England, the Methodists and Evangelicals, who now sprang forward to become the chief standard-bearers of the nationalist movement. And with its political advance stalled, there really was no alternative to 'moral reformation.' The respectability and piety of these Anglican 'saints' was the perfect camouflage, even though many, like Wilberforce, had been political reformers in the eighties. Though ostentatiously loyalist in politics, they were drastic moral and social revolutionaries; and to them the French Revolution was a godsend. Unworried about official persecution, indeed for a while receiving official encouragement, the Evangelicals, protected not only by their respectability but by the genuineness of their desire to discipline the masses, were permitted to flood the country with propaganda which was inwardly but profoundly subversive, perhaps more subversive indeed in total impact than anything produced in the pre–1789 period. Seizing the initiative, they cunningly fitted the dreadful vision of France to their own ambitions, and, to the increasingly horrified realization of the aristocracy, began to fight what must be regarded as one of the most remarkable moral and social battles of modern times.

Unerringly they saw that propaganda against the 'French' system of evils, though it was always to be dispensed from the patriotic—*and now seemingly conservative!*—pulpit of anti-Jacobinism, could be channeled also against aristocratic habits and social ascendancy; roughly in the same way, to suggest an obvious analogy from twentieth-century nationalism, that the Nazis, while incessantly alleging the danger of an international 'Jewish-Bolshevik conspiracy,' mounted a mammoth but sidelong social revolution against their country's elite establishments—the Prussian aristocracy, the army, schools, universities, existing systems of law, manners, morality, and so on.[6] The anti-Gallic stereotype of the 1790s, the ghastly caricature of 'French' traits hastily pasted up as a religious and political scarecrow to control the masses, was, just as soon as its tremendous new repressive power became evident, seized upon as a moral and social tool, and made an instrument, just as the pre–1789 anti-Gallic image had been earlier, for smearing the habits and undermining the ascendancy of Britain's own upper classes, for discrediting what were deliberately treated as the Gallic tastes and attitudes handed down by 'the better sort.'

Coleridge, commenting on the Foxite Whigs, knowingly remarked that their "coward whine and Frenchified slaver and slang" were extreme disabilities; "Fox's Gallicism," he observed, "was a treasury of weapons to Pitt."[7] But obviously the same treasury was open to anyone clever enough to raid and exploit it. Anti-French feeling was a loose cannon on a rolling deck. Upper-class reactionaries had employed it against radicalism in the nineties, and now it was seized by Evangelicalism and cunningly directed against them. It was in this way that from about 1800 the Evangelicals' extremely heavy yet ambiguous condemnation of 'French traits' became the convenient battering ram of a multifarious campaign against *analogous* tendencies of impurity, dishonesty, artificiality, worldliness, and moral irresponsibility in England, a stamp for promoting and enforcing the moral revolution already begun, a revolution which, though naturally modified in certain respects now (as in the new post–1789 dread of religious unbelief), amounted basically to the imposition of a counter-system, the system of 'English Sincerity' (Victorianism'). And with this moral revolution there went a social one, as we saw before. The Evangelical propagandists and their 'saintly' supporters—divines, bankers, barristers, entrepreneurs, missionaries, colonialists, preachers—did much more to subvert the established order than to uphold it. Abstractly evident in all their projects was a determined effort to strike down many of the fundamental traditions of the country—not just the 'nominal Christianity' but also the localism, the elitism, the structures of traditional deference, the sophisticated literary culture, the manners and morals and amusements customary to Britain's ancien régime.

Of course this was a very confusing development, and just as it deceived many contemporaries, so too it has deceived scholars unequipped to understand it. Professor Spring saw the essential fact. Speculating on the spread of 'Victorian' attitudes and the marked decline of aristocratic values during the first third of the nineteenth century, he pointed to the *deceptiveness* of this great process, observing that "it seems to have worked in such a fashion as to obscure its true nature and to preserve the illusion in many minds that all was well, or at least was not seriously deranged."[8] The explanation is that *an extremely radical process was now working under cover of an extremely conservative one.* The 'reaction against the French Revolution' was genuine enough, but it also marvelously camouflaged those moral revolutionaries who, following John Brown, had thirsted for decades to transform, nationalize, level, and make uniform their country's institutions.

Their avowed purpose seemed innocent enough. The announced principle was one of National Security. The principle, which they tirelessly reiterated, was that national 'quarantine' must be adopted against the 'moral plague' of France—a principle, as we recall, which English nationalists had been trying to inculcate for half a century already. But what did it mean *now*, in the hands of these particular propagandists under these supposedly perilous new conditions? In effect it amounted to a demand that many of the values most cherished by sophisticated Englishmen should be instantly thrown aside in favor of a bigoted provincialism on the pretext that upper-class sophistication led (as it allegedly had in France) to lower-class rebellion. For the sly exploitation of this principle one must examine the actual phraseology (and, behind that, the spirit) in which it was preached and inculcated. For example, in Hannah More's *Strictures on the Modern System of Female Education* (1799) one may study how the battle was managed through a counterpoint of suggestions and hints as to the dreadful infectiousness of the system of 'French' evils—or rather systems, for now the nationalist writer preached fear at both the more aristocratic and the more proletarian manifestations of the horrid Frenchness:

> Under a just impression of the evils which we are sustaining from the principles and the practices of *modern* France, we are apt to lose sight of those deep and lasting mischiefs which so long, so regularly, and so systematically we have been importing from the same country, though in another form, and under another government. In one respect, indeed, the first were the more formidable, because we embraced the ruin without suspecting it; while we defeat the malignity of the latter, by detecting the turpitude, and defending ourselves against its contagion. This is not the place to descant on that levity of manners, that contempt of the sabbath, that fatal familiarity with loose principles, and those relaxed notions of conjugal fidelity, which have often been transplanted into this country by women of fashion, as a too common effect of a long residence in a neighbouring country; but it is peculiarly suitable to my subject to advert to another domestic mischief derived from the same foreign extraction; I mean the risks that have been run, and the sacrifices which have been made, in order to furnish our young ladies with the means of acquiring the French language in the greatest possible purity.[9]

This passage typifies one of the main ways in which the traditional attitudes and mores of pre-industrial Britain were weakened and finally discredited by the modernizing nationalist propagandists. Those mores and attitudes were revolutionized under the suggestion, which contained just enough truth to make the strategy work, that they derived directly or indirectly 'from the same foreign extraction'; while, and this was equally important, counterattacks by *true* conservatives and traditionalists on the rising structure of Evangelical moral authority and worldly organization were repelled from the same anti-Gallic 'treasury,' so patriotically, so insidiously: "What!" exclaims Jack in Hannah More's *Village Politics*, "Why dost know they have no *Sabbath* in France?" "Do French principles make so slow a progress," demanded Arthur Young, "that you should lend them such helping hands?" The creeping, patriotic discomfiture of the aristocratic world of fashion was being felt by 1802, "when the *monde* flocked to Paris, to the horror of the Evangelicals." Down through the Consulate and Empire, down until after Waterloo, it was "customary," continues Ford Brown, "to put many immoralities down to French Jacobinism." Meanwhile, in the seemingly startled words of Halévy, there were "protests raised every day more loudly against the brutal amusements not only of the lower classes, but of the aristocracy itself."[10] Of course it was not only the 'brutal amusements' of agrarian society (and, more significant to the student of national modernization, the essentially feudal, the essentially seigneurial social gatherings connected with these hunts, dogfights, cockfights, bear-baitings, and so on) that were repressed with the crucial help of the anti-French propaganda. Irreligious, immoral, abstract and internationalist tendencies of thought and feeling were beaten down also, and so too was the armory of ridicule and criticism which had customarily been brought out to defend these values in the eighteenth century.[11]

The Evangelicals' attack was stealthy, sidelong, and untiring. The longer the French peril could be said to exist, the more deeply they entrenched themselves as dictators of the national morality. But of course not everyone was fooled by their attack. Some of its cleverer victims saw its nature, although, as time was to prove, they were nearly helpless to stop it. One clear-eyed witness was Charles Fox's niece, Lady Holland, who at the turn of the century stood with her husband Henry Fox at the very pinnacle of Whig society—still 'the World.' Commenting appreciatively in her diary on Voltaire, French philosophy, and "the freedom of discussion," she voiced her alarm that there was at that very moment (1799) arising in England "*an anti-conspiracy to that of which the philosophers are accused . . .* one that, if pursued with the ardour I see many enter into it with, will inevitably be the ruin of all taste, literature, and civil liberty."[12] This was prescient. The lady saw that the anti-French attack was being fitted to the purposes of a much larger but covert attack on values which she herself and many others of her station cherished.

They were not all Whigs. It was in 1800, only a year later, that the Tory Bishop Samuel Horsley, in a famous ecclesiastical charge, opened an attack upon the upstart religious propagandists as "conscious or unconscious agents of the Atheistic and Jacobin propaganda." By 1801 the *Anti-Jacobin Review* and many other defenders of the traditional social order had begun to fight the rapidly rising forces of Methodism and Evangelicalism through the Gallic stereotype, attempting to associate the 'saints' with French radicalism. Halévy, the celebrated historian whose writings have so largely conditioned our understanding of this era, pronounced these attacks ridiculous: "When the anti-Jacobins made their charges universal and attacked the Methodist preachers, the injustice became scandalous, the calumny almost self-evident; for the sect was on principle conservative."[13]

Here again, as with the supposed 'absurdity' and 'irrelevance' of the radical political ideology, modern historians have unjustly dismissed the instincts and good sense of eyewitnesses. The Evangelicals were certainly not 'on principle conservative' according to the conservative principles of William Windham, privy councillor and secretary at war, who denounced the "Methodist-Jacobin conspiracy to make the lower classes serious, gloomy, critical, and discontented." Nor were they on those of the *Annual Review*, which in 1804 began to scrutinize the zealous new Vice Society's contention that normal activities "on the Sabbath day have any connection with the French encyclopedists." The editors of major political journals, the Tory *Anti-Jacobin* and the Whig *Edinburgh Review*, though *political* enemies, were *socially* of one (conservative) mind concerning the subversive aspirations and ambiguously anti-'French' tactics of these rising bourgeois religious confederacies: "One rushes out of his chambers," declared a Whig attacker, "and tells us we are beaten by the French, because we do not abolish the slave trade. Another tells us we have no chance of victory till India is evangelized," and the India Board, which resisted this claim, were "all Atheists, and disciples of Voltaire, of course." "These very impudent people have one ruling canon, which pervades every thing they say and do. *Whoever is unfriendly to Methodism, is an infidel and an atheist.*" Evangelical patriotism was unimpeachable, but Evangelical loyalty to the status quo was a very different thing altogether. "Wolves are, indeed, prowling about in sheep's clothing," charged the *Anti-Jacobin.* They "will call us atheists, and disciples of the French school; but it is our decided opinion," declared the *Edinburgh,* "that there is some fraud in the prophetic visit." These "insidious manoeuvres," warned the former, were drawn up "for subverting the establishment." "Mankind hate the lust of power," cried the latter, "when it is veiled under the garb of piety."[14]

On the Halévy principle, it is true, these attacks appear ridiculous. The famous Halévy thesis is little more than an uncritical endorsement of the revivalists' own self-serving propaganda. Accepting this at face value, Halévy treated Methodism and Evangelicalism exactly as proponents of those kindred movements wished them to be regarded, i.e., as profoundly "conservative" in nature, emanating "a spirit from which the established order had nothing to fear," indeed as vital defenses against the infection of "French principles."[15] But there is now an accumulation of studies which show that it is high time to reject this false supposition.[16] Halévy's theory would surely have collapsed long ago from its own weakness had it not been so badly needed to help explain the rise of Victorian morality. Now we have a better theory, and may let it drift away to the dark resting place of historical fictions.

3. THE SPREADING ANTI-FRENCH REVOLUTION

Thus the 'religious revivalists,' sternly rejecting Fashion now on the supposedly proven ground that it led to moral rot and revolution, clambered aboard the nationalist bandwagon and helped to drive it. Again let us take note of the always growing breadth of the movement. What had begun as a cultural resentment and as an artistic and intellectual phenomenon first produced its own aesthetic and historical philosophy and then took on social, political, and now at last religious ramifications. But of course there is no reason to suppose that it thereby became in any real sense a religious movement. Though it may *appear* so, it was in fact carried along quite cheerfully after 1800 by agnostics and the religiously indifferent as well as believers, by sinners as well as saints. A sarcastic periodical notice of 1824 begins: "SAINTSHIP daily acquires vogue." And as its author implied, it is really very hard to say how many Englishmen were, by the 1820s, finding their way to Christ, and how many were, merely by adopting a severe (a Sincere) system of conduct, simply serving notice of their moral fitness, their Englishness, and hence their claim to respect and social equality. Although the Evangelical intelligentsia were now in the van of the great struggle, this 'transvaluation of values' as Nietzsche might have called it, there is no need to assume that others who participated in it were much interested in religion. Even Bentham, a determined atheist, said he would have been "a methodist . . . had I not been what I am." The historians have not taken to heart the statement of Wilberforce's biographer, who acknowledges that "the reforming movement was not specifically religious."[17] From beginning to end, the inner dynamics of the nationalist movement were essentially moral and social, not religious.

To appreciate this is to see dispelled another famous interpretative mystery (the period is so full of them!), for if the inner logic of the whole pre-Victorian moral revolution was indeed essentially secular (i.e., nationalist) rather than religious, then no contradiction arises from the fact, indeed it becomes altogether logical that, after the unhappy experiments with pantisocracy and 'universal' philanthropy in the 1790s, skeptics no less than believers should have gravitated to the movement's support. Halévy, who studied all this in the light not of nationalist but of religious ideology, pronounced the early nineteenth-century cooperation between reformers of antithetical religious views, atheists as well as true believers, "a strange paradox," and many succeeding writers have puzzled over how Evangelicalism's "influence," in the words of Best, "touched many who were themselves not evangelically-minded."[18] The explanation is that the true point of unity lay not in the realm of theology at all but in that of social ethics, the concept of the Englishman, the severe bourgeois 'code' of English Sincerity adopted in opposition to the exaggerated Frenchness and Insincerity of both the Quality and (after 1789) the spokesmen of the working class. As we saw in Chapter Six, it was to this concept of English National Character, rather than to any definable position in religion, that the whole people was now gravitating. There was a transforming power here, but there are reasons to believe that it inhered less in the Cross than in the wholesale consumption, for decades, of anti-French propaganda and of the accompanying doctrine of the seriousness, honesty, and moral independence of the native Englishman.

There are interesting signs that many propagandists understood very well the domestic impact and shaping value of their incessant anti-foreign vociferations. For example, in 1818 a writer for the pugnaciously bourgeois *British Review*, reciting the usual litany of 'French traits,' conceded in passing that the French people themselves might have found cause in this to "charge us with calumny," but then brushed the question aside by asserting that "we should be abandoning the best means of instruction, and the most forcible admonitions against certain dangers, if we were to make any such concession." To his mind the 'best means of instruction' was abhorrence of everything said to be 'French.' The 'danger' was what another reviewer frankly deplored as the persistently lopsided "intercourse of sentiment," the unfavorable balance of cultural influence, between France and Britain. The danger, according to another, was that "denationalising spirit" emanated by the French. It was what De Quincey, similarly deploring English "intercourse with France," in a striking phrase decried as "the transfiguration of our own ideals." The danger was, in short, the dissipation of anti-French feeling, which was intimately connected now with middle-class consciousness, by Francophilism, which was still associated with the habits of the aristocracy, and, ever since Tom Paine, with the radical spokesmen of the working class as well. Thus one finds, not only in the exhortations of the Evangelicals but in the productions of sophisticated young literary men, known skeptics like Hazlitt and Carlyle as well as an army of more obscure literary propagandists, the artful coupling of international censure with domestic social criticism, the elaborate invocation of France interlarded with patriotic condemnation of both "Jacobinism" and "our young men of fashion"—and again, just as before the Revolution, with Sincere declarations that "we who are plain men, and know no better, are disposed to contest French superiority."[19] As the decades of war drew to a close and international tourism again became an attractive possibility, British periodicals voiced an even more obsessive concern over "the peculiarly infectious nature" of the "moral disease of France," and repeatedly, sharp antitheses were drawn between 'English' and 'French' traits: "A woman who swerves from her sex's point of honour in England, is aware that she has committed an unpardonable offense. . . . But it is very different in France. A female there . . . experiences little, if any alteration, in consequence of the violation of her person." "The French act from feeling, and the British from principle." "They cannot feel as men, but only as Frenchmen." British readers were insistently coached to believe in "the utter non-existence among the French of those notions of delicacy and reserve . . . [which] no common degree of moral depravation can totally eradicate with us." These comparisons were kept up for decades.[20]

4. Triumph of the Native Poetry

The subject of the attitude taken toward France by sophisticated literary men brings us finally to the Poets' Corner of that early nineteenth-century 'morass' and provides a new guide to the lay of the land. It should be obvious, to begin with, that the so-called 'first generation of Romantic Poets,' the Lake Poets—Wordsworth, Coleridge, Southey—were the chief carriers in this era, indeed the last great theoreticians, of the English nationalist aesthetics; of the oracular, subjectivist, primitivistic, loco-descriptive, populist, anti-French aesthetic ideas developed earlier by Hurd and Warton, Thomson and Shenstone and Cowper. The three 'Lakists,' as they were called by Byron and their other literary enemies, were the supreme bards and aesthetic system-builders of the movement, and all three lived to see England's final deliverance from 'the yoke of French taste.'

Their work was all the more sapient and unanswerable because they themselves began as enthusiastic overnight Francophiles. Their intellectual evolution reflected that of many idealistic, college-educated young Englishmen still in their teens at the time of the fall of the Bastille. Originally swept up in the pro-French enthusiasm of 1789, then increasingly put off by the Terror and French military expansion, they gravitated in the later nineties through spiritual crises in which they recanted their Gallicism, their Jacobinism, their irreligion, their schemes for the regeneration of the world, and fervently embraced the culture of their own country. All this was but the natural effect of revolutionary disillusionment, the domestic tide of anti-French propaganda, and the nation's apparent peril as the nineties drew to a close. And so they turned from extreme Francophilism to equally extreme anti-Gallic patriotism. But what scholars have generally overlooked, and what is also obscured by the abnormal political tension of the wartime era, is the important fact that these new-clad Tories did not abandon their anti-aristocratic social philosophy so much as they simply 'recycled' it under the Union Jack. The newly Gallophobic Coleridge himself stated the fact fairly explicitly (though he elsewhere remarked that his was "a *disguised* System of Morals & Politics"), and it did not escape the attention of J. S. Mill and other careful observers. Hazlitt as late as 1825, with the bulk of Wordsworth's poetry before him, declared that "his Muse (it cannot be denied, and without this we cannot explain its character at all) is a levelling one." (And he saw that much the same was true of Southey.) Thus in their strident patriotism, Tory political leanings, progressive moral and social ideology, and even date of decisive new departure (circa 1800), the repentant Lake Poets, polite propagandists of the drawing room, were birds of a feather with the middle-brow Evangelicals and low-brow Methodists. Their triumph in public opinion also exactly matched that of Evangelicalism; De Quincey commented that "up to 1820 the name of Wordsworth was trampled under foot; from 1820 to 1830 it was militant; from 1830 to 1835 it has been triumphant." As to the propaganda content of their new writings, was it merely a coincidence that Wordsworth's great production *The Excursion* (1814) embodied, in the phrase of his friend Lamb, a system of "Natural Methodism"?—and that the symbolic framework which conveyed this was sturdily borne along on the same Gallic stereotype as that so productively exploited at the same time by the Evangelicals?—the menacing and 'sarcastically smiling' image of the Solitary, an immoral and misanthropic infidel, a cosmopolitan philosopher with "everlasting joy to France" on his lips, and, in his hand, as his most treasured possession, a dog-eared copy of *Candide!* In his other major work, *The Prelude*, Wordsworth projected the same nationalist poetics and ideology through equally invidious contrasts with what he called "the ape Philosophy" of France.[21]

It is thus a very serious mistake to consider these poets 'conservative,' as many literary critics, unfamiliar with nationalist ideology, have done. As with the misinterpretation of 'conservative' Evangelicalism, there has been a natural but misguided tendency to evaluate the ideological views of the Romantic 'bards and reviewers' solely along a *political* continuum inferred from the *debates over civil liberties* that raged from the 1790s to the 1820s (in which the Whigs, of course, occupy the best light, as 'friends of liberty'), without considering the need also for a *social* continuum inferred from the less conspicuous but much more important fact of *drastic moral and social change* during the same period. Politically, and especially in view of their strident patriotism (which many twentieth-century writers incorrectly identify with conservatism, forgetting that patriotism in the early nineteenth century was everywhere a progressive force), Wordsworth and the repentant Lake Poets may appear 'reactionary' to observers today; Byron and his friends may, for opposite reasons, appear 'liberal.' But *socially* (and this was really the more important dimension), it was Wordsworth and his friends who were the true radicals, and Byron and his who were the aristocratic reactionaries of contemporary letters. We may love them all the same, but it is important to see what they stood for. It is vital to recognize, as Wordsworth did no less than Wilberforce, that the long reign of 'Tory Repression' was, if unintentionally, Britain's own social Reign of Virtue: that the patriotic anti-French values of 1795–1820, if bigoted, anti-intellectual, and morally and politically repressive, for these very reasons tended to further the rapid *mental unification, moral reformation, and social reorganization of the country;* and that enlightened Whig values, on the other hand, though attractive to Lady Holland and many other devotees of 'taste, literature, and civil liberty,' tended nevertheless to sustain the sophistication, the literary refinement, the moral relaxation, the intellectual and social internationalism—in a word, the mental, moral and social divisions—of traditional and hierarchical society, the aristocratic society of eighteenth-century Europe.

In short, both a political measure and a social one need to be applied when evaluating opinion during that topsy-turvy age. The predicament of the Duke of Wellington, who, it is said, felt 'a social contempt for his intellectual equals and an intellectual contempt for his social equals,' was writ large in the literary world. The fact helps to explain some of the colorful eccentricity and strained personal relations that marked that world, and it is certain also that much of the tortuous complexity of literary reviewing and poetical criticism during this turbulent period, this time of drastic political contraction and social revolution, is attributable to hostility on political grounds between writers who in basic social attitudes had much in common, and vice versa.[22]

Thus Wordsworth too signed on with the long revolution, singing to and indoctrinating the sophisticated just as Hannah More instructed the simple and Cobbett lectured the workingman; and it this which explains the many striking resemblances in their ideas, sympathies, and homiletic tones. But inevitably under the circumstances, the social revolution which all three helped to lead was thrown out of focus, as was noted above, by sharp political debate over the question essentially of civil rights versus national unity. And it is understandable, in view of this abnormal *political* tension which marked the age, especially the Regency, that ardent young idealists of the 'second generation' like Hunt and Byron, Shelley and Peacock and Moore, were slow and unwilling to perceive the contrary, deeper, and more valuable *moral and social* implications of the 'bigoted' nationalist value system. Instead they wrote as defiant anti-nationalists and deliberately aligned themselves with 'the French'—that is, with the alarmed, intelligent, repressed, snobbish, whiggish, still cosmopolitan and still very glamorous denizens, friends, sympathizers, and assorted confederates of Holland House, the superior people of 'the World.' Finding humane and universal values—the true values of eighteenth-century 'Philosophy'—grotesquely distorted and repressed under the tide of anti-French propaganda, these young (and, some of them, rich and wellborn) writers were irresistibly tempted to vaunt the French, scorn their own country, castigate its Tory government, put their shoulders to the flimsy wheel of Whig 'liberty,' inveigh against the tremendous new advances of Evangelical 'bigotry,' dabble in atheism and immorality, reject the new, insular, anti-French and anticlassical aesthetics of the government's friends the Lake Poets, write in heroic couplets and satire, stigmatize Shakespeare and laud Voltaire, and protest the whole general flowering of bourgeois nationalism as an outrageous upsurge of 'cant.' Their attitudes are typified in Shelley's praise of "Man Equal, unclassed, tribeless, and nationless" (*Prometheus Unbound*, 1819). And it was not until this era of *abnormal political hatred* wore away in the twenties that these champions of 'universal' philanthropy, art and liberty, these 'intelligent admirers of Voltaire,' as their opponents sarcastically called them, began crossing over, as the Lake Poets themselves had done earlier, to adopt the new anti-French code of English morality and taste.[23]

This anti-nationalist, pro-French and pro-whiggish reaction, though it mirrored a larger uneasiness at the repression of free speech and the relentless moral coercion imposed by the 'saints,' was not, however, of much importance outside the sphere of belles letters. It achieved its greatest influence during the half-decade after Waterloo, then petered out. Naturally it alarmed the nationalist propagandists. In 1819 Hannah More voiced their fears:

> The middle class has now merged its distinctive character in the other two. . . . Numbers of a higher strain remain domiciliated in France, and too many who are returned, are more than ever assimilated with French manners. It is to be feared, that with French habits, French principles may be imported. French alliances are contracted, as almost every newspaper records. We are losing our national character. . . . In a few years, if things proceed in their present course . . . the strong and discriminating features of the English heart and mind will be obliterated. . . . This contagious intercourse has been too probably the cause of the recent multiplication of those great Sunday entertainments, in the diminution of which we had begun to rejoice. . . . What would Johnson have said had he been spared till now?[24]

But the evangelical lady need not have troubled herself so much. The social revolution had gone too far to be reversed, and the worldly counter-revolution rapidly disintegrated in the early 1820s. It was that decade that saw the final demise in England of the international ideas of the French Enlightenment. J. S. Mill, whose 'mental crisis' of the 1820s has received so much puzzled attention, was but one of several progressive intellectuals—Hazlitt, Moore, and Carlyle were others—who at about that time found themselves drawn over from what their opponents condemned as the ('French') philosophy of cosmopolitanism, universalism, infidelity, protest, scorn, 'negativity,' and the rest, toward the system of mystical and nationalist enthusiasm enunciated by Wordsworth. As Brinton wisely remarked of Hazlitt's later writings, there was an "almost instinctive modification of the revolutionary gospel of the rights of man into the Victorian gospel of the rights of Englishmen."[25] After two decades of Enlightened Reaction the last of England's intellectuals entered, not without anguish for what they had left behind, their own splendid century. The 1820s were inevitably a time of 'cant,' 'sham,' and the hiding of lights under the collective bushel, as well as of genuine spiritual crisis.

Thanks to the rise and then collapse of this 'pagan' and Gallicising current of 1800–1820 (a desperately 'Hellenising' current, as Matthew Arnold might have called it), the basic process of the later 1790s thus repeated itself in the souls of thoughtful young people in the twenties. Here is the reason why the unhappy young Mill, falling victim then to that 'Dejection' which, he said, was so perfectly described in Coleridge's ode of 1802, could no longer find solace in Byron's poetry, but responded with mounting enthusiasm to the ideas of the repentant Lake Poets. Like Coleridge in the late nineties, he was painfully finding his way home; he was making his way from the great broad idea of 'universal benevolence' to the narrower but surer one of 'national improvement.' It is equally significant that Carlyle, imaginatively tracing his own painful spiritual migration during nearly the same period, the early twenties, staged the critical phase of philosophical conversion in a dirty little street of Paris, locked in colloquy with the personified spirit of eighteenth-century France: "'Cease, my much-respected Herr von Voltaire,' thus apostrophises the Professor: 'shut thy sweet voice; for the task appointed thee seems finished.'"[26]

So indeed it was. Finished now at last, thanks to Carlyle and many before him, was la Belle France in England. Now it was England's turn to set the tone everywhere. Carlyle himself, oracle of the nineteenth century, would seduce legions of envying foreigners. Now they would learn the importance of English Sincerity, the power of being earnest.

NOTES

NOTE: in all book references, place of publication is London unless specified otherwise.

PREFACE

[1] K. R. Minogue, *Nationalism* (Baltimore, 1970), p. 29; Anthony D. Smith, "Introduction: The Formation of Nationalist Movements," in *Nationalist Movements*, ed. A. D. Smith (NY, 1976), p. 3; idem, *Theories of Nationalism* (1971), pp. 271–72; Berlin, "Nationalism: Past Neglect and Present Power," in Isaiah Berlin, *Against the Current: Essays in the History of Ideas* (NY, 1980), p. 350.

[2] See H. Kohn, "The Genesis and Character of English Nationalism," *Journal of the History of Ideas* 1 (1940): 69–94; for an example of older work see Esmé Wingfield-Stratford, *The History of English Patriotism* (Toronto and London, 1913).

[3] W. Houghton, *The Victorian Frame of Mind, 1830–1870* (New Haven and London, 1957), pp. 324–25.

[4] *Heads of the People: Or, Portraits of the English*, "Drawn by Kenny Meadows with Original Essays by Distinguished Writers" (1840), p. iv.

[5] J. G. A. Pocock, "The Limits and Divisions of British History: In Search of the Unknown Subject," *American Historical Review* 87, No. 2 (1982): 316; Ian R. Christie, *Wars and Revolutions: Britain, 1760–1815* (Cambridge, Mass., 1982), p. 2; C. P. Wormald, "Coming inevitably together," *Times Literary Supplement* No. 4,248 (31 Aug. 1984): 975.

[6] Pocock, "Limits and Divisions," pp. 314, 317; Porter, "The Enlightenment in England," in *The Enlightenment in National Context*, eds. Roy Porter and Mikulas Teich (Cambridge, 1981), p. 3; T. Zeldin, "Ourselves, as we see us," *Times Literary Supplement* No. 4,161 (31 Dec. 1982): 1435.

[7] A. Macfarlane, *The Origins of English Individualism: The Family, Property and Social Transition* (NY, 1979), p. 165; D. Greene, *The Age of Exuberance: Backgrounds to Eighteenth-Century English Literature* (NY, 1970), p. 4.

CHAPTER ONE

[1] Thomas J. Schlereth, *The Cosmopolitan Ideal in Enlightenment Thought: Its Form and Function in the Ideas of Franklin, Hume, and Voltaire, 1694–1790* (Notre Dame and London, 1977), p. xxi; *Encyclopedia of the Social Sciences*, s.v. "Cosmopolitanism," by Max Hilbert Boehm.

[2] Joseph Chiari, *Britain and France, The Unruly Twins* (1971), p. 49; Derek Jarrett, *The Begetters of Revolution: England's Involvement with France, 1759–1789* (1973); Leon Cahen, "The Prime Minister in France and England during

the Eighteenth Century," *Studies in Anglo-French History,* eds. Alfred
Colville and Harold Temperley (Freeport, N.Y., 1969), p. 31; Frederick C.
Green, *Minuet: A Critical Survey of French and English Literary Ideas in the
Eighteenth Century* (1935); also see Green's essay "Anglomaniacs and
Francophiles" in his *Eighteenth-Century France: Six Essays* (London and
Toronto, 1929); also Richard Faber, *French and English* (1975); and the
pioneering work by Joseph Texte, *Jean-Jacques Rousseau and the
Cosmopolitan Spirit in Literature: A Study of the Literary Relations between
France and England during the Eighteenth Century,* trans. J. W. Matthews
(London and NY, 1899).

[3] Over the past two centuries more than a dozen writers have published accounts
of Voltaire's sojourn in England; the definitive study is Part I of André-
Michel Rousseau's magisterial *L'Angleterre et Voltaire (1718–1789),* Studies
on Voltaire and the Eighteenth Century [vols. 145–47] (Oxford, 1976), 1:
75–156.

[4] See Sir Gavin de Beer and André-Michel Rousseau, eds., *Voltaire's British
Visitors,* Studies on Voltaire and the Eighteenth Century [vol. 49], ed.
Theodore Besterman (Geneva, 1967); and (for Adam Smith's comment) P.
W. Clayden, *The Early Life of Samuel Rogers* (Boston, 1888), p. 84.

[5] C. H. Glover, ed., *Dr. Charles Burney's Continental Travels, 1770–72* (1927), pp.
17–19; de Beer and Rousseau, *Voltaire's Visitors,* pp. 128, 95; Brian
Connell, *Portrait of a Whig Peer* (1957), p. 41.

[6] *Critical Review* 7 (1759): 550; *Extracts of the Journals and Correspondence of Miss
Berry,* ed. Lady Theresa Lewis (1865), 1: 7; John Andrews, *A Comparative
View of the French and English Nations, in their Manners, Politics, and Literature*
(1785), p. 425.

[7] W. E. H. Lecky, *A History of England in the Eighteenth Century* (NY, 1887), 5: 301;
Alan McKillop, "Local Attachment and Cosmopolitanism—The
Eighteenth-Century Pattern," in *From Sensibility to Romanticism: Essays
Presented to Frederick A. Pottle,* eds. Frederick W. Hilles and Harold Bloom
(NY, 1965), p. 191.

[8] Rousseau, *L'Angleterre et Voltaire,* 1: 241.

[9] See (for Wilkes) de Beer and Rousseau, *Voltaire's Visitors,* p. 102; *The Letters of
Horace Walpole, Fourth Earl of Orford,* ed. Mrs. Paget Toynbee (Oxford,
1904), 7: 206–07; H. N. Brailsford, *Voltaire* (1963), p. 104; Rousseau,
L'Angleterre et Voltaire, 1: 247–48; and for the complete list of subscribers
see (what is largely a translation of Voltaire's *Traité sur la tolérance*) *The
History of the Misfortunes of Jean Calas* (Edinburgh, 1776), pp. iii–viii.

[10] Besterman, *Voltaire* (NY, 1969), pp. 427, 120; (for Franklin) Schlereth,
Cosmopolitan Ideal, p. 4.

[11] John Moore, *View of the Causes and Progress of the French Revolution,* in *The Works
of John Moore, M.D.,* ed. Robert Anderson (Edinburgh, 1820), 4: 10;
Preserved Smith, *A History of Modern Culture* (NY, 1934), 2: 367; Hywel B.
Evans, *A Provisional Bibliography of English Editions and Translations of
Voltaire,* Studies on Voltaire and the Eighteenth Century [vol. 8], ed. T.
Besterman (Geneva, 1959), p. 30, index and passim; R. S. Crane,
"Diffusion of Voltaire's Writings in England, 1750–1800," *Modern Philology*
20 (1923): 261–74; *Free and Impartial Remarks upon the Letters written by the
. . . Earl of Chesterfield to his Son* (1774), p. 35; *Monthly Review* 58 (1778):
544.

12 E. Burke, *Two Letters on a Regicide Peace* (1796) in Robert A. Smith, *Edmund Burke on Revolution* (NY and Evanston, 1968), pp. 273–75; also see Thomas Preston Peardon, *The Transition in English Historical Writing, 1760–1830* (NY, 1933), p. 65.

13 David B. Horn, *Great Britain and Europe in the Eighteenth Century* (Oxford, 1967), p. 28.

14 Jean-Pierre Labatut, *Les noblesses Européenes: de la fin du XVe siècle à la fin du XVIIIe siècle* (Paris, 1978).

15 G. E. Mingay, *English Landed Society in the Eighteenth Century* (London and Toronto, 1963), pp. 138–41; Cahen, "Prime Minister in France and England," p. 42; Peter Gay, *The Enlightenment: An Interpretation* (New York, 1968), p. 16.

16 Hume, "Of National Character" (1748), in David Hume, *Essays and Treatises on Several Subjects,* new edn (1764), 1: 231; Labatut, *Les noblesses,* p. 177; Norman Hampson, *The Enlightenment* (NY, 1968), p. 71; R. R. Palmer, *The Age of the Democratic Revolution: A Political History of Europe and America, 1760–1800* (Princeton, 1959–64): see esp. vol. 1, *The Challenge,* ch. 3.

17 Lecky, *England in the Eighteenth Century,* 5: 445; A. Young, *Travels in France during the Years 1787, 1788, 1789,* ed. Miss Betham-Edwards (1912), p. 84.

18 H. A. L. Fisher, *A History of Europe,* rev. edn (Boston, 1939), pp. 297–98.

19 See Christopher Hill, "The Norman Yoke," in C. Hill, *Puritanism and Revolution: Studies in Interpretation of the English Revolution of the 17th Century* (NY, 1958), p. 59; Innes, *The Appleby File: Detective Stories* (NY, 1975), p. 14; Mitford, *The Blessing* (NY, 1951), p. 12.

20 Derek Jarrett, *England in the Age of Hogarth* (NY, 1974), p. 194; *Spectator,* No. 2 (1711); Mingay, *Landed Society,* p. 220.

21 A. F. B. Clark, *Boileau and the French Classical Critics in England (1660–1830)* (NY, 1970), p. 419; Stephen, "Dr. Johnson's Writings," in L. Stephen, *Hours in a Library,* new edn (1892), 2: 13; *Monthly Review* 21 (1759): 84; Young, *Travels,* p. 184; H. L. Bruce, *Voltaire on the English Stage* (Berkeley, 1918), p. 9.

22 Warton quoted in *Annual Register* 24 (1781): 146, and in Byron's "Note" to Canto V, v. cxlvii of *Don Juan; The Works of Sir William Jones,* eds. Lord Teignmouth and Lady Jones (1807), 5: 168, and 12: 328–30.

23 Jarrett, *England in the Age of Hogarth,* p. 195; Mingay, *Landed Society,* pp. 146–47; Rosamond Bayne-Powell, *Travellers in Eighteenth-Century England* (NY, 1972), pp. 134–38; Burke, *Reflections on the Revolution in France,* ed. T. Mahoney (NY, 1955), p. 90.

Chapter Two

1 G. M. Trevelyan, *English Social History: A Survey of Six Centuries* (NY, 1942), p. 376; Mingay, *English Landed Society,* p. 51; also see J. D. Chambers and G. E. Mingay, *The Agricultural Revolution, 1750–1880* (1966).

2 Trevelyan, op. cit., p. 376; Palmer, *Age of Democratic Revolution,* 1: 72; cf. J. V. Beckett, "English Landownership in the Late Seventeenth and Eighteenth Centuries: the Debate and the Problems," *Economic History Review,* 2d ser. 30 (1977): 567–81.

3 See (for J.P.'s) E. N. Williams, *The Eighteenth-Century Constitution, 1688–1815: Documents and Commentary* (Cambridge, 1965), p. 279; J. H. Plumb,

"Political Man," in *Man Versus Society in Eighteenth-Century Britain: Six Points of View*, ed. James L. Clifford (NY, 1972), pp. 8–9.

[4] For example, see Roger Hart, *English Life in the Eighteenth Century* (NY, 1970), p. 51; also see Douglas Hay, Peter Linebaugh, John G. Rule, E. P. Thompson, and Cal Winslow, *Albion's Fatal Tree: Crime and Society in Eighteenth-Century England* (NY, 1975).

[5] Harold Perkin, *The Origins of Modern English Society, 1780–1880* (1969), pp. 17, 49; for the critic (Rev. J. Brown) see Williams, op. cit., p. 140; L. B. Namier and John Brooke, *Charles Townshend* (NY, 1964), p. 104.

[6] Lord David Cecil, *Melbourne* (NY, 1954), p. 24; L. B. Namier, *The Structure of Politics at the Accession of George III* (1929), 1: 5, 22; Mingay, *Landed Society*, p. 114; R. R. Palmer, "Social and Psychological Foundations of the Revolutionary Era," *New Cambridge Modern History: Vol. VIII, The American and French Revolutions, 1763–93*, ed. A. Goodwin (Cambridge, 1965), p. 434; for the critics (Rev. J. Brown) see Williams, *Eighteenth-Century Constitution*, p. 140; for posts see Jacob Viner, "Man's Economic Status," in *Man Versus Society*, ed. Clifford, p. 24; for Baugh (and Guy Miege, preferments observer) see Daniel A. Baugh, *Aristocratic Government and Society in Eighteenth-Century England: The Foundations of Stability* (NY, 1975), pp. 21, 47; Jay B. Botsford, *English Society in the Eighteenth Century as Influenced from Oversea* (NY, 1924), p. 160; G. H. Guttridge, *English Whiggism and the American Revolution* (Berkeley and Los Angeles, 1963), pp. 103–04.

[7] Norman Sykes, *Church and State in England in the XVIIIth Century* (Hamden, Conn., 1962), p. 414; Trevelyan, *Social History*, p. 360; also see H. J. Habakkuk, "England," in *The European Nobility in the Eighteenth Century*, ed. Albert Goodwin (London and NY, 1953), p. 13.

[8] *OED*, "Enthusiasm"; Roland N. Stromberg, *Religious Liberalism in Eighteenth-Century England* (1954), p. 167; for Moritz see Hart, *English Life*, pp. 111–12.

[9] Quoted in Williams, *Eighteenth-Century Constitution*, p. 372.

[10] Meredith quoted in L. B. Namier, *England in the Age of the American Revolution*, 2d edn (1961), p. 181; John L. Sanford and Meredith Townsend, *The Great Governing Families of England* (Edinburgh and London, 1865), 1: 2–3; John Brooke, *King George III* (1972), p. 155; Peter Laslett, *The World We Have Lost* (NY, 1965), p. 52; Mingay, *Landed Society*, p. 131; E. P. Thompson, "Patrician Society, Plebian Culture," *Journal of Social History* 7, no. 4 (1974): 382–405.

[11] *Lord Chesterfield's Letters to his Son and Others*, ed. R. K. Root (1969), p. 81; (on 'manner') Chesterfield quoted in William B. Willcox and Walter Arnstein, *The Age of Aristocracy, 1688 to 1830*, 4th ed. (Lexington and Toronto, 1983), p. 83; N. Forster quoted in Richard Tames, *Josiah Wedgwood* (Aylesbury, 1972), p. 14.

[12] H. Perkin, *Origins of Modern English Society*, pp. 24–25; idem, "The Social Causes of the British Industrial Revolution," *Transactions of the Royal Historical Society*, 5th Ser. 18 (1968): 123–43; J. Jean Hecht, *The Domestic Servant Class in Eighteenth-Century England* (1956), pp. 203–06; Hart, *English Life*, p. 9; Mingay, *Landed Society*, p. 215; Roy Porter, *English Society in the Eighteenth Century* (Harmondsworth, 1982); Dorothy Marshall, "Manners, Meals, and Domestic Pastimes," in *Johnson's England: An Account*

of the Life & Manners of his Age, ed. A. S. Turberville (Oxford, 1967), 1: 336–60; idem, *Dr. Johnson's London* (NY, 1968), pp. 137–39; A. R. Humphreys, *The Augustan World: Society, Thought, and Letters in Eighteenth-Century England* (NY, 1963), p. 124; also see the excellent collection of essays in Neil McKendrick, John Brewer and J. H. Plumb, *The Birth of a Consumer Society: The Commercialization of Eighteenth-Century England* (Bloomington, Ind., 1982).

[13] See S. M. Lipset and Reinhard Bendix, *Social Mobility in Industrial Society* (Berkeley and Los Angeles, 1967), p. 2.

[14] Perkin, "Causes of the Industrial Revolution," pp. 127, 140; but cp. the important recent study by Lawrence Stone and Jeanne C. Fawtier Stone, *An Open Elite? England 1540–1880* (Oxford 1984), which furnishes strong indirect support for the interpretation advanced here.

[15] See Talcott Parsons, *Societies: Evolutionary and Comparative Perspectives* (Englewood Cliffs, N.Y., 1966), pp. 70–71, 73–74; also see Max Weber on 'Classes, Status Groups and Parties' in *Max Weber: Selections in Translation,* ed. W. G. Runciman, trans. E. Matthews (Cambridge, 1978), pp. 43–61.

[16] Frank Parkin, "Strategies of Social Closure in Class Formation," in *The Social Analysis of Class Structure,* ed. F. Parkin (London, 1974), pp. 4–6.

[17] Johnson quoted in Stella Margetson, *Leisure and Pleasure in the Eighteenth Century* (1970), p. 162; Palmer, "Social and Psychological Foundations," p. 433; also see idem, *Age of Democratic Revolution,* 1: 72–82.

[18] A. Goodwin, "Introductory Summary," *New Cambridge Modern History,* 8: 4; for France see (for example) John Lough, *An Introduction to Eighteenth Century France* (NY, 1960), pp. 11–12, 123–25.

[19] Palmer, *Age of Democratic Revolution,* 1: 80; Habakkuk, "England," p. 10; R. K. Webb, *Modern England: From the Eighteenth Century to the Present* (NY, 1968), p. 9; Mingay, *Landed Society,* p. 265; Marshall, *Johnson's London,* pp. 46, 100; Porter, *English Society in the Eighteenth Century,* p. 67; Baugh, *Aristocratic Government and Society,* p. 12; Lawrence Stone, "Social Mobility in England, 1500–1700," *Past and Present,* No. 33 (1966): 51; Lecky, *England in the Eighteenth Century,* 6: 144; Smith, *The Wealth of Nations,* Bk. V., ch. I, ii; Andrews, *Comparative View of the French and English Nations,* p. 383.

[20] Peter Burke, *Popular Culture in Early Modern Europe* (NY, 1978), pp. 275–81; Namier, *Structure of Politics,* pp. 279–80; Habakkuk, "England," pp. 16, 19; Palmer (citing Holdsworth, Clark), *Age of Democratic Revolution,* 1: 72; Baugh, op. cit., p. 10.

[21] Eric J. Evans, *The Forging of the Modern State: Early Industrial Britain 1783–1870* (London and NY, 1983), p. 7; italics added.

[22] Namier, *Structure of Politics,* p. 19n.

[23] M. Dorothy George, "London and the Life of the Town," in *Johnson's England,* ed. Turberville, 1: 163; George Rudé, *Hanoverian London, 1714–1808* (Berkeley and Los Angeles, 1971), pp. 9 (for Fielding), 10; Margetson, *Leisure and Pleasure,* pp. 198–99.

[24] Neil McKendrick, "The Commercialization of Fashion," in McKendrick et al, *Birth of a Consumer Society,* p. 64.

[25] Habakkuk, "England," p. 10.

[26] Walpole quotes from Rudé, *Hanoverian London,* p. 71, and H. D. Traill and J. S. Mann, *Social England: A Record of the Progress of the People* (NY and London,

1909), 5: 479; Clifford Geertz, "Deep Play: Notes on the Balinese Cockfight," in *Myth, Symbol, and Culture*, ed. C. Geertz (NY, 1971), pp. 1–37.

[27] For eating and sleeping habits and Walpole citation see Marshall, "Manners, Meals, and Pastimes," pp. 344–46; for Garrick see his epilogue to Cumberland's *West Indian* (1771) in *Eighteenth-Century Plays*, selected by John Hampden (London and Toronto, n.d.), p. 408.

[28] C. Willett Cunnington, "Costume," in *The Connoisseur's Complete Period Guides to the Houses, Decoration, Furnishing and Chattels of the Classic Periods*, eds. Ralph Edwards and L. G. G. Ramsey (NY, 1968), p. 717.

[29] Traill and Mann, *Social England*, 5: 479; Trevelyan, *Social History*, p. 355; Cecil, *Melbourne*, p. 21; Lawrence Stone, *The Family, Sex and Marriage In England, 1500–1800*, abridged edn (NY, 1979), pp. 331–33.

[30] Mingay, *Landed Society*, p. 265; George Martelli, *Jemmy Twitcher: A Life of the Fourth Earl of Sandwich, 1718–1792* (London, 1962), p. 19; Archenholz quoted in Rudé, *Hanoverian London*, pp. 55–56.

[31] G. M. Trevelyan, *History of England* (Garden City, NY, 1953), 3: 26.

[32] George Colman and David Garrick, *The Clandestine Marriage* (1766), in *Eighteenth-Century Plays*, Act II, sc. i; (for Kingston) Mingay, *Landed Society*, pp. 138–41; John W. Derry, *Charles James Fox* (NY, 1972), p. 15; (for Bingham) Cecil Woodham-Smith, *The Reason Why* (NY, 1953), pp. 18–19; Samuel Foote, *The Englishman Returned from Paris*, in *The Dramatic Works of Samuel Foote, Esq.* (London and NY, n.d.), pp. 16–17, 26–27, 30–32.

[33] See Mingay, *Landed Society*, p. 152; Christopher Hibbert, *The Grand Tour* (NY, 1969), p. 49; John Andrews, *Comparative View of the French and English Nations*, pp. 104–05; Rebecca West, "The Englishman Abroad," in *The Character of England*, ed. Ernest Barker (Oxford, 1947), p. 494; Reginald Blunt, *Mrs. Montagu, "Queen of the Blues": Her Letters and Friendships from 1762 to 1800* (1923), 1: 48–49; R. Bayne-Powell, *Travellers in Eighteenth-Century England*, pp. 138–39.

[34] *Gentleman's Magazine* 36 (1766): 592.

[35] Martin Sherlock (1781) quoted in William Edward Mead, *The Grand Tour in the Eighteenth Century* (Boston and NY, 1914), p. 224; in *Dramatic Works of Foote* see Garrick's prologue to Foote's *Taste* (1752), also *Taste*, pp. 13, 22–24, also the prologue to *The Englishman Returned from Paris* (1756); Cunnington, "Costume," p. 718; Charles Churchill, 'The Rosciad' (1761), in *English Poetry, 1700–1780: Contemporaries of Swift and Johnson*, ed. David W. Lindsay (Tottowa, N.J., 1974), p. 136.

[36] J. G. A. Pocock, [book reviews], *Eighteenth-Century Studies* 15 (1981): 96.

[37] For 'Quality' see *Clandestine Marriage*, Act I, also *OED*, "Quality"; Foote, *Taste* (1752), Act II; Burns cited in *OED*, "World"; for 'Fashion' see Mingay, *Landed Society*, p. 159, also John Langhorne's 'The Country Justice' in Lindsay, ed., *English Poetry*, p. 184, also Churchill, 'The Rosciad,' ibid., p. 140; also see Susie I. Tucker, *Protean Shape: A Study in Eighteenth-Century Vocabulary and Usage* (1967).

[38] See McKendrick's "The Commercialization of Fashion," p. 40.

[39] *OED*, "Ton"; Rupert Emerson, *From Empire to Nation: The Rise to Self-Assertion of Asian and African People* (Cambridge, Mass., 1967), p. 241; author's conversations with Dr. Innocent Uzoechi, Senior Lecturer in History, Alvan Ikoku College of Education, Owerri, Nigeria.

40 McKendrick, "The Commercialization of Fashion," pp. 54–55, 64; Mead, *Grand Tour*, pp. 104, 121.

41 Mead, op. cit., pp. 375–76, 10, 105.

42 Hibbert, *Grand Tour*, pp. 10, 44, 55–56.

43 Lecky, *England in the Eighteenth Century*, 6: 179; (Gibbon's trip) Geoffrey Trease, *The Grand Tour* (NY, 1967), p. 187; Walpole quoted in Mead, *Grand Tour*, p. 218; (for figures on travelers) F. C. Green, *Eighteenth-Century France: Six Essays*, p. 48. See also Jeremy Black, *The British and the Grand Tour* (London and Dover, N. H., 1985).

44 See Lecky, op. cit., 6: 179; (A. Smith) Hibbert, *Grand Tour*, p. 25; Mead, op. cit., pp. 407–08, 126.

45 Mead, op. cit., pp. 105, 108, 121, 401, 404 and passim; (for Cowper) Hibbert, op. cit., p. 233.

46 Ibid., pp. 104, 210; for voluminous material on Macaronis see *Catalogue of Prints and Drawings in the British Museum: Division I. Political and Personal Satires*, Vol. IV.—A.D. 1761 to *c.* A.D. 1770 (1883), pp. 711–836.

47 See Mead, *Grand Tour*, pp. 382–96.

48 Alexander Herzen, *My Past and Thoughts: The Memoirs of Alexander Herzen*, abridged and annotated by Dwight Macdonald, trans. Constance Garnett (NY, 1973), p. 450; Foote, *The Englishman in Paris*, in *Dramatic Works of Foote*, Act I, sc. i; for Moore see Mead, *Grand Tour*, pp. 125–26.

49 Mead, op. cit., p. 125.

50 Jarrett, *England in the Age of Hogarth*, p. 195.

51 For Lauraguais see F. C. Green, "Anglomaniacs and Francophiles," in Green's *Eighteenth-Century France*, p. 49; for Marivaux see Joseph Texte, *Rousseau and the Cosmopolitan Spirit in Literature*, p. 79.

52 Jean-René Suratteau, "Rapport de synthèse," *Transactions of the Fifth International Congress on the Enlightenment*, Studies on Voltaire and the Eighteenth Century [vol. 190] (Oxford, 1980), pp. 430, 435–36.

CHAPTER THREE

1 Joseph Texte, "L'Hégémonie littéraire de la France," in J. Texte, *Études de Littérature européene* (Paris, 1898), pp. 281, 284.

2 *Dictionary of the History of Ideas*, 1973 ed., s.v. "Nationalism," by Hans Kohn.

3 Isaiah Berlin, "Nationalism: Past Neglect and Present Power," in I. Berlin, *Against the Current*, p. 338; H. Munro Chadwick, *The Nationalities of Europe and the Growth of National Ideologies* (Cambridge, 1945), p. 3.

4 Leonard W. Doob, *Patriotism and Nationalism: Their Psychological Foundations* (New Haven and London, 1964), pp. 6–9; Ernest Gellner, *Nations and Nationalism* (Ithaca and London, 1983), p. 138; Elie Kedourie, *Nationalism*, rev. edn (NY, 1961), pp. 73–74; italics added.

5 V. Kiernan, "Nationalist Movements and Social Classes," in *Nationalist Movements*, ed. A. D. Smith, p. 112.

6 Eliot's *Impressions of Theophrastus Such*, quoted in W. Houghton, *Victorian Frame of Mind*, pp. 324–25.

7 Halvdan Koht, "The Dawn of Nationalism in Europe," *American Historical Review* 52 (1947): 279; Froude, "On Progress," quoted in Houghton, op. cit., p. 47.

[8] K. R. Minogue, "Nationalism and the Patriotism of City-States," in *Nationalist Movements*, ed. Smith, pp. 71–73; John Plamenatz, "Two Types of Nationalism," in *Nationalism: The Nature and Evolution of an Idea*, ed. Eugene Kamenka (Canberra, 1973), p. 23; for Snyder (italics added) and Carr et al, see *The Dynamics of Nationalism: Readings in its Meaning and Development*, ed. Louis L. Snyder (Princeton, 1964), pp. 23, 14; Gellner, *Nations and Nationalism*, pp. 24–38.

[9] K. Minogue, *Nationalism*, pp. 31–32.

[10] Hans Kohn, *The Idea of Nationalism: A Study of Its Origins and Background* (NY, 1944), pp. 10–11.

[11] Doob, *Patriotism and Nationalism*, p. 258 (italics added); Plamenatz, "Two Types of Nationalism," pp. 23–27 (italics in original).

[12] Minogue, *Nationalism*, pp. 23–24; Berlin, "Nationalism," p. 346.

[13] A. D. Smith, "Introduction," in *Nationalist Movements*, ed. Smith, p. 1; Chadwick, *Nationalities of Europe*, p. 3; Minogue, *Nationalism*, p. 26; Herzen, *My Past and Thoughts*, pp. 288–89; see also *Nationalism in Latin America*, ed. with an introduction by Samuel L. Baily (NY, 1971).

[14] Max S. Handman, "The Sentiment of Nationalism," *Political Science Quarterly* 36 (1921): 104–05; italics added.

[15] J. G. A. Pocock, *The Machiavellian Moment: Florentine Political Thought and the Atlantic Republican Tradition* (Princeton, 1975), Part Three; Berlin, "Nationalism," pp. 346–47.

[16] Caroline Robbins, *The Eighteenth-Century Commonwealthman* (Cambridge, Mass., 1959), p. 384; Walpole cited in Robert R. Rea, *The English Press in Politics, 1760–1774* (Lincoln, Neb., 1963), p. 224.

CHAPTER FOUR

[1] For example see Rudolf Wittkower, "The Artist," in *Man Versus Society in 18th-Century Britain*, ed. Clifford, pp. 70–84.

[2] William Gaunt, *The World of William Hogarth* (1978), p. 18; Robert E. Moore, *Hogarth's Literary Relationships* (Minneapolis, 1948), pp. 82–83; V. De S. Pinto, "William Hogarth," in Boris Ford, ed., *A Guide to English Literature*, Vol. 4: *From Dryden to Johnson* (1969), p. 279.

[3] Quoted in Pinto, loc. cit.; and *Encyclopaedia Britannica*, 11th ed., "Hogarth," by Austin Dobson.

[4] Gaunt, op. cit., p. 60.

[5] See Pinto, op. cit., pp. 282, 288–91.

[6] See Henry Fielding, *The History of the Adventures of Joseph Andrews and his Friend Mr. Abraham Adams* (NY, 1960), Bk. II, chaps. iv, vi.

[7] Tobias Smollett, *The Adventures of Ferdinand Count Fathom*, ed. with an intro. by Damian Grant (1971), chaps. i, xxiv.

[8] Ibid., chap. xxxi.

[9] Ibid., chap. xxxii.

[10] See Samuel Johnson, "London: A Poem In Imitation of . . . Juvenal," in *Johnson: Prose and Poetry*, selected by Mona Wilson (Cambridge, Mass., 1967), p. 30; (for Young) Laurence Goldstein, *Ruins and Empire: The Evolution of a Theme in Augustan and Romantic Literature* (Pittsburgh, 1977), p. 81.

[11] Ian Watt, *The Rise of the Novel: Studies in Defoe, Richardson and Fielding* (Berkeley and Los Angeles, 1964), pp. 299–300; also see Irma Z. Sherwood, "The

Novelists as Commentators," in *The Age of Johnson: Essays Presented to Chauncey Brewster Tinker,* ed. Frederick W. Hilles (New Haven and London, 1949), pp. 113–25; (for Fielding) Ernest A. Baker, *The History of the English Novel,* Vol. 4: *Intellectual Realism: from Richardson to Sterne* (NY, 1930), pp. 159, 166–70, 173, 191–92.

[12] See his Prologue to Foote's *Taste* in *Dramatic Works of Samuel Foote,* p. xi; also see Simon Trefman, *Sam. Foote, Comedian, 1772–1777* (NY, 1971), pp. 55–58.

[13] The two short plays are reprinted in Foote's *Dramatic Works;* in the references given below, let the date of performance stand for the whole title (*Englishman in Paris,* 1753; *Englishman Returned from Paris,* 1756).

[14] 1756: Act I (italics added); Garrick, *Lilliput,* sc. 1, in *The Plays of David Garrick,* eds. H. W. Pedicord and F. L. Bergmann (Carbondale and Edwardsville, Ill., 1980), 1: 114; also see Elizabeth P. Stein, *David Garrick, Dramatist* (NY, 1937), pp. 61, 64–65.

[15] 1753: Epilogue, Act I, Act II; 1756: Act I, Act II.

[16] John Cartwright, *Take Your Choice!* (1776), pp. 57, 61–62.

[17] 1756: Act I.

[18] Quoted by Frederick Hertz, "War and National Character," *Contemporary Review* 171, No. 977 (May, 1947): 275.

[19] 'The Progress of the French, In their Views of Universal Monarchy, (1756), quoted in Herbert M. Atherton, *Political Prints in the Age of Hogarth: A Study of the Ideographic Representation of Politics* (Oxford, 1974), p. 173; Young's *Theatre of the Present War,* quoted by John M. Gazley, "Arthur Young, British Patriot," in *Nationalism and Internationalism: Essays Inscribed to Carlton J. H. Hayes,* ed. Edward M. Earle (NY, 1950), p. 147.

[20] Gazley, op. cit., pp. 145, 155, 166–68 and passim.

[21] See Wittkower, "The Artist," p. 79.

[22] Atherton, *Political Prints,* pp. 263, 84–85.

[23] Ibid., pp. 91–96.

[24] Minogue, *Nationalism,* p. 7; Atherton, op. cit., pp. 96, 174–76.

[25] Atherton, op. cit., pp. 87, 96, 103, 173–77, 186–89, 197, 215–16, 235, 240, 246–47, 250 and passim.

[26] From Abbé le Blanc's *Letters on the English and French Nations* (1747), quoted by Horn, *Britain and Europe in the Eighteenth Century,* pp. 25–26.

[27] Atherton, *Political Prints,* p. 266.

[28] [John Brown], *An Estimate of the Manners and Principles of the Times,* 6th ed. (1757), 1: 24–26.

[29] Ibid., pp. 72, 89; 2: 82, 159–60.

[30] Ibid., 1: 34–35, 91, 181–82 and passim; 2: 73, 83–84, 158 and passim.

[31] Ibid., 1: 74; 2: 72–73.

[32] Ibid., 1: 75, 131, 180–83; 2: 69–70.

[33] Ibid., 1: 135–41.

[34] Ibid., 140.

[35] Ibid., 143–45.

[36] Ibid., 220.

[37] Ibid., 218–21.

CHAPTER FIVE

[1] Lois Whitney, *Primitivism and the Idea of Progress In English Popular Literature of the Eighteenth Century* (NY, 1965), p. 7.

[2] Northrop Frye, "Towards Defining an Age of Sensibility," in N. Frye, *Fables of Identity: Studies in Poetic Mythology* (NY, 1963), p. 130; D. Greene, *Age of Exuberance*, pp. vii, 160; Murray Cohen, "Eighteenth-Century English Literature and Modern Critical Methodologies," *The Eighteenth Century: Theory and Interpretation* 20 (1979): 5–7, 22; Alexander Gelley, "Character and Person: On the Presentation of Self in Some 18th-Century Novels," ibid. 21 (1980): 109–27; Clifford Siskin, "Personification and Community: Literary Change in the Mid and Late Eighteenth Century," *Eighteenth-Century Studies* 15, No. 4 (1982): 371–72, 387; John Barrell, *English Literature in History, 1730–80: An Equal, Wide Survey* (NY, 1983); Virginia C. Kenny, *The Country-House Ethos in English Literature, 1688–1750: Themes of Personal Retreat and National Expansion* (Brighton and NY, 1984); Pat Rogers, *Literature and Popular Culture in Eighteenth-Century England* (Brighton and Totowa, N. J., 1985); idem, *Eighteenth-Century Encounters: Studies in Literature and Society in the Age of Walpole* (Brighton and Totowa, N. J., 1985).

[3] The best recent summary: Roger Chartier, "Intellectual History or Sociocultural History? The French Trajectories," in *Modern European Intellectual History: Reappraisals and New Perspectives*, eds. Dominick LaCapra and Steven L. Kaplan (Ithaca and London, 1982), pp. 13–46.

[4] See Greene, *Age of Exuberance*, pp. 34, 49–50.

[5] Boyd C. Shafer, *Nationalism: Interpretations and Interpreters*, 3d edn, Service Center for Teachers of History No. 20 (Washington, D. C., 1966), p. 21; Frye, "Towards defining an Age of Sensibility," pp. 135–36; John Sitter, *Literary Loneliness in Mid-Eighteenth-Century England* (Ithaca and London, 1982); Pocock, *The Machiavellian Moment*, p. 462.

[6] H. Atherton, *Political Prints*, pp. 172–74, 186; Samuel Shellabarger, *Lord Chesterfield and His World* (Boston, 1951), pp. 287–90, 378–84; Hibbert, *The Grand Tour*, p. 234; Jarrett, *England in the Age of Hogarth*, p. 194; Derry, *Fox*, pp. 10, 16, 31–33, 50–52; Christopher Hobhouse, *Fox* (1964), pp. 1, 7, 27, 54–56; Robert A. Smith, *Eighteenth-Century English Politics: Patrons and Place-hunters* (NY, 1972), p. 3; and for many prints linking Fox, Macaronis, 'treatises on French Dress,' etc., see *Catalogue of Prints and Drawings in the British Museum . . . Political and Personal Satires*, IV: 792–829 and passim.

[7] D. Horn, *Britain and Europe in the Eighteenth Century*, p. 35.

[8] For example, see Watt, *Rise of the Novel*, pp. 52–59.

[9] W. Jackson Bate, *Samuel Johnson* (NY and London, 1977), p. 257.

[10] See Edward A. Bloom, *Samuel Johnson in Grub Street* (Providence, R.I., 1957), p. 172; S. Trefman, *Sam Foote*, pp. 143–50; Oliver Goldsmith, *The Vicar of Wakefield: A Tale Supposed to be Written by Himself* (Cambridge, Mass., 1895), chaps. ix, xxi, pp. 60, 132–33; Churchill's 'Rosciad' in *English Poetry*, ed. Lindsay, pp. 126, 129.

[11] Smollett, *Fathom*, pp. 7–8; Henry Fielding, *Amelia* (1930), 2: 141 [Bk. ix, ch. vii].

[12] Tames, *Josiah Wedgwood*, pp. 14, 23, 30; J. G. Crowther, *Scientists of the Industrial Revolution* (1962), pp. 113–14; also see John Brewer, "English Radicalism in the Age of George III," in *Three British Revolutions: 1641, 1688, 1776*, ed. J. G. A. Pocock (Princeton, 1980), pp. 339, 347.

[13] N. McKendrick, "The Commercialization of Fashion" in *Birth of a Consumer Society*, p. 57; Churchill, 'Rosciad,' *English Poetry*, ed. Lindsay, pp. 124,

134–35; J. Brown, *Estimate*, 1: 127–28; John Cartwright, *Take Your Choice!*, p. 5; (for Pitt) Sir Charles Grant Robertson, *Chatham and the British Empire* (1967), p. 85.

[14] Quoted in John Brewer, *Party Ideology and Popular Politics at the Accession of George III* (Cambridge, 1976), p. 71.

[15] For Bentham see John Brewer, "The member for Bristol and Malton," *Times Literary Supplement*, No. 4,099 (23 Oct. 1981): 1233; Edmund Burke, "A Letter to a Noble Lord" (1796) in *The Works of the Right Honourable Edmund Burke* (1854–62), 5: 129–30.

[16] Isaac Kramnick, *The Rage of Edmund Burke: Portrait of An Ambivalent Conservative* (NY, 1977), pp. 190–96.

[17] J. Brooke, *King George III*, pp. 138, 140.

[18] Eleanor Flexner, *Mary Wollstonecraft: A Biography* (Baltimore, 1973), p. 34.

[19] See *Karl Marx: Selected Writings in Sociology and Social Philosophy*, eds. T. B. Bottomore and Maximilien Rubel (1956), p. 80; Goldsmith, *Vicar of Wakefield*, chap. xix, pp. 120–21.

[20] Henry Mackenzie, *The Man of Feeling* (1967), pp. 39–41; see Lois Whitney, *Primitivism and the Idea of Progress in the English Popular Literature of the Eighteenth Century* (NY, 1965), pp. 46, 59–60.

[21] Langhorne, 'The Country Justice,' in *English Poetry*, ed. Lindsay, p. 185.

[22] Sir S. H. Scott, *The Exemplary Mr. Day, 1748–1789* (NY, 1935), p. 100.

[23] Ibid., pp. 104–06.

[24] Ibid., pp. 107–08.

[25] Ibid., pp. 186, 190; also Martin S. Day, *History of English Literature, 1660–1837* (NY, 1963), p. 249.

[26] Thomas Day, *The History of Sandford and Merton: A Book for the Young* (1860), pp. 47, 17, 264, 276, 261, 19.

[27] Ibid., pp. 266–68, 281–83, 19–20, 426, 290, 256, 202, 28, 311–12, 357.

[28] Ibid., pp. 20, 202, 28, 311–12, 357.

[29] Ibid., pp. 411, 279.

[30] Ibid., pp. 268, 277, 260–62, 183–84.

[31] Ibid., pp. 250, 387–88, 277, 100.

[32] Ibid., pp. 262–64, 271.

[33] Ibid., pp. 59, 303.

[34] Ibid., pp. 279, 284.

[35] Ibid., pp. 313, 267, 148–49, 270.

[36] Ibid., pp. 382–92.

[37] Ibid., pp. 243 (italics added), 11–12, 16–17, 262, 287–90.

[38] Ibid., pp. 11, 424–27.

[39] Ibid., pp. 386, 334, 321–30, 257, 44 and passim.

[40] Ibid., pp. 260, 252–53, 23–25.

[41] Leslie Stephen, *English Literature and Society in the Eighteenth Century* (1904), pp. 80–85.

[42] Minogue, *Nationalism*, pp. 26–27; *Dictionary of the History of Ideas*, 1973 ed., s.v. "Nationalism," by H. Kohn; A. F. B. Clark, *Boileau and the French Classical Critics in England*, p. 419.

[43] Richard Hurd, *Letters on Chivalry and Romance*, edited and introduced by Hoyt Trowbridge: The Augustan Reprint Society No. 101–102 (Los Angeles, 1963), pp. 2–4, 78–81, 83–86; italics added.

[44] See Montague Summers, *The Gothic Quest: A History of the Gothic Novel* (n.d.), pp. 17–18; Albert C. Baugh, gen. ed., *A Literary History of England*, 2d edn,

vol. 3: *The Restoration and Eighteenth Century (1660–1789)*, by George
        Sherburn and Donald F. Bond (NY, 1967), p. 949.

45 See Hoxie Neale Fairchild, *The Noble Savage: A Study in Romantic Naturalism*
        (NY, 1928), p. 62; for Thomson see (for example) H. T. Dickinson, ed.,
        Politics and Literature in the Eighteenth Century (1974), pp. 95–96; for J.
        Warton's 'Ode to Fancy' see (for example) G. B. Woods, ed., *English Poetry
        and Prose of the Romantic Movement* (Chicago, 1929), p. 85.

46 Anthony Smith, "Introduction," *Nationalist Movements*, ed. Smith, p. 8.

47 L. B. Namier, *England in the Age of American Revolution*, p. 33.

48 Samuel Johnson, *A Dictionary of the English Language: In Which the Words are
        deduced from their Originals* . . . (1755), "Preface"; also see the corrected
        version for the 4th edn (1773) in *Johnson: Prose and Poetry*, selected by
        Mona Wilson, pp. 301–23; and for other protests against the supposed
        Frenchification of English, see Tucker, *Protean Shape*, p. 35.

49 Quoted in Wittkower, "The Artist," in *Man Versus Society in 18th-Century Britain*,
        ed. Clifford, p. 78.

50 John Buston and Norman Davis, gen. eds., *The Oxford History of English
        Literature*, Vol. 8: *The Mid-Eighteenth Century*, by John Butt, edited and
        completed by Geoffrey Carnall (Oxford, 1979), pp. 5, 95; Minogue,
        Nationalism, p. 27.

51 Ramsay quoted in Ernest Bernbaum, *Guide Through the Romantic Movement*, 2d.
        edn, rev. (NY, 1949), p. 20; Bernbaum, ibid., p. 20; Thomas Warton,
        History of English Poetry, intro. by René Wellek (NY and London, 1968),
        1:1–7; Smart, *Rejoice in the Lamb*, in *Poems by Christopher Smart*, ed. Robert
        Brittain (Princeton, 1950), p. 112.

52 Smith, "Introduction," p. 8; G. M. Miller, *The Historical Point of View in English
        Literary Criticism from 1570–1770* (NY, 1968), p. 146; Peardon, *The
        Transition in English Historical Writing, 1760–1830*, pp. 295, 78, 162–64.

53 See Peardon, op. cit., pp. 114–18, 294.

54 Kedourie, *Nationalism*, pp. 73–74; (for J. Bull) Atherton, *Political Prints*, p. 216.

55 Hugh A. MacDougall, *Racial Myth in English History: Trojans, Teutons, and Anglo-
        Saxons* (Montreal, Hanover, N.H., and London, 1982), p. 82; Samuel
        Kliger, *The Goths in England: A Study in Seventeenth and Eighteenth Century
        Thought* (NY, 1972), pp. 1–3; Léon Poliakov, *The Aryan Myth: A History of
        Racist and Nationalist Ideas in Europe*, trans. Edmund Howard (NY, 1977), p.
        47 and (for Sieyès) p. 28.

56 Quoted in Poliakov, op, cit., p. 29.

57 [Obadiah Hulme] quoted in MacDougall, *Racial Myth*, p. 83.

58 Judith Shklar, "Subversive Genealogies," in *Myth, Symbol, and Culture*, ed.
        Clifford Geertz, p. 129; Kliger, *Goths in England*, pp. 208 and (for *World*
        writer) 27–28; also see Marilyn Butler, *Romantics, Rebels and Reactionaries:
        English Literature and its Background, 1760–1830* (NY and Oxford, 1981),
        pp. 29, 37.

59 See, in addition to the works of Greene and Butt noted above, Martin Price, *To
        the Place of Wisdom: Studies in Order and Energy from Dryden to Blake* (Garden
        City, NY, 1964).

60 Greene, *Age of Exuberance*, pp. 137–38.

61 Lawrence Lipking, *The Ordering of the Arts in Eighteenth-Century England*
        (Princeton, 1970), pp. 328–29.

CHAPTER SIX

[1] W. Houghton, *Victorian Frame of Mind*, p. 45n.

[2] Friedrich Meinecke, *Cosmopolitanism and the National State*, trans. Robert B. Kimber, introduced by Felix Gilbert (Princeton, 1970), p. 16.

[3] Allen Curnow, "Distraction and Definition: Centripetal Directions in New Zealand Poetry," in *National Identity: Papers delivered at the Commonwealth Literature Conference*, Brisbane, 1968, ed. K. L. Goodwin (London and Melbourne, 1970), pp. 176–77, 182.

[4] J. L. Talmon, *Political Messianism: The Romantic Phase* (NY, 1960), p. 285; C. Siskin, "Personification and Community," *Eighteenth-Century Studies* 15 (1982): 401; J. Butt and G. Carnall, *The Mid-Eighteenth Century*, p. 134; Frye, "The Romantic Myth," in Northrop Frye, *A Study of English Romanticism* (NY, 1968), p. 18.

[5] Meinecke, *Cosmopolitanism and the National State*, p. 14; also see Kedourie, *Nationalism*, p. 73.

[6] Jacques Barzun, "Cultural Nationalism and the Makings of Fame," in *Nationalism and Internationalism*, ed. E. M. Earle, p. 3; for Hampden and Sydney see Peter Karsten, *Patriot-Heroes in England and America: Political Symbolism and Changing Values over Three Centuries* (Madison, Wis., 1978), chaps. 3, 6; T. B. Macaulay, "Horace Walpole" (1833), in *The Complete Writings of Thomas Babington Macaulay* (Boston, 1901): *Critical and Historical Essays*, II: 195–96.

[7] A. D. Smith, "Introduction," in *Nationalist Movements*, ed. Smith; also see idem, *Theories of Nationalism*, pp. 90–93; for Bright see *OED*, "Nation."

[8] Leon Guilhamet, *The Sincere Ideal: Studies on Sincerity in Eighteenth-Century English Literature* (Montreal and London, 1974), pp. 1, 211, 207.

[9] McKillop, "Local Attachment and Cosmopolitanism," in *From Sensibility to Romanticism*, eds. F. W. Hilles and H. Bloom, p. 204; H. N. Fairchild, *The Noble Savage*, p. 52; Lionel Trilling, *Sincerity and Authenticity* (Cambridge, Mass., 1972), pp. 112, 110–14.

[10] Trilling, op. cit., p. 111; Guilhamet, *The Sincere Ideal*, pp. 211, 282.

[11] Guilhamet, op. cit., pp. 270, 284.

[12] See Trilling, op. cit., pp. 12–13; (for Godwin and Walker) Guilhamet, op. cit., pp. 297, 284.

[13] See Trilling, op. cit., p. 2; (for Wordsworth) Guilhamet, op. cit., p. 4; (for Carlyle) M. H. Abrams, *The Mirror and the Lamp: Romantic Theory and the Critical Tradition* (NY, 1953), p. 319.

[14] See Guilhamet, op. cit., pp. 1, 201, 273, 284; Abrams, op. cit., p. 318.

[15] For Sterne see Mead, *The Grand Tour*, p. 386; for Godwin see Guilhamet, op. cit., p. 286; for Carlyle see Abrams, op. cit., p. 319.

[16] See Aaron V. Cicourel, "Basic and Normative Rules in the Negotiation of Status and Role," in *Studies in Social Interaction*, ed. David Sudnow (NY, 1972), pp. 232–33; E. Flexner, *Mary Wollstonecraft*, p. 36; Foote, *The Englishman in Paris*, p. 28, and *The Englishman Returned from Paris*, p. 26.

[17] Richard Hurd, "On Sincerity in the Commerce of the World," in R. Hurd, *Moral and Political Dialogues; with Letters on Chivalry and Romance*, 5th ed. (1776), 1: 26–27.

[18] See Guilhamet, op. cit., pp. 160, 182, 202–03, 294; (for Rousseau) Trilling, op. cit., p. 62.

[19] See Guilhamet, op. cit., pp. 269, 217; (for Shenstone) Butt and Carnall, *The Mid-Eighteenth Century*, p. 60.

[20] See Guilhamet, op. cit., pp. 201, 256, 274, 284.

[21] See Garrick's epilogue to Cumberland's *The West Indian* in *Eighteenth-Century Plays*, selected by John Hampden, p. 408; Hurd, "On Sincerity," pp. 11, 37 and passim; (for Shenstone) Guilhamet, op. cit., pp. 207–09.

[22] Tobias Smollett, *The Expedition of Humphry Clinker* (NY and Toronto, 1950), pp. 212–14, 94–95, 114–116, 121, 86, 158, 374.

[23] Ibid., pp. 181, 177.

[24] Ibid., pp. 242, 332–48, 398–402.

[25] Ibid., pp. 86, 38–40, 99–102, 327, 112–15, 409.

[26] Fanny Burney, *Evelina* (London and NY, 1950), pp. 7–8, 118, 202, 313.

[27] Ibid., pp. 256, 45–48, 62.

[28] Ibid., pp. 45, 366, 103–06.

[29] Ibid., pp. 46, 372–73.

[30] Ibid., p. 55.

[31] Ibid., pp. 73, 244, 249.

[32] Ibid., pp. 267, 271.

[33] Guilhamet, op. cit., pp. 202, 282, 291.

[34] Letters CLXI (Sept. 5, O.S. 1748) and CLXVI (Oct. 19, O.S. 1748), in *The Letters of the Earl of Chesterfield to His Son*, ed. Charles Strachey (NY and London, 1925), 1: 259, 285; Alec Mellor, *Lord Chesterfield et sons temps, un grand européen* (Tours, 1970), p. 314.

[35] See Trilling, *Sincerity and Authenticity*, p. 69.

[36] For Shenstone and Blake see Guilhamet, *The Sincere Ideal*, pp. 214, 260; for Carlyle see Abrams, *Mirror and Lamp*, p. 319.

[37] Quoted in Trilling, *Sincerity and Authenticity*, pp. 118–19.

[38] W. J. Bate, *Samuel Johnson*, p. 591.

[39] John Andrews, *A Comparative View of the French and English Nations*, pp. 250–54, 77–79.

[40] Ibid., pp. 463, 291–92, 104–05, 207, 267–68.

[41] Ibid., pp. 268–71, 45–46, 84–86, 96–97, 140–47.

[42] Ibid., pp. 319–26, 340, 388, 276.

[43] Ibid., pp. 380, 143, 327, 357–59, 48, 366–67.

[44] Ibid., pp. 96, 73, 244, 358, 319, 63, 414, 328, 378, 170–71, 12, 142.

[45] Ibid., pp. 442–43.

[46] For example, see Ernest Baker, *History of the English Novel*, Vol. 5: *The Novel of Sentiment and the Gothic Romance*, esp. pp. 288–89.

[47] Peter Mathias, *The First Industrial Nation: An Economic History of Britain, 1700–1914* (NY, 1969), p. 3; R. M. Hartwell, "Introduction," *The Causes of the Industrial Revolution in England*, ed. R. M. Hartwell (1967), pp. 19–21.

[48] F. Crouzet, "England and France in the Eighteenth Century: A Comparative Analysis of Two Economic Growths," in *Causes of the Industrial Revolution*, ed. Hartwell, pp. 145–47, 154; Phyllis Deane, *The First Industrial Revolution*, 2d edn (Cambridge, 1979), p. 18.

[49] Deane, op. cit., p. 123.

[50] T. S. Ashton, *The Industrial Revolution, 1760–1830* (1948), p. 19.

[51] James Boswell, *Life of Johnson*, ed. R. W. Chapman (1953), p. 1211; Deane, op. cit., p. 135; Crouzet, op. cit., pp. 155–56.

[52] For Bentham see Giovanni Costigan, *Makers of Modern England: The Force of*

Individual Genius in History (NY and London, 1967), p. 7; Butt and Carnall, *The Mid-Eighteenth Century*, p. 502.

[53] See J. G. Crowther, *Scientists of the Industrial Revolution*, pp. 113–14, 171, 128, 104–05, 124, 95 and passim; for Robison's comments see Eric Robinson and A. E. Musson, *James Watt and the Steam Revolution* (NY, 1969), p. 25.

[54] See Robinson and Musson, op. cit., p. 21.

[55] Crouzet, "England and France," p. 156; Mathias, *The First Industrial Nation*, p. 9 (italics added).

[56] Crouzet, op. cit., pp. 157–61; see also A. Rupert Hall, "What did the Industrial Revolution in Britain owe to Science?" in *Historical Perspectives: Studies in English Thought and Society in honour of J. H. Plumb*, ed. Neil McKendrick (1974), pp. 144–45.

[57] Guilhamet, *The Sincere Ideal*, p. 6.

[58] See Mark Girouard, *The Return to Camelot: Chivalry and the English Gentleman* (New Haven and London, 1981), pp. 40–41; also see Terry Coleman, "Leveller heads than mine," *Manchester Guardian Weekly*, May 20, 1984, p. 4.

[59] See G. M. Young, *Victorian England: Portrait of an Age*, 2d edn (1960), p. 4.

CHAPTER SEVEN

[1] A. D. Smith, *Theories of Nationalism*, p. 330n.36 and passim; John Plamenatz, "Two Types of Nationalism," in *Nationalism*, ed. E. Kamenka, p. 28.

[2] A. D. Smith, "Introduction: The Formation of Nationalist Movements," in *Nationalist Movements*, ed. Smith, pp. 4–5; idem, *Theories of Nationalism*, pp. 216–17, 224–25, 321n., 327n.; K. R. Minogue, *Nationalism*, pp. 135, 154.

[3] Smith, "Introduction," p. 3.

[4] Minogue, *Nationalism*, p. 27; Eugene Kamenka, "Political Nationalism—The Evolution of the Idea," in *Nationalism*, ed. Kamenka, p. 14.

[5] Boyd C. Shafer, *Nationalism: Myth and Reality* (NY, 1955), pp. 108–09; Minogue, op. cit., p. 40; H. Kohn, *The Idea of Nationalism*, pp. 206, 229–31, 456.

[6] See E. Kedourie, *Nationalism*, pp. 12–15 (italics added); Minogue, op. cit., p. 46; Kohn, op. cit., pp. 207–08, 645–46; Jacques Barzun, *The French Race: Theories of its Origins and their Social and Political Implications Prior to the Revolution* (Port Washington, New York, 1966), pp. 228–35, 247–50.

[7] K. Minogue, "Nationalism and the Patriotism of City-States," in *Nationalist Movements*, ed. Smith, p. 71.

[8] V. Kiernan, "Nationalist Movements and Social Classes," in *Nationalist Movements*, ed. Smith, p. 111; A. D. Smith, "Neo-Classicist and Romantic Elements in the Emergence of Nationalist Conceptions," in *Nationalist Movements*, ed. Smith, p. 75; Max Handman, "The Sentiment of Nationalism, *Political Science Quarterly* 36 (1921): 104–05; H. M. Chadwick, *Nationalities of Europe and Growth of National Ideologies*, p. 3.

[9] Minogue, *Nationalism*, p. 154; Kedourie, *Nationalism*, p. 101; V. Kiernan, "Movements and Classes," p. 132.

[10] Minogue, "Nationalism and the Patriotism of City-States," p. 57.

[11] See W. J. Argyle, "Size and Scale as Factors in the Development of Nationalist Movements," in *Nationalist Movements*, ed. Smith, pp. 31–53.

[12] Smith, "Introduction," pp. 22–26; Kiernan, "Movements and Classes," p. 115;

Minogue, *Nationalism,* pp. 13, 24; idem, "Nationalism and the Patriotism of City-States," p. 72; Kedourie, *Nationalism,* p. 18.

13 See Argyle, "Size and Scale," pp. 47–50; George L. Mosse, "Mass Politics and the Political Liturgy of Nationalism," in *Nationalism,* ed. Kamenka, pp. 39–40, 50, 54.

14 Smith, *Theories of Nationalism,* pp. 226–27; Mosse, op. cit., pp. 40–57; Smith, "Introduction," p. 3.

15 Minogue, *Nationalism,* pp. 28–29; Smith, "Introduction," pp. 26–28.

16 Peter Calvert, "On Attaining Sovereignty," in *Nationalist Movements,* ed. Smith, p. 138.

17 Ibid., pp. 137–38; Minogue, *Nationalism,* p. 29; Smith, "Introduction," p. 27.

18 See (for Disraeli quotation) G. H. Guttridge, *English Whiggism and the American Revolution,* p. 4; for Pitt see Archibald S. Foord, *His Majesty's Opposition, 1714–1830* (Oxford, 1964), p. 308.

19 See Linda Colley, [review], *History* 67 (1982): 149–50.

20 Inscription on Blackfriars' Bridge (1760), quoted in R. J. White, *A Short History of England* (Cambridge, 1967), p. 203.

21 J. Brooke, *King George III,* p. 78; Marie Peters, *Pitt and Popularity: The Patriot Minister and London Opinion during the Seven Years' War* (Oxford, 1980), pp. 222–24.

22 See (for Bedford) D. Jarrett, *Begetters of Revolution,* pp. 37–38; Sir C. G. Robertson, *Chatham and the British Empire,* p. 132.

23 See Peters, op. cit., p. 147.

24 Ibid., p. 247; G. Rudé, *Hanoverian London,* p. 226; idem, *Wilkes and Liberty: A Social Study of 1763 to 1774* (Oxford, 1962), p. 98; Jarrett, *Begetters,* p. 58; (for Malmesbury) Albert Tucker, *A History of English Civilization* (NY, 1972), p. 477; J. Brewer, *Party Ideology and Popular Politics,* p. 153.

25 See Richard Pares, *King George III and the Politicians* (1967), pp. 58–60.

26 See Foord, *His Majesty's Opposition,* p. 304; Brooke, *George III,* p. 150; Pares, op. cit., p. 67.

27 See Foord, op. cit., p. 312; Pares, op. cit., p. 58.

28 See Foord, op. cit., pp. 308, 315; R. A. Smith, *Eighteenth-Century English Politics,* p. 132.

29 See Rudé, *Wilkes and Liberty,* pp. 25–36.

30 Brewer, *Party Ideology and Popular Politics,* chap. 9; Rudé, *Wilkes and Liberty,* p. 42.

31 Pares, *George III and the Politicians,* p. 57.

32 Alexander Stephens, *Memoirs of John Horne Tooke, Interspersed with Original Documents* (1813; NY, 1968), 1: 21, 38–39; William Hazlitt, *The Spirit of the Age, or Contemporary Portraits,* 4th ed. (1886), p. 79.

33 Stephens, op. cit., 1: 41, 54.

34 Ibid., pp. 57–66.

35 Ibid., pp. 97–100.

36 Ibid., pp. 147–53.

37 Ibid., pp. 161–66; Rudé, *Hanoverian London,* pp. 166–72; G. D. H. Cole and Raymond Postgate, *The British People, 1746–1946* (NY and London, 1961), pp. 103–04; Albert Goodwin, *The Friends of Liberty: The English Democratic Movement in the Age of the French Revolution* (Cambridge, Mass., 1979), p. 48.

38 For Rockingham see Rudé, *Wilkes and Liberty,* p. 165; for Horne's warning,

Stephens, *Memoirs of Horne Tooke*, 1: 78, 177; for the buttons see Lecky, *History of England*, 6: 139.

[39] Brewer, *Party Ideology and Popular Politics*, p. 19.

[40] Quoted in John W. Osborne, *William Cobbett: His Thought and his Times* (New Brunswick, N.J., 1966), p. 83.

[41] Jarrett, *Begetters*, p. 53.

[42] Obadiah Hulme, *An Historical Essay on the English Constitution: Or, An Impartial Inquiry into the Elective Power of the People, from the first Establishment of the Saxons in this Kingdom* (1771), p. iv.

[43] Ibid., pp. 4–9, 16, 19, 23–24, 31–32.

[44] Ibid., pp. 9, 37–38, 57, 72.

[45] Ibid., pp. 53–60, 64–68, 175–80, 109–14.

[46] Ibid., pp. 119–22, 124–25, 144.

[47] Ibid., pp. 115, 126, 141–48, 151.

[48] Ibid., pp. 126, 131–38, 140–41, 149.

[49] Ibid., pp. 143, 150–52, 164.

[50] Ibid., pp. 151–54, 158–64.

[51] Ibid., pp. 9–10, 47–50, 126, 130–32, 137–40, 178.

[52] Hill, "The Norman Yoke," in C. Hill, *Puritanism and Revolution*, pp. 57, 75, 94–100, 111–12.

[53] Ibid., pp. 73, 57–58.

[54] Ibid., pp. 67–69, 74.

[55] Alan Valentine, *Lord North* (Norman, Okla., 1967), 2: 180–81.

[56] Bernard Bailyn, *The Ideological Origins of the American Revolution* (Cambridge, Mass., 1967), pp. vi–x, 23–33, 40–54, 184–89.

[57] Ibid., pp. ix, 46, 51, 82n.

[58] G. Chinard, *The Commonplace Book of Thomas Jefferson*, quoted in Hill, "The Norman Yoke," p. 94.

[59] Indicative of current thinking is the fact that the published record of a recent conference on English and American radicalism, to which more than a dozen experts contributed essays dealing mainly with the eighteenth century, contains in its index no reference to nationalism or patriotism. See *The Origins of Anglo-American Radicalism*, eds. Margaret Jacob and James Jacob (1984).

[60] See, for example, Solomon Lutnick, *The American Revolution and the British Press, 1775–1783* (Columbia, Missouri, 1967), p. 210.

[61] Quoted in Valentine, *Lord North*, 2: 181.

[62] See Foord, *His Majesty's Opposition*, p. 323; Smith, *Eighteenth-Century Politics*, p. 102.

[63] Ian R. Christie, *Wilkes, Wyvill and Reform: The Parliamentary Reform Movement in British Politics, 1760–1785* (1962), p. 49.

[64] Hulme, *Historical Essay*, pp. 179–210.

[65] See Stephens, *Memoirs of Horne Tooke*, 1: 233, 380, 388–89.

[66] Ibid., 362–69, 381–82, 407–13.

[67] Ibid., pp. 240–41, 269, 289, 372; also see, for more on the internal divisions of the radical movement, H. T. Dickinson, *Liberty and Property: Political Ideology in Eighteenth-Century Britain* (1977), chap. 6; Brewer, *Party Ideology and Popular Politics*, pp. 197–200; John Brewer, "English Radicalism in the Age of George III," in *Three British Revolutions*, ed. Pocock, pp. 330–32, 342–43, 354.

68 See Christie, *Wilkes, Wyvill and Reform*, p. 64; Rudé, *Hanoverian London*, p. 172; George Stead Veitch, *The Genesis of Parliamentary Reform* (Hamden, Conn., 1965), p. 45; (for Chatham) Brewer, *Party Ideology and Popular Politics*, p. 261.

69 Robbins, *The Eighteenth-Century Commonwealthman*, pp. 363, 324; Stephens, *Memoirs of Horne Tooke*, 2: 31–33.

70 See Carla H. Hay, *James Burgh, Spokesman for Reform in Hanoverian England* (Washington, 1979), pp. 11–12, 27, 32–35, 77–100 and passim; Herbert Butterfield, *George III, Lord North and the People, 1779–1780* (NY, 1968), pp. 259–62.

71 Samuel Bamford, *Passages in the Life of a Radical* (1967), p. 31; Cartwright, *Take Your Choice!*, pp. 92–95.

72 Cartwright, op. cit., pp. x, xviin., xix, xxv, 12, 15, 50, 90–91.

73 Ibid., pp. xvii, 34n., 38–40, 51–52, 89, 96.

74 Ibid., pp. 19–22, 37.

75 See Robert E. Toohey, *Liberty and Empire: British Radical Solutions to the American Problem, 1774–76* (Lexington, Ky., 1978), p. 16; Stephens, *Memoirs of Horne Tooke*, 1: 434–35.

76 John Cartwright, *American Independence the Interest and Glory of Great-Britain*, new edn (1775; NY, 1970), p. 11.

77 See Dora Mae Clark, *British Opinion and the American Revolution* (NY, 1966), pp. 161–66, 170–71; Colin Bonwick, *English Radicals and the American Revolution* (Chapel Hill, 1977), pp. 90, 112.

78 See Bonwick, op. cit., pp. 103–04; Clark, op. cit., p. 159.

79 See Stephens, *Memoirs of Horne Tooke*, 1: 473; 2: 21–23; Toohey, *Liberty and Empire*, p. 105.

80 See Carl B. Cone, *The English Jacobins: Reformers in Late 18th Century England* (NY, 1968), pp. 53–54; Eugene Charlton Black, *The Association: British Extraparliamentary Political Organization, 1769–1793* (Cambridge, Mass., 1963), pp. 36–37; Butterfield, *George III, Lord North and the People*, pp. 188–89.

81 See Black, op. cit., pp. 36–37; Butterfield, op. cit., pp. 192, 258; Cone, op. cit., p. 54; and for more on Jebb see Philip Anthony Brown, *The French Revolution in English History* (NY, 1965), pp. 18–19.

82 Black, op. cit., p. 5.

83 Pares, *George III and the Politicians*, p. 53n.; also see T. M. Parssinen, "Association, convention, and anti-parliament in British radical politics, 1771–1848," *English Historical Review* 88 (1973): 504–33.

84 Quoted in Black, op. cit., p. 33.

85 Butterfield, op. cit., p. 271.

86 See Guttridge, *English Whiggism*, pp. 124–26; Veitch, *Genesis of Reform*, pp. 66, 76; Butterfield, op. cit., p. 296; Sir S. H. Scott, *The Exemplary Mr. Day*, p. 152.

87 Veitch, op. cit., p. 66.

88 See Butterfield, op. cit., pp. 239, 246, 250, 309, 326, 333; Veitch, op. cit., p. 59.

89 Butterfield, op. cit., pp. 238 (italics added), 227, 332; also see S. I. Tucker, *Protean Shape*, on the usage by the '80s of such words as 'bold,' 'candid,' and 'free.'

90 See Rudé, *Hanoverian London*, pp. 178–81, 220–27; Alan Valentine, *The British Establishment, 1760–1784: An Eighteenth-Century Biographical Dictionary* (Norman, Okla., 1970), s.v. "Bull, Frederick."

91 Butterfield, op. cit., pp. 374–75, 379.

92 See Edward Royle and James Walvin, *English Radicals and Reformers, 1760–1848* (Lexington, Ky., 1982), pp. 29–30; Veitch, op. cit., pp. 71–74; Moritz quoted in Hart, *English Life in the Eighteenth Century*, p. 18.

93 See Foord, *His Majesty's Opposition*, p. 365.

94 Ibid., pp. 373–74.

95 See Christie, *Wilkes, Wyvill and Reform*, p. 156; Veitch, *Genesis of Reform*, pp. 77, 84.

96 See (for the paucity of noble reformers) Christie, op. cit., p. 194; Veitch, op. cit., p. 83; Lord Rosebery, *Pitt* (1902), p. 61.

97 See Stephens, *Memoirs of Horne Tooke*, 2: 43–44; Christie, op. cit., p. 214.

98 See Stephens, op. cit., 2: 35; Christie, op. cit., p. 156; Veitch, op. cit., pp. 92–93.

99 See (for Wyvill) Christie, op. cit., p. 192; (for Horne) Stephens, op. cit., 2: 75.

100 Foord, op. cit., p. 384; John Cannon, *The Fox-North Coalition: Crisis of the Constitution, 1782–84* (Cambridge, 1969), pp. xi-xii; Stephens, op. cit., 2: 44.

101 See J. W. Derry, *Charles James Fox*, p. 139; Mrs. Eric George, "Fox's Martyrs; The General Election of 1784," *Transactions of the Royal Historical Society* 4th Ser. 21 (1939): 142–44.

102 See Derry, op. cit., p. 187; George, op. cit., p. 151; Rudé, *Hanoverian London*, p. 182.

103 Brooke, *King George III*, pp. 256–57; J. Steven Watson, *The Reign of George III, 1760–1815* (Oxford, 1960), p. 270; John Ehrman, *The Younger Pitt: The Years of Acclaim* (NY, 1969), p. 152.

104 See Cannon, *Fox-North*, p. 221; George, op. cit., pp. 166–67; Stephens, *Memoirs of Horne Tooke*, 2: 71–78.

105 See George, op. cit., pp. 157, 164; Foord, *His Majesty's Opposition*, pp. 402–03; Ehrman, op. cit., pp. 150–51; B. W. Hill, "Fox and Burke: the Whig party and the question of principles, 1784–1789," *English Historical Review* 89 (1974): 1–24; J. R. Dinwiddy, "Charles James Fox and the People," *History*, N.S. 55 (1970): 342–59; J. H. Plumb, "The Decent Tory Voice," *Times Literary Supplement* No. 3,942 (14 Oct. 1977): 1179.

106 Cannon, op. cit., pp. 230–31; George, op. cit., p. 140; Ehrman, op. cit., p. 55; Derry, op. cit., pp. 196–209; also see I. R. Christie, *Wars and Revolutions*, pp. 181–83.

107 Namier's *Manchester Guardian* article, "Pathological Nationalisms," is partially reprinted in *The Dynamics of Nationalism*, ed. L. L. Snyder, pp. 53–54.

108 Derry, *Fox*, p. 180; Cannon, *Fox-North*, p. 226.

109 Pares, *George III and the Politicians*, p. 135; Rosebery, *Pitt*, p. 61; Christie, *Wilkes, Wyvill and Reform*, p. 207; Cannon, op. cit., p. 229; Watson, *Reign of George III*, p. 274.

110 Daniel Baugh, [review], *Albion* 14 (1982): 180.

111 Smith, *Eighteenth-Century English Politics*, p. 157; and for French reaction to the treaty see Derry, *Fox*, p. 240; also see Christie, *Wars and Revolutions*, p. 168.

112 Smith, op. cit., p. 157; Christie, op. cit., pp. 207–10.

113 Royle and Walvin, *Radicals and Reformers*, p. 31.

114 See (for Cartwright) Veitch, *Genesis of Reform*, p. 107; (for Horne) Stephens, *Memoirs of Horne Tooke*, 2: 49.

115 See Linda Colley, "The Apotheosis of George III: Loyalty, Royalty and the British Nation," *Past & Present* No. 102 (Feb. 1984): 94–129; Michael

McCahill, "The Search for a United Kingdom Peerage," paper delivered
at the Oct. 30, 1982 Conference on British Studies meeting (Boston,
Mass.), p. 11.

[116]Some of the more valuable recent discussions, besides those already cited here,
are James E. Bradley, "Whigs and Nonconformists: 'Slumbering
Radicalism' in English politics 1739–89," *Eighteenth Century Studies* 9, 1
(1975): 1–27; Nicholas Rogers, "The Urban Opposition to Whig
Oligarchy, 1720–60," in *Origins of Anglo-American Radicalism*, eds. Jacob
and Jacob, pp. 132–48; J. G. A. Pocock, "Radical Criticisms of the Whig
Order in the Age between Revolutions," ibid., pp. 33–57; John Seed,
"Gentlemen Dissenters: The Social and Political Meanings of Rational
Dissent in the 1770s and 1780s," *Historical Journal* 28, 2 (1985): 299–325.

[117]Butterfield, *George III, Lord North and the People*, p. 344; also see Cone, *English
Jacobins*, pp. 23, 38–39, 45, 72.

[118]R. R. Palmer, *Age of the Democratic Revolution*, 1: 4; Jarrett, *Begetters*, p. 4.

[119]R. R. Palmer, "The World Revolution of the West: 1763–1801," in *The
Eighteenth-Century Revolution: French or Western?*, ed. Peter Amann (Boston,
1963), pp. 3–4.

[120]However, even though some historians continue to resist this, recent writing on
the French revolutionaries' creed has increasingly called attention to its
nationalist, rather than cosmopolitan, character. The older view is that
"the creed of French and American revolutionaries [was] cosmopolitan,"
regardless of what may have been "nationalistic overtones." (Peter H.
Merkl, *Modern Comparative Politics*, 2d edn [Hinsdale, Ill., 1977], p. 211.)
But more symptomatic of recent attitudes is the following: "The question
of how the revolutionaries came to abandon their initial pacific
cosmopolitanism for a kind of crusading that came to look very much like
imperialism, demands an answer." Norman Hampson, "Into military
channels," *TLS* No. 4,135 (2 July 1982): 723. See also Patrice Higonnet,
Class, Ideology, and the Rights of Nobles during the French Revolution (Oxford,
1981), p. 33; and Vivian R. Gruder, "A Mutation in Elite Political Culture:
The French Notables and the Defense of Property and Participation,
1787," *Journal of Modern History* 56, No. 4 (1984): 599.

[121]Goodwin, "Introductory Survey," p. 4.

[122]The reader should note that it is not necessary to insist that these similar but
individually different nationalist ideologies excluded every conceivable
'cosmopolitan' idea. Nor is it necessary to suggest that, before 1789,
contemporaries even distinguished sharply between what we would now
differentiate as nationalist and cosmopolitan philosophical tendencies. A
nationalist writer might, without sensing any of our modern feeling of
contradiction in this, don the costume of the 'philosophe' and argue the
rights of the citizen from man-in-general principles of Reason as well as
from more parochial ones of Religion and still more local ones of National
History. It is important to realize that to him, the same truths were all
taught by Truth in its varying guises, whether manifested in national
history, divine revelation, or the laws of nature. Horne was characteristic
in writing that he revered the "constitution and constitutional LAWS of
England" because they were "in conformity with the LAWS of God and
Nature." Upon this threefold base—the base of history, divine
dispensation, and natural law—rested the rights of his countrymen:
"Upon these are founded the rational RIGHTS of Englishmen." (Quoted

in Veitch, *Genesis of Reform,* p. 28) It was only after 1789, with the French Revolution being very unjustly blamed upon the much-exaggerated 'abstract ideas of the French philosophers,' that nationalist thinkers began to jettison completely the 'truths of nature' so beloved by the seventeenth and eighteenth centuries.

123 Plamenatz, "Two Types of Nationalism," in *Nationalism,* ed. Kamenka, p. 27.

CHAPTER EIGHT

1 R. K. Webb, *Modern England,* p. 180.

2 The present chapter is partly an abridgement of an article published earlier in *Victorian Studies,* whose editors the author hereby thanks for permission to use it. See Gerald Newman, "Anti-French Propaganda and British Liberal Nationalism in the Early Nineteenth Century: Suggestions toward a General Interpretation," *Victorian Studies* 18, No. 4 (1975): 385–418.

3 For example, it was Cartwright, not Burke, who, fifteen years before Burke's *Reflections,* wrote this encomium on the English 'body-politic': "Its natural tendency is consequently towards all the immortality which the duration of this world can afford it. It is not corporeal. It is not formed from the dust of the earth. It is purely intellectual; and its life-spring is truth." Cartwright, *Take Your Choice!,* p. 16.

4 For these and similar prints, see M. Dorothy George, *English Political Caricature: A Study of Opinion and Propaganda* (Oxford, 1959), I: Pl. 93; II: Pl. 1; *Catalogue of Political and Personal Satires . . . in the British Museum,* 6: 945–46; 7: 42–43, 159–60, 469, 529, 611–12; 8: 190–92; 9: 870, 883, 929; see also John Lord Campbell, *Lives of the Chief Justices* (1849), 2: 335n.

5 For Watt, see E. P. Thompson, *The Making of the English Working Class* (NY, 1963), p. 184; also see *OED,* 'Nationalization.' For middle-class consciousness see Asa Briggs, "Middle-Class Consciousness in English Politics, 1780–1846," *Past and Present* 9 (1956): 65–74; for the general evolution of political radicalism over these decades see the excellent recent study by J. Ann Hone, *For the Cause of Truth: Radicalism in London, 1796–1821* (Oxford, 1982).

6 See David Schoenbaum, *Hitler's Social Revolution: Class and Status in Nazi Germany, 1933–1939* (Garden City, NY, 1966); Richard Grunberger, *The 12-Year Reich: A Social History of Nazi Germany, 1933–1945* (NY, 1971).

7 *Specimens of the Table Talk of the late Samuel Taylor Coleridge* (n.d.), p. 154.

8 David Spring, "Some Reflections on Social History in the Nineteenth Century," *Victorian Studies* 4 (1960): 58.

9 *The Works of Hannah More* (NY, 1844) 1: 328–29; also see 59–61, 487; 2: 438–40; see also Maurice Quinlan, *Victorian Prelude: A History of English Manners, 1700–1830* (NY, 1965), pp. 69, 82, 97, 181; Bernard Semmel, *The Methodist Revolution* (NY, 1973), pp. 128–31, 135–36, 143, 226–28, 231–32.

10 More, *Works,* 1: 62; Arthur Young, *A General View of the Agriculture of the County of Lincoln* (1799), p. 439; Ford K. Brown, *Fathers of the Victorians: The Age of Wilberforce* (Cambridge, 1961), pp. 15, 27, 440; Elie Halévy, *England in 1815,* trans. by E. I. Watkin and D. A. Barker (1961), p. 453.

11 See G. Kitson Clark, "The Romantic Element, 1830–1850," in *Studies in Social History,* ed. J. H. Plumb (1955), p. 226; also see idem, *The Making of Victorian England* (NY, 1967), pp. 36–39; O. F. Christie, *The Transition from*

Aristocracy, 1832–1867 (NY, 1928), pp. 12, 79–88; Eric Williams, *Capitalism and Slavery* (NY, 1966), pp. 135–36, 169–86.

[12] *The Journal of Elizabeth Lady Holland, 1791–1811*, ed. by the Earl of Ilchester (1908), 2: 16; italics added.

[13] Halévy, *England in 1815*, pp. 426–27.

[14] Ibid., p. 454; *Annual Review for 1804* 3: 129, 225ff.; Sydney Smith, "Methodism," *Edinburgh Review* (1809), reprinted in *The Works of the Rev. Sydney Smith* (1869), pp. 156–63; *Anti-Jacobin Review* 3 (1799): 319–21; see the scathing attack in *Gentleman's Magazine* 90 (1820): 609; also see *British Critic* 34 (1810): 199; 41 (1813): 509–12; 2d Ser. 2 (1814): 127, 284; 5 (1816): 69, 357, 493.

[15] See Halévy, op. cit., pp. 424–25, 459, and in general Part III, ch. i.

[16] The Halévy thesis is now nearly demolished by a variety of works which examine the profound structural impacts throughout society of Evangelicalism and Methodism. Some of the most important of these are: Geoffrey Best, "Evangelicalism and the Victorians," in *The Victorian Crisis of Faith*, ed. Anthony Symondson (1970), pp. 37–56; idem, "The Evangelicals and the Established Church in the Early Nineteenth Century," *Journal of Theological Studies* N.S. 10 (April, 1959): 63–78; W. R. Ward, *Religion and Society in England, 1790–1850* (1972), esp. pp. 44–54; Semmel, *The Methodist Revolution*, esp. pp. 112–14, 125–43, 178–84; E. M. Howse, *Saints in Politics: The Clapham Sect and the Growth of Freedom* (1952), pp. 118–37, 176–82; also see the strangely neglected but very penetrating study by Muriel Jaeger, *Before Victoria: Changing Standards and Behaviour, 1787–1837* (1956).

[17] *New Monthly Magazine and Literary Journal* 10 (1824): 47; (for Bentham) Elie Halévy, *The Growth of Philosophic Radicalism*, trans. by M. Morris (Boston, 1955), p. 493; John Pollock, *Wilberforce* (NY, 1977), p. 64. In 1873, Leslie Stephen, himself a son of one of the most prominent Evangelical 'saints,' interestingly remarked (with himself in mind) that the mental growth of agnosticism was "not, in fact, an abandonment of beliefs seriously held and firmly implanted in the mind, but a gradual recognition of the truth that you never really held them." See W. Houghton, *Victorian Frame of Mind*, p. 397.

[18] Halévy, *England in 1815*, p. 438; Best, "Evangelicalism and the Victorians," p. 44.

[19] A characteristic approach was to condemn the "moral disease of France," to lament its particular infectiousness among "the young of the higher ranks," and to recommend "that instead of being corrupted into Frenchmen themselves, they will infuse an English spirit into strangers." *British Critic* 2d Ser. 2 (1814): 32–33; 9 (1818): 20; *British Review* 2 (1811): 149–60; 11 (1818): 330, 552; *The Collected Writings of Thomas De Quincey*, ed. David Masson (Edinburgh, 1889–90), 14: 333–34; *The Complete Works of William Hazlitt*, ed. P. P. Howe (London, 1930–34), 5: 111–14; 12: 314, 323.

[20] See the *British Critic* 2d Ser. 2 (1814): 32–33; 4 (1815): 102; 5 (1816): 429; 6 (1816): 377; 11 (1819): 157; *British Review* 10 (1817): 467ff.; 12 (1818): 67ff.; *Quarterly Review* 28 (1820): 156, 160; *Gentleman's Magazine* 86 (1816): 119; *Blackwood's Edinburgh Magazine* 2 (1818): 486–90; 26 (1829): 314; *Monthly Review* 2d Ser. 107 (1825): 334–35; and for examples from the 1830s see the laughable assertions in Macaulay's essay "Horace Walpole,"

in Macaulay's *Complete Writings* (Boston, 1900–01), *Critical and Historical Essays*, 2: 195–96; and in De Quincey, *Collected Writings*, 4: 83; 5: 375n. Very doubtful is the reliability of Bulwer's protestation in 1833 that *"we no longer hate the French."* See, together with the editor's comments, Bulwer's *England and the English,* ed. Standish Meacham (Chicago, 1970), pp. xxv, 38–39.

21 See Alfred Cobban, *Edmund Burke and the Revolt against the Eighteenth Century,* 2d edn (1960), pp. 144, 150–51, 183, 201; Crane Brinton, *The Political Ideas of the English Romanticists* (Ann Arbor, 1966), pp. 83, 107, 227–30; Carl Woodring, *Politics in English Romantic Poetry* (Cambridge, Mass., 1970), pp. 11, 328–29; Thomas M. Raysor, ed., *Coleridge's Miscellaneous Criticism* (Cambridge, Mass., 1936), p. 441n.; Coleridge, *Biographia Literaria* (1965), p. 104; J. S. Mill, "Coleridge," *Essays on Politics and Culture,* ed. Gertrude Himmelfarb (Garden City, N.Y., 1963), pp. 151, 155, 163–64; Elizabeth Sewell, "Coleridge on Revolution," *Studies in Romanticism* 11 (1972): 342–59; Hazlitt, *The Spirit of the Age,* pp. 144, 152; (for De Quincey) E. Bernbaum, *Guide through the Romantic Movement,* p. 87n.; [Lamb], "Wordsworth's *Excursion,*" *Quarterly Review,* 12 (1814): 105; Wordsworth, *The Excursion* ii.442–45, 480–86 and passim, e.g. iv. 995–1007, where Voltaire is explicitly characterized at length; *The Prelude* v.525–26 and passim; also see Richard E. Brantley, *Wordsworth's 'Natural Methodism'* (New Haven and London, 1975); idem, *Locke, Wesley, and the Method of English Romanticism* (Gainesville, 1984).

22 Consider, for example, Hazlitt's attacks on Wordsworth's "bigotry," strangely mixed with applause for his social ethics; and Lockhart's attempts to vilify Hunt, "this most profound Universalist," without damaging Hunt's friend "the noble lord Byron"; and Shelley's major criticism of his friend Byron: "He has many generous and exalted qualities," but "the canker of aristocracy wants to be cut out." *Examiner* No. 348 (28 August 1814): 556; *Quarterly Review* 37 (1828): 408, 418–22; H. J. C. Grierson, "Byron and English Society," in *Byron, The Poet,* ed. W. A. Briscoe (New York, 1967), p. 63; see also Philip W. Martin, *Byron: a poet before his public* (Cambridge, 1982), pp. 38–41, 137–39; and Hone, *For the Cause of Truth,* pp. 361–62.

23 For a basic trend of the '20s see *Monthly Review* 2d Ser. 94 (1821): 496–97; 105 (1824): 43, 126; 107 (1825): 4, 333–35, 536; 108 (1825): 379–80; "New and Improved Series" 5 (1827): 430–32; 12 (1829): 72–77. For fuller documentation of some of the assertions here see Newman, "Anti-French Propaganda," pp. 415–17, notes.

24 *Sketches of Foreign Manners,* in More, *Works,* 2: 438–39.

25 Briton, *Political Ideas of the Romanticists* p. 130.

26 See Mill's *Autobiography,* ch. v; Carlyle, *Sartor Resartus* (1833–34), ch. ix, "The Everlasting Yea."

SELECTED BIBLIOGRAPHY

NOTE: for books, place of publication is London unless specified otherwise.

A. REFERENCES AND ANTHOLOGIES

Catalogue of Prints and Drawings in the British Museum: Division I. Political and Personal Satires, vols. 4–11 (A.D. 1761–1832).

George, M. Dorothy, *English Political Caricature: A Study of Opinion and Propaganda,* 2 vols. (Oxford, 1959).

Eighteenth-Century Plays, selected by John Hampden (London and Toronto, n.d.).

English Poetry, 1700–1780: Contemporaries of Swift and Johnson, ed. David W. Lindsay (Totowa, N.J.: 1974).

Oxford English Dictionary (OED).

Politics and Literature in the Eighteenth Century, ed. H. T. Dickinson (1974).

Valentine, Alan, *The British Establishment, 1760–1784: An Eighteenth-Century Biographical Dictionary,* 2 vols. (Norman, Okla.: 1970).

B. PERIODICALS

Anti-Jacobin Review
Blackwood's Edinburgh Magazine
British Critic
British Review
Critical Review
Edinburgh Review
Examiner
Gentleman's Magazine
Monthly Review
New Monthly Magazine and Literary Journal
Quarterly Review

C. PRIMARY SOURCES

Andrews, John, *A Comparative View of the French and English Nations, in their Manners, Politics, and Literature* (1785).

Bamford, Samuel, *Passages in the Life of a Radical* (1967).

Boswell, James, *Life of Johnson,* ed R. W. Chapman (1953).

Brown, John, *An Estimate of the Manners and Principles of the Times,* 6th ed., 2 vols. (1757).

Burke, Edmund, *Two Letters on a Regicide Peace* (1796) in Robert A. Smith, ed., *Edmund Burke on Revolution* (NY and Evanston, 1968).

———, *Reflections on the Revolution in France,* ed. T. Mahoney (NY, 1955).

———, *The Works of the Right Honourable Edmund Burke*, 12 vols. (1854–62).

Burney, Fanny, *Evelina* (London and NY, 1950).

Carlyle, Thomas, *Sartor Resartus* (Everyman's, NY, n.d.)

Cartwright, John, *Take Your Choice!* (1776).

———, *American Independence the Interest and Glory of Great-Britain*, new edn (1775; NY, 1970).

Chesterfield, Philip Dormer Stanhope, 4th earl of, *Lord Chesterfield's Letters to his Son and Others*, ed. R. K. Root (1969).

———, *The Letters of the Earl of Chesterfield to His Son*, ed. Charles Strachey (NY and London, 1925).

Coleridge, S. T., *Biographia Literaria* (1965).

———, *Specimens of the Table Talk of the late Samuel Taylor Coleridge* (Routledge, n.d.).

———, *Coleridge's Miscellaneous Criticism*, ed. Thomas M. Raysor (Cambridge, Mass., 1936).

Day, Thomas, *The History of Sandford and Merton: A Book for the Young* (1860).

De Quincey, *The Collected Writings of Thomas De Quincey*, ed. David Masson, 14 vols. (Edinburgh, 1889–90).

Fielding, Henry, *The History of the Adventures of Joseph Andrews and his Friend Mr. Abraham Adams* (NY, 1960).

———, *Amelia*, 2 vols. (1930).

Foote, Samuel, *The Dramatic Works of Samuel Foote, Esq.* (London and NY, n.d.).

Garrick, David, *The Plays of David Garrick*, eds. H. W. Pedicord and F. L. Bergmann, 7 vols. (Carbondale and Edwardsville, Ill., 1980–82).

Goldsmith, Oliver, *The Vicar of Wakefield: A Tale Supposed to be Written by Himself* (Cambridge, Mass., 1895).

Hazlitt, William, *The Spirit of the Age, or Contemporary Portraits*, 4th edn (1886).

———, *The Complete Works of William Hazlitt*, ed. P. P. Howe, 21 vols. (London, 1930–34).

Holland, Elizabeth, Lady, *The Journal of Elizabeth Lady Holland, 1791–1811*, ed. by the Earl of Ilchester, 2 vols. (1908).

[Hulme, Obadiah], *An Historical Essay on the English Constitution: Or, An Impartial Inquiry into the Elective Power of the People, from the first Establishment of the Saxons in this Kingdom* (1771).

Hume, David, *Essays and Treatises on Several Subjects*, new edn, 4 vols. (1764).

Hurd, Richard, *Letters on Chivalry and Romance*, edited and introduced by Hoyt Trowbridge (Augustan Reprint Society No. 101–102, Los Angeles, 1963).

———, *Moral and Political Dialogues; with Letters on Chivalry and Romance*, 5th ed., 3 vols. (1776).

Johnson, Samuel, *Johnson: Prose and Poetry*, selected by Mona Wilson (Cambridge, Mass., 1967).

———, *A Dictionary of the English Language: In Which the Words are deduced from their Originals . . .* (1755).

Jones, William, *The Works of Sir William Jones*, eds. Lord Teignmouth and Lady Jones, 12 vols. (1807).

Lytton, Edward G. E. L. Bulwer, *England and the English*, ed Standish Meacham (Chicago, 1970).

Macaulay, T. B., *The Complete Writings of Thomas Babington Macaulay*, 10 vols. (Boston, 1901).

Mackenzie, Henry, *The Man of Feeling* (1967).

Mill, J. S., "Coleridge," *Essays on Politics and Culture,* ed. Gertrude Himmelfarb (Garden City, NY, 1963).

——, *Autobiography* (NY, 1964).

Moore, John, *The Works of John Moore, M.D.,* ed. Robert Anderson, 7 vols. (Edinburgh, 1820).

More, Hannah, *The Works of Hannah More,* 2 vols. (NY, 1844).

Smart, Christopher, *Poems by Christopher Smart,* ed. Robert Brittain (Princeton, 1950).

Smith, Sydney, *The Works of the Rev. Sydney Smith* (1869).

Smollett, Tobias, *The Adventures of Ferdinand Count Fathom,* ed. with an intro. by Damian Grant (1971).

——, *The Expedition of Humphry Clinker* (NY and Toronto, 1950).

Walpole, Horace, *The Letters of Horace Walpole, Fourth Earl of Orford,* ed. Mrs. Paget Toynbee, 16 vols. (Oxford, 1904).

Warton, Thomas, *History of English Poetry,* intro. by René Wellek, 2 vols. (NY and London, 1968).

Wordsworth, William, *The Excursion.*

——, *The Prelude.*

Young, Arthur, *Travels in France during the Years 1787, 1788, 1789,* ed. Miss Betham-Edwards (1912).

——, *A General View of the Agriculture of the County of Lincoln* (1799).

D. SECONDARY SOURCES

Abrams, M. H., *The Mirror and the Lamp: Romantic Theory and the Critical Tradition* (NY, 1953).

Argyle, W. J., "Size and Scale as Factors in the Development of Nationalist Movements," in *Nationalist Movements,* ed. A. D. Smith (NY, 1976).

Ashton, T. S., *The Industrial Revolution, 1760–1830* (1948).

Atherton, Herbert M., *Political Prints in the Age of Hogarth: A Study of the Ideographic Representation of Politics* (Oxford, 1974).

Bailyn, Bernard, *The Ideological Origins of the American Revolution* (Cambridge, Mass., 1967).

Barker, Ernest A., *The History of the English Novel,* 10 vols. (NY, 1957).

Baker, Ernest, ed., *The Character of England* (Oxford, 1947).

Barrell, John, *English Literature in History, 1730–80: An Equal, Wide Survey* (NY, 1983).

Barzun, Jacques, "Cultural Nationalism and the Makings of Fame," in *Nationalism and Internationalism:* Essays Inscribed to Carlton J. H. Hayes, ed. Edward M. Earle (NY, 1950).

——, *The French Race: Theories of its Origins and their Social and Political Implications Prior to the Revolution* (Port Washington, New York, 1966).

Bate, W. Jackson, *Samuel Johnson* (NY and London, 1977).

Baugh, Daniel A., ed., *Aristocratic Government and Society in Eighteenth-Century England: The Foundations of Stability* (NY, 1972).

Bayne-Powell, Rosamond, *Travellers in Eighteenth-Century England* (NY, 1972).

de Beer, Sir Gavin, and André-Michel Rousseau, eds., *Voltaire's British Visitors,* Studies on Voltaire and the Eighteenth Century, vol. 49, ed. Theodore Besterman (Geneva, 1967).

Berlin, Isaiah, *Against the Current: Essays in the History of Ideas* (NY, 1980).

Bernbaum, Ernest, *Guide Through the Romantic Movement,* 2d edn, rev. (NY, 1949).

Best, Geoffrey, "Evangelicalism and the Victorians," in *The Victorian Crisis of Faith,* ed. Anthony Symondson (1970).

———, "The Evangelicals and the Established Church in the Early Nineteenth Century," *Journal of Theological Studies* N.S. 10 (April, 1959): 63–78.

Besterman, Theodore, *Voltaire* (NY, 1969).

Black, Jeremy, *The British and the Grand Tour* (London and Dover, N.H., 1985).

Bloom, Edward A., *Samuel Johnson in Grub Street* (Providence, R.I., 1957).

Black, Eugene C., *The Association: British Extraparliamentary Political Organization, 1769–1793* (Cambridge, Mass., 1963).

Blumer, Herbert, "Social Movements," in *Taking State Power: The Sources and Consequences of Political Challenge,* ed. John C. Leggett (NY, 1973).

Blunt, Reginald, *Mrs. Montagu, "Queen of the Blues": Her Letters and Friendships from 1762 to 1800* (1923).

Bonwick, Colin, *English Radicals and the American Revolution* (Chapel Hill, 1977).

Brantley, Richard E., *Wordsworth's 'Natural Methodism'* (New Haven and London, 1975).

———, *Locke, Wesley, and the Method of English Romanticism* (Gainesville, 1984).

Brewer, John, *Party Ideology and Popular Politics at the Accession of George III* (Cambridge, 1976).

———, "English Radicalism in the Age of George III," in *Three British Revolutions: 1641, 1688, 1776,* ed. J. G. A. Pocock (Princeton, 1980).

Briggs, Asa, "Middle-Class Consciousness in English Politics, 1780–1846," *Past and Present* 9 (1956): 65–74.

Brinton, Crane, *The Political Ideas of the English Romanticists* (Ann Arbor, 1966).

Brooke, John, *King George III* (1972).

Brown, Ford K., *Fathers of the Victorians: The Age of Wilberforce* (Cambridge, 1961).

Brown, Peter, *The Chathamites: A Study in the Relationship between Personalities and Ideas in the Second Half of the Eighteenth Century* (London and NY, 1967).

Brown, Phillip Anthony, *The French Revolution in English History* (NY, 1965).

Burke, Peter, *Popular Culture in Early Modern Europe* (NY, 1978).

Butler, Marilyn, *Romantics, Rebels and Reactionaries: English Literature and its Background, 1760–1830* (NY and Oxford, 1981).

Butt, John, and Geoffrey Carnall, *The Mid-Eighteenth Century* (Oxford, 1979), in *The Oxford History of English Literature,* eds. John Buston and Norman Davis.

Butterfield, Herbert, *George III, Lord North and the People, 1779–1780* (NY, 1968).

———, *George III and the Historians* (1957).

Calvert, Peter, "On Attaining Sovereignty," in *Nationalist Movements,* ed. A. D. Smith, (NY, 1976).

Cannon, John, *The Fox-North Coalition: Crisis of the Constitution, 1782–84* (Cambridge, 1969).

———, "New lamps for old: the end of Hanoverian England," in *The Whig Ascendancy: Colloquies on Hanoverian England,* ed. J. Cannon (NY, 1981).

Cecil, David, Lord, *Melbourne* (NY, 1954).

Chadwick, H. Munro, *The Nationalities of Europe and the Growth of National Ideologies* (Cambridge, 1945).

Chartier, Roger, "Intellectual History or Sociocultural History? The French Trajectories," in *Modern European Intellectual History: Reappraisals and New Perspectives,* eds. Dominick LaCapra and Steven L. Kaplan (Ithaca and London, 1982).

Christie, Ian R., *Wilkes, Wyvill and Reform: The Parliamentary Reform Movement in British Politics, 1760–1785* (1962).

————, "Introduction," in G. S. Veitch, *The Genesis of Parliamentary Reform* (1965).

————, *Wars and Revolutions: Britain, 1760–1815* (Cambridge, Mass., 1982).

Christie, O. F., *The Transition from Aristocracy, 1832–1867* (NY, 1928).

Clark, A. F. B., *Boileau and the French Classical Critics in England (1660–1830)* (NY, 1970).

Clark, Dora Mae, *British Opinion and the American Revolution* (NY, 1966).

Clark, G. Kitson, "The Romantic Element, 1830–1850," in *Studies in Social History*, ed. J. H. Plumb (1955).

————, *The Making of Victorian England* (NY, 1967).

Clifford, James L., ed. *Man versus Society in 18th-Century Britain: Six Points of View* (NY, 1972).

Cobban, Alfred, *Edmund Burke and the Revolt against the Eighteenth Century*, 2d edn (1960).

Cohen, Murray, "Eighteenth-Century English Literature and Modern Critical Methodologies," *The Eighteenth Century: Theory and Interpretation* 20 (1979): 5–23.

Colley, Linda, "The Apotheosis of George III: Loyalty, Royalty and the British Nation," *Past & Present* No. 102 (Feb. 1984): 94–129.

Colville, Alfred, and Harold Temperley, eds., *Studies in Anglo-French History* (Freeport, N.Y., 1969).

Cone, Carl B., *The English Jacobins: Reformers in Late 18th Century England* (NY, 1968).

Connell, Brian, *Portrait of a Whig Peer* (1957).

Costigan, Giovanni, *Makers of Modern England: The Force of Individual Genius in History* (NY and London, 1967).

Crane, R. S., "Diffusion of Voltaire's Writings in England, 1750–1800," *Modern Philology* 20 (1923): 261–74.

Crouzet, F., "England and France in the Eighteenth Century: A Comparative Analysis of Two Economic Growths," in *The Causes of the Industrial Revolution in England*, ed. R. M. Hartwell (1967).

Crowther, J. G., *Scientists of the Industrial Revolution* (1962).

Cunnington, Willett, "Costume," in *The Connoisseur's Complete Period Guides to the Houses, Decoration, Furnishing and Chattels of the Classic Periods*, eds. Ralph Edwards and L. G. G. Ramsey (NY, 1968).

Curnow, Allen, "Distraction and Definition: Centripetal Directions in New Zealand Poetry," in *National Identity: Papers delivered at the Commonwealth Literature Conference*, University of Queensland, Brisbane, 9th–15th August, 1968, ed. K. L. Goodwin (London and Melbourne, 1970).

Day, Martin S., *History of English Literature, 1660–1837* (NY, 1963).

Deane, Phillis, *The First Industrial Revolution*, 2d edn (Cambridge, 1979).

Derry, John W., *Charles James Fox* (NY, 1972).

Dickinson, H. T., *Liberty and Property: Political Ideology in Eighteenth-Century Britain* 1977).

Dinwiddy, J. R., "Charles James Fox and the People," *History*, N.S. 55 (1970): 342–59.

Doob, Leonard W., *Patriotism and Nationalism: Their Psychological Foundations* (New Haven and London, 1964).

Earle, Edward M., ed., *Nationalism and Internationalism: Essays Inscribed to Carlton J. H. Hayes* (NY, 1950).

Evans, Eric J., *The Forging of the Modern State: Early Industrial Britain 1783–1870* (London and NY, 1983).

Ehrman, John, *The Younger Pitt: The Years of Acclaim* (NY, 1969).

Emerson, Rupert, *From Empire to Nation: The Rise to Self-Assertion of Asian and African Peoples* (Cambridge, Mass., 1967).

Faber, Richard, *French and English* (1975).

Fairchild, Hoxie Neale, *The Noble Savage: A Study in Romantic Naturalism* (NY, 1928).

Foord, Archibald S., *His Majesty's Opposition, 1714–1830* (Oxford, 1964).

Ford, Boris, ed., *A Guide to English Literature*, Vol. 4: *From Dryden to Johnson* (1969).

Flexner, Eleanor, *Mary Wollstonecraft: A Biography* (Baltimore, 1973).

Frye, Northrop, *Fables of Identity: Studies in Poetic Mythology* (NY, 1963).

———, *A Study of English Romanticism* (NY, 1968).

Gaunt, William, *The World of William Hogarth* (1978).

Gay, Peter, *The Enlightenment: An Interpretation* (New York, 1968).

Gazley, John M., "Arthur Young, British Patriot," in *Nationalism and Internationalism: Essays Inscribed to Carlton J. H. Hayes*, ed. Edward M. Earle (NY, 1950).

Gelley, Alexander, "Character and Person: On the Presentation of Self in Some 18th-Century Novels," *The Eighteenth Century: Theory and Interpretation* 21 (1980): 109–27.

Gellner, Ernest, *Nations and Nationalism* (Ithaca and London, 1983).

George, Mrs. Eric, "Fox's Martyrs; The General Election of 1784," *Transactions of the Royal Historical Society* 4th Ser. 21 (1939): 133–68.

———, [M. Dorothy], "London and the Life of the Town," in *Johnson's England: An Account of the Life & Manners of his Age*, ed. A. S. Turberville (Oxford, 1967).

Girouard, Mark, *The Return to Camelot: Chivalry and the English Gentleman* (New Haven and London, 1981).

Glover, C. H., ed., *Dr. Charles Burney's Continental Travels, 1770–72* (1927).

Goldstein, Laurence, *Ruins and Empire: The Evolution of a Theme in Augustan and Romantic Literature* (Pittsburgh, 1977).

Goodwin, Albert, ed., *The European Nobility in the Eighteenth Century* (London and NY, 1953).

———, "Introductory Survey," *New Cambridge Modern History: Volume VIII, The American and French Revolutions, 1763–93* (Cambridge, 1965).

———, *The Friends of Liberty: The English Democratic Movement in the Age of the French Revolution* (Cambridge, Mass., 1979).

Green, Frederick C., *Minuet: A Critical Survey of French and English Literary Ideas in the Eighteenth Century* (1935).

———, *Eighteenth-Century France: Six Essays* (London and Toronto, 1929).

Greene, Donald, *The Age of Exuberance: Backgrounds to Eighteenth-Century English Literature* (NY, 1970).

Grierson, H. J. C., "Byron and English Society," in *Byron, The Poet*, ed. W. A. Briscoe (New York, 1967).

Guilhamet, Leon, *The Sincere Ideal: Studies on Sincerity in Eighteenth-Century English Literature* (Montreal and London, 1974).

Guttridge, G. H., *English Whiggism and the American Revolution* (Berkeley and Los Angeles, 1963).

Habakkuk, H. J., "England," in *The European Nobility in the Eighteenth Century*, ed. A. Goodwin (London and NY, 1953).

Halévy, Elie, *England in 1815*, trans. by E. I. Watkin and D. A. Barker (1961).

———, *The Growth of Philosophic Radicalism*, trans. by M. Morris (Boston, 1955).

Hall, A. Rupert, "What did the Industrial Revolution in Britain owe to Science?" in *Historical Perspectives: Studies in English Thought and Society in honour of J. H. Plumb,* ed. Neil McKendrick (1974).

Hampson, Norman, *The Enlightenment: An Interpretation* (NY, 1968).

Handman, Max S., "The Sentiment of Nationalism," *Political Science Quarterly* 36 (1921): 104–21.

Hart, Roger, *English Life in the Eighteenth Century* (NY, 1970).

Hartwell, R. M., ed., *The Causes of the Industrial Revolution in England* (1967).

Hay, Carla H., *James Burgh, Spokesman for Reform in Hanoverian England* (Washington, 1979).

Hay, Douglas, Peter Linebaugh, John G. Rule, E. P. Thompson, and Cal Winslow, *Albion's Fatal Tree: Crime and Society in Eighteenth-Century England* (NY, 1975).

Hecht, J. Jean, *The Domestic Servant Class in Eighteenth-Century England* (1956).

Herzen, Alexander, *My Past and Thoughts: The Memoirs of Alexander Herzen,* abridged and annotated by Dwight Macdonald, trans. Constance Garnett (NY, 1973).

Hibbert, Christopher, *The Grand Tour* (NY, 1969).

Hill, B. W., "Fox and Burke: the Whig party and the question of principles, 1784–1789," *English Historical Review* 89 (1974): 1–24.

Hill, Christopher, "The Norman Yoke," in C. Hill, *Puritanism and Revolution: Studies in Interpretation of the English Revolution of the 17th Century* (NY, 1958).

Hilles, Frederick W., ed., *The Age of Johnson: Essays Presented to Chauncey Brewster Tinker* (New Haven and London, 1949).

———, and Harold Bloom, eds., *From Sensibility to Romanticism: Essays Presented to Frederick A. Pottle* (NY, 1965).

Hone, J. Ann, *For the Cause of Truth: Radicalism in London, 1796–1821* (Oxford, 1982).

Horn, David B., *Great Britain and Europe in the Eighteenth Century* (Oxford, 1967).

Houghton, Walter, *The Victorian Frame of Mind, 1830–1870* (New Haven and London, 1957).

Howse, E. M., *Saints in Politics: The Clapham Sect and the Growth of Freedom* (1952).

Humphreys, A. R., *The Augustan World: Society, Thought, and Letters in Eighteenth-Century England* (NY, 1963).

Jacob, Margaret, and James Jacob, eds., *The Origins of Anglo-American Radicalism* (1984).

Jaeger, Muriel, *Before Victoria: Changing Standards and Behaviour, 1787–1837* (1956).

Jarrett, Derek, *The Begetters of Revolution: England's Involvement with France, 1759–1789* (1973).

———, *England in the Age of Hogarth* (NY, 1974).

Kamenka, Eugene, ed., *Nationalism: The Nature and Evolution of an Idea* (Canberra, 1973).

———, "Political Nationalism—The Evolution of the Idea," in *Nationalism,* ed. E. Kamenka (Canberra, 1973).

Karsten, Peter, *Patriot-Heroes in England and America: Political Symbolism and Changing Values over Three Centuries* (Madison, Wis., 1978).

Kedourie, Elie, *Nationalism,* rev. edn (NY, 1961).

Kenny, Virginia C., *The Country-House Ethos in English Literature, 1688–1750: Themes of Personal Retreat and National Expansion* (Brighton and NY, 1984).

Kiernan, V., "Nationalist Movements and Social Classes," in *Nationalist Movements,* ed. A. D. Smith, (NY, 1976).

Kohn, Hans, "The Genesis and Character of English Nationalism," *Journal of the History of Ideas* 1 (1940): 69–94.

——, *The Idea of Nationalism: A Study of Its Origins and Background* (NY, 1944).

Koht, Halvdan, "The Dawn of Nationalism in Europe," *American Historical Review* 52 (1947): 265–80.

Kliger, Samuel, *The Goths in England: A Study in Seventeenth and Eighteenth Century Thought* (NY, 1972).

Kramnick, Isaac, *The Rage of Edmund Burke: Portrait of an Ambivalent Conservative* (NY, 1977).

——, "Republican Revisionism Revisited," *American Historical Review* 87, No. 3 (1982): 629–64.

Labatut, Jean-Pierre, *Les noblesses Européenes: de la fin du XVᵉ siècle a la fin du XVIIIᵉ siècle* (Paris, 1978).

Laslett, Peter, *The World We Have Lost* (NY, 1965).

Lecky, W. E. H., *A History of England in the Eighteenth Century*, 8 vols. (NY, 1878–90).

Lipking, Lawrence, *The Ordering of the Arts in Eighteenth-Century England* (Princeton, 1970).

Lutnick, Solomon, *The American Revolution and the British Press, 1775–1783* (Columbia, Missouri, 1967).

MacDougall, Hugh A., *Racial Myth in English History: Trojans, Teutons, and Anglo-Saxons* (Montreal, Hanover, N.H., and London, 1982).

Margetson, Stella, *Leisure and Pleasure in the Eighteenth Century* (1970).

Marshall, Dorothy, *Dr. Johnson's London* (NY, 1968).

——, "Manners, Meals, and Domestic Pastimes," in *Johnson's England: An Account of the Life & Manners of his Age*, ed. A. S. Turberville (Oxford, 1967).

Martelli, George, *Jemmy Twitcher: A Life of the Fourth Earl of Sandwich, 1718–1792* (London, 1962).

Martin, Philip W., *Byron: A Poet before his Public* (Cambridge, 1982).

Mathias, Peter, *The First Industrial Nation: An Economic History of Britain, 1700–1914* (NY, 1969).

McCahill, Michael, "The Search for a United Kingdom Peerage," paper delivered on Oct. 30, 1982 at the Conference on British Studies meeting (Boston, Mass.).

McKendrick, Neil, John Brewer and J. H. Plumb, *The Birth of a Consumer Society: The Commercialization of Eighteenth-Century England* (Bloomington, Ind., 1982).

——, "The Commercialization of Fashion," in *The Birth of a Consumer Society: The Commercialization of Eighteenth-Century England*, eds. N. McKendrick, J. Brewer and J. H. Plumb (Bloomington, Ind., 1982), pp. 34–99.

McKillop, Alan, "Local Attachment and Cosmopolitanism—The Eighteenth-Century Pattern," in *From Sensibility to Romanticism: Essays Presented to Frederick A. Pottle*, eds. Frederick W. Hilles and Harold Bloom (NY, 1965).

Mead, William Edward, *The Grand Tour in the Eighteenth Century* (Boston and NY, 1914).

Meinecke, Friedrich, *Cosmopolitanism and the National State*, trans. Robert B. Kimber, introduced by Felix Gilbert (Princeton, 1970).

Mellor, Alec, *Lord Chesterfield et son temps, un grand européen* (Tours, 1970).

Mingay, G. E., *English Landed Society in the Eighteenth Century* (London and Toronto, 1963).

Miller, G. M., *The Historical Point of View in English Literary Criticism from 1570–1770* (NY, 1968).

Minogue, K. R., *Nationalism* (Baltimore, 1970).

——, "Nationalism and the Patriotism of City-States," in *Nationalist Movements*, ed. A. D. Smith, (NY, 1976).

Moore, Robert E., *Hogarth's Literary Relationships* (Minneapolis, 1948).

Mosse, George L., "Mass Politics and the Political Liturgy of Nationalism," in *Nationalism*, ed. E. Kamenka (Canberra, 1973).

Namier, L. B., *The Structure of Politics at the Accession of George III*, 2 vols. (1929).

——, *England in the Age of the American Revolution*, 2d edn (1961).

——, and John Brooke, *Charles Townshend* (NY, 1964)

Newman, Gerald, "Anti-French Propaganda and British Liberal Nationalism in the Early Nineteenth Century: Suggestions toward a General Interpretation," *Victorian Studies* 18, No. 4 (1975): 385–418.

Osborne, John W., *William Cobbett: His Thought and his Times* (New Brunswick, N.J., 1966).

——, *John Cartwright* (Cambridge, 1972).

Palmer, R. R., *The Age of the Democratic Revolution: A Political History of Europe and America, 1760–1800*, 2 vols. (Princeton, 1959–64).

——, "Social and Psychological Foundations of the Revolutionary Era," ch. xv of *The New Cambridge Modern History: Vol. VIII, The American and French Revolutions, 1763–93*, ed. A. Goodwin (Cambridge, 1965).

——, "The World Revolution of the West: 1763–1801," in *The Eighteenth-Century Revolution: French or Western?*, ed. Peter Amann (Boston, 1963).

Pares, Richard, *King George III and the Politicians* (1967).

Parkin, Frank, "Strategies of Social Closure in Class Formation," in *The Social Analysis of Class Structure*, ed. F. Parkin (London, 1974).

Parsons, Talcott, *Societies: Evolutionary and Comparative Perspectives* (Englewood Cliffs, N.Y., 1966).

Parssinen, T. M., "Association, convention, and anti-parliament in British radical politics, 1771–1848," *English Historical Review* 88 (1973): 504–33.

Peardon, Thomas P., *The Transition in English Historical Writing, 1760–1830* (NY, 1933).

Perkin, Harold, *The Origins of Modern English Society, 1780–1880* (1969).

——, "The Social Causes of the British Industrial Revolution," *Transactions of the Royal Historical Society* 5th Ser. 18 (1968): 123–43.

Peters, Marie, *Pitt and Popularity: The Patriot Minister and London Opinion during the Seven Years' War* (Oxford, 1980).

Plamenatz, John, "Two Types of Nationalism," in *Nationalism*, ed. E. Kamenka (Canberra, 1973).

Plumb, J. H., "Political Man," in *Man Versus Society in Eighteenth-Century Britain: Six Points of View*, ed. J. L. Clifford (NY, 1972).

Pocock, J. G. A., *The Machiavellian Moment: Florentine Political Thought and the Atlantic Republican Tradition* (Princeton, 1975).

——, "The Limits and Divisions of British History: In Search of the Unknown Subject," *American Historical Review* 87, No. 2 (1982): 311–36.

——, "Radical Criticisms of the Whig Order in the Age between Revolutions," in *The Origins of Anglo-American Radicalism*, eds. Margaret Jacob and James Jacob (1984).

——, ed., *Three British Revolutions: 1641, 1688, 1776* (Princeton, 1980).

Poliakov, Léon, *The Aryan Myth: A History of Racist and Nationalist Ideas in Europe*, trans. Edmund Howard (NY, 1977).

Pollock, John, *Wilberforce* (NY, 1977).

Porter, Roy, *English Society in the Eighteenth Century* (Harmondsworth, 1982).

————, and Teich, Mikulas, eds., *The Enlightenment in National Context* (Cambridge, 1981).

Price, Martin, *To the Palace of Wisdom: Studies in Order and Energy from Dryden to Blake* (Garden City, NY, 1964).

Quinlan, Maurice, *Victorian Prelude: A History of English Manners, 1700–1830* (NY, 1965).

Rea, Robert R., *The English Press in Politics, 1760–1774* (Lincoln, Neb., 1963).

Robbins, Caroline, *The Eighteenth-Century Commonwealthman* (Cambridge, Mass., 1959).

Robinson, Eric, and A. E. Musson, *James Watt and the Steam Revolution* (NY, 1969).

Rogers, Nicholas, "The Urban Opposition to Whig Oligarchy, 1720–60," in *The Origins of Anglo-American Radicalism*, eds. Margaret Jacob and James Jacob (1984).

Rogers, Pat, *Literature and Popular Culture in Eighteenth-Century England* (Brighton and Totowa, N.J., 1985).

————, *Eighteenth-Century Encounters: Studies in Literature and Society in the Age of Walpole* (Brighton and Totowa, N.J., 1985).

Rousseau, André-Michel, *L'Angleterre et Voltaire (1718–1789)*, Studies on Voltaire and the Eighteenth Century, vols. 145–47 (Oxford, 1976).

Royle, Edward, and James Walvin, *English Radicals and Reformers, 1760–1848* (Lexington, Ky., 1982).

Rudé, George, *Wilkes and Liberty: A Social Study of 1763 to 1774* (Oxford, 1962).

————, *Hanoverian London, 1714–1808* (Berkeley and Los Angeles, 1971).

Sanford, John L., and Meredith Townsend, *The Great Governing Families of England*, 2 vols. (Edinburgh and London, 1865).

Schlereth, Thomas J., *The Cosmopolitan Ideal in Enlightenment Thought: Its Form and Function in the Ideas of Franklin, Hume, and Voltaire, 1694–1790* (Notre Dame and London, 1977).

Scott, Sir S. H., *The Exemplary Mr. Day, 1748–1789* (NY, 1935).

Semmel, Bernard, *The Methodist Revolution* (NY, 1973).

Sewell, Elizabeth, "Coleridge on Revolution," *Studies in Romanticism* 11 (1972): 342–59.

Shafer, Boyd C., *Nationalism: Interpretations and Interpreters*, 3d edn, Service Center for Teachers of History No. 20 (Washington, D. C., 1966).

————, *Nationalism: Myth and Reality* (NY, 1955).

Shellabarger, Samuel, *Lord Chesterfield and His World* (Boston, 1951).

Shklar, Judith, "Subversive Genealogies," in *Myth, Symbol, and Culture*, ed. Clifford Geertz (NY, 1971).

Siskin, Clifford, "Personification and Community: Literary Change in the Mid and Late Eighteenth Century," *Eighteenth-Century Studies* 15, No. 4 (1982): 371–401.

Sitter, John, *Literary Loneliness in Mid-Eighteenth-Century England* (Ithaca and London, 1982).

Smith, Anthony D., *Theories of Nationalism* (1971).

————, ed., *Nationalist Movements*, (NY, 1976).

————, "Introduction: The Formation of Nationalist Movements," in *Nationalist Movements*, ed. A. D. Smith (NY, 1976).

Smith, Robert A., *Eighteenth-Century English Politics: Patrons and Place-hunters* (NY, 1972).

Snyder, Louis L., ed., *The Dynamics of Nationalism: Readings in its Meaning and Development* (Princeton, 1964).

Spring, David, "Some Reflections on Social History in the Nineteenth Century," *Victorian Studies* 4 (1960): 55–64.

Stephens, Alexander, *Memoirs of John Horne Tooke, Interspersed with Original Documents,* 2 vols. (1813; NY, 1968).

Stephen, Leslie, *English Literature and Society in the Eighteenth Century* (1904).

Stone, Lawrence, *The Family, Sex and Marriage In England, 1500–1800,* abridged edn (NY, 1979).

———, and Jeanne C. Fawtier Stone, *An Open Elite? England 1540–1880* (Oxford, 1984).

———, "Social Mobility in England, 1500–1700," *Past and Present* 33 (1966): 16–55.

Stromberg, Roland N., *Religious Liberalism in Eighteenth-Century England* (1954).

Sudnow, David, ed., *Studies in Social Interaction,* (NY, 1972).

Suratteau, Jean-René, "Rapport de synthèse," *Transactions of the Fifth International Congress on the Enlightenment,* Studies on Voltaire and the Eighteenth Century, vol. 190 (Oxford, 1980): 411–40.

Sykes, Norman, *Church and State in England in the XVIIIth Century* (Hamden, Conn., 1962).

Talmon, J. L., *Political Messianism: The Romantic Phase* (NY, 1960).

Tames, Richard, *Josiah Wedgwood* (Aylesbury, 1972).

Texte, Joseph, *Jean-Jacques Rousseau and the Cosmopolitan Spirit in Literature: A Study of the Literary Relations between France and England during the Eighteenth Century,* trans. J. W. Matthews (London and NY, 1899).

———, *Études de Litterature européene* (Paris, 1898).

Thompson, E. P., *The Making of the English Working Class* (NY, 1963).

———, "Patrician Society, Plebeian Culture," *Journal of Social History* 7, No. 4 (1974): 382–405.

———, *Whigs and Hunters: The Origins of the Black Act* (NY, 1975).

Toohey, Robert E., *Liberty and Empire: British Radical Solutions to the American Problem, 1774–76* (Lexington, Ky., 1978).

Traill, H. D. and J. S. Mann, *Social England: A Record of the Progress of the People* (NY and London, 1909), 6 vols.

Trease, Geoffrey, *The Grand Tour* (NY, 1967).

Trefman, Simon, *Sam. Foote, Comedian, 1772–1777* (NY, 1971).

Trevelyan, G. M., *English Social History: A Survey of Six Centuries* (NY, 1942).

Trilling, Lionel, *Sincerity and Authenticity* (Cambridge, Mass., 1972).

Tucker, Susie I., *Protean Shape: A Study in Eighteenth-Century Vocabulary and Usage* (1967).

Tuberville, A. S., ed., *Johnson's England: An Account of the Life & Manners of his Age,* 2 vols. (Oxford, 1967).

Valentine, Alan, *Lord North* (Norman, Okla., 1967).

Veitch, George Stead, *The Genesis of Parliamentary Reform* (Hamden, Conn., 1965).

Ward, W. R., *Religion and Society in England, 1790–1850* (1972).

Watson, J. Steven, *The Reign of George III, 1760–1815* (Oxford, 1960).

Watt, Ian, *The Rise of the Novel: Studies in Defoe, Richardson and Fielding* (Berkeley and Los Angeles, 1964).

Webb, R. K., *Modern England: From the Eighteenth Century to the Present* (NY, 1968).

Weber, Max, *Max Weber: Selections in Translation,* ed. W. G. Runciman, trans. E. Matthews (Cambridge, 1978).

Whitney, Lois, *Primitivism and the Idea of Progress in the English Popular Literature of the Eighteenth Century* (NY, 1965).

Williams, E. N., *The Eighteenth-Century Constitution, 1688–1815: Documents and Commentary* (Cambridge, 1965).

Wittkower, Rudolf, "The Artist," in *Man versus Society in 18th-Century Britain: Six Points of View,* ed. L. Clifford (NY, 1972).

Woodring, Carl, *Politics in English Romantic Poetry* (Cambridge, Mass., 1970).

Young, G. M., *Victorian England: Portrait of an Age,* 2d edn (1960).

INDEX